T0314308

THE

PUBLICATIONS

OF THE

SURTEES SOCIETY

VOL. CCII

At a COUNCIL MEETING of the SURTEES SOCIETY, held on 9 December 1993, it was ORDERED —

"That the edition of the Newcastle customs accounts surviving from the later fifteenth century prepared by Mr John Wade M.Phil. should be printed as a volume of the Society's publications."

A.J.Piper, *Secretary*
5 The College
Durham

THE

PUBLICATIONS

OF THE

SURTEES SOCIETY

ESTABLISHED IN THE YEAR
M.DCCC.XXXIV

VOL. CCII

THE CUSTOMS ACCOUNTS OF NEWCASTLE UPON TYNE 1454–1500

EDITED
BY

J. F. WADE

TYPESET FROM DISC BY
ROGER BOOTH ASSOCIATES, KEYMER, WEST SUSSEX

PRINTED FOR THE SOCIETY BY
ATHENÆUM PRESS LIMITED, GATESHEAD
1995

ISBN 0–85444–059–3

CONTENTS

ACKNOWLEDGEMENTS

All the original documents published here are lodged in the Public Record Office and are Crown copyright; they are reproduced with the permission of the Controller of Her Majesty's Stationary Office. Texts of them formed the core of the thesis for the degree of Master of Philosophy at the University of Leeds which I submitted in December 1991; I wish to thank Dr W. R. Childs, my supervisor, for advice and encouragement over the previous five years, and to express my gratitude to Mr G. C. F. Forster and Dr C. M. Fraser. For help in preparing the text for publication I am greatly indebted to the Secretary of the Society. The maps were prepared by Mr T. P. Hadwin.

NOTE ON EDITING

Customs accounts contain many marginal notes, almost all apparently added to assist in the compilation or checking of a final account from the particulars. These are printed inside { } brackets. In the earlier accounts such marginal notes are generally the only indication of whether a merchant was a denizen or alien. Only when they give information not found in the main text are they reproduced in this edition, and, since all merchants were designated as either aliens or denizens, the notes for the denizens are omitted. Also omitted are the few instances of "auditors use", the system of dots in place of numerals in checking totals.

Erasures and deletions are printed inside < > brackets, and additions inside ( ) brackets, with any accompanying editorial comment italicized. [ ] brackets are used to enclose other editorial comments, again italicized; and, in roman, text lost in the original collectors' rolls that can be supplied from a surviving controller's roll. Loss of text is indicated by ..., with an accompanying note where the loss is extensive. Punctuation has been added only in cash amounts and in the few passages of continuous prose. Capitals have been normalized, including *M*, *D* and *C* in roman numerals. Cash amounts are printed as found in the documents, except that "q" for "quadrans" is rendered as "qu". In the names of persons and places, and vernacular words, contractions of the original that can be expanded with certainty are expanded silently, with the exact spelling retained, except that a final mark of suspension is generally omitted. For other words *v* for a vowel is rendered *u* and consonantal *u* as *v*, while *i* is used for the vowel, and *j* for the consonant; thorn is rendered *th*, and the single instance of yogh as *y*. Contractions of Latin words are expanded silently, save in cases of uncertainty, which are italicized, but nouns preceded by a collective expression are extended in the genitive, and units of quantity preceded by verbs such *pondere, facere* and *continere* are extended in the accusative. Latin was the language of the customs service, and so words which, as abbreviated in the documents, might be either English or Latin are taken to be Latin, but Latin adjectives qualifying English words are not extended.

INTRODUCTION

I

Medieval Newcastle upon Tyne has been characterized as 'the most mysterious as well as the most successful of all the "new towns" of post-conquest England'[1]. The town's dual role as a market centre and as a port was a major factor in that success. To the profits of internal trade centred on an important river crossing were added the commercial opportunities afforded by navigable access along the Tyne to the North Sea. Development was aided by the presence after 1080 of the town's eponymous castle, and in the Pipe Roll for 1204 there was noted the expense of hiring a ship to bring to the garrison corn purchased in Lynn.[2] The presence of a royal castle with the functions of a military outpost of government ensured that logistics played some part in early shipping activity on the Tyne. The same Pipe Roll shows that trade had, as it were, spread from castle bailey to river and thence to continental Europe. King John's levy of a fifteenth on the goods of alien merchants in twenty-four English seaports showed Newcastle returning £158-5s-11d[3]. This was less than London, Southampton, Boston, Lincoln, Hull and York, but Newcastle had already established a commanding lead in foreign trade over the other north-eastern ports of Yarm, Coatham (near the modern Redcar), and Whitby. Newcastle lay on the route along which wool from counties north of the Tees, including Cumberland and Westmorland by way of the Tyne Gap, was shipped to Flanders and perhaps to Italy. Thus in 1270, when the goods of Flemish merchants were seized as part of a diplomatic offensive, Jean de Boinebroke had lying at Newcastle ninety-two sacks of Newminster Abbey wool.[4]

It was this leading position as a port for shipment of wool that led to Newcastle's designation as a customs port in 1275, when a royal tax was introduced on all exports of wool, wool-fells and hides. The tax immediately became a valuable source of revenue, and further customs and subsidies on exports and imports were introduced in the course of the fourteenth century. The documentation of collection which has survived among Exchequer records is useful not only for the history of English overseas trade as a whole but also for local history. For Newcastle upon Tyne the interest of the records of the medieval customs is enhanced because there is scarcely any original material prior to the sixteenth century in the archives of the city, probably as a result of a destruction of corporation muniments when the Scots

1. R. B. Dobson, 'Urban Decline in late Medieval England', *Transactions of the Royal Historical Society*, Fifth Series, 27, (1977), 19.
2. *The Great Roll of the Pipe for the Sixth Year of the Reign of King John, Michaelmas 1204, Pipe Roll 50*, ed. D. M. Stenton, Pipe Roll Society, vol. LVI = New Series vol. XVIII, (1940), 234.
3. *Pipe Roll 6 John*, Pipe Roll Society LVI (1940), 218
4. T. H. Lloyd, *The English Wool Trade in the Middle Ages*, (Cambridge, 1977), p. 36

occupied Newcastle in 1640[5]. It is consequently worthwhile to print in as much detail as practicable representative documents from national archives which relate directly to Newcastle.

The documentation of national customs collection preserved among Exchequer papers at the Public Record Office can be divided into four groups: cockets, particular accounts of collectors and controllers, collectors' summary accounts, and enrolled accounts. A cocket was a receipt for duty paid, and the word is thought to derive from a corruption of 'quo quietus est'.[6] Cockets recorded the name of the merchant responsible for payment, a description of the goods taxed, an identification of the carrying vessel, and the amount of duty charged. The collectors made out the cockets in duplicate. One was taken away by the merchant as proof of payment, and the counterpart was retained. At the end of the collectors' period of office, or of the Exchequer's financial year, all the particulars on the counterparts were entered, ship by ship, and merchant by merchant, in rolls or ledgers to form the particular accounts. One roll was compiled by the collectors, generally two in number except in the port of London, and another by the controller. The controller used the same source of information as the collectors, namely the cockets, but he was not required to record the duty paid. In all other respects the roll of the controller was normally a duplicate of the collectors', so that both collectors' and controller's rolls are of equal value for the student of trade; they have come to be known collectively as particular customs accounts. The third group of documents are the summary accounts of the collectors submitted to the Exchequer. These begin with a note of the collectors' authority and period of appointment, followed by a statement of their total indebtedness for each of the royal customs or subsidies against which duties had been received. These summaries of account, after the collectors' and controller's rolls of particulars had been checked one against the other, formed the basis of agreement between the collectors and the barons of the Exchequer. After audit they were enrolled by an Exchequer clerk, and it is these enrolled accounts which are the final group of documents.

Of the four groups, it is the enrolled accounts that have survived best, not merely in great numbers but with so few losses that for exports of wool and cloth a series from 1275 to 1547 has been constructed covering all major customs ports.[7] Such a series was possible because wool and cloth were subject to specific duties and the quantities exported were included in the enrolled account with the

5. *The Accounts of the Chamberlains of Newcastle upon Tyne 1508–1511*, ed. C. M. Fraser, The Society of Antiquaries of Newcastle upon Tyne Record Series No. 3, (Newcastle, 1987), p. xi.
6. R. C. Jarvis, 'The Archival History of the Customs Records', in *Prisca Munimenta – Studies in Archival History presented to Dr A. E. J. Hollaender*, ed. F. Ranger, (1973), p. 204, note 15.
7. E. M. Carus-Wilson and O.Coleman, *England's Export Trade 1275–1547*, (Oxford, 1963).

amount of duty collected. Wine, wax, tin and pewter similarly attracted specific duties. All the myriad other commodities of trade were charged on an *ad valorem* basis, and of these the enrolled accounts give their total value. The enrolled accounts provide an excellent general picture of the course of England's external trade, and all the totals for each custom or subsidy from 1399 to 1482 have been tabulated and published.[8] For more detailed information, however, the student must turn to the particular accounts, since cockets are not available in significant quantities.

In the day to day events of overseas business in late medieval England, particular accounts have much to offer. Because of the dearth of private mercantile records in England, the accounts are indeed arguably the best available source, since the memorandum and account book of Gilbert Maghfeld, and the Cely papers are among the few private business documents from the Middle Ages so far discovered.[9] A wealth of references to trade exists in administrative and legal records, but many of these are concerned with regulation or with actions for debt. The special merit of particular customs accounts lies in their recording of the routine and repetitive transactions on which commerce depends. Whereas the legal records are largely concerned with occasions when business trust had failed, particular accounts are devoted to the normal and unremarkable. They therefore do something to counter the impression which diplomatic sources can create, that maritime trade was almost perpetually disrupted by war or indiscriminate violence. Above all, these accounts describe discrete events, which are dated and with which the names of individual merchants can be connected.

Nevertheless, in using the accounts as historical sources, it is important to recall that all the evidence they contain was determined by fiscal requirements. As a result, only the imports and exports on which custom was paid were recorded, and the accounts cannot be used as a shipping register, because vessels entering or leaving in ballast were not noticed. Trade between English ports received no mention, so that coastal trade, of the greatest importance for Newcastle, is missing. Happily, the discovery in 1978, and the publication in 1987, of the account of the Chamberlains of Newcastle from 1508 to 1511 supplies a wealth of information about maritime trade between Newcastle and other English ports.[10]

Another problem is caused by the patchy survival of particular accounts, which of course ceased to have any value as documents of record in the archives of the Exchequer once the corresponding

8. 'Tables of Enrolled Customs and Subsidy Accounts, 1399–1482' in *Studies in English Trade in the Fifteenth Century*, ed. E. Power and M. M. Postan, (1933), pp. 321–60.
9. M. K. James, 'Gilbert Maghfeld, a London Merchant of the Fourteenth Century', *Economic History Review*, Second Series, VIII (1956), 364–76. *The Cely Letters 1472–1488*, ed. A. Hanham, Early English Text Society no. 273 (Oxford, 1975).

collectors' summary accounts had been enrolled. Although the particular accounts of collectors and controllers occupy a substantial part of two index volumes at the Public Record Office,[11] it is hard to construct a series for any one customs port, or to find accounts from several ports that are contemporary and so permit comparisons to be made. While one must be grateful for the good fortune that some accounts do survive, a further difficulty is caused by their condition. While the enrolled accounts are still almost as legible as when the Pipe office clerks laid down their pens, many particular accounts are damaged, and some have portions missing. These considerations may have a bearing on why so few particular accounts have been published in full.

In the case of Newcastle upon Tyne, only one particular account covering the period 1294–97 is in print, together with a discussion of three more from the reign of Edward I.[12] Features of the fourteenth century accounts have been described in an unpublished thesis.[13] From the fifteenth century eight accounts survive from 1400–11. After a gap of over forty years, there are thirteen accounts extant between 1454 and 1500, but two of these are by controllers which merely duplicate information from the corresponding collectors' rolls. This latter group has been chosen for publication.

II

Most of the lordships of medieval England levied taxes on trade within their franchise, and when this included facilities for ships to anchor, local customs on maritime trade were also in force. In the few instances where accounts of these local taxes have survived in quantity, as for example they have at Southampton, they yield valuable information. Such local customs, however, generally granted exemption to all the trade of merchants who were free of the town, and their transactions were then wholly omitted. These omissions invalidate estimates of volumes of trade that can be made from local customs accounts. To these, the royal customs form a contrast, because they were intended from the start to be levied throughout the realm, 'dedenz franchise et dehors'.[14] Nobody trading in the classes of goods to which the royal customs applied were to be excused payment of duties as a matter of course. In the maintenance of this principle, collectors were required by the exchequer to include in their accounts notice of all goods, including those belonging to merchants who from time to time did

---

10. *Newcastle Chamberlains' Accounts 1508–1511* ed. C. M. Fraser, (Newcastle, 1987).
11. *Exchequer K. R. Customs Accounts (E122),* List and Index Society, vol 43 (1969), and vol. 60 (1970).
12. J. Conway Davies, 'The Wool Customs Accounts for Newcastle upon Tyne for the Reign of Edward I', *Archaeologia Aeliana*, Fouth Series, XXXII, (1954). 220–308.
13. J. B. Blake, 'Some Aspects of the Trade of Newcastle upon Tyne in the Fourteenth Century', unpublished M.A. thesis, (University of Bristol 1962).
14. *Parliamentary Writs* ed. F. Palgrave (2 vols., Record Commission, 1827–1830), I. l.

succeed in obtaining from the Crown abatements of duty. The enrolled accounts then stated the tax payable on the total volume of trade, followed by disclaimers in respect of the reductions in moneys received as a result of licences of exemption or abatement from the Crown. The national customs accounts can therefore be used to supply quantitative evidence with more confidence than local customs accounts which may contain wide ranging and unstated omissions.

The number of commodities in overseas trade which attracted tax increased between 1275 and 1350. In 1275, only fleece-wool, the wool-bearing sheepskins known as wool-fells, and hides were taxed. Fleece-wool was reckoned by weight. Seven pounds made a nail or clove, and fifty-two nails made a sack. The sack was a fiscal unit of 364 pounds to be distinguished from the canvas container in which wool was actually packed, known as a sarpler. Wool-fells were reckoned by tale in hundreds of six score, but the framers of the 1275 custom, seeking the administrative simplicity of a unified rate, laid down that 300 wool-fells were to be reckoned as of equivalent weight to a sack of wool. This approximation must have been to the Crown's disadvantage, for in 1368, the number of fells was reduced to 240, where it remained.[15] The duty payable by all exporters was 6s 8d for each sack and 13s 4d for a last containing 200 hides.

Alien merchants obtained an improved legal status in the *Carta Mercatoria* of 1303, but the *quid pro quo* was more taxes. They paid a further 3s 4d custom on each sack of wool, and 6s 8d more on the last of hides. Woollen cloth was taxed at one shilling for a cloth of assize measuring twenty-four yards in length by between sixty-three and seventy-two inches in width. This rate was for cloths dyed without grain. Grain was a very costly dye, so that cloths dyed wholly in grain attracted a duty of two shillings, and if dyed partly in grain, of one and sixpence. Cloths of different dimensions were charged *pro rata* according to their relationship to the cloth of assize. Wax attracted a custom of one shilling for each quintal of approximately one hundredweight. The Crown held ancient rights of prise on the wine imports of both denizens and aliens. (Denizens were native-born merchants and the few foreign merchants privileged to enjoy the same status for taxation as natives). For aliens, the Crown renounced the right of prise for custom of two shillings on each wine tun of 252 gallons. In addition to these specific customs, all other goods were subject to an *ad valorem* duty of threepence in the pound.

After 1303, therefore, all the trade of aliens was taxed, even though merchants of the Hanseatic League resisted with some success the payment of customs and subsidies introduced subsequently. At a meeting of representatives of towns held in York on 25 July 1303, Edward I tried to extend to denizen merchants the same duties to which the aliens had just agreed. Peter Graper and Richard Emeldon

15. *Rotuli Parliamentorum ut et Petitiones et Placita in Parliamento* (6 vols., Record Commission, 1767–77), IV, 302.

represented Newcastle upon Tyne in an assembly which rejected the royal proposals, calling the increase in wool custom a maltote and resisting any addition to 'the due and established customs of old'.[16] The distinction between alien and denizen was retained throughout medieval customs records.

In 1347, a custom on cloth exported by both denizen and alien merchants was introduced. Cloths without grain paid a custom of ls 2d, cloths in part grain 1s 9d, and those wholly in grain 2s 4d. There were also small duties on single and double worsteds and worsted bed-cloths, but none of these were to approach woollen cloth in commercial importance before the sixteenth century.

The remainder of the taxes on overseas trade were in the form of subsidies granted to the crown by parliament, originally for a specific purpose and a delimited period. Around the subsidy of wool, wool-fells and hides, major political conflicts occurred in 1294–97 and continued intermittently until the later parliaments of Edward III. The rate of subsidy which was in force for much of the fifteenth century and was unchanged after 1471, was, on each sack, 33s 4d for denizens and 66s 8d for aliens. When the custom of 1275 had been added to this subsidy, the total tax could be equated with an *ad valorem* duty of approximately 25% for denizens and 48% for aliens, on good quality Cotswold wool like that in which the Celys traded.[17] On wools of lower price, such as those shipped by Newcastle merchants, the tax could amount to an unacceptable proportion of the selling price. The other subsidies were tunnage and poundage, granted with increasing frequency after 1350, and applicable to both denizen and alien imports and exports. Tunnage became a duty of three shillings per tun on non-sweet wine, and six shillings per tun on sweet wine. Poundage was an *ad valorem* duty of one shilling in the pound on all goods not included in the other subsidies, although denizen exporters succeeded in gaining exemption for their cloth which already paid the cloth custom of 1347.

The mature national customs system, in force throughout the period from which the accounts published here have been taken, was arranged in three groups. The first was the custom, and subsidy, of wool. By this time the custom of 1275 was known as the great or ancient custom and the second group therefore was distinguished by the name of the petty custom. This comprehended the custom of 1303, and the cloth custom of 1347. The third group was tunnage and poundage, now granted as a single subsidy. Early in the fifteenth century the grant of subsidies was made regularly by Parliament. Henry VI received a life grant in 1454. Edward IV received a similar grant in 1465, although the customs and subsidies had been collected from his accession in 1461. Richard III and Henry VII had life grants from the start of their reigns. The administrative framework was

16. *Parliamentary Writs*, I, 134–35.
17. Carus-Wilson and Coleman, *England's Export Trade 1275–1547*, p. 194.

therefore in place throughout the second half of the fifteenth century for all overseas trade to come to the notice of the collectors of the national customs. Only the personal effects of seamen and passengers, goods of the Crown, and victuals for Calais were exempt.

III

Particular accounts thus provided a comprehensive listing of external trade, provided that the accounts were reliably kept, and that there was no evasion by merchants. Fraud or neglect by officials, and smuggling by traders only gained a place in the records when detected. The amount of successful breaking of the law can never be known, and customs accounts, in common with all other sources from taxation records, cannot be used without qualifications. What case can be made for their accuracy and reliability?

Perhaps the most important point is that, with the exception of wool, the duties imposed by the medieval customs and subsidies were not at all punitive. The cloth custom was equivalent to some 3% of the cost price for denizens. Tunnage also rarely exceeded 3% of cost. The impact of the *ad valorem* duties, 5% for denizens and 7.5% for aliens, was lessened by the conservative basis of valuation. Goods were required to be valued at the cost of first buying, and these prices were to be given on oath, or by letters from factors acting for the merchants. In practice, conventional valuations were often adopted, as the regularity with which the same values appear over several accounts can hardly have reflected the reality of commerce. (As a result particular customs accounts are not useful to the historian of prices).

Given the penalties of forfeiture and fine awaiting detection, there was little financial gain to be made from smuggling except in wool. In the first half of the fourteenth century, research has certainly uncovered large scale evasions of wool duty, notably by William de la Pole and his associates.[18] By the end of the century, the drop in demand for English wool as alternative supplies became available to continental cloth makers, coupled with the monopoly distribution powers given by the Crown to the merchants of the Staple at Calais, made smuggling wool less profitable and more difficult also to organize discreetly. The sheer bulk of sarplers each weighing up to 1000 pounds inhibited large clandestine shipments. When the medieval customs system was reformed during the reign of Elizabeth I, with books of rates replacing the lax 1303 provisions for valuation and with higher rates of duty on a wide range of commodities, prosecutions for smuggling brought in the Exchequer courts increased in number. Lack of adequate incentive to carry out extensive systematic evasion of the medieval customs is one reason for accepting the general reliability of the collectors' accounts.

---

18. E. B. Fryde, *William de la Pole Merchant and King's Banker, d. 1366*, (Gloucester, 1988).

A second reason is the care taken by the Exchequer in administering the customs. Their yield was an important part of royal revenue, and made up no less than half of Edward IV's regular income.[19] There was therefore pressure from central government to minimize losses through evasion.

The methods adopted were proven over time. Collection was never entrusted to a single man. The keeping of a counter roll was a check on the collectors. The cocket seal used to authenticate receipts was in two halves, one half to be held by the collectors, the other by the controller. Among the customs staff there was generally a tronager, in charge of weighing, and the collectors often employed clerks. The most important of these officials was the searcher. His duties were described in 1545 as taking the cockets made out by the collectors and then 'he doth peruse the cocketts and ladings of every marchaunt in the said straung ship, whether they doe justly agree or no.'[20] When agreement was lacking, the searchers were encouraged by shares in the value of forfeited goods to bring prosecutions in the Exchequer courts.

With the aid of a contemporary index,[21] records of these cases for individual customs ports can be identified, and a comparison of Newcastle with the next adjacent head customs port, Kingston upon Hull, shows that fewer prosecutions originated at Newcastle than at Hull between 1450 and 1500. The few cases that were reported at Newcastle include the following. On 7 February 1456, William Underwood found in the *Mary* of Newcastle a pipe filled with linen cloth, spices, and other merchandise to the value of twenty pounds, the property of William Roos, a merchant; Underwood impounded the pipe, but William Roos came 'with many other unknown men' and took it out of the searcher's possession.Thomas Moll, acting as servant to John Frizley, a collector from 1476 to 1478, was sent by Frizley to seize cloth which Walter Bray and William Junour had shipped uncustomed in a ship of Lynn. Moll evidently did not get his timing right, as the petition stated that Bray and Junour 'were departed almost out of the said port' when Moll made the seizure. They proceeded to take out an action for trespass against Moll for taking away the cloth, which was by then forfeited to the Crown.[23]

The customs officers were not always unsuccessful. William Underwood in 1456 found six small pokes of uncustomed wool belonging to William Bird aboard the *Mary* of Antwerp on the bank of the river at North Shields 'which is a suspected locality'.[24] Three times in 1453 William Hurlbat of Newcastle was charged with smuggling

---

19. C. Ross, *Edward IV*, (1974), p. 384.
20. Georg Schanz, *Englische Handelspolitik gegen Ende des Mittelalters*, (2 vols., Leipzig, 1881), II, 359–60.
21. PRO IND 7040 IND 7041, K.R.Memoranda Repertory Rolls.
22. PRO E 159/232 34 Henry VI, Recorda Pasche, m. 14d.
23. PRO C 1/64/184.
24. PRO E 159/232, 34 Henry VI, Recorda Pasche, m. 15.

wool. On March 5 he had one uncustomed sack aboard the *Katherine* of Schiedam, where William Cuthbert and William Scott, both of Newcastle, had smuggled respectively two and three sacks. On the following day, Hurlbat had three uncustomed sacks on the *Saint Maryknight* of Schiedam, and on April 30th, he had a sack 'or more' aboard the *Anne* of Arnemuiden.[25] An enterprising arrest was made by the searcher Nicholas Turpin on 20 September 1490. On the high seas 'against the town of Hartlepool' he arrested the crayer of Robert Stokall, a Newcastle merchant, in which were twenty-two packs called 'horse cariours', each containing sixteen stones of wool. These were the property of George Carr who had evidently loaded almost fourteen sackweights of wool on to horses, and transferred them to Stokall's ship for uncustomed export at 'Teyse in the Water'. [26] Only one case was related to unsatisfactory administration by a Newcastle official. William Chauntrell, an example of whose work as controller is included among the accounts printed here, was required to present himself at the Exchequer bringing with him whatever books or particulars he had during the time that he was controller. The writ was endorsed that he was not found.[27]

That the number of cases reaching the Exchequer from Newcastle between 1450 and 1500 was small may indicate good administration, but it may merely bear witness to effective evasion. For this reason, the quantities in the accounts must be seen as minimum quantities. That done, one can emphasize that the accounts are wholly reliable as the record of goods on which custom and subsidy was paid. The accounts were not composed to justify a farmed tax. They recorded real quantities, real sailings and real payments. Once a cocket had been issued, the collectors were liable at the Exchequer for the relevant duties and were aware that heavy penalties awaited officials found to be fraudulent. In a small community, fraud and collusion would not have been easy to conceal, and prosecutions were initiated by the laying of information. Informants, like searchers, were rewarded with a share of any forfeited goods. Finally, the accuracy of Exchequer auditing was a further spur for the collectors to work carefully and conscientiously, so far as all trade in the port of Newcastle upon Tyne was concerned. The collectors' responsibilities, however, extended from Berwick to Scarborough. Where the amount of customable trade was small, it cannot have been economically practicable for a government with severe financial problems to maintain officials permanently other than at the head port. One may doubt whether occasional surveillance was sufficient to deter some merchants from

---

25. *Bronnen tot de Geschiedenis van dem Handel met England, Schotland en Ierland, 1150–1485*, ed. H. J. Smit, two vols. Rijks Geschiedkundige Publicatiën 65, 66, (The Hague, 1928), document nos. 1422, 1477, 1416.
26. PRO E 159/267, 6 Henry VII, Recorda Michaelmas, m. 21.
27. PRO E 159/248, 11 Edward IV, Recorda Michaelmas, m. 18.

using the outports, although these were legally closed to overseas trade. With that proviso, it is not unreasonable to conclude that these particular customs accounts offer a substantially reliable impression of Newcastle's overseas trade between 1450 and 1500.

IV

That trade was carried on in a harsh economic climate. Depression in Europe was widespread for much of the fifteenth century. To population decline consequent on recurrent epidemic disease was added the difficulty caused by bullion shortages as sources of precious metals became exhausted. Although England's exports of wool cloth may have offset some of the losses caused by a steep decline in demand for English wool, these were not sufficient for England to escape the prevalent slowing of business activity. The weakness of the Lancastrian government after Henry V's death caused merchants effectively to become excluded from the markets of the Baltic. Gascony was lost and Burgundian hegemony in the Low Countries created periodic problems for traders in the most important of English markets overseas. Some English merchants were forced into seeking trade in Iceland, and in the customs account for 1456–57 a Newcastle ship setting out in such a voyage is recorded.[28] The drop in demand was exacerbated for all east coast ports by the steady increase in the maritime trade of the port of London. The value of goods which paid the poundage subsidy there in the year to Michaelmas 1466 was £42,899, when the combined value of goods in Ipswich, Yarmouth, Lynn, Boston, Hull and Newcastle was £11,336. Newcastle's share was £1,487.[29]

A recent study of the North-East during the Wars of the Roses has concluded that the region 'passed through an extended economic crisis in the later middle ages. The major factors were climatic deterioration, war damage and above all, population decline'.[30] The last of these may explain why the merchants of Newcastle failed to share in the expansion of woollen cloth exports. While English exports were exceeding 50,000 cloths in some years, Newcastle's contribution rarely rose above fifty cloths. Imports of woad, madder and other textile adjuncts showed that there was some cloth manufacture in or near Newcastle. If, however, rural depopulation was such that spinning and weaving could not be organized in the countryside, the ability to create an exportable surplus of manufactured goods was destroyed. In Newcastle itself, the evidence from late fifteenth century rentals

---

28. Thomas Castell and William Haysand of Newcastle were granted a licence to trade in Iceland for seven years from Michaelmas, 1455, *Diplomatarium Islandicum* (16 vols. Reykjavik, 1857–1972), vol. XVI, (1415–1589), pp. 384–385.
29. 'Tables of Enrolled Customs Accounts', in *English Trade in the Fifteenth Century*, pp. 331, 340, 342, 346, 348, 352, 360.
30. A. J. Pollard, *North Eastern England during the Wars of the Roses*, (Oxford, 1990), p. 43.

suggests that the market in urban property was weak,[31] and it is unlikely that Newcastle escaped the decline which affected many hitherto prosperous centres of population at the close of the Middle Ages, including both York and Hull in the North. The customs accounts provide one set of figures, whose implication for the prosperity of Newcastle merchants is clear. Between 1299–1339, which admittedly were boom times, Newcastle merchants had shipped 38,000 sacks of wool through the royal customs, and the great majority were shipped by denizens. In 1399–1439, the total of sacks exported, all by denizens, was 7932.[32] From the evidence of surviving particular accounts, even in the one seaborne trade for which Newcastle had outstanding natural resources, that of coal, exports were disappointing. The lowest total out of four late fourteenth-century accounts was an export of 4843 chalders in the thirteen months to Michaelmas 1391.[33] In the thirteen months to April 1466, only 2281 chalders were exported, and this was the highest total observable between 1450 and 1500.

In this unpromising situation, the resourcefulness of Newcastle's merchant community secured exemption from the requirement common to all other ports save Berwick that all wool for Northern Europe should be shipped to the Company of the Staple at Calais. Licences were regularly recorded after 1410 in the enrolled accounts for the wools of Northumberland, Cumberland, Westmorland, the bishopric of Durham and of Richmondshire and Allertonshire to be shipped to Bruges and to Middelburg through Newcastle. Not surprisingly, the Staplers fought in defence of their monopoly. Even after the special position of Northern wools had received statutory recognition in 1463,[34] a petition to Parliament in 1476 began 'A grete noyse renneth by men of ye Newcastell and Berwick that if they brought their woolles to the Staple they should be undone and destroyed', and goes on to the charge that Newcastle merchants were 'abating the price of the commoditie'.[35]

Parallel with the privileges of avoiding the Staple at Calais were those for shipping inferior fells – shorlings, morlings and lamb fells – without paying the wool custom and subsidy on them. A licence of 1452 awarded for 'the defence of our seide town against the Scots' specified that the duty on inferior fells was only to be one shilling in the pound by value, or the standard rate of the subsidy of poundage.[36] It was followed by many more licences of this type. Newcastle merchants were clearly successful in marketing their coarse wools and inferior fells to the makers of medium price cloth in towns like Gouda,

31. A. F. Butcher, 'Rent, Population and Economic Change in Late Medieval Newcastle', *Northern History*XIV, (1979), 71–73.
32. Carus-Wilson and Coleman, *England's Export Trade 1275–1547*, pp. 40–60.
33. J. B. Blake, 'The Medieval Coal Trade of Northeast England', *Northern History*, II, (1967), 17–20.
34. *The Statutes of the Realm*, ed. A. Luders et al. (11 vols., 1810–1828), II, 393.
35. *Rotuli Parliamentorum*, IV, 360.
36. *Proceedings and Ordinances of the Privy Council of England*, ed. Sir H. Nicholas, (7 vols., Record Commission, 1834–7), IV, 117–18.

Hoorn and the Hague. In Leyden, where high quality cloths were produced, an ordinance of 1434 proscribed the mixing of Newcastle wools with Staple wools.[37] Such regulations often were a sign that the materials forbidden were in fact being used and that Newcastle wool had acquired a recognizable commercial identity. There is an entry in the toll of Iersekeroord for 1493 for a crayer loaded with 'Casteels' wool belonging to William Davell, Thomas Lilburn and Thomas Green.[38] When in 1505 Henry VII opened Calais to trading, among the commodities to be sold without restriction were 'Newcastle wool and fell, accustomed to be sold in the Archduke's countries'.[39]

Perhaps the greatest success for the merchants had come at the start of Henry VII's reign. The account for 1488–89, printed below, shows them enjoying complete exemption from wool custom and subsidy, and in 1489 they received a licence by which northern wool was for seven years to pay custom and subsidy at one quarter of the standard rate. The king, said the letters patent, was 'informed . . . that wool of the said counties is so coarse and of so little value that the ordinary duties thereon are excessive and the trade is carried on at a loss'.[40] The combination of royal favour and commercial enterprise by the merchants led to a brief Indian summer in wool exports from Newcastle. At a time when exports of wool to the Staple at Calais were in terminal decline, Newcastle's independent share of the total market actually rose. In 1391–1400, the decennial average for the whole of England, was 17,679, to which Newcastle's contribution was only 213 sacks. In 1491–1500, when the decennial average was more than halved at 8,149 sacks, Newcastle's share doubled to 444 sacks.[41]

Probably the proceeds of this wool went to finance the importing of the greatly increased quantity and range of imported products for the consumer, seen in the account for 1499–1500. Another encouraging sign in that account, and in the preceding one for 1494–95, was the increase in the number of French ships, especially from Boulogne and Dieppe. Many of these entered in ballast and left with coal. They marked the start of what was to become in the sixteenth century a most significant new export market for Newcastle's hostmen.

The evidence of the customs accounts is too slight to indicate whether this greater activity in the port at the end of the fifteenth century reflected an improvement in Newcastle's fortunes, but if it did, this was in line with the general improvement in international trade at that time. In any case, one must constantly recall that overseas trade

37. E. Power, 'The Wool Trade in the Fifteenth Century,' in *Studies in English Trade in the Fifteenth Century*, ed. E. Power and M.M.Postan, (1933), p. 43.

38. *De Tol van Iersekeroord – Document ed Rekeningen 1321–1572*, ed. W. S. Unger, Rijks Geschiedkundige Publicatiën, Kleine Serie 29, (The Hague, 1939), p. 431.

39. *Tudor Royal Proclamations*, ed. P. L. Hughes and J. F. Larkin, (3 vols., New Haven and London, 1969), I, 68.

40. *Calendar of Patent Rolls, 1272–1509*, (52 vols. 1891–1916), 1476–85, pp. 159–60.

41. Carus-Wilson and Coleman, *England's Export Trade 1275–1547*, pp. 53–69.

was only one aspect, and that not the most important, of Newcastle's commercial activity in the later Middle Ages. The marketing of Tyne coal by sea to other English ports, and the maintenance of the town's position as a leading market for the North-East, especially in the distribution of corn and other foodstuffs, were central to economic success. The men named in the customs accounts were merchant adventurers in their own justified estimation. Most of them were also boothmen as familiar with Bigg Market as with the Quayside. Lacking records of their domestic business, the history of Newcastle upon Tyne's trade in the later Middle Ages will remain a mystery. All that is claimed for the particular customs accounts is that they fill in one small section of a jigsaw from which, regrettably, so many of the pieces are missing.

For discussion of the information contained in the accounts printed below, and in four further accounts for the period 1500–1509, see J. F. Wade, 'The overseas trade of Newcastle upon Tyne in the late Middle Ages', *Northern History*, 30, (1994), 31–48

1. Particulars of Account of Thomas Weltden, controller, from Michaelmas 1454 to 31 March 1455

E 122/107/48

The three membranes, sewn Exchequer style, measure 225 mm. in width by 710 mm. in length, 225 mm. by 620 mm., and 220 mm. by 580 mm. They are stained and worn, but all but a few words can be read with the help of ultra violet light. The large holes and the damaged edges are noticed where they occur below. There is no record of the document's delivery to the Exchequer on the final membrane, but dating of entries suggests the account is complete.

Although, in the manuscript, denizens and aliens were both designated by marginal comments, only those relating to aliens have been printed. Merchants whose name immediately follows the word *alienigena* are aliens. All others are denizens. In this, and the three collectors' accounts that follow it, there are no records of customs and subsidies paid. These are only found in collectors' accounts.

In the title to the account, there is no mark of suspension on *contrarotulator* to indicate the genitive case. Unusually in these accounts 'barels' occurs twice fully written out, so the abbreviated forms have been extended as English words. The phrase *redys an*^{ce} *slays* occurs once and *custellorum an*^{ce} *brages* three times. The outer words are synonyms, so the conjunction, left unextended, has the general sense of 'alternatively'. Possibly *antecedenter* is intended if Latin is being used. In English, *ance* is a Northern dialect form of 'once', but the use of superscript letters for abbreviations of English words does not occur elsewhere in this account.

[*Membrane 1 face*]

Rotulus Thome Weltden, contrarotulator custume et subsidii lanarum, corriorum et pellium lanutarum necnon subsidii tonagii et pondagii ac parve custume, in portu ville Novi Castri super Tynam et in singulis portubus et locis eidem portui adiacentibus, videlicet de huiusmodo custumis et subsidiis domini regis ibidem a festo Sancti Michaelis Archangeli anno regni regis Henrici sexti post conquestum Anglie xxxiij^{o} usque ultimam diem Marcii tunc proximo sequentem, quo tempore Ricardus Weltden et Johannes Baxster fuerunt custumarii dicti domini regis in portubus et locis predictis.

Navis vocata Cristofyr de Skyddam unde Johannes Jonson est magister applicuit ix° die Octobris
{alienigena}

Idem pro iiij barelles smigmatis	valor xl s.
Idem pro j sacco hope	valor x s.
Alanus Byrde pro xxx barelles ceparum	valor x s.
Idem pro C bundellis allei	valor vj s. viij d.
Idem pro xiiij barelles bituminis	valor xl s.
Idem pro vij barelles osmundes	valor xl s.
Idem pro vj schyf tasyls	valor iij s. iiij d.
Johannes Byrde pro viij barelles bituminis	valor lx s.
Idem pro M et j quarterio libris ferri	valor xl s.
Idem pro vij barelles osmondes	valor xl s.
Willelmus Rothom senior pro di' last bituminis	valor xx s.
Willelmus Byrd pro xviij barelles bituminis	valor lx s.

Summa valoris xviij li. x s.

Navis vocata Michaell de Leythe unde Thomas Orkeney est magister applicuit xix die Octobris

Willelmus Brankston pro iiij last ostrium	valor xxvj s. viij d.

Summa valoris patet

Navis vocata Cristofyr de Skyddam unde Johannes Jonson est magister exivit xxj° die Octobris
{alienigena}

Idem pro vj celdris carbonum	valor x s.
Johannes Richardson pro ij dossenis gryndstonys	valor xl s.
Johannes Forster pro j foder plumbi	valor liij s. iiij d.
Robertus Baxster pro j foder plumbi	valor lx s.
Willelmus Rothom senior pro ij fother plumbi	valor cvj s. viij d.
Thomas Cuthbert pro iij gryndstanys	valor v s.
Johannes Spense pro CCxl schorlynges	valor xxxv s.
Idem pro CCCxx pellibus agnellorum	valor xlj s. viij d.
Nicholaus Haynyng pro CC schorlynges	valor xxx s.
Idem pro CCCCxl pellibus agnellorum	valor lviij s. iiij d.
Johannes Penrethe pro CClx schorlynges	valor xxxvij s. vj d.
Idem pro Cxlviij pellibus agnellorum	valor xviij s. iiij d.
Thomas Castell pro CCC schorlynges	valor xlv s.
Thomas Wardley pro CCCC schorlynges	valor lxs.
Idem pro iiij^{xx} pellibus agnellorum	valor x s.

Summa valoris xxxli. x s. x d.

Ricardus comes Saresburie pro vj saccis lane in v pokes
Johannes Spense pro ij saccis [lane] in ij pokes

Nicholaus Haynyng pro j sacco et viij clavis lane in j pok
Johannes Richardson pro j sacco iij quarteriis xj clavis lane in iij pokes
Johannes Penreth pro j sacco iij quarteriis xj clavis lane in iij pokes
Idem pro xx pellibus lanutis
Willelmus Byrde pro j sacco iij quarteriis iij clavis lane in iij pokes
Johannes Forster pro iij quarteriis et v clavis lane in ij pokes
Johannes Byrde pro dimidio sacco lane in j poke
Thomas Castell pro j s[acco et *hole in membrane 30 x 40 mm.*] dimidio lane in ij pokes
Johannes Matson pro ... clavis lane in j poke
Willelmus Roos pro ... ij pokes
Thomas Cuthbert pro di...[midio] ... ij pokes

Summa { saccorum lane xx sacci iij quarteria vij clavi
pellium lanutarum patet }

{Novembris}
Navis vocata Cristofir de Camfer unde Jacob Frees est magister applicuit x die Novembris
{alienigena}

Idem pro vj barelles bituminis	valor xxiij s. iiij d.
Idem pro xij barelles ceparum	valor v s.
Willelmus Byrde pro M et di' libris ferri	valor xlv s.
Idem pro C ulnis canvasse	valor xiij s. iiij d.
Idem pro ij dossenis felthattes	valor v s.
Johannes Penreth pro vij C libris ferri	valor xxv s.
Idem pro j barelle smigmatis	valor x s.
Idem pro ij barelles osmundes	valor xiij s. iiij d.
Thomas Brigham pro x barelles ceparum	valor iij s. iiij d.
Johannes Richardson pro M et di' libris ferri	valor xlv s.
Idem pro j barelle smygmatis	valor xs.
Idem pro xij bundellis lini	valor x s.
Johannes La... pro ij saccis hope	valor xiij s. iiij d.
Alanus Byrde pro M libris ferri	valor xxxs.
Willelmus Stokton pro iiij doliis wadde	valor xij li.
Idem pro C et di' libris c...	valor xl s.
Thomas Castell pro j poke madour	valor...
...	
...	

[Summa valoris] xxviij li. xx d.

Navis vocata Cristofyr de Camfer unde Jacob Frees est magister exivit xx die Novembris
[*50 mm. missing from left edge of membrane; right edge heavily rubbed.*]

... Richardson pro vj celdris carbonum	...
... ...	
... pro CClx pellibus agnellorum	...
... ...iij fothyr plumbi	...
... ...v fothyr plumbi	...
... ...CC shorlynges	...

... ...vij C lx pellibus agnellorum ...
... ...x... ...
Summa valoris xxiij li. xs.

[*Membrane l dorse*]
... pro j quarterio et viij clavis lane in j pok
Summa saccorum lane patet

[Navis] vocata Mary de Lethe unde Henricus Bylbye est magister...
... Chambre pro ij last ostrium ...
Idem pro xxx... ...
Idem pro xl ulnis panni linei ...
Johannes Richardson pro j barelle olei ...
Idem pro j barelle litmos ...
Idem pro ij coopertoriis ......
... Wytte pro C horschon ...
... ...
Summa ... xlj s. viij d.

{Decembris}
Navis vocata Marye de Andwarpe unde Mattheus Colle est magister applicuit iij die Decembris
{alienigena}
Idem pro xij skytfattes ...
{alienigena}

Johannes Danherus pro M speculis	valor xxx s.
Idem pro xx payntyd clothys	valor x s.
Idem pro C par precularum	valor xx s.
Idem pro viij dossenis bruschys	valor xj s. viij d.
Idem pro V dakyr custellorum	valor x s.
Idem pro iiij M spinctris	valor x s .
Idem pro iiij gros lasyngpoyntes	valor vj s. viij d.
Idem pro v pauper punctorum	valor...
Idem pro xij redys an[ce] slays	valor v s.
Idem pro vj M acubus	valor iij s. iiij d.
Idem pro vj dossenis felthattes	valor xx s.
Idem pro j barell bituminis	valor x s.
Idem pro j magnum speculum	valor xx d.
Idem pro ij dossenis bursarum	valor iij s. iiij d.
Idem pro iij dossenis pilleorum	valor xs.
Johannes Ellyson pro ij barelles allecis albi	valor xiij s. iiij d.
Willelmus Roos pro j last bituminis	valor xv s.
Idem pro iij barelles osmundes	valor xx s.
Thomas Cuthbert pro iiij barelles allecis albi	valor xxvj s. viij d.
Willelmus Horsley pro v...	
[*hole in membrane 20 x 40 mm.*]	valor xxiij s. iiij d
Willelmus Hewet pro iii...	valor xxvj. viij d.

Summa valoris xvij li. vj s. viij d.

{Januarii}

Navis vocata Jacob de Camfer unde Mattheus Person est magister applicuit x° die Januarii

{alienigena}

Idem pro xx barelles ceparum valor vj s. viijd.

Summa valoris patet

Navis vocata Cristofyr de Camfer unde Willelmus Stobe est magister applicuit xvj° die Januarii

{alienigena}

Idem pro iij ferkyns allecis albi valor v s.
Idem pro di' barell allecis albi valor iij s. iiij d.
Idem pro xxv bundellis allei valor xx d.
Idem pro iiij[or] aughtyndeles angwillarum valor xiij s. iiij d.

Summa valoris xxiij s iiij d.

Navis vocata Maryknight de Amsterdam unde Jacob Jonson est magister applicuit xxvij° die Januarii

{alienigena}

Idem pro xx last berre valor xxiij li. vj s.viij d.
Idem pro ij C clapholt valor xiij s. iiij d.
Idem pro iij barelles ottmell valor v s.
Idem pro xx salt hydys valor xl s.
Idem pro iij barelles littmos valor v s.

Summa valoris xxvj li. xs.

Navis vocata Mary de Andwarppe unde Matheus Coll est magister exivit xxvij° die Januarii

Willelmus Hurlbad pro iiij[or] celdris carbonum valor v s.
Idem pro Cxiiij schorlynges valor xvj s. viij d.
Alanus Karre pro [j] fothyr plumbi valor liij s. iiij d.
Robertus Maltby pro ij C xxx schorlynges valor liij s. iiij d.
Ricardus Stevynson pro iiij[xx] schorlynges valor x s.
Idem pro CC pellibus agnellorum valor xxvj s. viiij d.
Idem pro dimidia pecia panni lanei stricti
Johannes Waels pro v[xx] schorlynges valor xij s. vj d.

Summa { valoris vij li. xvi js. vj d.
panni lanei sine grano patet

Willelmus Hurlbad pro iij quarteriis et v clavis lane in ij pokes
Idem pro v pellibus lanutis
Robertus Maltby pro j sacco iij quarteriis v clavis lane in iiij pokes
Idem pro x pellibus lanutis
Ricardus Stevynson pro j quarterio et v clavis lane in j pok
Johannes Waels pro v pellibus lanutis
Johannes Firle pro j sacco lane in ij pokes
Johannes Robynson pro j sacco lane in ij pokes
Thomas Pykden pro j sacco iij quarteriis lane in iij pokes

Johannes Spense pro iij quarteriis et ij clavis lane in ij pokes
Johannes Richardson pro j quarterio lane in j poke
Willelmus Rothom senior pro iij quarteriis lane in ij pokes
Nicholaus Haynyng pro j quarterio et v clavis lane in j poke
Willelmus Scott pro j quarterio iiij clavis lane in j poke
Summa { saccorum lane ix sacci et j quarterium lane
pellium lanutarum xx pelles }

Navis vocata Cristofir de Novo Castro unde Henricus Driffeld est magister applicuit penultimo die Januarii

Johannes Richardson pro M libris ferri	valor xxx s.
Idem pro j pipa avalanarum	valor xx s.
Idem pro ij barelles smigmatis	valor xx s.
Idem pro xl bundellis lini	valor xxvj s. viij d
Idem pro di' last allecis albi	valor xxvj s. viij d.
Willelmus Lawes senior pro di' M libris ferri	valor xv s.
Idem pro j barell smigmatis	valor x s.
Idem pro j pok madyr	valor xx s.
Idem pro j barell alome	valor xx s.
[*Membrane 2 face*]	
Idem pro j fulle ketylles	valor xxvj s. viij d.
Idem pro CCC ulnis canvasse	valor xxx s.
Idem pro viij dossenis felthattes	valor xxiij s. iiij d.
Idem pro iij dossenis [librarum] amigdalarum	valor vjs. viij d.
Idem pro vj salettes	valor vj s. viij d.
Robertus Baker pro viij libris piperis	valor vj s. viij d.
Idem pro dimidia pecia fustian	valor iiij s. ij d.
Idem pro j quarterio safaron	valor ij s. vj d.
Willelmus Hewet pro j last allecis albi	valor iiij li.
Idem pro ij bales alom	valor xxx s.
Idem pro j fatt avalanarum	valor xx s.
Thomas Durham pro C ulnis kanvase	valor xiij s. iiij d.
Idem pro ij C ulnis panni linii	valor xxvj s. viij d.
Idem pro C et di' ulnis panni linei	valor xx s.
Idem pro vj felthattes	valor ij s. vj d.
Idem pro vj daker custellorum an[ce] brages	valor xx d.
Idem pro M spinctris	valor ij s. vj d.
Idem pro vj libris fili blodii	valor iij s. iiij d.
Johannes Makpas pro ij M libris ferri	valor lx s.
Idem pro j barell alom	valor xx s.
Idem pro j barell smigmatis	valor x s.
Idem pro ij schyf tasyls	valor xx d.
Idem pro di' M libris ferri	valor xv s.
Idem pro j barell olei	valor xx s.
Idem pro ij barels drosse	valor v s.
Thomas Cuthbert pro MM libris ferri	valor lx s.
Idem pro xl bundellis lini	valor xl s.

Idem pro ij barelles smigmatis valor xx s.
Idem pro j pok madour valor xx s.
Idem pro j barell olei valor xx s.
Thomas Burton pro ij dossenis felthattes valor x s.
Idem pro xij libris piperis valor vj s. viij d.
Idem pro xxv libris amigdalarum valor ij s. vj d.
Idem pro xij libris rice valor xx d.
Idem pro j gros lasyng poyntes valor iij s. iiij d.
Willelmus Rothom senior pro M et di' libris ferri valor xlv s.
Idem pro j pipa avelanarum valor x s.
Idem pro j barell allecis albi valor vj s. viij d.
Idem pro j pok madour valour xx s.
Idem pro j quarterio de C pakthred valor xx d.
Idem pro di' C ulnis canvasse valor vj s. viij d.
Idem pro xij felthattes valor v s.
Idem pro j grosse lasyng poyntes valor xx d.
Johannes ...de pro ij dossenis felthattes valor x s.
Idem pro j last allecis albi valor lx s.
Idem pro v barelles smigmatis valor l s.
Idem pro ij barelles alome valor xl s.
Idem pro iij M libris ferri valor iiij li. x s.
Idem pro ij sortes fices et rasenis valor xiij s. iiij d.
Johannes Byrde pro C ulnis canvasse valor xiij s. iiij d.
Idem pro iij dossenis felthattes valor iij s. iiij d.
Idem pro vj libris fili blodii valor iij s. iiij d.
Idem pro vj dakyr cultellorum an^{ce}brages valor xx d.
Idem pro j barell alom valor xx s.
Idem pro j full ketylles valor xx s.
Idem pro j quarterio C seminis ceparum valor ij s. vj d.
Idem pro j pipa avalanarum valor x s.
Idem pro MM libris ferri valor lx s.
Idem pro vij dossenis bowstaves valor xiij s. iiij d.
Idem pro vj barelles olei valor xx s.
Johannes Forster pro di' M libris ferri valor xv s.
Idem pro j barell smigmatis valor x s.
Johannes Byge pro xv bundellis lini valor xijs. vjd.
Johannes Spense pro M libris ferri valor xxx s.
Idem pro ij barelles smigmatis valor xx s.
Thomas Morby pro j [barell] smigmatis valor x s.
Idem pro ij barelles bituminis valor v s.
Idem pro j pipa avalanarum valor x s.
Idem pro di' M libris ferri valor xv s.
Johannes Yonger pro iij barelles smigmatis valor xxx s.
Idem pro M libris ferri valor xxx s.
Idem pro iij barelles drosse valor vj s. viij d.
Idem pro j poke madour valor xx s.
Idem pro j barell selesmoth valor iij s. iiij d.
Idem pro ij dossenis felthattes valor x s.

Idem pro xxv libris seminis ceparum valor ij s. vjd.
Idem pro l bundellis lini valor xl s.
Idem pro j pipa avalanarum valor x s.
Johannes Waels pro M et dimidio libris ferri valor xlv s.
Nicholaus Haynyng pro M libris ferri valor xxx s.
Idem pro l bundellis lini valor xl s.
Idem pro j pipa avalanarum valor xv s.
Idem pro j barell olei valor v s.
Willelmus Thomson junior pro j dossena felthattes valor v s.
Idem pro dimidio C ulnis canvasse valor vj s. viij d.
Idem pro j barelle smigmatis valor x s.
Idem pro j barell avalanarum valor ij s. vj d.
Alanus Karre pro MMM libris ferri valor iij li. x s.
Idem pro ij pokes madour valor xl s.
Idem pro j barell alom valor xx s.
Idem pro j barell smigmatis valor x s.
Idem pro C et di' ulnis canvase valor xx s.
Idem pro ij peciis panni linii vocata butclothe valor v s.
Idem pro ij barelles dros valor x s.
Idem pro iij quarteriis cere valor xxvj s. viij d.
Willelmus Rothom junior pro MM libris ferri valor lx s.
Idem pro ij barelles alom valor xl s.
Idem pro j poke madour valor xx s.
Idem pro xxx bundellis lini valor xxv s.
Idem pro j last bituminis valor xxvj s. viij d.
Idem pro ij fattes avelanarum valor xx s.
Idem pro iij dossenis calapodiis valor ij s. vj d.
Idem pro xiij brusches valor ijs. vjd.
[*Damage extending 80 mm. down left edge of membranes*]
... pro xij dossenis strahattes valor x s.
... pro CC ulnis canvas valor xxvj s. viij d.
... pro iiij^or remis papyri spendabilis valor...
... pro v dossenis felthattes valor...
... pro j full ketylles valor ...
... pro C ulnis canvasse valor vj s. viij d.
... pro CC ulnis panni linii valor xiij s. iiij d.
... pro iiij dossenis felthattes valor xx s.
[*Membrane 2 dorse*]
... pro C libris canabi valor vj s. viij d.
... pro CC pectannis valor ij s. vj d.
... pro ij dossenis librarum amigdalarum valor ij s. vj d.
... pro j pecia et dimidia fustian valor xiij s. iiij d.
... pro C ulnis panni linii valor x s.
... pro j pipa avelanarum valor x s.
... pro xx bundellis lini valor xx s.
... pro j full ketylles valor xx s.
Idem pro j pok madour valor xxs.
Idem pro ij barelles smigmatis valor xx s.

Idem pro j barell alom	valor xx s.
Idem ro ij barelles dros	valor x s.
Idem pro iij M libris ferri	valor iiij li. x s.
Thomas Wylkynson pro j pok madour	valor xx s.
Idem pro iij barelles allecis albi	valor xxs.
Idem pro ij di' barelles bituminis	valor x s.
Thomas Wardley pro di' M libris ferri	valor xv s.
Idem pro iiij barelles bituminis	valor xiij s. iiij d.
Idem pro ij barelles de landyrne	valor x s.
Idem pro j barell smigmatis	valor x s.
Thomas Castell pro j pipa avalanarum	valor x s.
Idem pro M libris ferri	valor xxx s.
Idem pro ij barelles bituminis	valor vj s. viij d.
Willelmus Byrde pro M libris ferri	valor xxx s.
Idem pro ij barelles smigmatis	valor xx s.
Idem pro dimidia pipa avalanarum	valor v s.
Idem pro ij dossenis librarum piperis	valor xiij s. iiij d.
Robertus Maltby pro di' M libris ferri	valor xv s.
Idem pro j pipa avalanarum	valor x s.
Idem pro xx bundellis lini	valor xx s.
Willelmus Haynyng pro j barell smigmatis	valor x s.
Idem pro j full ketylles	valor xx s.
Willelmus Roos pro di' C ulnis canvas	valor vj s. viij d.
Idem pro CC ulnis panni linii	valor lx s.
Idem pro j dossena felthattes	valor v s.
Idem pro vij libris fili albi	valor iij s. iiij d.
Idem pro dimidia pecia fustian	valor vj s. viij d.
Idem pro M spinctris	valor vj s. viij d.
Idem pro xij dakyrs cultellorum an[ce] brages	valor ij s. vj d.
Ide pro j rema papiri spendabilis	valor ij s. vj d.
Idem pro xx bundellis lini	valor xx s.
Idem pro j pok madour	valor xx s.
Idem pro j fulle ketylles	valor xx s.
Idem pro j pipa avalanarum	valor x s.
Johannes Yonge pro M libris ferri	valor xxx s.
Idem pro ij barelles smigmatis	valor xx s.
Thomas Cathe pro M libris ferri	valor xxx s.
Idem pro j barelle alom	valor xx s.
Idem pro x bundellis lini	valor x s.
Jacobus Lystor pro C ulnis canvasse	valor vj s. viij d.
Idem pro j dossena felthattes	valor v s.
Idem pro di' [M] libris ferri	valor xv s.
Willelmus Haysand pro iiij barelles picis et bituminis	valor x s.
Idem pro j pok madour	valor xx s.
Idem pro j barell smigmatis	valor x s.
Robertus Penrethe pro xx bundellis lini	valor xx s.
Idem pro (di') C bowestavis	valor xiij s. iiij d.
Alanus Byrde pro ij pipis avalanarum	valor xl s.

Idem pro ij barels drosse	valor xx s.
Idem pro ij fulles ketylles	valor xl s.
Idem pro MM libris ferri	valor lx s.
Idem pro di' C libris seminis ceparum	valor xiij s. iiij d.
Jacobus Ketelay pro iij peciis cere	valor viij li.
Idem pro iiij pokes madour	valor iiij li.
Willelmus Hudson pro xx bundellis lini	valor xxs.
Idem pro j barell stelle	valor xl s.
Idem pro ij barelles dross	valor xiij s. iiij d.
Idem pro j pok madour	valor xx s.
Idem pro j barell alome	valor xx s.
Idem pro iiij peciis linii	valor xxx s.
Idem pro ij dossenis librarum piperis	valor xiij s. iiij d.
Idem pro iiij dossenis [librarum] amigdalarum	valor iij s. iiij d.
Idem pro iij libris croci	valor xv s.
Idem pro viij libris rice	valor x d.
Idem pro xij grosse lasyng poyntes	valor vj s. viij d.
Idem pro xM spinctris	valor iij s. iiij d.
Idem pro xx pauper poyntes	valor xiij s. iiij d.
Idem pro di' M elsyn blades	valor ij s. vj d.
Henricus Driffeld pro j barelle smigmatis	valor x s.
Idem pro x bundellis lini	valor x s.
Johannes Todde pro di' M libris ferri	valor xv s.
Johannes Yong pro j barelle smigmatis	valor x s.
Willelmus Robynson pro di' M libris ferri	valor xv s.
Johannes ... pro di' M libris ferri	valor xv s
Willelmus Boyde pro lx ulnis sewys cloth	valor x s.
Idem pro iiij^{or} peciis panni linei	valor xl s.
Idem pro iiij cofyrs	valor ij s. vj d.
Idem pro ij dossenis felthattes	valor x s.
Idem pro di' C ulnis canvasse	valor vj s. viij d.
Idem pro ij dossenis brusches	valor x d.
Idem pro j dossena kanns	valor ij s. vj d.
Willelmus Wryght pro CC libris ferri	valor vj s. viij d.
Robertus Baxster pro iiij M libris ferri	valor vj li.
Summa valoris ccvjli. iijs. iiijd.	

{Februarii}

Navis vocata Nicholaus de Camfer unde Lam Adrianson est magister applicuit j^{o} die Februarii

{alienigena}

Idem pro di' C bundellis allei	valor iij s. iiij d.
Willelmus Lawes senior pro iiij barelles allecis albi	valor xxvj s. viij d.
Willelmus Hewet pro j barell bituminis	valor iij s. iiij d.
Idem pro xxvij barelles ceparum	valor xiij s. iiij d.
Johannes Makpas pro ij sort fices et racenis	valor x s.
Nicholaus Haynyng pro xvj peciis rosyn	valor vj s. viij d.
Idem pro lx libris seminis ceparum	valor x s.

Idem pro j dossena felthattes valor v s.
Idem pro j pok madour valor xx s.
Johannes Byrde pro ij barelles allecis albi valor xiij s. iiij d.
Idem pro ij sort fices et rasenis valor x s.
[*Membrane 3 face*]
Johannes Forster pro di' M libris ferri valor xv s.
Idem pro ij sort fices et rasenis valor x s.
Johannes Spense pro ij barelles bituminis valor vj s. viij d.
Idem pro ij sorte fices et rasenis valor x s.
Idem pro j barell alom valor xx s.
Johannes Yonger pro ij sorte fices et rasenis valor x s.
Thomas Castell pro j laste allecis albi valor lx s.
Idem pro ij sorte fices et rasenis valor x s.
Willelmus Tomson junior pro j barelle bituminis valor iij s. iiij d.
Idem pro xx bundellis allei valor xx d.
Alanus Karre pro M libris ferri valor xxx s.
Willelmus Roos pro ij barelles allecis albi valor xiij s. iiij d.
Idem pro j barell smigmatis valor x s.
Alanus Byrde pro iiij barellis allecis albi valor xxxvj s. viij d.
Idem pro j barell alome valor xxs.
Idem pro ij sorte fices et rasenis valor xiij s. iiij d.
Idem pro iij sort fices et rasenis valor xxxvj s. viij d.
Thomas Wylkynson pro iij barelles osmundes valor xx s.
Idem pro j barell alom valor xx s.
Willelmus Byrde pro iij barelles olei valor xxx s.
Summa valoris xxiij li. xviij s. iiij d.

Navis vocata Petyr de Sandwyche unde Willelmus Stokes est magister exivit xiiij die Februarii
Willelmus dominus de Faconbryge pro xx celdris carbonum valor l s.
Idem pro di' last corrii
Idem pro iiij foder plumbi valor xij li.
Idem pro ij dossenis gryndstonys valor xx s.
Alanus Byrde pro vij C clapholt valor xiij s. iiij d.
Idem pro xxx alviolis valor v s.
Johannes Sempyll pro ix dacris corii tannati valor vj li.
Summa { valoris xxij li. viij s. iiij d.
corrii patet

Navis vocata Nicholaus de Camfer unde Lam Adryanson est magister exivit penultimo die Februarii
{alienigena}
Idem pro iij celdris carbonum valor v s.
Willelmus Byrde pro xij gryndstanys valor xiij s. iiij d.
Willelmus Roos pro xij gryndstanys valor xiijs. iiijd.
Alanus Karr pro i fothyr plumbi valor liij s. iiij d.
Summa valoris iiij li. vs.

{Marcii}
Navis vocata Cristofyr de Brell unde Johannes Robertson est magister exivit j die Marcii
Idem pro xxx celdris carbonum valor l s.
Summa valoris patet

{Marcii}
Navis vocata Cristofyr de Yermothe unde Willelmus Carne est magister applicuit iiij° die Marcii
{alienigena}
Idem pro ij last ostrium valor xiij s. iiij d.
Idem pro iij barelles allecis albi valor xiij s. iiij d.
{alienigena}
Thomas Clapyrton pro j dossena par sotularium valor ij s. vj d.
Idem pro j dossena dagars valor viij s. iiij d.
{alienigena}
Jacobus Cothrwon pro iij dossenis et vj pars sotularium valor viij s. iiij d.
Idem pro iij peciis panni linei grossi valor x s.
Nicholas Barre pro j pipa wadde valor xxxvj s. viij d.
Idem pro xx dossenis rollys jeschys pro capis valor xxij s. vj d.
Idem pro xij barelles salis albi valor viij s. iiij d.
Idem pro iij dossenis et viij pars sotularium valor v s.
Idem pro xv dagars valor vj s. viij d.
Summa valoris vj li. xv s.

Navis vocata Cristofir de Novo Castro unde Henricus Dryffeld est magister exivit vj^to die Marcii
Willelmus Hewet pro vj celdris carbonum valor vj s. viij d.
Idem pro ij foder plumbi valor vj li.
Johannes C... pro v gryndstanis valor v s. vii d.
Alanus Byrde pro iij foder plumbi valor ix li.
Alanus Karre pro ij foder... valor v li. vj s. viij d.
Idem pro CCCC... schorlynges valor lxxij s. vj d.
Idem pro CCCC xx pellibus agnellorum valor lv s.
Johannes Richardson pro vj grindstanys valor x s.
Idem pro MDCxxx schorlynges valor xij li. iiij s. ij d.
Idem pro DCCClx pellibus agnellorum valor v li. xiij s. iiij d.
Willelmus Lawes senior pro Mxl schorlynges valor xij li. xv s.
Idem pro DCCCC pellibus agnellorum valor vj li.
Robertus Baxster pro CCClxx schorlynges valor liiij s. ij d.
Johannes Chambre pro MCCCClxx schorlynges valor x li. xviij s. x d.
Thomas Wylkynson pro CCCxx schorlynges valor xlvijs. vj d.
Idem pro vijCxx pellibus agnellorum valor iiij li. xv s. x d.
Thomas Durham pro Cxx schorlynges valor xvij s. vj d.
Johannes Ryddisdale pro vCiiij^xx schorlynges valor v li.
Idem pro CCCCxl pellibus agnellorum valor lvij s. vj d.
Alexander Pescod pro CCl schorlynges valor xxxvj s. viij d.

Ricardus Stevynson pro CCCiiij^{xx}x schorlynges valor lvj s. viij d.
Summa valoris iiij^{xx}xiij li. xv s. vj d.
Johannes Richardson pro ij saccis et dimidio lane in v pokes
Idem pro v^{xx} pellibus lanutis continentibus j quarterium dimidium quarterium et x pelles.
Willelmus Lawes senior pro x^{xx} pellibus lanutis continentibus dimidium saccum et j quarterium
Robertus Baxster pro dimidio sacco et v clavibus lane in l poke
Idem pro lxx pellibus lanutis continentibus j quarterium et x pelles
Alanus Karre pro ij saccis iij quarteriis et viij clavibus lane in vj pokes
Idem pro lxx pellibus lanutis continentibus j quarterium et x pelles.
Johannes Chambre pro iiij saccis lane in iiij pokes
Idem pro viij^{xx} pellibus lanutis continentibus dimidium saccum dimidium quarterium et x pelles
Thomas Wylby pro ij quarteriis lane in j poke
Idem pro xxx pellibus lanutis continentibus dimidium quarterium
Thomas Cuthbe[rt *hole in membrane 50 x 60 mm.*] ... saccis dimidio et ij clavis lane in ij pokes
Willelmus Scott ... saccis et iij clavis lane in iiij pokes
Thomas ... ... saccis viij clavis lane in iij pokes
[*Membrane 3 dorse*]
Willelmus H... ... j quarterio lane in ij pokes
Johannes Riddy ... ... iij quarteriis lane in j poke
Idem ... pellibus lanutis continentibus dimidium quarterium et xxx pelles
Alexander Pes... ... quarteriis et ij clavis lane ...
Idem ... pellibus lanutis ...
Robertus Sto... ... dimidio sacco lane in ij pokes
Idem ... xxx pellibus lanutis continentibus dimidium quarterium
Jacobus Lystor pro dimidio sacco lane in j poke
Nicholaus Haynyng pro iij quarteriis et ij clavis lane in ij pokes
Summa { saccorum lane xxxij sacci dimidius vij clavi
pellium lanutarum DClxx continentibus ij saccos iij quarteria x pelles

Navis vocata Mary de Novo Castro unde Ricardus Thomson est magister [exivit] ...
Henricus Fowler pro viij celdris carbonum valor viij s. iiij d.
Willelmus Berton pro x gryndstones valor xxxiij s. iiij d.
Alanus Byrde pro iij fothers plumbi valor ix li.
Idem pro CCxv schorlynges valor xxxj s. viij d.
Idem pro vC pellibus agnellorum valor lxvj s. viij d.
Willelmus Byrde pro xx gryndstones valor xxvj s. viij d.
Idem pro j foder et di' plumbi valor iiij li. x s.
Idem pro vCxxv schorlynges valor iij li. viij s. iiij d.
Idem pro DCC pellibus agnellorum valor iiij li. xiij s iiij d.
Thomas Cutbert pro Cxl schorlynges valor xxx s.
Johannes Byrd pro DCCCxlv schorlynges valor vj li.

Johannes Yonger pro Cv^{xx} schorlynges	valor xxx s. viij d.
Thomas Hedlam pro CCxv schorlynges	valor xxxj s. viij d.
Ricardus Stevynson pro CCClxxvj schorlynges	valor lv s.
Johannes Spense pro DCCxlv schorlynges	valor v li. x s. x d.
Nicholaus Haynyng pro CC schorlynges	valor xxx s.
Willelmus Roos pro DCCCxx schorlynges	valor vj li. ij s. iij d.
Idem pro DClx pellibus agnellorum	valor viij li. vj s. vij d.
Johannes Schelton pro CCv^{xx}... schorlynges	valor xliij s. vj d.
Alexander Pescod pro Cv^{xx}... schorlynges	valor xxx s.
Willelmus Byrde pro CC schorlynges	valor xxx s.
Alanus Karre pro vC schorlynges	valor lxxv s.
Thomas Castell pro CCCCx schorlynges	valor lxj s. viij d.

Summa valoris lxxiij li. x s. x d.

Johannes Byrde pro ij saccis j quarterio et x clavis lane in v pokes
Idem pro lxxv pellibus lanutis continentibus j quarterium et xv pelles
Thomas Hanson pro j quarterio et ij clavis lane in j poke
Alanus Byrde pro iiij saccis et dimidio lane in iiij pokes
Idem pro xxx pellibus lanutis continentibus dimidium quarterium
Johannes Yonge pro xv pellibus lanutis continentibus xv pelles
Johannes Hedlam pro j quarterio et x clavis lane in j poke
Idem pro xv pellibus lanutis
Ricardus Stevynson pro xx pellibus lanutis
Johannes Spense pro iij quarteriis et v clavis lane in ij pokes
Idem pro lxxv pellibus lanutis continentibus j quarterium et xv pelles
Nicholaus Haynyng pro xv pellibus lanutis
Willelmus Roos pro iiij saccis et dimidio lane in vij pokes
Idem pro Cxx pellibus lanutis continentibus dimidium saccum
Willelmus Byrde pro iij quarteriis lane in j poke
Idem pro lxxv pellibus lanutis continentibus j quarterium et xv pelles
Thomas Cuthbert pro dimidio sacco et iij clavis lane in j pok
Alexander Pescod pro V pellibus lanutis
Willelmus Rothom senior pro dimidio sacco et iij clavis lane in j poke
Alanus Karre pro j sacco j quarterio et iij clavis lane in iij pokes
Idem pro Cxx pellibus lanutis continentibus dimidium saccum
Johannes Foster pro j sacco et j clavo lane in iij pokes
Johannes Reddysdall pro j sacco et iij clavis lane in ij pokes
Robertus Pykden pro j quarterio et viij clavis lane in j pok
Johannes Richardson pro ij saccis et viij clavis lane in v pokes
Willelmus Boydde pro j quarterio et iiij clavis lane in j pok
Idem pro x pellibus lanutis
Thomas Castell pro lxx pellibus lanutis continentibus j quarterium et x pelles
Johannes Waels pro dimidio sacco et ij clavis lane in j pok

Sacci lane xxj sacci et dimidius et ix clavi lane

Pelles lanute DCxlv continentes ij saccos dimidium et dimidium quarterium et xv pelles

2. Particulars of Account of William Bynchestyr, controller, from 20 November 1456 to 17 May 1457

E122/107/50

The two membranes, both 250 mm. wide, are 650 mm. and 630 mm. long, and are sewn Chancery style. They are rubbed in places, but are legible under ultra-violet light. There is a hole at the foot of the second membrane. The account appears to be complete.

The marginal notes identifying merchants who were denizens have been not been printed.

Piss' salsis has been extended as pissibus salsis, though the context demands the genitive case. In *ij buc' sylke*, *buc'* has not been extended, but is probably *buckes* (books). *Bundys* was found spelt out, and has therefore been retained in this account, in the sense of bonds, or bundles. In other accounts *bund'* has been extended as *bundellus*.

[*Membrane 1 face*]

{Novum Castrum}

Roluli Willelmi Bynchestyr, contrarotulatoris custume et subsidii lanarum, coriorum et pellium lanutarum necnon tonagii et pondagii ac parve custume, in portu ville Novi Castri super Tynam et in singulis portubus et locis eidem portui adiacentibus, videlicet de huiusquid custumis et subsidiis domini regis ibidem a vicesimo die Novembris anno regni regis (nunc) Henrici sexti post conquestum Anglie tricesimo quinto usque decimo septimo die Maii ex tunc proximo futuro. Willelmus Overton et Johannes Penrethe fuerunt custumarii dicti domini regis in portubus et locis predictis per idem tempus.

{Decembris}

Navis vocata Mychaell de Scheles unde Robertus Fawsyde est magister exivit iiij^to^ die Decembris

Alanus Byrde pro ij fodyr et dimidio plumbi	valor vij li. x s.
Idem pro vj dossenis rubstanys	valor iij s. iiij d.

Johannes Forster pro C pellibus agnellorum valor xiij s. iiij d.
Robertus Baxster pro C iiij^{xx} schorlynges valor xxv s.
Summa valoris ix li. xj s. viij d.
Johannes Robynson pro ij saccis iij quarteriis ij clavis lane in v pokys
Thomas Rothom pro iij saccis x clavis lane in vj pokys
Thomas Davell pro j quarterio et viij clavis lane in j pokett
Thomas Dorham pro iij quarteriis et viij clavis lane in j pokett
Robertus Baxster pro xx pellibus lanutis
Willelmus Hewet pro j sacco dimidio xj clavis lane in ij pokys
Johannes Younger pro j sacco dimidio xj clavis lane in iij pokys
Summa { saccorum lane x sacci dimidius xj clavi
pellium lanutarum patet

{Januarii}
Navis vocata Kateryn de Newport unde Jacobus Mayll est magister applicuit xviij^{o} die Januarii
{alienigena}
Idem pro vC libris ferri valor xx s.
Idem pro vjC <ferri *struck through*> hoppe valor xxv s.
Idem pro j barello cum C ulnis canves valor xviij s. iiij d.
Idem pro xviij mandys valor ijs. vjd.
Idem pro iij barellis alager valor x s.
Summa valoris lxxvs. x d.

{Marcii}
Navis vocata Valentyn de Novo Castro unde Willelmus Slego est magister applicuit primo dei Marcii
Johannes Byrde pro Cxxv libris licores valor v s.
Idem pro ij qwytt fulles ketylles valor vj s. viijd .
Idem pro j poke madyr valor xx s.
Idem pro di' alme vini renensis valor xiij s. iiij d.
Nicholaus Wettwang pro j sacco hoppe valor xiij s. iiij d.
Johannes Richardson pro iiij barellis smygmatis valor xl s.
Idem pro j pok madyr valor xx s.
Idem pro iiij sortes fructus valor xxvj s. viij d.
Idem pro C libris seminis separum valor x s.
Idem pro j fulle ketylles valor xx s.
Willelmus Blaxton pro iiij barellis osmundes valor xxvj s. viij d.
Idem pro xxx bundys lini valor xxx s.
Idem pro di' barello alome valor xx s.
Idem pro vj barellis bituminis valor xvj s. viij d.
Idem pro j fulle ketylles valor xx s.
Idem pro lx libris canabi valor v s.
Idem pro di' C ulnis canvess valor vj s. viij d.
Idem pro xxx libris pakthrede valor ij s. vj d.
Richardus Stevynson pro ij M libris ferri valor lxvj s. viij d.
Idem pro j barello smygmatis valor x s.
Idem pro vj barellis osmundes valor xl s.

Willelmus Thomson pro M libris ferri	valor xxxiij s. iiij d.
Idem pro ij barellis smigmatis	valor xx s.
Idem pro iij barellis bituminis	valor viij s. iiij d.
Idem pro xj felthattes	valor v s.
Willelmus Roose pro j lasto bituminis	valor xxxj s. viij d.
Idem pro C libris canabi	valor xiij s. iiij d.
Idem pro j barello smygmatis	valor x s.
Idem pro dimidio barello olei	valor vj s. viij d.
Henricus Fowler pro j lasto osmundes	valor iiij li.
Thomas Rothom pro ij pok madyr	valor xl s.
Idem pro iij barellis bituminis	valor viij s. iiij d.
Idem pro j barello smygmatis	valor x s.
Thomas Castell pro xxx bundis lini	valor xxx s.
Idem pro dimidio lasto allecis albi	valor xl s.
Idem pro iij sort fructus	valor xx s.
Idem pro iij barellis osmundes	valor xx s.
Idem pro iij C libris hoppe	valor xv s.
Johannes Esyngton pro vj sortes fructus	valor xl s.
Idem pro vj barellis osmundes	valor xl s.
Idem pro vij M libris ferri	valor xj li. xiij s. iiij d.
Idem pro iij barellis olei	valor xxx s.
Idem pro iiij barellis smygmatis	valor xl s.
Idem pro j barello alom	valor xl s.
Idem pro j barello madyr	valor xxx s.
Idem pro j poke seminis ceparum	valor x s.
Idem pro iiij^{xx} bundis lini	valor iiij li. x s.

Summa valoris lxvij li. xiij s. ij d.

{Marcii}

Navis vocata Mary de Novo Castro unde Robertus Symson est magister applicuit primo die Marcii

Johannes Byrde pro j lasto bituminis	valor xxx s.
Idem pro M libris rosyn	valor xx s.
Idem pro iij barellis smigmatis	valor xl s.
Willelmus Haysande pro iij barellis bituminis	valor vj s. viij d.
Willelmus Rothom pro viij barellis bituminis	valor xx s.
Idem pro iij barellis picis	valor xiij s. iiij d.
Johannes Wales pro vj barellis bituminis	valor xviij s. iiij d.
Thomas Cuthebert pro vj barellis bituminis	valor xviij s. iiij d.
Idem pro iij barellis allecis albi	valor xx s.
Idem pro parva pipa avelanarum	valor x s.
Idem pro iiij barellis bituminis	valor x s. x d.
Johannes Esyngton pro j lasto bituminis	valor xxxj s. viij d.
Idem pro j lasto osmundes	valor iiij li.
Johannes Richerdson pro j lasto picis	valor xxxj s. viij d.
Idem pro j fatte avelanarum	valor v s.

[*Membrane 1 dorse*]

Idem pro xx bundys lini	valor xx s.

Robertus Garton pro M libris ferri valor xxxiij s. iiij d.
Idem pro iij barellis smigmatis valor xxx s.
Idem pro ij barellis picis valor v s.
Idem pro ij barellis pomorum valor xx d.
Idem pro xxiij libris lini valor iij s. iiij d.
Idem pro j aghtyndelle anguillarum valor x d.
Idem pro j dossena bastes valor x d.
Willelmus Blaxton pro j barello smigmatis valor x s.
Robertus Nottyng pro ij barellis picis valor v s.
Summa valoris xxiij li. v s. x d.

Navis vocata Jacobus de Camfer unde Adrianus Colle est magister applicuit xij^{o} die Marcii
{alienigena}
Idem pro ij lastis et dimidio pissibus salsis valor C s.
{alienigena}
Goddard Wynner pro vj last stokfyche valor xiij li.
Idem pro ij lastis et dimidio pissibus salsis valor C s.
Summa valoris xxiij li.

Navis vocata Mary de Novo Castro unde Johannes Ferthyng est magister exivit xx die Marcii
Johannes Chambre pro iiiC et lx lamfelles valor xlvj s. viij d.
Idem pro ijM schorlynges valor xv li.
Thomas Burton pro x gryndstayns
et v dossenis robstans valor xxiij s. iiij d.
Thomas Filopson pro xx gryndstayns valor xxvj s. viij d.
Thomas Cathe pro xviij gryndstayns valor xxv s.
Johannes Pager pro MijClxx schorlynges valor ix li. vij s. iiij d.
Nicholaus Haynyng pro xlviij lamfelles valor iij s. iiij d.
Idem pro ijCxx schorlynges valor xxxij s. vj d.
Idem pro vj gryndstayns valor x s.
Alanus Byrde pro iijCiiij^{xx} lamfelles valor l s.
Idem pro iiijC et xxiiij schorlynges valor lxiij s. iiij d.
Willelmus Roose pro MC et xx schorlynges valor viij li. vij s. vj d.
Thomas Wilkynson pro iiijC lamfelles valor liij s. iiij d.
Idem pro vjCiiij^{xx}x schorlynges valor Cj s. viij d.
Thomas Doram pro ixC pellibus
<ang' *struck through*> agnellorum valor xxvj s. viij d.
Idem pro M iiijC lxx schorlynges valor x li. xviij s. iiij d.
Idem pro Clx schorlynges valor xxij s. vj d.
Willelmus Rothom junior pro vjCxx schorlynges valor iiij li. xij s. vj d.
Johannes Byrde pro CCCC schorlynges valor lx s.
Thomas Hanson pro iiijC schorlynges valor lx s.
Thomas Cuthbert pro ijClx schorlynges valor xxxvij s. vj d.
Willelmus Hewet pro M et C schorlynges valor viij li. v s.
Thomas Berton pro iiijCiiij^{xx}v schorlynges valor lxxij s. vj d.

Willelmus Clrake [*? for* Clarke]
pro C pellibus agnellorum valor iiij s. ij d.
Idem pro Cv^{xx}vj schorlynges valor xxviij s. iiij d.
Johannes Pounde pro xviij gryndstayns valor xxj s. viij d.
Summa valoris iiij^{xx} et xv li. x d.

Johannes Yong pro j sacco dimidio et v clavis lane in ij pokys valor ['valor' *entered in error*]
Idem pro ijClx pellibus lanutis continentibus j saccum et xx pelles
Johannes Esyngton pro vij saccis dimidio xj clavis in ix pokys
Robertus Baxster pro j sacco lane in ij pokys
Idem pro iiij^{xx} et x pellibus lanutis continentibus j quarterium et dimidium quarterium
Willelmus Roose pro iijC pellibus lanutis continentibus j saccum et j quarterium
Johannes Chambre pro iij saccis et v clavis lane in iij pokys
Idem pro vijCxx pellibus lanutis continentibus iij saccos
Thomas Cutbert pro j sacco iij quarteriis lane in ij pokys
Idem pro lx pellibus lanutis continentibus j quarterium
Robertus Pykdayn pro ij saccis v clavis lane in iij pokys
Idem pro xl pellibus lanutis continentibus dimidium quarterium et x pelles
Willelmus Hewet pro v saccis et viij clavis lane in v pokys
Idem pro CCCxx pellibus lanutis continentibus j saccum j quarterium et xx pelles
Thomas Hanson pro ij saccis dimidio et v clavis lane in iij pokys
Richardus Stevynson pro ij saccis iij quarteriis lane in iiij pokys
Nicholaus Haynyng pro iij saccis iij quarteriis lane in v pokys
Idem pro xl pellibus lanutis continentibus dimidium quarterium et x pelles
Johannes Spense pro iij quarteriis lane in j poke
Alanus Byrde pro ij saccis iij quarteriis v clavis lane in iij pokys
Idem pro Cxx pellibus lanutis continentibus dimidium saccum
Thomas Doram pro CClx pellibus lanutis continentibus j saccum et xx pelles
Idem pro j sacco j quarterio viij clavis lane in iij pokys
Idem pro iij saccis viij clavis lane in iiij pokys
Idem pro ijC pellibus lanutis continentibus iij quarteria et xx pelles
Willelmus Rothom junior pro iij saccis lane in iij pokys
Idem pro Cxl pellibus lanutis continentibus dimidium saccum et xx pelles
Thomas Burton pro Cxxxv pellibus lanutis continentibus dimidium saccum et xv pelles
Willelmus Clerke pro xl pellibus lanutis continentibus dimidium quarterium et x pelles

Summa { saccorum lane xlj sacci dimidius et viij clavi lane
pellium lanutarum ijMvijCxxv pelles continentes xj saccos j quarterium et xxv pelles

{Aprilis}

Navis vocata Crystofyr de Novo Castro super Tynam unde Henricus Dreffeld est magister exivit vj^{o} die Aprilis

Johannes Richerdson pro di' fodyr plumbi	valor xxx s.
Idem pro vijCiiij^{xx} schorlynges	valor Cxv s.
Willelmus Lawys pro xlv petris plumbi	valor xv s.
Idem pro vij C et lx schorlynges	valor Cxij s. vj d.
Willelmus Blakston pro vjCxxx schorlynges	valor iiij li. xiij s. iiij d.
Ricardus Browne pro vCxxx schorlynges	valor lxxviij s. iiij d.
Idem pro C pellibus agnellorum	valor vj s. viij d.
Alanus Carre pro ijC lamfelles	valor xxvj s. viij d.
Idem pro CClx schorlynges	valor xxxvj s. viij d.
Johannes Esynton pro viijCxl schorlynges	valor vj li. v s.

Summa valoris xxix [*for* xxxj] li. xix s. ij d.

Johannes Byrde pro j sacco dimidio lane in ij pokys
Johannes Esyngton pro dimidio sacco viij clavis lane in j poke
Idem pro CCC pellibus lanutis continentibus j saccum et j quarterium
Willelmus Haysande pro ij saccis et dimidio lane in iiij pokys
Alanus Carre pro j sacco iij quarteriis lane in ij pokys
Idem pro lx pellibus lanutis continentibus j quarterium
Alanus Byrde pro j sacco iij quarteriis v clavis lane in ij pokys
Willelmus Blaxston pro CCxl pellibus continentibus j saccum
Thomas Doram pro iij quarteriis lane in j poke
Johannes Richardson pro CCCCiiij^{xx} pellibus lanutis continentibus ij saccos
Willelmus Lawys pro CCClx pellibus lanutis continentibus j saccum et dimidium

Summa { saccorum lane ix sacci lane
pellium lanutarum MiiijCxl pelles continentes vj saccos }

[*Membrane 2 face*]

{Aprilis}

Navis vocata Kateryn de Newporte unde Jacobus Maylle est magister exivit xxv^{to} die Aprilis

{alienigena}

Idem pro xxiiij celdris carbonum	valor xl s.

Summa valoris patet

{Aprilis}

Navis vocata Kateryn de <Sch *struck through*> Seryksee unde Herman Jacobson est magister applicuit xxvij^{mo} die Aprilis

{alienigena}

Idem pro iijM pavyng tylles	valor xx s.
Idem pro j parvo barello vini dulcis	
Idem pro j bede tyke	valor iij s. iiij d.
Idem pro j dossena maundes	valor vj d.

Summa { vini patet
valoris xxiij s. x d. }

{Aprilis}
Navis vocata Kateryn de Seryksee unde Herman Jacobson est magister exivit ultimo die Aprilis
{alienigena}

Idem pro xxviij celdris carbonum	valor xlvj s. viij d.
Summa valoris patet	

{Maii}
Navis vocata Valentyn de Novo Castro unde Johannes Bygge est magister exivit iiij[to] die Mayi

Thomas Castell pro xiiij pannis panni lanii largii sine grano	
Idem pro iij lastis barlymelle	valor xlviij s. iij d.
Idem pro x barellis bere	valor xiij s. iiij d.
Idem pro iij dossenis ulnis panni lini	valor xiij s. iiij d.
Idem pro iij dossenis beltes	valor x d.
Idem pro iij dossenis cultellorum	valor x d.
Idem pro j grose et di' punctorum	valor xx d.
Idem pro CC nedyls	valor x d.
Idem pro iiij felthattes	valor xx d.
Idem pro vj quarteriis ordii	valor xv s.
Idem pro ij barellis vini	valor v s.
Idem pro vj kagges hony	valor x s.
Idem pro viij kagges butter	valor xiij s. iiij d.
Idem pro x ketyls	valor xviij s. iiij d.
Idem pro iij dossenis ulnis panni lanii	valor iij s. iiij d.
Idem pro vj barellis osmundes	valor xl s.
Johannes Warde pro xij pannis panni lanii largii sine grano	
Idem pro ij lastes barlymelle	valor xxxij s. vj d.
Idem pro iij dossenis ulnis panni lanii	valor xiij s. iiij d.
Idem pro iij dossenis beltes	valor x d.
Idem pro ij dossenis cultellorum	valor x d.
Idem pro ij grosse punctorum	valor x d.
Idem pro CCC nedyls	valor x d.
Idem pro v felthattes	valor xx d.
Idem pro v quarteriis ordii	valor xij s. vj d.
Idem pro vj kagges hony	valor x s.
Idem pro vj ferkyns butter	valor x s.
Idem pro v kettyls	valors xv s.
Idem pro iij barellis osmundes	valor xx s.
Archebald Whytton pro xij pannis panni lanii sine grano	
Idem pro iij lastis barly mell	valor xl s.
Idem pro viij kagges hony	valor xij s. vj d.
Idem pro vj quarteriis ordii	valor xv s.
Idem pro iij dossenis beltes	valor x d.
Idem pro xij kettyls	valor xx s.
Idem pro viij dakyres cultellorum	valor iij s. iiij d.
Idem pro iij dossenis cappys	valor v s.
Idem pro j clute nedyls	valor x d.

Idem pro iij barellis osmundes valor xx s.
Idem pro ij M spinctris valor x d.
Idem pro j dossena dagers valor v s.
Idem pro ij buc' sylke valor xx d.
Willelmus Haysand pro xij pannis panni lanii largii sine grano
Idem pro iij lastis et iiij barellis melle valor liij s. iiij d.
Idem pro j lasto bere valor xvj s. viij d.
Idem pro ij dossenis ulnarum panni linii valor x s.
Idem pro iiij dossenis beltes valor xx d.
Idem pro v dossenis cultellorum valor ij s. vj d.
Idem pro ij grosse punctorum valor xx d.
Idem pro iiij C nedyls valor xx d.
Idem pro vj felthattes valor iij s. iiij d.
Idem pro xij par sotularium valor iij s. iiij d.
Idem pro vj quarteriis ordii valor xv s.
Idem pro pipa vini valor x s.
Idem pro iiij kagges hony valor viij s. iiij d.
Idem pro j barello butter valor xx s.
Idem pro iij barellis osmundes valor xx s.
Johannes Waeles pro v pannis panni lanii largii sino grano
Idem pro vj barellis melle valor viij s. iiij d.
Idem pro ij kagges hony valor ij s. vj d.
Idem pro j quarterio ordii valor ij s. vj d.
Idem pro vj dagers valor xx d.
Idem pro ijM spinctris valor x d.
Idem pro ij dossenis cappys valor xx d.
Idem pro ij dossenis beltes valor x d.
Idem pro dị' grosse punctorum valor x d.
Radulphus Berton pro iij pannis panni lanii largii sine grano
Johannes Whytton [*blank*]
Idem pro j barello cramery valor xx s.
Johannes Scotte pro ij pannis panni lanii largii sine grano
Willelmus Rose pro j panno et dimidio panno panni lanii stricti sine grano
Idem pro j grosse punctorum valor x d.
Idem pro viij barellis melle valor x s.
Idem pro iij barellis bere valor iij s. iiij d.
Idem pro ij dossenis ulnarum panni linii valor v s.
Idem pro ij dossenis cultellorum valor x d.
Idem pro j dossena cappys valor xx d.
Idem pro j dossena beltes valor x d.
Idem pro j dossena libris fili valor x s.
Idem pro iij felt hattes valor x d.
Johannes Cook pro j panno et dimidio panno panni lanii strycti sine grano
Idem pro xvj barellis melle valor xxj s.
Idem pro ij barellis bere valor iij s. iiij d.
Idem pro j barello osmundes valor vj s. vij d.

Idem pro j barello bituminis	valor v s.
Idem pro ij quarteriis ordii	valor vj s.
Idem pro dimidio barello bituminis	valor iiij s. ij d.
Idem [*hole in membrane 30 x 30 mm.*] ...	valor ij s. vj d.
Idem ...	valor lij s. iiij d.

Summa { [pannorum lanii] sine grano lxiij panni
[valoris] xxxv li. xiij s. iiij d.

3. Particulars of Account of Robert Folbery, controller, from 30 July 1459 to 24 December 1459

E122/107/52

The two membranes are sewn Chancery style. The first is 259 mm. wide and 640 mm. long; the second varies in width between 242 and 253 mm. and is 390 mm. long. The first 80 mm. contain four holes each 30 mm. across, and six smaller holes. The missing words have been supplied either from the common form of other heads of account or from the enrolled account (E356/21 m. 58) where the corresponding collectors' account is summarized. It is clear from the enrolled account that Folbery's colleagues as collectors, Alan Bird and John Penreth, accounted only for the wool custom. Tunnage and poundage were collected separately by John Richardson, for whom Folbery acted as controller again.

All the merchants named were denizens. Folbery's account uses Latin more freely and with fewer suspensions than other accounts, and *Georgeus Chaumbre* for *Georgius Chaumbre* is probably a slip of the pen.

[*Membrane 1 face*]
Rotulus contrarotulatoris Roberti Folbery [contrarotulatoris in portu] ville Novi Castri super Tynam et in [diversis portubus] et locis eidem portui [adiacentibus] custume et subsidii domini regis lanarum, coriorum et pellium [lanutarum], necnon tonagii et pondagii [ac] parve custume in portu predicto et in singulis portubus et locis [predictis], a penultimo die Julii anno regni regis Henrici sexti post conquestum Anglie tricesimo [septimo usque] vicesimum quartum diem Decembris extunc proximo sequentem, quo tempore Alanus Birde et [Johannes] Penreth fuerunt collectores custume et subsidii predictorum.

Navis vocata le Volantyne de Novo Castro super Tynam unde Henricus Driffeld est magister exivit ultimo die Julii
Nicholaus Haynyng pro ij saccis lane in ij pokes
Thomas Edean pro iij quarteriis unius sacci lane in j poke

Thomas Cadechyff pro ... dimidio sacco lane in j poke
Thomas More [pro] ... unius sacci lane in j poke
Ricardus Stok ... [pro] ... unius sacci et iij clavis lane in j poke
Thomas Cast ... [pro] ... unius sacci lane in viij pokes
Summa saccorum lane xj sacci dimidius et iij clavi

{Julii}

Navis vocata le Cristofer de Novo Castro super Tynam unde Robertus Symson est magister exivit ultimo die Julii
Thomas Davell pro iij saccis lane in iij pokes
Willelmus Scot pro iij quarteriis unius sacci lane et iij clavis lane in j poke
Johannes Mappas pro j sacco lane in j poke
Johannes Forster pro ij saccis et dimidio et viij clavis lane in iij pokes
Johannes Wales pro j sacco lane in j poke
Robertus Baxster pro iij quarteriis unius sacci lane et viij clavis lane in j poke
Willelmus Brotherwyk pro j sacco et iij quarteriis unius sacci et viij clavis lane in j poke
Johannes Ryddisdale pro j sacco lane et viij clavis lane in j poke
Willelmus Roos pro j sacco et j quarterio unius sacci lane in ij pokes
Idem Willelmus pro CCC pellibus lanutis continentibus j saccum et j quarterium lane
Summa { saccorum lane xiij sacci et dimidius saccus et x clavi
pellium lanutarum patet }

{Augusti}

Navis vocata le Ive alias vocata le carvell de Novo Castro super Tynam unde Johannes Marshall est magister exivit xxviij die mensis Augusti
Johannes Mappas pro ij saccis et iij quarteriis unius sacci et viij clavis lane in iij pokes
Willelmus Haysand pro ij saccis lane in ij pokes
Willelmus Brotherwyke pro j sacco et j quarterio unius sacci lane in j poke
Johannes Ryddesdale pro ij saccis et j quarterio unius sacci lane in ij pokes
Johannes Wales pro j sacco et iij quarteriis unius sacci et viij clavis lane in ij pokes
Nicholaus Haynyng pro j sacco et iij quarteriis unius sacci lane in ij pokes
Willelmus Scot pro iij quarteriis unius sacci et viij clavis lane in j poke
Robertus Harden pro ij saccis et j quarterio unius sacci lane in ij pokes
Johannes Esyngton pro iij saccis et dimidio unius sacci lane in iiij pokes
Willelmus Byrde pro ij saccis lane in ij pokes
Willelmus Rothum Junior pro ij saccis et j quarterio unius sacci lane in iij pokes

Robertus Baxster pro j sacco et dimidio unius sacci lane in ij pokes
Johannes Sample pro j sacco et j quarterio unius sacci lane in ij pokes
Alexander Byrde pro j sacco lane in j poke
Johannes Syde pro j quarterio unius sacci et viij clavis lane in j poke
Willelmus Watson pro iij quarteriis unius sacci lane in j poke
Johannes Yonger pro dimidio unius sacci lane in j poke
Thomas Swan pro j sacco et viij clavis lane in ij pokes
George Chaumbre pro j sacco et j quarterio unius sacci lane in j poke
Willelmus Hunter pro j sacco et dimidio unius sacci et v clavis lane in ij pokes
Ricardus Stevynson pro j sacco et j quarterio unius sacci et viij clavis lane in ij pokes
Johannes Brigham pro dimidio sacco lane in j poke
Idem Johannes pro Cxx pellibus lanutis continentibus dimidium saccum lane

Summa { saccorum lane xxxiiij sacci j quarterium unius sacci et j clavus
pellium lanutarum patet }

{Septembris}

Navis vocata le Edward de Novo Castro super Tynam unde Johannes Big est magister exivit primo die mensis Septembris
Robertus Pykden pro ij saccis lane in ij pokes
Thomas Castell pro j sacco lane et iij quarteriis unius sacci et v clavis lane in ij pokes
Willelmus Rothum junior pro iij saccis et iij quarteriis unius sacci lane in vj pokes
Thomas Burton pro iiij saccis et viij clavis lane in iiij pokes
Thomas Davell pro iij quarteriis unius sacci et viij clavis lane in ij pokes
Willelmus Haysand pro ij saccis et viij clavis lane in ij pokes
Willelmus Birde pro iij quarteriis unius sacci lane in j poke
Willelmus Scot pro iij quarteriis unius sacci et viij clavis lane in j poke
Willelmus Hunter pro iij quarteriis unius sacci lane in j poke
Robertus Harden pro j sacco lane in j poke
Nicholaus Haynyng pro j sacco lane in j poke
Thomas Wryght pro iij quarteriis unius sacci lane in j poke
Johannes Esyngton pro j sacco et dimidio unius sacci et v clavis lane in ij pokes
Thomas Cuthbert pro j sacco et dimidio unius sacci lane in ij pokes
Petrus Bewyk pro ij saccis lane in ij pokes
Georgius Brygham pro iij quarteriis unius sacci lane in ij pokes
Willelmus Rothum senior pro viij clavis lane in j poke
Robertus Musgrave pro iij saccis et iij quarteriis unius sacci lane in iiij pokes
Willelmus Hurlebat pro j sacco et iij quarteriis unius sacci lane in ij pokes

Summa saccorum lane xxxij sacci et j quarterium unius sacci et xj clavi

{Septembris}

Navis vocata le Kateryn de Novo Castro super Tynam unde Johannes Dawson est magister exivit v^to^ die Septembris

Johannes Wales pro iij saccis et j quarterio unius sacci et v clavis lane in iiij pokes

Willelmus Rothum junior pro ij saccis et dimidio unius sacci lane in iij pokes

Thomas Cudbert pro iiij saccis lane in v pokes

Johannes Sample pro j sacco lane in j poke

Johannes Mappas pro ij saccis et dimidio sacco lane in iij pokes

Thomas Swan pro dimidio sacco lane in ij pokettes

Willelmus Bird pro iij quarteriis unius sacco lane in j poke

Willelmus Scot pro j sacco et j quarterio unius sacci et viij clavis lane in ij pokes

Petrus Baxster pro j sacco lane in j poke

Johannes Rydesdale pro dimidio sacco lane in j poke

Nicholas Haynyng pro j sacco et j quarterio unius sacci lane in ij pokes

[*Membrane 2 face*]

Johanna Spens pro dimidio sacco lane in j poke

Thomas Burton pro j sacco et j quarterio unius sacci lane in iij pokes

Thomas Bothe pro iij quarteriis unius sacci lane in j poke

Willelmus Watson pro j sacco lane in j poke

Willelmus Thomson pro xxx pellibus lanutis continentibus dimidium quarterium unius sacci lane

Summa { saccorum lane xxij sacci et j quarterium unius sacci
pellum lanutarum patet

{Septembris}

Navis vocata le parve carvale de Novo Castro super Tynam unde Adam Forman est magister exivit v^to^ die Septembris

Willelmus Scot pro j quarterio unius sacci lane in j poke

Robertus Baxster pro dimidio sacco lane in j poke

Thomas Hanson pro dimidio unius sacco et viij clavis lane in ij pokes

Thomas Burton pro j sacco et viij clavis lane in ij pokes

Willelmus Byrde pro iij saccis et iij quarteriis unius sacci lane in iiij pokes

Johannes Syde pro dimidio unius sacci lane in j poke

Willelmus Hunter pro dimidio sacco lane in j poke

Willelmus Watson pro iij saccis et j quarterio unius sacci et viij clavis lane in iiij pokes

Georgeus Chaumbre pro iij saccis et viij clavis lane in iiij pokes

Willelmus Byrde pro iij quarteriis unius sacci lane in j poke

Nicholaus Haynyng pro dimidio sacco et viij clavis lane in j poke

Robertus Harden pro ij saccis et j quarterio unius sacci lane in iij pokes

Johannes Yonger pro uno quarterio unius sacci et viij clavis lane in j poke

Willelmus Blaxston pro iij quarteriis unius sacci et iij clavis lane in j poke

Thomas Bothe pro dimidio sacco et viij clavis lane in j poke
Johannes Hygele pro j quarterio unius sacci et viij clavis lane in j poke
Willelmus Haysand pro iij quarteriis unius sacci lane in j poke
Summa saccorum lane xx sacci et dimidius et ij clavi

{Octobris}
Navis vocata le Ann de Novo Castro super Tynam unde Johannes Rumbald est magister exivit xiij die Octobris
Johannes Sample pro j sacco et dimidio sacco lane in ij pokes
Johannes Esyngton pro j sacco et dimidio sacco lane in ij pokes
Thomas Castell pro iij quarteriis unius sacci et viij clavis lane in j poke
Thomas Hanson pro dimidio sacco et viij clavis lane in ij pokes
Willelmus Blaxston pro iij quarteriis unius sacci et v clavis lane in j poke
Johannes Cawchesyde pro dimidio sacco et viij clavis lane in j poke
Thomas Cudbert pro j quarterio unius sacci et iij clavis lane in j poke
Thomas Burton pro j quarterio unius sacci et viij clavis lane in j poke
Johannes Wales pro j quarterio unius sacci et iij clavis lane in j poke
Thomas Wryght pro iij quarteriis unius sacci et viij clavis lane in j poke
Willelmus Brotherwyk pro j sacco lane in j poke
Thomas Swan pro j quarterio unius sacci et viij clavis lane in j poke
Henricus Fouler pro dimidio sacco et viij clavis lane in j poke
Robertus Maltby pro iij saccis et dimidio sacco et viij clavis lane in iij pokes
Summa saccorum lane xiij sacci et dimidius et x clavi

{Octobris}
Navis vocata le Mary de Novo Castro unde Johannes Ryder est magister exivit xix die Octobris
Petrus Baxster pro j sacco et j quarterio unius sacci et viij clavis lane in ij pokes
Willelmus Blaxston pro iij quarteriis unius sacci et iij clavis lane in ij pokes
Johannes Robynson pro iiij saccis et dimidio sacco lane in iiij pokes
Alexander Byrde pro tribus quarteriis unius sacci et v clavis lane in ij pokes
Johannes Mappas pro dimidio sacco lane in j poke
Johannes Foster pro j sacco et dimidio sacco et iij clavis lane in ij pokes
Thomas Castell pro dimidio sacco et v clavis lane in j poke
Thomas Wardle pro C et xx pellibus lanutis continentibus dimidium saccum lane
Alanus Birde pro dimidio sacco et viij clavis lane in j poke
Summa { saccorum lane x sacci iij quarteria unius sacci et vj clavi
pellum lanutarum patet }

4. Particulars of Account of John Richardson and Thomas Spens, collectors, 10 May 1461 to 18 February 1462

E122/107/53

The account consists of two membranes sewn Exchequer style. The first membrane is 278 mm. wide and 711 mm. long. The head of account and entries to 3rd June are on the face, but the dorse is blank except for an incomplete summary or foot of account, on which the clerk noted 'All the figures are struck out because they are entered in the following roll'; the text of this section is printed as 4* below. The second membrane is 290 mm. wide and 880 mm. long, and includes the foot of account covering both membranes.

The account as it stands is incomplete: the summaries for each ship when added together are less than the total in the final summary. The latter refers to 'two rolls', but there must be some missing material, as additions were carefully checked at the Exchequer.

Both membranes are rubbed in places, but these are legible under ultra-violet light. There are a number of small holes and an area 90 mm. square is missing from the bottom of the first membrane.

The marginal notes identifying denizens are not printed here.

The superscript *mi*, for *minor*, is used twice, to distinguish the lesser hundred of five score, by which woolfells were counted, from the great hundred, or long hundred, of six score, by which shorlings and lambfells were counted.

[*Membrane 1 face*]

Particule compoti Johannis Richardson et Thome Spens, nuper collectorum custumarum et subsidiorum domini regis in portu ville Novi Castri super Tinam et in singulis portubus et locis eidem portui adiacentibus, videlicet de huius custumis et subsidiis regis ibidem a x^{mo} die Maii anno primo regis nunc Edwardi quarti usque xviij^{mo} diem Februarii tunc proximo sequentem, scilicet per tria quarteria anni et xij dies absque contrarotulamento.

{Maii}
Navis vocata Kateryn de Camfere unde Cornelius Mychelson est magister exivit xj die Maii
{alienigena}

Idem pro x celdris carbonum	valor xvj s. viij d.
custuma ij d.ob. subsidium x d.	
Idem pro vj grindstones	valor xxd.
custuma ob. subsidium j d.ob.	
Idem pro xviij rubstones	valor xx d.
custuma ob. subsidium j d.ob.	
Willelmus Hunter pro j plaustro et dimidio plumbi	valor iiij li. x s.
subsidium iiij s. vj d.	
Idem pro CC shorlynges	valor xxx s.
subsidium xviij d.	
Idem pro ij pannis panni lanei sine grano	
custuma ij s. iiij d.	

Summa	valoris	vij li.
	panni lanei sine grano	ij panni
	custume panni	ij s. <vij d.ob. *struck out*> iiij d.
	custume iijd de libra	iij d.ob.
	subsidii	vij s. j d.

Willelmus Hunter pro xl pellibus lanutis continentibus dimidium quarterium et x pelles
custuma xiij d.ob subsidium vs. vij d.

Summa	pellium lanutarum xl continentes dimidium quarterium et x pelles	
	custume	xiij d.ob.
	subsidii	v s. <j d.ob. *struck out*> vij d.
	denariorum Calesii	j d.ob.
	exitus coketti	ij d.

{Maii}
Navis vocata Kateryn de Camfere unde Adrianus Coll est magister exivit xj die Maii
{Alienigena}

Idem pro xvj celdris carbonum	valor xxvj s. viij d.
Idem pro xvj grindstones	valor xx s.
custuma iij d. subsidium xij d.	
Idem pro iij dossenis rubstones	valor ij s. vj d.
custuma ob. subsidium ij d.	

Summa	valoris	xlix s. ij d.
	custume	vij d.ob.
	subsidii	ij s. vj d.

{Maii}

Navis vocata Michel de Sheles, unde David Pereson est magister exivit xj die Maii

Robertus Harden pro j plaustro plumbi valor xxx s.
subsidium xviij d.

Robertus Baxter pro j plaustro plumbi valor lx s.
subsidium iij s.

Idem pro Ciiij^{xx} shorlynges valor xxv s.
subsidium xv d.

Willelmus Blaxton pro j plaustro plumbi valor lx s.
Subsidium iij s.

Willelmus Thomson pro dimidio plaustro plumbi valor xxx s.
subsidium xviij d.

Alanus Bird pro iiij plaustris plumbi valor xij li.
subsidium xij s.

Willelmus Conyngham pro CC shorlynges valor xxx s.
subsidium xviij d.

Robertus Baxter pro Ciiij^{xx} shorlynges valor xxv s.
subsidium xv d.

Summa { valoris xxv li.
subsidii xxv s.

Robertus Baxter pro xl pellibus lanutis continentibus dimidium quarterium sacci et x pelles
custuma xiij d.ob. subsidium v s. vij d.

Thomas Swan pro iij quarteriis iiij clavis lane in j poke
custuma v s. vj d.ob. subsidium xxvij s. viij d.

Johannes Mappas pro ij saccis lane in ij pokes
custuma xiij s. iiij d. subsidium lxvj s. viij d.

Johannes Sample pro j sacco j quarterio ij clavis lane in ij pokes
custuma viij s. x d.ob. subsidium xliiij s. iiij d.

... [*hole in membrane 25 x 15 mm.*] Blaxton pro iij saccis j quarterio iiij clavis lane in v pokes
custuma xxij s. ij d.ob. subsidium Cx s. xj d.

... Burton pro j sacco lane in j poke
custuma vj s. viij d. subsidium xxxiij s. iiij d.

... Rothom pro iij quarteriis viij clavis lane in j poke
custuma vj s. ob. subsidium xxx s. ij d.ob.

... Yonger pro dimidio sacco viij clavis lane in j poke
custuma iiij s. iiij d.ob. subsidium xxj s. viij d.ob.

Willelmus Thomson pro iij quarteriis iiij clavis lane in j poke
custuma v s. vj d.ob. subsidium xxvij s. viij d.

Thomas Wright pro j sacco iij quarteriis lane in ij pokes
custuma xj s. viij d. subsidium lviij s. iiij d.

Idem pro Ciiij^{xx} pellibus lanutis continentibus iij quarteria unius sacci
custuma v s. subsidium xxv s.

Robertus Harden pro iij quarteriis lane in j poke
custuma v s. subsidium xxv s.

Summa
- saccorum lane xiij sacci j quarterium <vj clavi *struck out*> iiij clavi
- pellium lanutarum CCxx continentes iij quarteria dimidium quarterium et x pelles
- custume lane iiij li. ix s. <j d.ob. *struck out*> ij d.
- custume pellium lanutarum vj s. j d.ob.
- subsidii lane xxij li. v s. <vj d.ob. *struck out*> vij d.
- subsidii pellium xxx s. vij d.
- denariorum Calesii ix s. vj d.ob.
- exituum coketti xxij d.

{Maii}

Navis vocata George de Durdright unde Adrianus Skynner est magister exivit xij die Maii

{alienigena}

Idem pro vj celdris carbonum custuma j d.ob. subsidium vj d.	valor x s.
Willelmus Hunter pro vj grindstones subsidium ix d.	valor xv s.
Thomas Cudbert pro xvj grindstones subsidium vj d.	valor x s.
Idem pro CCC shorlynges subsidium ij s. iij d.	valor xlv s.
Thomas Dayvell pro CCiiij^{xx}x shorlinges subsidium ij s. j d.	valor xlj s. viij d.
Willelmus Hurlbad pro CCC shorlinges subsidium iij s. iij d	valor xlv s.
Robertus Chambre pro C shorlynges subsidium ix d.	valor xv s.
Idem pro CCCClx lambskyns subsidium iij s.	valor lx s.
Johannes Robynson pro CCC shorlinges subsidium ij s. iij d.	valor xlv s.
Georgius Brigham pro CClx shorlinges subsidium xxij d.ob.	valor xxxvij s. vj d.
Robertus Heley pro C shorlinges subsidium ix d.	valor xv s.
Johannes Esyngton pro Dlx shorlinges subsidium iiij s. j d.ob.	valor iiij li. ij s. vj d.
Willelmus Scot pro Clx shorlinges subsidium xiij d.ob.	valor xxij s. vj d.
Robertus Harden pro C shorlinges subsidium ix d.	valor xv s.
Nicholaus Haynyng pro CCC shorlinges subsidium ij s. iij d.	valor xlv s.
Johannes Side pro Dlx shorlinges subsidium ij s. j d.ob.	valor iiij li. ij s. ij d.

Summma { valoris xxix li. vj s. viij d.
custume j d.ob.
subsidii xxix s. iiij d. }

Thomas Cudbert pro j sacco viij clavis lane in ij pokes
custuma vij s. viij d.ob. subsidium xxxviij s. v d.ob.
Idem pro iiij^{xx} pellibus lanutis continentibus j quarterium et xx pelles
custuma ij s. iij d. subsidium xj s. j d.ob.
Robertus Pykden pro iij quarteriis viij clavis lane in j poke
custuma vj s. ob. subsidium xxx s. ij d.ob.
Idem pro C pellibus lanutis continentibus j quarterium dimidium quarterium et x pelles
custuma ij s. ix d. subsidium xiij s. xj d.
Willelmus Hurlbad pro lx pellibus lanutis continentibus j quarterium
custuma xx d. subsidium viij s. iiij d.
Johannes Yonger pro dimidio sacco lane in j poke
custuma iij s. iiij d. subsidium xvj s. viij d.
Idem pro CCxl pellibus lanutis continentibus j saccum
custuma vj s. viij d. subsidium xxxiij s. iiij d.
Robertus Chambre pro xx pellibus lanutis
custuma vij d. subsidium ij s. ix d.ob.
Alanus Carr pro ij saccis j quarterio viij clavis lane in iiij pokes
custuma xvj s. ob. subsidium iiij li. j d.ob.
Johannes Robynson pro j sacco dimidio in ij pokes
custuma x s. subsidium l s.
Idem pro iiij^{xx} pellibus lanutis continentibus j quarterium et xx pelles
custuma ij s. iij d. subsidium xj s. j d. ob
Thomas Burton pro j sacco dimidio viij clavis lane in ij pokes
custuma xj s. ob. subsidium lv s. j d.ob.
Thomas Swan pro dimidio sacco lane in j poke
custuma iij s. iiij d. subsidium xvj s. viij d.
Willelmus Haysand pro lx pellibus lanutis continentibus j quarterium sacci
custuma xx d. subsidium viij s. iiij d.
Georgius Brigham pro lx pellibus lanutis continentibus j quarterium
custuma xx d. subsidium viij s. iiij d.
Willelmus Hunter pro Cxx pellibus lanutis continentibus dimidium saccum
custuma iij s. iiij d. subsidium xvj s. viij d.
Johannes Sample pro Cxx pellibus lanutis continentibus dimidium saccum
custuma iij s. iiij d. subsidium xvj s. viij d.
Willelmus Scot pro xxx pellibus lanutis continentibus dimidium quarterium
custuma x d. subsidium iij s. ij d.
Robertus Harden pro xx pellibus lanutis
custuma vij d. subsidium ij s. ix d.ob.
Johannes Side pro Cxl pellibus lanutis continentibus dimidium saccum et xx pelles
custuma iij s. xj d. subsidium xix s. v d.ob.

Nicholas Haynyng pro lx pellibus lanutis continentibus j quarterium
custuma xx d. subsidium viij s. iiij d.
Willelmus Lawes pro ij saccis lane in ij pokes
custuma xiij s. iiij d. subsidium lxvj s. viij d.

Summa
- saccorum lane x sacci dimidius vj clavi
- pellium lanutarum MCiiij^{xxx}x continentes iiij saccos iij quarteria dimidium xx pelles
- custume lane iij li. x s. <ix d.ob. *struck out*> x d.
- custume pellium lanutarum xxxvj s. <j d. *struck out*> ij d.ob.
- subsidii lane xvij li. xiij s. x d.<ob. *struck out*>
- subsidii pellium lanutarum viij li. v s. iiij d.ob.
- denariorum Calesii <vij s. j d. *struck out*> x s. iiij d.
- exituum coketti iij s.

{Maii}
Navis vocata Valentine de Novo Castro super Tynam unde Robertus Symson est magister exivit xx die Maii

Willelmus Lawes pro MCCClx shorlinges subsidium x s. j d.ob.	valor x li. ij s. vj d.
Idem pro MCCCC lambskyns subsidium ix s. iiij d.	valor ix li. vj s. viij d.
Johannes Mappas pro Mxl shorlinges subsidium vij s. ix d.	valor vij li. xv s.
Idem pro CCCClx lambskyns subsidium iij s.	valor lx s.
Georgius Brigham pro CCCCxl shorlinges subsidium iij s. iij d.	valor lxv s.
Johannes Redesdale pro DCiiij^{xx} shorlinges subsidium v s.	valor C s.
Willelmus Conyngham pro CCCC shorlynges subsidium iij s.	valor lx s.
Robertus Brigham pro Dxl shorlinges subsidium iiij s.	valor iiij li.
Willelmus Faucus pro CCCC lambskyns subsidium ij s. viij d.	valor liij s. iiij d.
Idem pro xl shorlinges subsidium iij d.	valor v s.
Johannes Belt pro CCCC shorlinges subsidium iij s.	valor lx s.
Robertus Bulmer pro xxvj grindstones subsidium ij s. iij d.	valor xlv s.
Robertus Baxter pro j plaustro et dimidio plumbi subsidium iiij s. vj d.	valor iiij li. x s.
Johannes Bee pro j plaustro et dimidio plumbi subsidium iij s. vj d.	valor iiij li. x s.

Alanus Bird pro dimidio plaustro plumbi valor xxx s.
subsidium xviij d.
Willelmus Haysand pro j plaustro plumbi valor lx s.
subsidium iij s.
Willelmus Thomson pro ij plaustris plumbi valor vj li.
subsidium vj s.
Nicholaus Haynyng pro iij quarteriis unius panni panni lanei sine grano
custuma x d.ob.
Johannes Side pro j plaustro et dimidio plumbi valor iiij li. x s.
subsidium iiij s. vj d.

Summa {
valoris lxxvij li. xij s. vj d.
panni lanei sine grano iij quarteriis unius panni
custume x d.ob.
subsidii lxxvij s. vij d.ob.

Willelmus Lawes pro CCC^{minor} pellibus lanutis continentibus j saccum j quarterium
custuma viij s. iiij d. subsidium clj s. viij d.
Johannes Mappas pro ij saccis j quarterio viij clavis lane in iij pokes
custuma xvj s. ob. subsidium iiij li. j d.ob.
Idem pro CC^{minor} pellibus lanutis continentibus iij quarteria et xx pelles
custuma v s. vij d. subsidium xxvij s. ix d. ob
Jacobus Clerk pro CCxl pellibus lanutis continentibus j saccum
custuma vj s. viij d. subsidium xxxiij s. iiij d.
Georgius Brigham pro dimidio sacco viij clavis lane in j poke
custuma iiij s. iiij d.ob. subsidium xxj s. ix d.ob.
Idem pro Cxl pellibus lanutis continentibus dimidium saccum et xx pelles
custuma iij s. xj d. subsidium xix s. v d.ob.
Willelmus Conyngham pro iij quarteriis viij clavis lane in ij pokes
custuma vj s. ob. subsidium xxx s. j d.ob.
Idem pro iiij^{xx} pellibus lanutis continentibus j quarterium et xx pelles
custuma ij s. iij d. subsidium xj s. j d.ob.
Johannes Sample pro ij saccis dimidio lane in iiij pokes
custuma xvj s. viij d. subsidium iiij li. iij s. iiij d.
Johannes Esyngton pro v saccis j quarterio iij clavis et dimidio lane in v pokes
custuma xxxv s. vj d. subsidium viij li. xvij s. iij d.
Agnes Rothom pro iij saccis iij quarteriis iij clavis et dimidio lane in iiij pokes
custuma xxv s. vij d.ob. subsidium vj li. vij s. <iij d. *struck out*> ij d.ob.
Thomas Burton pro iiij saccis lane in iiij pokes
custuma xxvj s. viij d. subsidium vj li. xiij s. iiij d.
Thomas Dayvell pro iij quarteriis iij clavis lane in j poke
custuma v s. v d. subsidium xxvj s. xj d.
Johannes Belt pro j sacco et dimidio lane in ij pokes
custuma x s. subsidium l s.

Willelmus Hurlbad pro j sacco j quarterio lane in ij pokes
custuma viij s. iiij d. subsidium xlj s. viij d.
Willelmus Scot pro vj saccis lane in vij pokes
custuma xl s. subsidium x li.
Thomas Swan pro dimidio sacco lane in j poke
custuma iij s. iij d. subsidium xvj s. viij d.
Robertus Brigham pro ij saccis viij clavis lane in iij pokes
custuma xiiij s. iiij d.ob. subsidium lxxj s. ix d.ob.
Idem pro Cxx pellibus lanutis continentibus dimidium saccum lane
custuma iij s. iiij d. subsidium xvj s. viij d.
Robertus Harden pro ij saccis j quarterio viij clavis lane in iiij pokes
custuma xvj s. ob. subsidium iiij li. j d.ob.
Johannes Cacherside pro j sacco j quarterio lane in ij pokes
custuma viij s. iiij d. subsidium xlj s. viij d.
Robertus Baxter pro j sacco j quarterio lane in ij pokes
custuma viij s. iiij d. subsidium xlj s. viij d.
Nicholaus Haynyng pro dimidio sacco lane in j poke
custuma iij s. iiij d. subsidium xvj s. viij d.
Willelmus Lawes pro iij saccis lane in iij pokes
custuma xx s. subsidium C s.
Willelmus Esyngton pro ij saccis dimidio lane in iij pokes
custuma xvj s. viij d. subsidium iiij li. iij s. iiij d.
Robertus Brigham pro iij quarteriis lane in j poke
custuma v s. subsidium xxv s.
Idem pro j sacco dimidio lane in iij pokes
custuma x s. subsidium l s.
Idem pro dimidio sacco lane in j poke
custuma iij s. iiij d. subsidium xvj s. viij d.
Willelmus Blaxton pro dimidio sacco viij clavis lane in j poke
custuma iiij s. iiij d.ob. subsidium xxij s. ix d.ob.

Summa {
saccorum lane xlvj sacci vj clavi
pellium lanutarum Miiij^{xx} continentes iiij saccos dimidium
custume lane xv li. vij s. vij d.
custume pellium lanutarum xxx s. iij d.ob.
subsidii lane <lxxij li. xj s. *struck out*> lxxv li. vijs. vj d.ob.
<subsidium iiij^{xx}iiij li. vj s. x d.qu. *struck out*>
subsidii pellium lanutarum vij li. xs. vij d.ob. qu.
denariorum Calesii xxxiij s. ix d.ob.
exituum coketti iij s. x d.
}

{Junii}
Navis vocata Cristofre de Broweshaven unde Van Harryson est magister exivit tercio die Junii
Alanus Carr pro j plaustro et dimidio plumbi valor iiij li. x s.
subsidium iiij s. vj d.
Willelmus Richardson pro MC shorlynges valor viij li. v s.
subsidium viij s. iij d.

Robertus Chambre pro Cl shorlynges valor xxj s. viij d.
subsidium xiij d.
Idem pro CCCCiiij^{xx} lambskyns valor xlviij s. iiij d.
subsidium ij s. v d.
Robertus Brigham pro CClx shorlinges valor xxxvij s. vj d.
subsidium xxij d.ob.
Idem pro CClx lambskyns valor xxxiij s. iiij d.
subsidium xx d.
Willelmus Faucus pro CCCC shorlynges valor lx s.
subsidium iij s.
Summa { valoris xxij li. xv s. x d.
subsidii xxij s. ix d.ob.
Robertus Chambre pro xx pellibus lanutis
... [*From this point to the foot of the first membrane 90 mm. is missing from the right-hand side.*]
Robertus Brigham pro xl pellibus lanutis continentibus dimidium quarterium sacci et x pelles
Willelmus Faucus pro lx pellibus lanutis continentibus j quarterium
Summa { pellium lanutarum cxx continentes ...
custume pellium lanutarum ...
subsidii pellium lanutarum ...
denariorum Calesii ...
exituum coketti ...

Navis vocata Maryknyght de Camfere unde Andreas Johnson ...
{alienigena}
Idem pro viij celdris carbonum valor xiij s. ...

[*Membrane 2 face*]
{Octobris}
Navis vocata Cristofre de Novo Castro super Tynam unde Germenus Harssh est magister exivit tercio die Octobris
Alanus Bird pro iiij plaustris et dimidio plumbi valor xiij li. x s.
subsidium xiij s. vj d.
Johannes Stele pro j plaustro et dimidio plumbi valor iiij li. x s.
subsidium iiij s. vj d.
Nicholaus Haynyng pro CCCC shorlynges valor lx s.
subsidium iij s.
Idem pro D lambskyns valor x li.
subsidium x s.
Alanus Carr pro vj dossenis grindstones valor xl s.
subsidium ij s.
Idem pro iij plaustris plumbi valor ix li.
subsidium ix s.
Petrus Baxter pro CCiiij^{xx} shorlinges valor xl s.
subsidium ij s.
Robertus Bulmer pro xvj grindstones valor xxx s.
subsidium xviij d.

Summma { valoris xlv li. x s.
subsidii xlv s. vj d.

Nicholaus Haynyng pro vj saccis lane in viij pokes
custuma xl s. subsidium x li.

Idem pro Cxx pellibus lanutis continentibus dimidium saccum
custuma iij s. iiij d. subsidium xvj s. viij d.

Robertus Huet pro dimidio sacco viij clavis lane in ij pokes
custuma iiij s. iiij d.ob. subsidium xxj s. ix d.ob.

Petrus Baxter pro ij saccis lane in iij pokes
custuma xiij s. iiij d. subsidium lxvj s. viij d.

Idem pro xl pellibus lanutis continentibus dimidium quarterium x pelles
custuma xiij d.ob. subsidium vs. vij d.

Johannes Shilton pro dimidio sacco lane in j poke
custuma iij s. iiij d. subsidium xvj s. viij d.

Willelmus Conyngham pro iij quarteriis lane in j poke
custuma v s. subsidium xxv s.

Willelmus Broderwyk pro ij saccis j quarterio lane in v pokes
custuma xv s. subsidium lxxv s.

Alanus Carr pro viij clavis lane in j poke
custuma xij d.ob. subsidium vs. ij d.ob.

Idem pro xx pellibus lanutis
custuma vij d. subsidium ij s. ix d.ob.

Willelmus Blaxton pro v saccis dimidio j clavo lane in viij pokes
custuma xxxvj s. x d. subsidium ix li. iiij s.

Johannes Riddyng pro iij saccis dimidio lane in iiij pokes
custuma xxiij s. iiij d. subsidium Cxvj s. viij d.

Willelmus Bird pro iij quarteriis lane in j poke
custuma v s. subsidium xxv s.

Robertus Musgrave pro iij quarteriis viij clavis lane in ij pokes
custuma vj s. ob. subsidium xxx s. j d.ob.

Johannes Penreth pro j quarterio lane in j poke
custuma xx d. subsidium viij s. iiij d.

Willelmus Rothom pro dimidio sacco lane in j poke
custuma iij s. iiij d. subsidium xvj s. viij d.

Robertus Craufurd pro j quarterio viij clavis lane in j poke
custuma ij s. viij d.ob. subsidium xiij s. v d.ob.

Hugo Watson pro dimidio sacco viij clavis lane in j poke
custuma iiij s. iiij d.ob. subsidium xxj s. ix d.ob.

Robertus Baxter pro ij saccis dimidio lane in iij pokes
custuma xvj s. viij d. subsidium iiij li. iij s. iiij d.

Alanus Bird pro ij saccis iij quarteriis iij clavis lane in iiij pokes
custuma xviij s. ix d. subsidium iiij li. xiij s. vij d.

Robertus Harden pro iij quarteriis viij clavis lane in ij pokes
custuma vj s. ob. subsidium xxx s. j d.ob.

Willelmus Thomson pro iij quarteriis lane in j poke
custuma v s. subsidium xxv s.

Agnes Rothom pro j sacco lane in j poke
custuma vj s. viij d. subsidium xxxiij s. iiij d.

Summa {
saccorum lane xxxij sacci iiij quarteria
Pellium lanutarum Ciiij^{xx} continentes iij quarteria sacci
custume lane x li. xviij s. iiij d.
custume pellium lanutarum v s.
subsidii lane liiij li. x s. viij d.
subsidii pellium lanutarum xxv s.
denariorum Calesii xxij s. iiij d.
exituum coketti iij s. iiij d.

Navis vocata Valentine de Novo Castro super Tynam unde Robertus Symson est magister applicuit tercio die Octobris

Johannes Robynson pro MM libris ferri	valor lxvj s. viij d.
subsidium iij s. iij d.	
Alanus Carr pro MMMM libris ferri	valor vj li. xiij s. iiij d.
subsidium vj s. viij d.	
Idem pro ij barellis smigmatis	valor xx s.
subsidium xij d.	
Idem pro CC ulnis panni linii	valor l s.
subsidium ij s. vj d.	
Thomas Cudbert pro MMMM libris ferri	valor vj li. iij s. iiij d.
Idem pro C ulnis panni linii de holand	valor xx s.
subsidium xij d.	
Johannes Redesdale pro j fulle ketilles	valor xxx s.
subsidium xviij d.	
Idem pro MM di' libris ferri	valor iiij li. iij s. iiij d.
subsidium iiij s. ij d.	
Johannes Bee pro iiij barellis smigmatis	valor xl s.
subsidium ij s.	
Idem pro MM libris ferri	valor lxvjs. viij d.
subsidium iij s. iij d.	
Idem pro viij dossenis felthattes	valor xxiiij s. iiij d.
subsidium xiiij d.	
Idem pro iij peciis de bricusy	valor xxiiij s. iiij d.
subsidium viij d.	
Willelmus Thomson pro M libris ferri	valor xxxiij s. iiij d.
subsidium xx d.	
Idem pro x dossenis felthattes	valor xxx s.
subsidium xviij d.	
Willelmus Faucus pro MMM di' libris ferri	valor C xvj s. viij d.
subsidium v s. x d.	
Nicholaus Haynyng pro MM libris ferri	valor lxvj s. viij d.
subsidium iij s. iiij d.	
Idem pro C ulnis de sayecloth	valor xv s.
subsidium ix d.	
Johannes Sample pro MM libris ferri	valor lxvj s viijd.
subsidium iij s. iiij d.	

Idem pro xij dossenis felthattes valor xxx s.
subsidium xviij d.
Johannes Brigham pro M libris ferri valor xxxiij s. iiij d.
subsidium xx d.
Idem pro CC libris canabi valor xx s.
subsidium xij d.
Jacobus Clerk pro x dossenis ulnis panni linii valor xlvj s. viij d.
subsidium ij s. iiij d.
Idem pro xij libris piperis valor x s.
subsidium vj d.
Robertus Chambre pro vj M libris ferri valor x li.
subsidium x s.
Idem pro j mat de ketilles valor xxx s.
subsidium xviij d.
Idem pro xx bundellis lini valor xx s.
subsidium xij d.
Idem pro CC di'ulnis de canvas valor xxv s.
subsidium xv d.
Idem pro di' [? C *omitted*] libris de alome valor xxvj s. viij d.
subsidium xvj d.
Willelmus Conyngham pro M libris ferri valor xxxiij s. iiij d.
subsidium xx d.
Thomas Rede pro MMM di' libris ferri valor Cxvj s. viij d.
subsidium v s. x d.
Idem pro j barello smigmatis valor x s.
subsidium vj d.
Robertus Symson pro M libris ferri valor xxxiij s. iiij d.
subsidium xx d.
Idem pro xxx bundellis lini valor xxx s.
subsidium xviij d.
Idem pro j fulle ketilles valor xx s.
subsidium xij d.
Johannes Barow pro MM libris ferri valor lxvj s. viij d.
subsidium iij s. iiij d.
Thomas Cathy pro MM di' libris ferri valor iiij li. iij s. iiij d.
subsidium iiij s. ij d.
Idem pro ijj barellis de osmondes valor xx s.
subsidium xij d.
Willelmus Robynson pro M libris ferri valor xxxiij s. iiij d.
subsidium xx d.
Thomas Davell pro iiij M libris ferri valor vj li. xiij s. iiij d.
subsidium vj s. viij d.
Idem pro iiij dossenis felthattes valor x s.
subsidium vj d.
Idem pro C di'ulnis panni linii valor lx s.
subsidium iij s.
Idem pro xii libris piperis valor xiij s. iiij d.
subsidium viij d.

Thomas Godeyere pro xl bundellis lini valor xl s.
subsidium ij s.
Idem pro M libris ferri valor xxxiij s. iiij d.
subsidium xx d.
Thomas Burton pro iiij M libris ferri valor vj li. xiij s. iiij d.
subsidium vj s. viij d.
Idem pro iij barellis de osmondes valor xx s.
subsidium xij d.
Idem pro j barello olei valor xiij s. iiij d.
subsidium viij d.
Agnes Rothom pro x dossenis felthattes valor xiij s. iiij d.
subsidium viij d.
Eadem pro C ulnis panni linii valor xvs.
subsidium ix d.
Eadem pro vj M libris ferri valor x li.
subsidium x s.
Johannes Esyngton pro C ulnis panni linii valor xv s.
subsidium ix d.
Idem pro xij dossenis felthattes valor xl s.
subsidium ij s.
Idem pro viij whyte fulles de ketilles valor xx s.
subsidium xij d.
Idem pro vj peciis de fustyane de Naples valor xxvj s. viiij d.
subsidium xvj d.
Idem pro dimidio barello de alome valor xl s.
subsidium ij s.
Idem pro iij barellis olei valor xxx s.
subsidium xviij d.
Idem pro j pipa olei valor xxxiij s. iiij d.
subsidium xx d.
Idem pro xx M libris ferri valor xxxiij li. vj s. viij d.
subsidium xxxiij s. iiij d.
Idem pro xij barellis de osmondes valor iiij li.
subsidium iiij s.
Willelmus Blaxton pro C ulnis de canvas valor x s.
subsidiium vj d.
Idem pro iiij M. libris ferri valor xj li.xiij s. iiij d.
subsidium vj s. viij d.
Willelmus Hurlbad pro lx bundellis linii valor lx s.
subsidium iiij s.
Thomas Wright pro xij dossenis felthattes valor xxx s.
subsidium xviij d.
Item pro iij peciis de fustyan valor xvj s. viij d.
subsidium x d.
Willelmus Scott pro ij dossenis felthattes valor vj s. viij d.
subsidium iiij d.
Idem pro v M libris ferri valor viij li. vj s. viij d.
subsidium viij s. iiij d.

Johannes Yonger pro x M libris ferri valor xvj li. xiij s. iiij d.
subsidium xvj s. viij d.
Idem pro xij barellis de osmondes valor iiij li.
subsidium iiij s.
Idem pro j fulle di' kettilles valor xl s.
subsidium ij s.
Idem pro xij dossenis felthattes valor xl s.
subsidium ij s.
Idem pro CCC elles de canvas valor xl s.
subsidium lj s.
Andreas Lommesden pro j barello smigmatis valor x s.
subsidium vj d.
Idem pro xvj bundellis lini valor xxvj s. viij d.
subsidium xvj d.
Idem pro M libris ferri valor xxxiij s. iiij d.
subsidium xx d.

Summa { valoris CCxxviij li. xvj s. viij d.
subsidii xj li. viij s. x d.

[*Membrane 2 dorse*]

{Octobris}

Navis vocata Maryknyght de Horne unde Maynard Florenson est magister applicuit xxij die Octobris

{alienigena}

Idem pro iij M pavyngtile valor xxvj s. viij d.
custuma iiij d. subsidium xvj d.
Idem pro C caseis valor viij s. iiij d.
custuma j d.ob. subsidium v d.
Idem pro xx barellis ceparum valor viij s. iiij d.
custuma j d.ob. subsidium v d.
Idem pro vj barellis pomorum valor xx d.
custuma ob. subsidium j d.
Idem pro ij lastis cinerum valor xl s.
custuma vj d. subsidium ij s.

Summa { valoris iiij li. v s.
custume xiij d.ob.
subsidii iiij s. iij d.

{Octobris}

Navis vocata Michel de Sheles unde David Pereson est magister exivit xxiij die Octobris

Alanus Bird pro iij quarteriis unius plaustri plumbi valor xlv s.
subsidium ij s. iij d.
Johannes Neuton pro iij quarteriis unius plaustri plumbi valor xlv s.
subsidium ij s. iij d.
Robertus Chambre pro Ciiij[xx] shorlinges valor xxv s. x d.
subsidium xv d.ob.

Idem pro C lambskynnes valor xiij s. iiij d.
subsidium viij d.
Willelmus Richardson pro CC shorlinges valor xxx s.
subsidium xviij d.
Robert Brigham pro C shorlinges valor xv s.
subsidium ix d.
Summa { valoris viij li. xiiij s. ij d.
subsidii viij s. viij d.ob.
Agnes Rothom pro j quarterio lane in j poke
custuma xx d. subsidium viij s. iiij d.
Robertus Baxter pro dimidio sacco lane in j poke
custuma iij s. iiij d. subsidium xvj s. viij d.
Thomas Burton pro j sacco dimidio iiij clavis lane in ij pokes
custuma x s. vij d. subsidium lij s. vij d.
Willelmus Hunter pro j sacco j quarterio lane in ij pokes
custuma viij s. iiij d. subsidium xlj s. viij d.
Thomas Cudbert pro viij clavis lane in j poke
custuma xij d.ob. subsidium vs. j d.ob.
Robertus Harden pro j sacco j quarterio iij clavis lane in ij pokes
custuma viij s. ix d. subsidium xliij s. vij d.
Willelmus Richardson pro dimidio sacco lane in j poke
custuma iij s. iiij d. subsidium xvj s. viij d.
Johannes Mappas pro dimidio sacco lane in j poke
custuma iij s. iiij d. subsidium xvj s. viij d.
Johannes Riddyng pro j quarterio viij clavis lane in j poke
custuma ij s. viij d.ob. subsidium xiij s. v d.ob.
Summa { saccorum lane vj sacci j quarterium x clavi
custume lane xlij s. xj d.ob.
subsidii lane x li. xiiij s. ix d.
denariorum Calesie iiij s. iiij d.
exituum coketti xviij d.

{Octobris}
Navis vocata James de Durdright unde Johannes Skynner est magister exivit ultimo die Octobris
Agnes Lawes pro CC shorlynges valor xxx s.
subsidium xviij d.
Alanus Byrd pro di' last de clapholt valor x s.
subsidium vj d.
Johannes Esyngton pro CC lambskyns valor xxvj s. viij d.
subsidium xvj d.
Idem pro CClx shorlynges valor xxxv s. vj d.
subsidium xxj d.ob.
Summa { valoris Cij s. ij d.
subsidii v s. j d.ob.
Johannes Robynson pro j sacco lane in j poke
custuma vj s. viij d. subsidium xxxiij s. iiij d.

Johannes Sample pro j quarterio viij clavis lane in j poke
custuma ij s. viij d.ob. subsidium xiij s. v d.ob.
Nicholaus Haynyng pro j quarterio viij clavis lane in j poke
custuma ij s. viij d.ob. subsidium xiij s. v d.ob.
Thomas Cudbert pro j quarterio lane in j poke
custuma xx d. subsidium viij s. iiij d.
Ricardus Brown pro j sacco viij clavis lane in ij pokes
custuma vij s. viij d.ob. subsidium xxxviij s. v d.ob.
Johannes Esyngton pro ij saccis j quarterio lane in ij pokes
custuma xv s. subsidium lxxv s.
Idem pro iij saccis lane in iij pokes
custuma xx s. subsidium C s.
Robertus Huet pro ij saccis vj clavis lane in iiij pokes
custuma xvij s. v d. subsidium iiij li. vij s. ij d.ob.

Summa { saccorum lane xj sacci iiij clavi
custume lane lxxiij s. x d.ob.
subsidii lane xviij li. ix s. iij d.
denariorum Calesii vij s. v d.
exituum coketti xvj d.

{Decembris}

Navis vocata John de Durdright unde Simon Frithland est magister applicuit xiiij die Decembris

{alienigena}

Idem pro ij rodes vini de Ryne valor vj li. v s.
custuma xix d. subsidium vj s. iij d.
Idem pro j lasto de bere valor xiij s. iiij d.
custuma ij d. subsidium viij d.
Idem pro j lasto allecis albi valor l s.
custuma vij d.ob. subsidium ij s. vj d.
Idem pro lx waynscott valor x s.
custuma j d.ob. subsidium vj d.
Idem pro vj barellis pomorum valor vj s. viij d.
custuma j d. subsidium iiij d.
Idem pro CCCC ollis terrenis valor vj s. viij d.
custuma j d. subsidium iiij d.
Idem pro xv ulnis panni linii valor vj s. viij d.
custuma j d. subsidium ij d.
Idem pro CCC bowestaves valor xl s.
custuma vj d. subsidium ij s.

Summa { valoris xij li. xviij s. iiij d.
custume iij s. iiij d.
subsidii xij s. xj d.

{Januarii}

Navis vocata le Pynke de Novo Castro super Tynam unde Mattheus Henryson est magister applicuit ix die Januarii

Thomas Cudbert pro vj barellis bituminis valor xx s.
subsidium xij d.

Johannes Robynson pro iiij barellis bituminis valor xiij s. iiij d.
subsidium viij d.

Agnes Rothom pro iiij barellis bituminis valor xiij s. iiij d.
subsidium viij d.

Georgius Brigham pro C libris rosen valor vj s. viij d.
subsidium iiij d.

Johannes Esyngton pro di' C avelanarum valor xx s.
subsidium xij d.

Summa { valoris lxxiij s. iiij d
subsidii iij s. viij d.

Navis vocata George de Ostend unde Andreas Coll est magister exivit xvj die Januarii

{alienigena}

Idem pro liiij celdris carbonum valor iiij li. x s.
custuma xiij d.ob. subsidium iiij s. vj d.

Idem pro vj grindstones valor ij s. vj d.
custuma ob. subsidium j d.ob.

Summa { valoris iiij li. xij s. vj d.ob.
custume xiiij d.
subsidii iiij s. vij d.ob.

{Summa horum ij rotulorum}

Lane indigenarum
CCxxiiij sacci iij quarteria iij clavi
custuma lxxv li. xx d.qu.
subsidium CCClxxiiij li. xv s. vij d.ob.

Pelles lanute indigenarum
vMxx facientes xx saccos iij quarteria xl pelles
custuma vij li. iiij d.qu.
subsidium xxxiiij li. xvij s. xj d.qu.

Exitus coketti
provenientes de Clxxvj mercatoribus lanarum et pellium lanutarum predictarum in portubus et locis predictis videlicet de quolibet mercatore ij d.
xxix s. iiij d.

Denaria Calesii
contingentia lanas et pelles lanutas predictas videlicet de quolibet sacco lane viij d. et de quibuslicet CCxx pellibus lanutis predictis viij d.
viij li. iij s. ob.

Pelles vocate shorlynges et lambfelles
xxxvMDlxx pelles facientes Cxlviij saccos et l pelles
custuma oneratur lxxiiij li. ij s. ij d.qu.
Subsidium oneratur ultra xij li. x s. xj d. de subsidio pondagii earundem de quibus onerant se gratis
DCCxxviij li. ix s. xj d.
Exitus coketti
provenientes de Cv mercatoribus earundem pellium
estimantur ad xvij s. vj d.
Denaria Calesii
contingentia easdem pelles
onerantur iiij li. xviij s. viij d.ob.
Valor alienigarum
unde iij d. de libra iiij^{xx}iiij li. xiij s. iiij d.
xxj s. ij d.
Panni indigenarum sine grano
x panni iij quarteria
custuma xij s. vj d.ob.
Valor indigenarum et alienigarum
unde xij d. de libra cum xij li. x s. xj d. de subsidio pondagii pellium vocatarum shorlynges et lambfelles superdictarum DCCxxix li. iij s. ij d.
xxxvj li. xix s. ij d.ob.
Summa Totalis Omnis MCCCxlviij li. ix s. ij d.ob.

unde
Custuma lanarum et pellium lanutarum
cum lxxix li. xviij s. iiij d.ob.q. Pro pellibus vocatis shorlynges et lambfelles
Clxxj li. xij s. ix d.ob.qu.
Subsidium earundem
cum DCCxxiviij li. ix s. xj d. superoneratis pro predictis pellibus vocatis shorlynges et lambfelles ultra xij li. x s. xj d. de subsidio pondagii earundem de quibus onerant se gratis inferius in titulo subsidii pondagii
MCxxxviij li. iij s. v d.ob.qu.
Parva custuma xxxiij s. viij d.ob.
Subsidium pondagii
cum xij li. x s. xj d. pro pellibus vocatis shorlynges et lambfelles
xxxvj li. xix s. ij d.ob.

4*. Unfinished summary of account.

E 122/107/53 membrane 1 dorse

This was written on the dorse of the first membrane of no. 4 above, Particulars of Account for 10 May 1461 – 18 February 1462. The totals are almost all somewhat smaller than those given at the end of that account, with none larger, suggesting that this summary covers a rather shorter period. All the words and figures have been neatly struck out. The right of the membrane is damaged for 90 mm. and there is some heavy staining, so that the text is not fully recoverable. The number of merchants to be charged for the cockets was left blank by the scribe.

{Summa Totalis Recepte'}
... huius rotuli ... te omnia cancellantur hic quia titulantur in rotulo sequente.

Sacci lane indigenarum
Clxxiiij sacci dimidio ...
Pelles lanute indigenarum
iiijMDCCCxl facientes xx saccos x pelles ...
Exitus coketti
provenientes de mercatoribus lanarum et pellium lanutarum ... [ex portu] predicto traductarum videlicet de quolibet mercatore iij d. ...
Pelles vocate shorlynges et lambfelles indigenarum
xxxijMCxl facientes [Cxxiij saccos] iij quarteria xl pelles ...

de subsidio continente in pondagio ...
denaria calesii
onerantur — iiij li. ix s. iij d.ob.
exitus coketti
provenientes de iiij^{xx} xviij mercatoribus — xvj s. iiij d.

Valor alienigarum
unde iij d. de libra lxij li. x s.
Custuma — xv s. vij d.ob.
Panni indigenarum sine grano
x panni iij quarteria
Custuma — xij s. vj d.ob.

Valor indigenarum et alienigarum
unde xij d. de libra
iiijCxxv li. x s. viij d.ob.
Subsidium cum xj li. vij s. j d. de subsidio pondagii pellium vocatarum shorlinges et lambfelles
xxj li. v s. vij d.
Summa Totalis Recepte MCl li. xix d.ob.qu.

unde
Custuma lanarum et pellium lanutarum
cum lxxij li. iiij s. ix d.ob. superoneratis pro pellibus vocatis shorlinges et lambfelles
Cxliiij li. xviij s. ix d.ob.
Subsidium earundem
cum DCxxvj li. vj s. iij d. superoneratis pro pellibus vocatis shorlinges et lambfelles
ixCiiij[xx] ij li. ix s. j d.qu.
Parva custuma xxviij s. ij d.
Subsidium pondagii
cum xj li. vij s. j d. pro pellibus vocatis shorlinges et lambfelles
xxj li. v s. vij d.

5. Particulars of Account of John Herbotell and William Rothom, collectors, from 4 March 1465 to 11 April, 1466.

E 122/107/57

The six membranes, sewn Exchequer style, are each 232 mm. wide, and respectively 717, 715, 717, 641, 699 and 660 mm. long. The account is complete and well preserved. Almost all the manuscript proved legible, although ultra-violet light was necessary to read the text at the foot of each membrane.

The scribe consistently wrote out *seldre* in full; in other accounts this is abbreviated to *celdr'* or *cheldr'*. On membrane 2d, he wrote *salis* in full so that *salis alb'* could be extended as *salis albi*. Subsequently *sal* was written without suspension mark, so that *alb'* had to be extended in the nominative. The fourth entry for 30 April and the sixth for 10 June were marked with a cross, to remind the collector that subsidy as well as custom was charged on cloth exported by aliens. *Will'mson* has been extended as *Willemson* in the case of masters of ships from ports in Holland and Zeeland.

[*Membrane 1 face*]

Particule compoti Johannis Herbotell et Willelmi Rothom collectorum custume et subsidii lanarum et corriorum et pellium lanuturam necnon subsidii tonagii et pondagii ac parve custume, in portu ville Novi Castri super Tynam et in diversis portubus et locis eidem portui adiacentibus, videlicet de huius custumis et subsidiis domini regis ibidem, a quarto die Marcii anno regni regis [Edwardi] quarti post conquestum Anglie quinto usque undecimum diem Aprilis anno regni regis predicti sexto, scilicet per unum annum integrum et xxxviij dies, quo tempore Thomas Weltden (fuit) contrarotulator dicti domini regis in portubus et locis predictis, a quo quidem xj^{mo} die Aprilis dicto anno vj^{to}, prefatus Willelmus Rothom et Thomas Spence nunc collectores custumarum et subsidiorum regis ibidem, per visum et testimonium contrarotulatoris predicti, sunt inde computaturi.

Navis vocata Laurence de Novo Castro super Tynam unde Willelmus Jonson est magister applicuit xx° die Marcii

Thomas Lokwood pro lx toppes rasemorum valor xl s.
subsidium ij s.
Idem pro j barello olei rape valor xiiij s. iiij d.
subsidium viij d
Georgius Chambre pro x toppes rasemorum valor vj s. viij d.
subsidium iiij d.
Wilelmus Hunter pro viij barellis avelanarum valor iiij li.
subsidium iij s.
Idem pro j dolio vini dulcis
tonnagium iij s.
Willelmus Hurbald pro iij pokes hoppe valor xl s.
subsidium ij s.
Idem pro iij barellis olei valor xl s.
Idem pro ij sortes fructus valor xiij s. iiij d.
subsidium viij d.
Robertus Brigham pro ij quarteriis avelanarum valor xx s.
subsidium xij d.
Idem pro iij pokes hoppe valor xl s.
subsidium ij s.
Idem pro vj sortes fructus valor xl s.
subsidium ij s.
Johannes Alyn pro xij sortes fructus valor iiij li.
subsidium iiij s.
Idem pro ix barellis allecis valor iij li.
subsidium iij s.
Idem pro xij augkindelles anguillarum valor l s.
subsidium ij s. vj d.
Idem pro ij pokes hoppe valor xl s.
subsidium ij s.
Johanna Horne pro vj sortes fructus valor xl s.
subsidium xvj d.
Idem pro ij barellis olei valor xxvj s. viij d.
subsidium xvj d.
Johannes Mappas pro di' M avelanarum valor xx s.
subsidium xij d.
Idem pro ix barellis allecis valor lx s.
subsidium iij s.
Idem pro xj barellis separum valor vj s. viij d.
subsidium iij d.
Johannes Batmanson pro xj sortes fructus valor xl s.
subsidium xij d.
Nicholaus Hanyng pro di' M avelanarum valor xx s.
subsidium xij d.
Idem pro vj sortes fructus valor xl s.
subsidium iij s.

Idem pro ix barellis allecis subsidium iij s.	valor lx s.
Idem pro iij pokes hoppe subsidium ij s.	valor xl s.
Idem pro j pipe olei rape subsidium ij s.	valor xl s.
Philipus Johnson pro iiij sortes fructus subsidium xvj d.	valor xxvj s. viij d.
Idem pro xxvij barellis pomorum subsidium ij s.	valor xl s.
Idem pro ix barellis separum subsidium ij d.ob.	valor iiij s. ij d.
Thomas Davell pro ix barellis allecis subsidium iij s.	valor lx s.
Idem pro xj barellis separum subsidium iiij d.	valor vj s. viij d.
Idem pro lx toppes rasemorum subsidium ij s.	valor xl s.
Henricus Fouler pro j barello olei rape subsidium viij d.	valor xiij s. iiij d.
Idem pro iiij sortes fructus subsidium xvj d.	valor xxvj s. viij d.
Thomas Cudbert pro di' M avelanarum subsidium xij d.	valor xx s.
Idem pro xxiiij aughkindelles anguillarum subsidium v s.	valor v li.
Idem pro lx toppes rasemorum subsidium ij s.	valor xl s.
Willelmus Lawes pro ij quarteriis avelanarum subsidium xij d.	valor xx s.
Idem pro vj barellis allecis subsidium ij s.	valor xl s.
Idem pro lx toppes rasemorum subsidium ij s.	valor xl s.
Thomas Gudyer pro viij sortes fructus subsidium ij s. viij d.	valor liij s. iiij d.
Idem pro j barello et dimidio olei rape subsidium xij d.	valor xx s.
Johannes Esyngton pro viij sortes fructus subsidium ij s. viij d.	valor liij s. iiij d.
Idem pro iij barellis avelanarum subsidium xviij d.	valor xxx s.
Idem pro iij pokes hoppe subsidium ij s.	valor xl s.
Willelmus Scot pro iij barellis olei subsidium xvj d.	valor xxvj s. viij d.
Idem pro lx toppes rasemorum subsidium ij s.	valor xl s.

Idem pro iiij barellis avelanarum   valor xl s.
    subsidium ij s.
Idem pro j dolio vini dulcis
    tonnagium iij s.
Ricardus Hogeson pro vj sortes fructus   valor xl s.
    subsidium ij s.
Idem pro iiij et dimidio barellis allecis   valor xxx s.
    subsidium xviij d.
Idem pro xij barellis separum   valor vj s. viij d.
    subsidium iiij d.
Idem pro xij libris piperis   valor xj s. viij d.
    subsidium <vj d.ob. *struck out*> vij d.

Summa { valoris iiij^{xx}xj li. vs.xd.
subsidii iiij li dj s. iij d.ob.
vini indigenarum ij dolia
tonnagii vj s. }

Navis vocata George de Novo Castro super Tynam unde Ricardus Dobson est magister applicuit xxviij die Marcii
Nicholaus Hanyng pro vi sortes fructus   valor xl s.
    subsidium ij s.
Idem pro iij barellis olei   valor xl s.
    subsidium ij s.
Idem pro j dolio vini dulcis
    tonnagium iij s.
Idem pro xij aughkindelles anguillarum   valor l s.
    subsidium ij s. vj d.
Idem pro iij pokes hoppe   valor xl s.
    subsidium ij s.
Idem pro iij^{xx} vj [libris] piperis   valor iiij li.
    subsidium iiij s.
Idem pro iij barellis avelanarum   valor xl s.
    subsidiium ij s.
Johannes Ridisdale pro vj sortes fructus   valor xl s.
    subsidium ij s.
Idem pro di' M avelanarum   valor xx s.
    subsidium xij d.
Idem pro xx seldre frumenti   valor xiij li. vj s. viij d.
    subsidium xiij s. iiij d.

plus in tergo

[*Membrane 1 dorse*]
Johannes Rydisdale pro vj sortes fructus   valor xl s.
    subsidium ij s.
Idem pro di' M avelanarum   valor xx s.
    subsidium xij d.

Idem pro xxxiiij libris piperis valor xx s.
subsidium xviij d.
Idem pro xx seldre frumenti valor xiij li. vj s. viij d.
subsidium xiij s. iiij d.
Idem pro iiij pipes farini valor xxvj s. viij d.
subsidium xvj d.
Idem pro xj barellis berre valor xxj s.
subsidium xij d.ob.
Johannes Sampill pro v doliis vini Rochelle
tonnagium xv s.
Idem pro xx seldre frumenti valor xiij li. vj s. viij d.
subsidium xiij s. iiij d.
Idem pro iiij^{xx}vj [libris] piperis valor iiij li.
subsidium iiij s.
Idem pro iij pipes farini valor xx s.
subsidium xij d.
Idem pro ix barellis allecis valor lx s.
subsidium iij s.
Robertus Harkesse pro lx toppes rasemorum valor xl s.
subsidium ij s.
Idem pro xij libris piperis valor x s.
subsidium vj d.
Idem pro iij pokes hoppe valor xl s.
subsidium ij s.
Idem pro j dolio vini dulcis
tonnagium iij s.
Thomas Cudbert pro xx seldre frumenti valor xiij li. vj s. viij d.
subsidium xiij s. iiij d.
Idem pro v dossenis librarum piperis valor xlviij s. iiij d.
subsidium ij s. v d.
Idem pro ij doliis vini dulcis
tonnagium vj s.
Idem pro iij pokes hoppe valor xl s.
subsidium ij s.
Idem pro vj sortes fructus valor xl s.
subsidium ij s.
Willelmus Conynghame pro xx seldre frumenti valor xiij li. vj s. viij d.
subsidium xiij s. iiij d.
Idem pro ij barellis olei valor xxvj s. viij d.
subsidium xvj d.
Idem pro lx toppes rasemorum valor xl s.
subsidium iij s.
Idem pro ix barellis allecis valor lx s.
subsidium iij s.
Idem pro j dolio vini dulcis
tonnagium iij s.
Robertus Stokall pro x seldre frumenti valor xj li. xiij s. iiij d.
subsidium vj s. viij d.

Idem pro xij barellis allecis	valor iiij li.
subsidium iiij s.	
Idem pro ij pipes farini	valor xiij s. iiij d.
subsidium viij d.	
Willelmus Blaxton pro ij doliis vini dulcis	
tonnagium vj s.	
Idem pro vj sortes fructus	valor xl s.
subsidium ij s.	
Idem pro viij barellis separum	valor iiij s. ij d.
subsidium ij d.ob.	
Idem pro iij last berre	valor iij li.
subsidium iij s.	
Johannes Gamelson pro ij barellis olei	valor xxvj s. viij d.
subsidium xvj d.	
Idem pro xij aughkindelles anguillarum	valor l s.
subsidium ij s. vj d.	
Idem pro vj sortes fructus	valor xl s.
subsidium ij s.	
Thomas Wright pro lx toppes rasemorum	valor xl s.
subsidium ij s.	
Idem pro iiij sortes fructus	valor xxvj s. viij d.
subsidium xvj d.	
Idem pro j poke et di' hop	valor xx s.
subsidium xij d.	
Idem pro ix barellis allecis	valor iij li.
subsidium iij s.	
Johannes Mappas pro xx seldre frumenti	valor xiij li. vj s. viij d.
subsidium xiij s. iiij d.	
Idem pro iij pokes hop	valor xl s.
subsidium ij s.	
Idem pro lx toppes rasemorum	valor xl s.
subsidium ij s.	
Idem pro j dolio vini dulcis	
tonnagium iij s.	
Idem pro ij barellis olei rape	valor xxvj s. viij d.
Thomas Swan pro v doliis vini Rochelle	
tonnagium vj s.	
Idem pro iij barellis olei rape	valor xl s.
subsidium ij s.	
Idem pro ix barellis allecis	valor lx s.
subsidium iij s.	
Idem pro vj sortes fructus	valor xl s.
subsidium ij s.	
Robertus Brighame pro iij dossenis librarum piperis	valor xxxj s.
subsidium xviij d.	
Idem pro xiij aughkindelles anguillarum	valor xxxj s.
subsidium xviij d.ob.	

Idem pro vj sortes fructus	valor xl s.
subsidium ij s.	
Idem pro ij barellis olei rape	valor xxvj s. viij d.
subsidium xvj d.	
Ricardus Hogeson pro iij barellis olei rape	valor xl s.
subsidium ij s.	
Idem pro j dolio vini dulcis	
tonnagium iij s.	
Idem pro ij dossenis librarum piperis	valor xx s.
subsidium xij d.	
Idem pro vj sortes fructus	valor xl s.
subsidium ij s.	
Thomas Davell pro xx seldre frumenti	valor xiij li. vj s. viij d.
subsidium xiij s. iiij d.	
Idem pro vj sortes fructus	valor xl s.
subsidium ij s.	
Idem pro xij barellis allecis	valor iiij li.
subsidium iij s.	
Idem pro ij doliis vini Rochelle	
tonnagium vj s.	
Idem pro iij barellis olei rape	valor xl s.
subsidium ij s.	
Idem pro j poke hop	valor xx s.
subsidium xij d.	
Willelmus Fyssewyke pro xx seldre frumenti	valor xiij li. vj s. viij d.
subsidium xiij s. iiiij d.	
Idem pro ij doliis vini dulcis	
tonnagium vj s.	
Idem pro ij barellis olei rape	valor xl s.
subsidium ij s.	
Idem pro ix barellis allecis	valor lx s.
subsidium ij s.	
Willelmus Lawes pro xv seldre frumenti	valor xjli. xiij s. iiij d.
subsidium xj s. viij d.	
Idem pro vj sortes fructus	valor xl s.
subsidium ij s.	
Idem pro v last berre	valor x li.
subsidium v s.	
Idem pro iij pokes hoppe	valor xl s.
subsidium ij s.	
Henricus Fowler pro iij dossenis librarum piperis	valor xxx s.
subsidium xviij d.	
Idem pro iij barellis olei rape	valor xl s.
subsidium ij s.	
Petrus Bewyk pro xx seldre frumenti	valor xiij li. vj s. viij d.
subsidium xiij s. iiij d.	
Idem pro j dolio vini dulcis	
tonnagium iij s.	

Idem pro vj sortes fructus	valor xl s.
subsidium ij s.	
Idem pro vj dossenis librarum piperis	valor lx s.
subsidium iij s.	
Idem pro iij pokes hoppe	valor xl s.
subsidium ij s.	
Idem pro vij barellis allecis	valor iiij li.
subsidium iiij s.	
Johannes Belt pro j dolio vini dulcis	
tonnagium iij s.	
Idem pro vj sortes fructus	valor xl s.
subsidium ij s.	
Idem pro xij aughkindelles anguillarum	valor l s.
subsidium <xviij d. *struck out*> ij s vj d.	
Idem pro xxvij barellis pomorum	valor xl s.
subsidium ij s.	
Idem pro ix barellis allecis	valor lx s.
subsidium <xviij d. *struck out*> iij s.	
Johannes Alyn pro x dossenis librarum piperis	valor v li.
subsidium v s.	
Idem pro j dolio vini dulcis	
tonnagium iij s.	
Idem pro xx seldre frumenti	valor xiij li vj s. viij d.
subsidium xiij s. iiij d.	
Idem pro vj sortes fructus	valor xl s.
subsidium ij s.	
Idem pro ij barellis olei rape	valor xxvj s. viij d.
subsidium xvj d.	
Idem pro vj last berre	valor vj li.
subsidium vj s.	

[*Membrane 2 face*]
ad huc de nave de George.
summa totalis rotuli precedentis xxiiij li. iiij s. viij d.ob.

Robertus Chambre pro iij sortes fructus	valor xxvj s. viij d.
subsidium xvj d.	
Idem pro ij dossenis librarum piperis	valor xx s.
subsidium xij d.	
Idem pro xij barellis separum	valor xj s. viij d.
subsidium iiij d.	
Idem pro viij last berre	valor v li. xviij s.
subsidium v s. xj d.ob.	

Summa {
valoris CCCxvij li xix s. ij d.
subsidii xv li xviiij s.
vini xxvj dolia
tonnagii iij li. xviij s.

Navis vocata Mare de Novo Castro super Tynam unde Johannes (Yoke) est magister exivit ultimo die Marcii

Johannes Cokk pro j seldre carbonum valor xx d.
subsidium j d.

Idem pro xx grindstones valor xxvj s. viij d.
subsidium xvj d.

Idem pro vj dossenis rubstones valor vj s. viij d.
subsidium iiij d.

Robertus Brighame pro DCC shorlynges valor xij li. xij s. vj d.
subsidium xij s vij d.ob.

Johannes Brighame pro Cxxx shorlynges valor xviij s. iij d.
subsidium xj d.

Petrus Bewyk pro Dxxv shorlynges valor lxxvij s. vj d.
subsidium iij s. x d.ob.

Johannes Belt pro DC x shorlynges valor iij li. xj s. viij d.
subsidium iiij s. viij d.

Johannes Colwell pro Diiij^{xx} shorlynges valor iiij li. v s.
subsidium iiij s. iij d.

Robertus Crawford pro DCCCC xl shorlynges valor vij li.
subsidium vij s.

Willelmus Thomson pro CCC shorlynges valor xlv s.
subsidium ij s. iij d.

Willelmus Brotherwyk pro CCC xl shorlinges valor l s.
subsidium ij s. vj d.

Willelmus Langton pro DC shorlinges valor iiij li. vij s. vj d.
subsidium iiij s. iiij d.ob.

Robertus Baxster pro Cxl shorlinges valor xxij s. vj d.
subsidium xiij d.ob.

Nicholaus Hanyng pro CC shorlynges valor xxvij s. vj d.
subsidium xvj d.ob.

Willelmus Fawcus pro C xl shorlinges valor xx s.
subsidium xij d.

Idem pro CCC lamfelles valor xl s.
subsidium ij s.

Robertus Chambre pro CCiiij^{xx}x shorlinges valor xl s. x d.
subsidium ij s. ob.

Thomas Kokk pro Clx shorlinges valor xxij s vj d.
subsidium xiij d.ob.

Thomas Cudbert pro CCxl shorlinges valor xxxv s.
subsidium xxj d.

Johannes Mappas pro C shorlinges valor xv s.
subsidium ix d.

Idem pro CCCxxx lamfelles valor liij s. iiij d.
subsidium ij s. ij d.

Thomas Swan pro Dlx shorlinges valor iiij li. ij s. vj d.
subsidium iiij s. j d.ob.

Robertus Helay pro CCClx shorlinges valor lij s. vj d.
subsidium ij s. vij d.ob.

Robertus Stokkall pro DCCCiiij^{xx} shorlinges valor vj li. x s.
subsidium vj s. vj d.
Robertus Lovell pro CCxxx shorlinges valor xxiij s iiij d.
subsidium xx d
Summa { valoris lxxij li. vij s. vj d.
subsidii lxxij s. iiij d.ob.

Summa pellium lanutarum vocatarum shorylnges et lamfelles viijMDClv pelles facientes xxxvj saccos xv pelles
custuma
subsidium
denaria calesii
exitus coketti } Cxxxix li. xij s. ij d.

Robertus Brighame pro CCCiiij^{xx} pellibus lanutis continentibus ij saccos
custuma xiij s. iiij d. subsidium lxvj s. viij d.
Johannes Brighame pro xxx pellibus lanutis continentibus dimidium quarterium
custuma xd. subsidium iiij s. ij d.
Petrus Bewyk pro C^{mi}xxv pellibus lanutis continentibus dimidium saccum
custuma iij s. vj d. subsidium xvij s. iiij d.ob.
Johannes Belt pro C^{mi}xl pellibus lanutis continentibus dimidium saccum et xx pelles
custuma iij s. xj d. subsidium xix s. v d.ob.
Johannes Colwell pro C^{mi}xl pellibus lanutis continentibus dimidium saccum et xx pelles
custuma iij s. xj d. subsidium xix s. v d.ob.
Robertus Crawford pro CC xl pellibus lanutis continentibus j saccum
custuma vj s. viij d. subsidium xxxiij s. iiij d.
Willelmus Thomson pro lxx pellibus lanutis continentibus j quarterium et x pelles
custuma xxiij d.ob. subsidium id s. ix d.
Willelmus Brothirwyke pro iiij^{xx} pellibus lanutis continentibus j quarterium xx pelles
custuma ij s. iij d. subsidium xj s. j d.ob.
Willelmus Langton pro Cxx pellibus lanutis continentibus dimidium saccum
custuma iij s. iiij d. subsidium xvj s viij d.
Robertus Baxster pro xl pellibus lanutis continentibus dimidium quarterium et x pelles
custuma xiij d.ob. subsidium v s. vij d.
Nicholaus Hanyng pro lx pellibus lanutis continentibus j quarterium
custuma xx d. subsidium viij s. iiij d.
Willelmus Fawcose pro xxx pellibus lanutis continentibus dimidium quarterium
custuma x d. subsidium iiij s. ij d.

Robertus Chambre pro lxiiij pellibus lanutis continentibus j quarterium iiij pelles

custuma xxj d.ob. subsidium viij s. xj d.

Thomas Cokk pro xxxv pellibus lanutis continentibus dimidium quarterium v pelles

custuma xij d. subsidium iiij s. x d.ob.

Thomas Cudbert pro j quarterio viij clavis lane in j poke

custuma ij s. viij d.ob. subsidium xiij s. v d.ob.

Idem pro lx pellibus lanutis continentibus j quarterium

custuma xx d. subsidium viij s. iiij d.

Willelmus Hudson pro iij saccis et dimidio lane in iiij pokes

custuma xxiij s. iiij d. subsidium Cxxvj s. viij d.

Johannes Mappas pro j sacco lane in j poke

custuma xv s. viij d. subsidium xxxiij s. iiij d.

Idem pro xxv pellibus lanutis

custuma viij d.ob. subsidium iij s. vj d.

Thomas Swan pro C^{mi}xxxv pellibus lanutis continentibus dimidium saccum xv pelles

custume iij s. ix d. subsidium xviij s. ix d.

Robertus Helay pro iiij ^{xx}v pellibus lanutis continentibus j quarterium xxv pelles

custuma ij s.v d. subsidium xi s. x d.

Robertus Brone pro v saccis lane in viij pokes

custuma xxxiij s. iiij d. subsidium viij li. vj s. viij d.

Robertus Stokall pro CCC^{mi}x pellibus lanutis continentibus j saccum j quarterium et x pelles

custuma viij s. vij d.ob. subsidium xliij s. x d.

Summa {
lane ix sacci iij quarteria viij clavi lane
pellium lanutarum ijMCClxix continentes ix saccos j quarterium dimidium quarterium xix pelles
custume lane lxvj s. ob.
custume pellium lanutarum lxiij s. iij d.ob.
subsidii lane xvj li. x s. j d.ob.
subsidii pellium lanutarum xv li. xv s. iiij d.ob.
denariorum Calesii xij s. xj d.
exituum coketti iij s. vj d.

Navis vocata Katrin de Yermouth unde Johannes Stanford est magister applicuit xxvj die Aprilis

{alienigena}

Willelmus Michell pro l seldre ordei valor xiiij li. iij s.iiij d.

custuma iij s. vj d.ob. subsidium xiiij s. ij d.

Summa {
valoris xiiij li. iij s. iiij d.
custume iij s. vj d.ob.
subsidii xiiij s. ij d.

Navis vocata Katrin de Camfer unde Cornelius Michelson est magister exivit ultimo die Aprilis
{alienigena}
Idem magister pro vj seldre carbonum valor x s.
custuma j d.ob. subsidium vj d.
Idem pro xx grindstones valor xv s.
custuma ij d.ob. subsidium ix d.
Idem pro vj dossenis rubstones valor vj s. viij d.
custuma j d. subsidium iiij d.
Idem pro j (X) panno panni lanei stricti (valor xx s.)
custuma ij s. ix d. subsidium xij d.
Willelmus Hunter pro vj pannis panni lanei stricti
custuma vij s.
Willelmus Blaxton pro ij pannis panni lanei stricti
custuma ij s. iiij d.
Thomas Lokwod pro iiij pannis panni lanei stricti
custuma iij s. viij d.

Summa { valoris alienigene xxxj s. viij d.
custume v d.
subsidii xix d.
panni alienigene j pannus panni lanei stricti valor xx s.
custume ij s. ix d.
pannorum indigenarum xij panni panni lanei stricti
custume xiiij s.
subsidii panni alienigene xij d.

[*Membrane 2 dorse*]
Navis vocata Willibord de Weststapill unde Reginald Fedrikson est magister exivit ultimo die Aprilis
{alienigena}
Idem magister pro xx seldre carbonum valor xxxiij s. iiij d.
custuma v d. subsidium xx d.
Idem pro xx grindstones valor xviij s. iiij d.
custuma iij d. subsidium xj d.

Summa { valoris lj s. viij d.
custume viij d.
subsidii ij s. vij d.

Navis vocata Katryn de Campe unde Cemon Burman est magister exivit ultimo die Aprilis.
{alienigena}
Idem magister pro lxix seldre carbonum valor Cxv s.
custume xvij d.ob. subsidium v s. ix d.
Alanus Byrd pro xxiij seldre carbonum valor xxiij s. iij d.
subsidium xiiij d.

Summa { valoris alienigenarum C xv s.
custume xvij d.ob. subsidii v s. ix d.
valoris indigenarum xxiij s. iiij d. <custuma *struck out*>
subsidii xiiij d. }

Navis vocata Katrin de Rone unde Vincent Archer est magister applicuit vij die Maii

{alienigena}

Andreas Drew pro xxx seldre ordei valor vij li. x s.
custuma xxij d.ob. subsidium vij s. vj d.

Idem pro iij barellis pomorum valor xxx d.
custuma j d. subsidium j d.ob.

Summa { valoris vij li. xij s. vj d.
custume xxiij d.ob.
subsidii vij s. vij d.ob. }

Navis vocata Mary de Leyth unde Robertus Ballone est magister applicuit xiij die Maii

{alienigena}

Idem magister pro x seldre salis albi valor iij li. vj s. viij d.
custuma x d. subsidium iij s. iiij d.

{alienigena}

Georgius Abernethe pro viij barellis sal albus valor iiij s. ij d.
custuma j d. subsidium ij d.ob.

Idem pro iij barellis olei valor xxx s.
custuma iiij d.ob. subsidium xviij d.

{alienigena}

Jacobus Murhall pro ij mantilles valor iij s. iiij d.
custuma ob. subsidium ij d.

Idem pro C pissibus salsis valor x s. x d.
custuma ij d. subsidium vj d.ob.

Idem pro j barello sal albus valor x d.
custuma ob. subsidium ob.

Willelmus Conyngham pro xij wey sal albus valor iiij li.
subsidium iiij s.

Idem pro viij barellis olei valor iiij li.
subsidium iiij s.

Summa { valoris alienigenum C xv s. x d.
custume xviij d.ob. subsidiii vs. ix d.ob.
valoris indigene viij li.
(subsidii <iij s. vj d. *struck out*> viij s. }

Navis vocata George de Gow unde Nicholaus Ebrightson est magister applicuit xviij die Maii.

{alienigena}

Idem pro xij seldre ordei valor iij li. x s.
custuma x d.ob. subsidium iij s. vj d.

Summma { valoris iij li. x s.
custume x d.ob.
subsidii iij s. vj d. }

Navis vocata Hors de Gow unde Esmot Johnson est magister applicuit xviij die Maii.
{alienigena}
Idem magister pro iiij seldre mixtillionis valor iiij li. viij s. iiij d.
custuma xiij d.ob. subsidium iiij s. v d.

Summa { valoris iiij li. viij s. iiij d.
custume xiij d.ob.
subsidii iiij s. v d. }

Navis vocata Roos de Gow unde Johannes Lubertson est magister applicuit xxiij die Maii.
{alienigena}
Idem pro ij pokes hop valor xxx s.
custuma iiij d.ob. subsidium xviij d.

Summa valoris xxx s.
custume iiij d.ob.
subsidii xviij d.

Navis vocata Horse de Gow unde Esmot Jonson est magister exivit xxvij die Maii
{alienigena}
Idem magister pro xxxij seldre carbonum valor liij s. iiij d.
custuma viij d. subsidium ij s. viij d.

Summa { valoris liij s. iiij d.
custume viij d.
subsidii ij s. viij d. }

Navis vocata George de Gow unde Nicholaus Ebrightson est magister exivit xxvij die Maii
{alienigena}
Idem pro lij seldre carbonum valor iiij li. vj s. viij d.
custuma xiij d. subsidium iiij s. iiij d.

Summa { valoris iiij li. vj s. viij d.
custume xiij d.
subsidii iiij s. iiij d. }

Navis vocata Gerome de Brell unde Down Borwerson est magister applicuit xxxix die Maii.
{alienigena}
Idem pro iiij wey sal grose valor iij li.
custume ix d. subsidium iij s.

Summa { valoris iij li.
custume ix d.
subsidii iij s. }

Navis vocata Gerome de Brele unde Down Borwerson est magister exivit xxx die Maii
{alienigena}
Idem pro xij seldre carbonum valor liij s. iiij d.
custume viij d. subsidium ij s. viij d.

Summa
valoris liij s. iiij d.
custume viij d.
subsidii ij s. viij d.

Navis vocata Mary de Leth unde Robertus Ballone est magister exivit xxx die Maii
{alienigena}
Idem pro iiij [doliis] farini valor xxxvij s. vj d.
custume vj d. subsidium xxij d.ob.
Idem pro j seldre frumenti valor xiiij s. ij d.
custuma ij d.ob. subsidium viij d.ob.
Willelmus Conyngham pro iij seldre frumenti valor xl s.
subsidium ij s.
Idem pro vj doliis farini valor l s.
subsidium ij s. vj d.

Summa
valoris alienigene <vij li. xx d. *struck out*> lj s. viij d.
custume viij d.ob. subsidii ij s. vij d.
valoris indigene <viij d.ob. *struck out*> iiij li. x s.
subsidii iiij s. vj d.

Navis vocata Roos de Gow unde Johannes Lubertson est magister exivit ultimo die Maii
{alienigena}
Idem pro xxx seldre carbonum valor l s.
custuma viij d.ob. subsidium ij s. vj d.

Summa
valoris l s.
custume viij d.ob.
subsidii ij s. vj d.

Navis vocata Katryn de Rone unde Vincent Archer est magister exivit ultimo die Maii
{alienigena}
Idem pro lxiiij seldre carbonum valor vj li.
custuma xviij d. subsidium vj s.
Idem pro iiij^{xx}xij grindstones valor vj li. iij s. iiij d.
customa xviij d.ob. subsidium vj s. ij d.
Idem pro xj dossenis rubstones valor xiij s. iiij d.
custuma ij d. subsidium viij d.
Idem pro CCCC libris hop valor xl s.
custuma vj d. subsidium ij s.

Summa
valoris xiiij li. xvj s. viij d.
custume iij s. viij d.ob.
subsidii xiiij s. x d.

summa huius rotuli Ciiij^{xx}ix li. xv s. vj d.

[*Membrane 3 face*]

Navis vocata Michaell de Schelys unde David Person est magister exivit primo die Junii

Johannes Robynson pro xx seldre carbonum — valor xxxiij s. iiij d.
subsidium xx d.
Johannes Reddyng pro DC di' shorlinges — valor iiij li. xvij s. vj d.
Willelmus Haysand pro CCCxl shorlinges — valor l s.
subsidium ij s. vj d.
Idem pro C iiiij^{xx} lamfelles — valor xvij s. iiij d.
subsidium xj d
Willelmus Hunter pro DCCCC di' shorlinges — valor vj li. xv s.
subsidium vj s. ix d.
Idem pro lx lamfelles — valor vj s. viij d.
subsidium iiij d.
Georgius Chambre pro C iiij^{xx} shorlinges — valor xxvj s.
subsidium xv d.
Willelmus Lilborne pro CC shorlinges — valor xxx s.
subsidium xviij d.
Idem pro iiij pannis panni lanei sine grano — <valor *struck out*>
custuma iiij s. viij d.
Johannes Penreth pro Ciiij^{xx} shorlinges — valor xxv s.
subsidium xv d.
Thomas Cromer pro Ciiij^{xx} shorlinges — valor xxv s.
subsidium xv d.
Idem pro C lamfelles — valor xiij s. iiij d.
subsidium viij d.
Johannes Chachersyd pro Ciiij^{xx} shorlinges — valor xxv s.
subsidium xv d.
Willelmus Faucus pro Cxxx shorlinges — valor xviij s. iiij d.
subsidium xj d.
Idem pro xl lamfelles — valor iiij s. ij d.
subsidium ij d.
Thomas Lokwod pro DCC shorlinges — valor Cij s. vj d.
subsidium v s. j d.ob.
Willelmus Blaxton pro DCCxxvj shorlinges — valor Cxvij s. vj d.
subsidium v s. x d.
Nicholaus Haynyng pro CCC shorlinges — valor xlv s.
subsidium ij s. iij d.
Robertus Brigham pro CC di' shorlinges — valor xxxvij s. vj d.
subsidium xxij d.ob.
Idem pro CCC di' lamfelles — valor xlvij s. ij d.
subsidium ij s. ij d.
Johannes Mappas pro iiij^{xx} shorlinges — valor x s.
subsidium vj d.
Idem pro C lamfelles — valor xiij s. iiij d.
subsidium viij d.
Johannes Colwell pro iiij^{xx} shorlinges — valor x s.
subsidium vj d.

Idem pro Cxl lamfelles valor xvij s. vj d.
subsidium x d.ob.
Ricardus Hogeson pro Ciiij^{xx} shorlinges valor xxv s.
subsidium xv d.
Robertus Helay pro iiij^{xx} shorlinges valor x s.
subsidium vj d.
Idem pro CCC lamfelles valor xl s.
subsidium ij s.
Thomas Cudbert pro C shorlinges valor xv s.
subsidium ix d.
Idem pro CC lamfelles valor xxvj s. viij d.
subsidium xvj d.
Johannes Cok pro C xxx shorlinges valor xviij s. iiij d.
Willelmus Hurlband pro v^{xx} shorlinges valor xij s. vj d.
subsidium vij d.ob.
Johannes Brighame pro C shorlinges valor xv s.
subsidium ix d.

Summa {
valoris liij li. vj s. viij d.
subsidii liij s. iiij d.
panni iiij panni sine grano
custume iiij s. viij d.

Summa pellium lanutarum vocatarum shorlynges et lamfelles vij MDC lxxvj facientes xxxj saccos iij quarteria lvj pelles
custuma nihil oneratur xvli. xix s. x d.ob.
subsidium nihil oneratur Cvj li. xij s. ij d. lb.
denaria Calesii nihil oneratur xxj s. iiij d.
exitus coketti nihil oneratur iij s. viij d.

Johannes Reddyng pro Ciiij^{xx}xij pellibus lanutis continentibus iij quarteria xij pelles
custuma v s. iiij d. subsidium xxvj s. viij d.
Willelmus Haysand pro j sacco j clavo lane in j poke
custume vj s. x d. subsidium xxxiiij s. ij d.
Idem pro iiij^{xx} pellibus lanutis continentibus j quarterium xx pelles
custuma ij s. iij d. subsidium xj s. j d.ob.
Willelmus Hunter pro dimidio sacco viij clavis lane in j poke
custuma iij s. iij d. qu. subsidium xxj s. ix d.ob.
Idem pro Ciiij^{xx} pellibus lanutis continentibus iij quarteria
custume v s. subsidium xxv s.
Georgius Chambre pro iij quarteria (sacci) lane in j poke
custuma v s. subsidium xxv s.
Idem pro xl pellibus lanutis continentibus dimidium quarterium x pelles
custuma xiij d.ob. subsidium v s. vij d.
Willelmus Lilborn pro xl pellibus lanutis continentibus dimidium quarterium x pelles
custuma viij d.ob. subsidium v s. vij d.

Johannes Penreth pro xxx pellibus lanutis continentibus dimidium quarterium
custuma x d. subsidium iiij s. ij d.
Thomas Cromer pro lx pellibus lanutis continentibus j quarterium
custuma xx d. subsidium viij s. iiij d.
Johannes Cachersyd pro xl pellibus lanutis continentibus dimidium quarterium x pelles
custuma ix d. subsidium iij s. vij d.ob.
Wilelmus Fawcose pro xxvj pellibus lanutis
custuma ix d. subsidium iij s. vij d.ob.
Thomas Lokwod pro Clx pellibus lanutis continentibus dimidium saccum dimidium quarterium x pelles
custuma iiij s v d.ob. subsidium xxij s. iij d.
Willelmus Blaxton pro j sacco j quarterio lane in ij poke
custuma viij s iiij d. subsidium xlj s. viij d.
Idem pro Cxl pellibus lanutis continentibus dimidium saccum xx pelles
custuma iij s xj d. subsidium xix s. v d.ob.
Robertus Baxster pro x pellibus lanutis
custuma iij d.ob. subsidium xvij d.
Nicholaus Haynyng pro lx pellibus lanutis continentibus j quarterium
custuma xx d. subsidium viij s. iij d.
Robertus Brighame pro lvj pellibus lanutis continentibus dimidium quarterium xxvj pelles
custuma xviij d.ob.q. subsidium vij s. ix d.qu.
Johannes Mappas pro iij quarteriis iiij clavis lane in j poke
custuma v s. vj d.ob. subsidium xxvij s. vij d.
Idem pro xij pellibus lanutis
custuma iiij d. q. subsidium xx d.
Robertus Harden pro j sacco viij clavis lane in j poke
custuma vij s. viij d.ob. subsidium xxxvij s. v d.ob.
Johannes Colwell pro xv pellibus lanutis
custuma v d. qu. subsidium ij s. j d.
Ricardus Hogeson pro xl pellibus lanutis continentibus dimidium quarterium x pelles
custuma xiij d.ob. subsidium v s. vij d.
Robertus Helay pro xv pellibus lanutis
custuma v d. q. subsidium ij s. j d.
Thomas Cudbert pro xxv pellibus lanutis
custuma viij d.ob. subsidium iij s. vj d.
Johannes Cok pro xxx pellibus lanutis continentibus dimidium quarterium
custuma x d.ob. subsidium iiij s. ij d.
Willelmus Hurband pro xv pellibus lanutis
custuma v d.q. subsidium ij s. j d.
Johannes Brighame pro xx pellibus lanutis
custuma vij d. subsidium ij s. ix d.ob.

Summa	lane v sacci dimidius viij clavi lane	
	pellium lanutarum MCCiiij^{xx}vj continentes v saccos j quarterium xxvj pelles	
	custume	xxxvij s. viij d.ob.
	custuma pellium lanutarum	xxxv s. ix d.
	subsidii lane	ixli viij s. v d.ob.
	subsidii pellium lanutarum	viij li. xviij s. vij d.ob.
	denariorum Calesii	viij s. v d.ob.
	exituum coketti	iij s. x d.

Navis vocata Nicholaus de Leith unde Alexander Harward est magister applicuit vij die Junii

{alienigena}

Idem pro vj wey sal albus valor xxxj s. viij d.
custuma v d. subsidium xix d.

Summa { valoris xxxj s. viij d.
custume v d.
subsidii xix d.

Navis vocata Nicholaus de Leith unde Alexander Harward est magister exivit viij die Junii

{alienigena}

Idem pro iiij seldre siliginis valor xl s.
custuma vj d. subsidium ij s.

Summa { valoris xl s.
custume vj d.
subsidii ij s.

Navis vocata Margaret de Bullen unde Phelipot Gerard est magister applicuit vij die Junii

{alienigena}

Idem pro xviij wey sal grose valor ix li.
custuma ij s. iij d. subsidium ix s.

Summa { valoris ix li.
custume ii s. iij d.
subsidii ix s.

Navis vocata Kamyse de Bullen unde Johannes Thomas est magister applicuit viij die Junii

{alienigena}

Idem pro xxxiij wey sal grose valor xvij li vj s. viij d.
custuma iiij s. iiij d. subsidium xvij s. iiij d.

Summa { valoris xvij li. vj s. viij d.
custume iiij s. iiij d.
subsidii xvij s. iiij d.

Navis vocata Jerome de Breele unde Down Borwerson est magister exivit viij die Junii
{alienigena}
Idem pro viij seldre carbonum valor xxx s.
custuma iiij d.ob. subsidium xviij d.

Summa { valoris xxx s.
custume iiij d.ob.
subsidii xviij d.

[*Membrane 3 dorse*]
Navis vocata Olifant de Gowe unde Thomas Browne est magister applicuit viij die Junii
{alienigena}
Idem magister pro vj wey sal grose valor iij li.
custuma ix d. subsidium iij s.

Idem pro C libris hoppe valor x s.
custuma ij d. subsidium vj d.

Summa { valoris iij li x s.
custume xj d.
subsidii iij s. vj d.

Navis vocata Mare de Flaynburgh unde Adrian Manson est magister applicuit viij die Junii

Robertus Castell pro lx wey sal grose valor xxx s.
subsidium xxx s.
Idem pro iij pokes hoppe valor xl s.
subsidium ij s.
Robertus Pykden pro x wey sal grose valor x li.
subsidium v s.
Alanus Carr pro iij doliis (vini) Rochelle
tonnagium ix s.

Summa { valoris xxxvij li.
subsidii xxxvij s.
vini iij dolia
tonnagii ix s.

Navis vocata James de Camfer unde Johannes Person est magister exivit viij die Junii
{alienigena}
Idem pro xxx seldre carbonum l s.
custuma vij d.ob. subsidium ij s. vj d.

Summa { valoris l s.
custume vij d.ob.
subsidii ij s. vj d.

Navis vocata Nicholaus de Depe unde Prochyn Sur est magister exivit x die Junii
{alienigena}
Willelmus Michell pro lx seldre carbonum valor vj li.
custuma xviij d. subsidium vj s.
Idem pro xl grindstones valor v li.
custume xv d. subsidium v s.
Idem pro viij dossenis rubstones valor vj s. viij d.
custuma j d. subsidium iiij d.
Idem pro iij barellis salmonis valor lvj s. viij d.
custuma viij d.ob. subsidium ij s. i d.
Idem pro xl pissibus salsis xiij s. iiij d.
custuma ij d. subsidium viij d.
Idem pro j (X) panno panni lane sine grano valor xx s.
custuma ij s. ix d. subsidium xij d.

Summa { valoris xiiij li. xvj s. viij d.
custume iij s. viij d.ob.
subsidii xiiij s. x d.
panni j pannus sine grano
custume ij s ix d.
subsidii dicti j panni alienigene xij d. }

Navis vocata Bastell de Dep unde Willelmus More est magister exivit x die Junii.
{alienigena}
Idem pro vj^xx seldre carbonum valor xij li.
custuma iij s. subsidium xij s.
Idem pro lx grindstones valor vij li. x s.
custuma xxij d.ob. subsidium vij s. vj d.
Idem pro xvj dossenis rubstones valor xvj s. iiij d.
ij d.ob. subsidium x d.
Idem pro vj barellis salmonis valor vj li. ij s. x d.
custuma xix d. subsidium vj s. j d.ob.
Idem pro xvj pissibus salsis valor v s.
custuma j d. subsidium iij d.

Summa { valoris xxvj li. xiij s. ij d.
custume vj s. viij d. ob.
subsidii xxvj s. viij d. ob. }

Navis vocata James de Goos unde Johannes Henrikson est magister applicuit x die Junii.
{alienigena}
Idem pro DC libris hoppe valor xxvj s. viij d.
custuma iiij d. subsidium xvj d.

Summa { valoris xxvj s. viij d.
custume iiij d.
subsidii xvj d. }

Navis vocata Godisgrace de Gosford unde Thomas Stones est magister exivit xj die Junii
{alienigena}
Johannes Galiard pro iiij^{xx} seldre carbonum valor vij li.
custuma xxj d. subsidium vij s.
Idem pro xl pissibus salsis valor xiij s iiij d.
custuma ij d. subsidium viij d.
Idem pro viij dossenis rubstones valor vj s. viij d.
custuma j d. subsidium iiij d.
Summa { valoris viij li. / custume ij s. / subsidii viij s.

Navis vocata Jacobus de Goos unde Johannes Henrykson est magister exivit xj die Junii
{alienigena}
Idem pro xx seldre carbonum valor xxxiij s. iiij d.
custuma v d. subsidium xx d.
Summa { valoris xxxiij s. iiij d. / custume v d. / subsidii xx d.

Navis vocata Maudelyn de Camfer unde Adriane Johnson est magister exivit xiiij die Junii
{alienigena}
Idem pro xij seldre carbonum valor xx s.
custuma iij d. subsidium xij d.
{ valoris xx s. / custume iij d. / subsidii xij d.

Navis vocata Maudelyn de Camfer unde Henricus Johnson est magister exivit xiiij die Junii
{alienigena}
Idem pro xij seldre carbonum valor xx s.
custuma iij d. subsidium xij d.
Summa { valoris iiij li. / custume xij d. / subsidii iiij s.

Navis vocata Mary de Novo Castro super Tynam unde Johannes Broune est magister appliciut xvij die Junii
Idem magister pro j dolio j hogeshed [vini]
tonnagium iii s. ix d.
Nicholaus Hayning pro xl doliis vini
tonnagium vj li.
Willelmus Blaxton pro xl doliis vini
tonnagium vi li.

Willelmus Thomson pro xx doliis vini
tonnagium iij li.
Johannes Robynson pro x doliis vini
tonnagium xxx s.
Thomas Davell pro xx doliis vini
tonnagium iij li.
Willelmus Brodyrwick pro j dolio j pipe vini
tonnagium iiij s. vj d.
Thomas Lokwood pro j dolio vini
tonnagium iij s.
Summa { vini Cxxxiij dolia j pipe j hogeshed
tonnagii xx li. xv d.

Navis vocata Margaret de Bulleyn unde Philipp Gerome est magister exivit xxij die Junii
{alienigena}
Adam Mercer pro xx seldre carbonum valor xxxiij s. iiij d.
custuma v d. subsidium xx d.
Idem pro v dacre di' corriorum tannatorum valor vj li. viij s. vj d.
custuma xix d.ob.q. subsidium vj s. v d. qu.
Idem pro dimidio panno panni lanei stricti valor x s.
custume xvij d. subsidium vj d.
Summa { valoris viij li xxij d.
custume ij s. ob.qu.
subsidii viij s. j d.qu.
panni dimidius pannus sine grano
custume xvij d.
subsidii dimidius pannnus alienigena vj d.

Summa totalis huius rotuli Clxxviij li. viij s. ix d.ob.
[*Membrane 4 face*]
Navis vocata Kamys de Bulleyn unde Johannes Thomas est magister exivit xxvj die Junii
{alienigena}
Franchkyn Cosset pro xxiiij seldre carbonum valor xliij s iiij d.
custuma xij d.ob. subsidium ij s. ij d.
Idem pro v dacre corriorum tannatorum valor iiij li. iij s. iiij d.
custuma xij d.ob. subsidium iiij s. ij d.
Idem pro CCC libris hoppe valor xxv s.
custuma iiij d. subsidium xv d.
Summa { valoris vij li. xj s. viij d.
custume xxiij d.
subsidiii vij s vij d.

Navis vocata Trinite de Holme under Galfridus Paliser est magister exivit viij die Julii
Willelmus Kyrton pro lx quarteriis brasii valor vj li. x s.
subsidium vj s. vj d.

Idem pro xx quarteriis mixtillionis valor xxxiij s. iiij d.
subsidium xx d.

Summa { valoris viij li. iij s. iiij d.
subsidii viij s. ij d.

Navis vocata Cristofur de Dordright unde Petrus Reynoldson est magister exivit xij die Julii

{alienigena}

Idem pro xxxij seldre carbonum valor liij s. iij d.
custuma viij d. subsidium ij s. viij d.

Summa { valoris liij s. iiij d.
custume viij d.
subsidii ij s. viij d.

Navis vocata Kamys de Bulleyn unde Johannes Thomas est magister exivit xxvj die Julii

{alienigena}

Franchkyn Cosset pro xiij seldre carbonum valor xxiij s. iiij d.
custuma iij d.ob. subsidium xiiij d.
pro vj grindstones valor xx d.
custuma ob. subsidium j d.

Summa { valoris xxv s.
custume iiij d.
subsidii xv d.

Navis vocata Michell de Sheles unde Davyd Person est magister applicuit xviij die Augusti

Johannes Neuton pro xl seldre frumenti valor xxvj li. xiij s. iiij d.
subsidium xxvj s. viij d.
pro iiij last allecis valor xvj li.
subsidium xvj s.
pro iij pokes hoppe valor lx s.
subsidium iij s.
Idem pro xx seldre mixtillionis valor x li.
subsidium x s.
Idem pro ij doliis vini dulcis
tonnagium vj s.
Thomas Cudbert pro xx seldre frumenti valor xiij li. vj s. viij d.
subsidium xiij s. iiij d.
Idem pro iij barellis olei rape valor xl s.
subsidium ij s.
Idem pro vj sortes fructus valor xl s.
subsidium ij s.
Thomas Burton pro DC waynscotes valor vj li.
subsidium vj s.
Idem pro ij last allecis valor iiij li.
subsidium iiij s.
Idem pro xvj barellis pomorum valor x s. vj d.
subsidium vj d. q.

Summa
valoris iiij^{xx}iij li. x s. vj d.
subsidii iiij li. iij s. vj d. qu.
vini dulcis ij dolia
tonnagii vj s.

Navis vocata Petir de Gowe unde Jacobus Willemson est magister exivit xxiiij die Augusti
Roland Southryn pro x seldre carbonum valor xvj s. viij d.
subsidium x d.
Idem pro xvj grindstones valor xiij s. iiij d.
subsidium viij d.
{alienigena}
Henricus Snellenbergh pro x seldre carbonum valor xvj s. viij d.
custuma ij d.ob. subsidium x d.
{alienigena}
Jacobus Willemson pro viij seldre carbonum valor xiij s. iiij d.
custuma ij d. subsidium viij d.

Summa
valoris alienigene <iij li. *struck out*> xxx s.
custume iiij d.ob.
valoris indigene et alienigene pro subsidio lx s.
subsidii iij s.

Navis vocata James de Adam unde Adrian Petrison est magister exivit xxiiij die Augusti
{alienigena}
Idem pro iiij^{xx}x seldre carbonum valor vij li.
custuma xxj d. subsidium vij s.
Idem pro j dacre corriorum tannatorum valor xvj s viij d.
custuma ij d.ob. subsidium x d.
Johannes Pound pro xiij grindstones valor xiij s iiij d.
subsidium viij d.

Summa
valoris indigene et alienigene viij li. x s.
valoris alienigene pro custuma vij li. xvj s. viij d.
custume xxiij d.ob.
subsidii viij s. vj d.

Navis vocata Jesus de Hamsterdam unde Nicholaus Jamson est magister applicuit xx die Septembris
{alienigena}
Idem pro iiij lastes beer valor vj li vj s. viij d.
custuma xix d. subsidium vj s. iiij d.
Idem pro xlvj barellis pomorum valor xl s.
custuma vj d. subsidium ij s.
Idem pro ij sortes fructus valor xxv s.
custuma iiij d. subsidium xv d.

Summa
valoris ix li. xj s. viij d.
custume ij s. v d.
subsidii ix s. vij d.

Navis vocata cogschip de Gowe unde Johannes Derykson est magister exivit iiij die Octobris
{alienigena}
Idem pro xxx seldre carbonum valor l s.
custuma vij d.ob. subsidium ij s. vj d.
Summa { valoris l s. custume vij d.ob. subsidii ij s. vj d.

Navis vocata Horse de Gowe unde Esmot Jonson est magister exivit iiij die Octobris
{alienigena}
Idem pro xlij seldre carbonum valor iij li. x s.
custuma x d.ob. subsidium iij s. vj d.
Summa { valoris iij li. x s. custume x d.ob. subsidii iij s. vj d.

Navis vocata Mary de Solens unde Daniell Gerard est magister exivit iij die Octobris
{alienigena}
Idem pro l seldre carbonum valor iiij li. iij s. iiij d.
Summa { valoris iiij li. iij s. iiij d. custume xij d.ob. subsidii iiij s. ij d.

Navis vocata Jesus de Hamsterdam unde Nicholaus Jamson est magister exivit xiij die Octobris
{alienigena}
Idem pro xliiij seldre carbonum valor iij li. xiij s. iiij d.
custuma xj d. subsidium iij s. viij d.
Idem pro x grindstones valor xxx s.
custuma iiij d.ob. subsidium xviij d.
Idem pro x dossenis rubstones valor ix s. ij d.
custuma j d.ob. subsidium vj d.
Summa { valoris v li. vij s. vj d. custume xvij d. subsidii v s. viij d.

Navis vocata Nycholas de Petinweme unde Symon Waugh est magister applicuit xxj die Octobris
{alienigena}
Idem pro j barello allecis valor vj s. viij d.
custuma j d. subsidium iiij d.

Johannes Coke pro xxj last ostrearum valor xiiij li. xvj s. viij d.
subsidium xiiij s. x d.

Summa { valoris indigene et alienigene xv li. iij s. iiij d.
valoris alienigene pro custuma vj s. viij d.
custume j d.
subsidii xv s. ij d. }

[*Membrane 4 dorse*]

Navis vocata Cristofir de Camfer unde Petrus Gelison est magister applicuit xxij die Octobris

Johannes Foster pro CCCC waynscotes valor iij li.
subsidium iij s.

Idem pro xij quarteriis mixtillionis valor xviij s. iiij d.
subsidium xj d.

Nicholaus Haynyng pro DCC waynscotes valor v li. v s.
subsidium v s. iij d.

Idem pro xxC clapholt valor xj s. viij d.
subsidium vij d.

{alienigena}

Petrus Gelyson pro xxvj quarteriis mixtilionis valor xxxviij s. iiij d.
custuma v d.ob.q. subsidium xxiij d.

Johannes Mappas pro xij quarteriis mixtillionis valor xviij s. iiij d.
subsidium xj d.

Summa { valoris alienigene pro custume xxxviij s. iiij d.
valoris indigenarum et
alienigene pro subsidio xij li. xj s. vii d.
custume v d.ob.qu.
subsidii xij s. viij d. }

Navis vocata Nicholaus de Petinweme unde Symon Waugh est magister exivit ij die Novembris

Thomas Alder pro vj^{xx} seldre carbonum valor ix li. vj s. viij d.
subsidium ix s. iiij d.

Idem pro lx grindstones valor vij li. x s.
subsidium vij s. vj d.

Idem pro xviij dossenis rubstones valor xx s.
subsidium xij d.

Johannes Cok pro iij ^{xx}iij [seldre] carbonum valor v li. iij s. iiij d.
subsidium v s. ij d.

[Summa] { valor xxiij li.
subsidium xxiij s. }

Navis vocata Olifant de Gowe unde Thomas Brown est magister exivit iiij^{to} die Novembris
{alienigena}
Idem pro lij seldre carbonum valor iiij li. vj s. viij d.
custuma xiij d. subsidium iiij s. iiij d.

[Summa] valor iiiij li. vj s. viij d.
custuma xiij d.
subsidium iiij s. iiij d.

Navis vocata James de Medilburgh unde Pauk Person est magister applicuit vij die Novembris
{alienigena}
Idem pro l barellis separum valor xx s.
custuma iij d. subsidium xij d.
Idem pro ij barellis allecis valor xij s. vj d.
custuma ij d. subsidium vij d.ob.
Nicholaus Haynyng pro xxviij barellis separum valor x s.
subsidium vj d.

Summa valoris alienigene pro custuma xxxij s. vj d.
valoris indigene et alienigene pro subsidio xlij s. vj d.
custume v d.
subsidii ij s. j d.ob.

Navis vocata Mary de Brankaster unde Henricus Calverd est magister exivit vij die Novembris
Idem pro C quarteriis brasii valor xx li.
subsidium xx s.

Summa valoris xx li.
subsidii xx s.

Navis vocata le Cristofyr de Lyn unde Nicholaus Skowle est magister applicuit vij die Novembris.
Idem pro ij M stokfisch valor vij li.
subsidium vij s.
Idem pro iiij barellis olei rape valor iij li.
subsidium iij s.

Summa valoris x li.
subsidii x s.

Navis vocata Cristofir de Camfer unde Petrus Gelison est magister exivit vij die Novembris
{alienigena}
Idem pro xxxvj seldre carbonum valor iij li.
custuma <iij s.*struck out*> ix d. subsidium iij s.

Summa valoris iij li.
custume ix d.
subsidii iij s.

Navis vocata Cristofir de Gowe under Galfridus Johnson est magister exivit vij die Novembris
{alienigena}
Idem pro xxx seldre carbonum valor l s.
custuma vij d.ob. subsidium ij s. vj d.

Summa { valoris l s.
custume vij d.ob.
subsidii ij s. vj d.

Navis vocata George de Gowe under Jasper von Mure est magister exivit vij die Novembris.
{alienigena}
Idem pro lxiij seldre carbonum valor v li. xj s. viij d.
custuma xvij d.ob. subsidium v s. vij d.
Idem pro xxj grindstones valor xxj s. viij d.
custuma iij d.ob. subsidium xiij d.

Summa { valoris vj li. xiij s. viij d.
custume xxj d.
subsidii vj s. viij d.

Navis vocata Barlamew de Stonos unde Gerard Young Clayson est magister applicuit vij die Novembris
{alienigena}
Idem pro xlvj waynscottes valor xvj s. viij d.
custuma ij d.ob. subsidium x d.

Summa { valoris xvj s. viij d.
custume ij d.ob.
subsidii x d.

Navis vocata Barlamew de Stonos unde Gerard Yong Clayson [est magister] exivit xij die Novembris
{alienigena}
Idem pro lviij seldre carbonum valor iiij li xvj s. viij d.
custuma xiiiij d.ob. subsidium iiij s. x d.

Summa { valoris iiij li. xvj s. viij d.
custume xiij d.ob.
subsidii iiij s. x d.

Navis vocata Katrin de Camfer unde Cornelius Michelson est magister applicuit xij die Novembris
Robertus Watson pro iij barellis olei rape valor xxv s.
subsidium xxj d.

Summa { valoris xxxv s.
subsidii xxj d.

Navis vocata James de Medilburgh unde Pauk Person est magister exivit xiiij die Novembris
{alienigena}
Idem pro xxviiij seldre carbonum valor xlvj s. viij d.
custuma viij d. subsidium ij s. iiiij d.
Summa { valoris xlvj s. viij d.
custume vij d.
subsidii ij s. iiij d.

Navis vocata Mary de Leth unde Andreas Hook est magister applicuit xxiij die Novembris
{alienigena}
Thomas Pimerery pro x last ostrearum valor xl s.
custuma vj d. subsidium ij s.
Idem pro iij barellis salmonis valor xliij s. iiij d.
custuma vj d.ob. subsidium ij s. ij d.
Willelmus Welles pro viij barellis allecis valor xliij s. iiiij d.
subsidium ij s. ij d.
Summa { valoris indigene et alienigene vj li vj s. viij d.
valoris alienigene pro custuma iiij li. iij s. iiij d.
custume xij d.ob.
subsidii vj s. iiij d.

Navis vocata George de Andwarp unde Cornelius Lambson est magister applicuit xxvij die Novembris
{alienigena}
Idem pro xviij barellis [*right side of membrane stained*]
{alienigena}
Johannes Michelson pro CC et dimidio waynscotes ...
Summa { valoris iij li vj s. viij d.
custume xiij d.
subsidii iiij s. iiij d.

Navis vocata George de Andwarpe unde Cornelius Lambson est magister exivit x die Decembris
{alienigena}
Idem pro xlviij seldre carbonum valor iiij li.
custume xij d. subsidium iiij s.
Summa { valoris iiij li.
custume xij d.
subsidii iiij s.

Summa huius rotuli xiij li. xs. vij d.
[*Membrane 5 face*]
Navis vocata Mary de Brankaster unde Henricus Calverd est magister applicuit xvj die Decembris
Idem pro iiij last allecis albi valor x li.
subsidium x s.

Idem pro DC saltfisch valor iiij li.
subsidium iiij s.

Summa {valoris xiiij li.
subsidii xiiij s.

Navis vocata Michaell de Shelis unde Willelmus Robynson est magister exivit xxiij° die Decembris

Johannes Ridding pro CCxl shorlinges valor xxxvij s. vj d.
subsidium xxij d.ob.
Idem pro CCCiiij[xx] lambfelles valor xxxv s. x d.
subsidium xxj d.ob.
Idem pro xl seldre carbonum valor iij li. vj s. viij d.
subsidium iij s. iiij d.
Willelmus Blaxton pro v grindstones valor x s.
subsidium vj d.ob.
Johannes Batmanson pro xx shorlinges valor ijs. vj d.
subsidium j d.ob.
Idem pro CC di' lambfelles valor xxxiij s. iij d.
subsidium xx d.
Robertus Harden pro D shorlinges valor iij li. xv s.
subsidium iij s. ix d.
Robertus Baxster pro v[xx] shorlinges valor xij s. vj d.
subsidium vij d.ob.
Idem pro C di' lambfelles valor xx s.
subsidium xij d.
Georgius Bird pro xl seldre carbonum valor iij li. vj s. viij d.
subsidium iij s. iiij d.
Antonius Hogeson pro CC shorlinges valor xxx s.
subsidium xviij d.
Nicholaus Haynyng pro C shorlinges valor xv s.
subsidium ix d.
Alan Byrd pro C shorlinges valor xv s.
subsidium ix d.
Idem pro iiij[xx] seldre carbonum valor vj li. xiij s. iiij d.
subsidium vj s. viij d.
Georgius Carr pro CCC shorlinges valor xlv s.
subsidium ij s. iij d.
Johannes Neuton pro xl seldre carbonum valor iij li.
subsidium iij s.
Robertus Helay pro CC shorlinges valor xxxvij s. vj d.
subsidium xxij d.ob.

Summa {valoris xxxv li. ij s. vj d.
subsidii xxxv s. j d. ob

Summa pellium lanutarum vocatarum shorlinges et lamfelles MMiijClx pelles facientes x saccos j quarterium

custuma
subsidium
denaria Calesii
exitus coketti } xxxix li. xv s. ij d.

Johannes Ridding pro j sacco dimidio iiij clavis lane in ij pokes
custuma x s. v d. subsidium lij s. vj d.
Idem pro lx pellibus lanutis continentibus j quarterium
custuma xx d. subsidium viij s. iiij d.
Petrus Baxster pro j sacco viij clavis lane in ij pokes
custuma vij s. viij d.ob. subsidium xxxviij s. v d.ob.
Robertus Musgrave pro iij quarteriis viij clavis lane in j poke
custuma vj s. ob. subsidium xxx s. j d.ob.
Willelmus Blaxton pro vj saccis lane in viij pokes
custuma xl s. subsidium x li.
Robertus Harden pro iiij[xx] pellibus lanutis continentibus j quarterium et dimidium quarterium
custuma ij s. vj d.ob. subsidium xij s. vj d.
Willelmus Langton pro iij quarteriis viij clavis lane in j poke
custuma vj s. ob. subsidium xxx s. j d.ob.
Thomas Gudyer pro j quarterio lane in j poke
custuma xx d. subsidium viij s. iiij d.
Robertus Baxster pro xx pellibus lanutis
custuma vij d. subsidium ij s. ix d.ob.
Willelmus Richerdson pro dimidio sacco viij clavis lane in j poke
custuma iiij s. iiij d.ob. subsidium xxj s. ix d.ob.
Georgius Byrd pro j sacco j quarterio iij clavis lane in ij pokes
custume viij s. ix d. subsidium xl iij s. vj d.
Thomas Colt pro ij saccis j quarterio x clavis lane in iij pokes
custuma xvj s. iij d.ob. subsidium iiij li. xvij d.
Antonius Hogeson pro xl pellibus lanutis continentibus dimidium quarterium x pelles
custuma xiij d.ob. subsidium v s. vij d.
Nicholaus Haynyng pro xxx pellibus lanutis continentibus dimidium quarterium
custuma x d. subsidium iiij s. ij d.
Alanus Byrd pro j sacco lane in ij pokes
custuma vj s. viij d. subsidium xxxiij s. iiij d.
Idem pro xv pellibus lanutis
custuma v d. subsidium ij s. j d.
Willelmus Haysand pro j sacco viij clavis lane in ij pokes
custuma vij s viij d.ob. subsidium xxxviij s. vd.ob.
Georgius Carr pro C[mi]xx pellibus lanutis continentibus dimidium saccum
custuma iij s. iiij d. subsidium xvj s. viij d.
Johannes Mappas pro iij quarteriis viij clavis lane in j poke
custuma vj s. ob. subsidium xxx s. j d.ob.

Robertus Stokall pro dimidio sacco ij clavis lane in j poke
custuma iij s vij d.ob. subsidium xvij s. xj d.ob.
Robertus Helay pro lx pellibus lanutis continentibus j quarterium
custuma xx d. subsidium viij s. iiij d.
Willelmus Hurband pro j quarterio lane in j poke
custuma xx d. subsidium viij s. iiij d.
Johannes Scot pro dimidio sacco lane in j poke
custuma iij s. iiij d. subsidium xvj s. viij d.

Summa {
lane xix sacci dimidius ij clavi lane
pellium lanutarum CCCxxxxv pelles continentes j saccum iij quarteria xv pelles
custume lane vj li. x s. iij d.ob.
custume pellium lanutarum xij s. j d.
subsidii lane xxxij li. xj s. iij d.ob.
subsidii pellium lanutarum lx s. v d.
denariorum Calesii xiiij s. iij d.
exituum coketti iij s. vj d.
}

Navis vocata George de Breel unde Fop Willemson est magister applicuit ij die Januarii
{alienigena}

Idem pro iij last berre custuma x d.ob. subsidium iij s. vj d.	valor iij li. x s.
Idem pro iij barellis pomorum custuma ob. subsidium j d.	valor xx d.
Idem pro dimidio barello butiri custuma j d. subsidium iij d.	valor v s.

Summa {
valoris iij li xvj s. viij d.
custume xij d.
subsidii iij s. x d.
}

Navis vocata Katrin de Novo Castro super Tynam unde Cornelius Michelson est magister exivit ij die Januarii.

Robertus Stokall pro CCC di' shorlinges subsidium ij s. vij d.ob.	valor lij s. vj d.
Idem pro DC iiij[xx] lambfelles subsidium iiij s. v d.	valor iiij li. viij s. iiij d.
Willelmus Hurband pro DCCCC shorlinges subsidium vj s. idx d.	valor vj li. xv s.
Willelmus Brothirwyk pro CC di' shorlinges subsidium xx ij d.ob.	valor xxxvij s. vj d.
Idem pro DCC di' lambfelles subsidium v s.	valor C s.
Thomas Cudbert pro iiij[xx] shorlynges subsidium vj d.	valor x s.
Idem pro CC lambfelles subsidium xvj d.	valor xxvj s. viij d.
Willelmus Blaxton pro viij grindstones subsidium xij d.	valor xx s.

Johannes Scot pro CCl shorlinges valor xxxvj s. viij d.
subsidium xxij d.
Thomas Gudyer pro C iiij^{xx} shorlinges valor xxv s.
subsidium xv d.
Idem pro CC lambfelles valor xxvj s. viij d.
subsidium xvj d.
Thomas Ridell pro C di' shorlinges valor xxij s. vj d.
subsidium xiij d.ob.
Willelmus Richerdson pro CCx shorlinges valor xxxj s. viij d.
subsidium xix d.
Georgius Byrd pro CC di' shorlinges valor xxxvij s. vj d.
subsidium xxij d.ob.
Willelmus Hunter pro CCl shorlinges valor xxx j s. viij d.
subsidium xix d.
Idem pro CCC lambfelles valor xl s.
subsidium ij s.
Willelmus Haysand pro C shorlinges valor xij s. vj d.
subsidium vij d.ob.
Idem pro C lambfelles valor xiij s. iiij d.
subsidium viij d.
Johannes Sampill pro Ciiij^{xx} shorlinges valor xxv s.
subsidium xv d.
{alienigena}
Jasper Croner pro v^{xx} seldre carbonum valor ix li. xiij s. iiij d.
custume ij s. v d. subsidium ix s. viij d.
{alienigena}
Cornelius Michelson pro x seldre carbonum valor xvj s. viij d.
custuma ij d.ob. subsidium x d.
Idem pro CC cornubus boum valor ij s. vj d.
custuma ob. subsidium j d.ob.
Johannes Ridding pro DCCCC et di' shorlinges valor vj li. xiij s. iiij d.
subsidium vj s. viij d.
Johannes Foster pro iiij^{xx} shorlinges valor x s.
subsidium xj d.

Summa {
valoris indigenarum et alienigenarum lvj li. viij s. viij d.
valoris alienigenarum x li. xij s. vj d.
custume ij s. viij d.
subsidii lvj s. v d.
}

Summa pellium vocatarum shorlynges et lambfelles vjMCCCx facientes xxvj saccos j quarterium x pelles

custume
subsidium
denaria Calesii
exitus coketti
} cj li. xiiij s. vij d.ob.q.

Robertus Stokall pro j sacco iiij clavis lane in ij pokes
custuma vij s. ij d.ob. subsidium xxxv s. xj d.
Idem pro C xl pellibus lanutis continentibus dimidium saccum xx pelles
custuma iij s. xj d. subsidium xix s. vj d.ob.
Willelmus Hurband pro dimidio sacco ij clavis lane in j poke
custuma iij s. vij d.ob. subsidium xvj s. xj d.ob.
Idem pro Clxx pellibus lanutis continentibus dimidium saccum dimidium quarterium xx pelles
custuma iiij s. x d. subsidium xxj s. ij d.ob.
Willelmus Brotherwyk pro lx pellibus lanutis
custuma xx d. subsidium viij s. iiij d.

plus in dorse de ista navi

[*Membrane 5 dorse*]
Thomas Cudbert pro xx pellibus lanutis
custuma vij d. subsidium ij s. x d.
Willelmus Blaxton pro j sacco lane in ij pokes
custuma vj s. viij d. subsidium xxxiij s. iiij d.
Johannes Scot pro j sacco et j clavo lane in j poke
custuma iij s. vj d. subsidium xvij s. iiij d.
Idem pro xxx pellibus lanutis continentibus dimidium quarterium
custuma x d. subsidium iiij s iij d.
Thomas Gudyer pro l pellibus lanutis continentibus dimidium quarterium et xx pelles
custuma xvij d. subsidium vj s. xj d.ob.
Thomas Ridell pro dimidio sacco lane in j poke
custuma iij s. iiij d. subsidium xvj s. viij d.
Idem pro xx pellibus lanutis
custuma vij d. subsidium ij s. ix d.
Willelmus Richerdson pro iij quarteriis lane in j poke
custuma v s. subsidium xx v s.
Idem pro l pellibus lanutis continentibus dimidium quarterium x pelles
custuma xvij d. subsidium vj s. xj d.ob.
Georgius Bird pro iij quarteriis vij clavis lane in ij pokes
custuma vj s. ob. subsidium xxx s. j d.ob.
pro lx pellibus lanutis continentibus j quarterium
custuma xx d. subsidium viij s. iiij d.
Rogerus Lilburn pro dimidio sacco lane in j poke
custuma iij s. iiij d. subsidium xvj s. viij d.
Willelmus Hunter pro j sacco iij quarteriis iiij clavis lane in ij pokes
custuma xij s. ij d. subsidium [lx s.x d.]
Idem pro l pellibus lanutis continentibus dimidium quarterium xx pelles
custuma xvij d. subsidium vj s. xj d.ob.
Thomas Davell pro j sacco et dimidio lane in ij pokes
custuma x s. subsidium l s.
Willelmus Haysand pro dimidio sacco viij clavis lane in j poke
custuma iiij s. iiij d.ob. subsidium xxj s. x d.

Idem pro xv pellibus lanutis
custuma v d. subsidium ij s. j d.
Johannes Mappas pro j sacco dimidio viij clavis lane in ij pokes
custuma xj s.ob. subsidium lv s. j d.ob.
Johannes Sampill pro iij quarteriis lane in j poke
custuma v s. subsidium xx v s.
Idem pro xl pellibus lanutis continentibus dimidium quarterium x pelles
custuma xiij d.ob. subsidium v s. v d.ob.
Thomas Colt pro j sacco dimidio iij clavis lane in ij pokes
custuma x s. v d. subsidium lj s. xj d.
Nicholaus Haynyng pro dimidio sacco viij clavis lane in j poke
custuma iij s. iiij d.ob. subsidium xx j s. ix d.ob.
Johannes Foster pro xv pellibus lanutis
custuma v d. subsidium ij s. j d.

Summa {
lane xiiij sacci j quarterium vij clavi lane
pellium lanutarum DCC xx continentes iij saccos
custume lane iiij li xv s. ij d.
custume pellium lanutarum xx s.
subsidii lane xxiij li. xix s. vj d.
subsidii pellum lanutarum v li.
denariorum Calesii xj s. viij d.ob.
exituum coketti iij s. ij d.

Navis vocata Nicholaus de Leith unde Symon Clolk est magister applicuit xv die Januarii
Johannes Aleyn pro j last ostrearum et di' valor xiij s. iiij d.
subsidium viij d.
Johannes Coke pro ij barellis salmonis valor xxvj s. viij d.
subsidium xv j d.

Summa {
valoris xl s.
subsidii ij s.

Navis vocata Barbara de Goos unde Adrian Cornelius est magister exivit xxiij die Januarii
{alienigena}
Idem pro xxxij seldre carbonum valor xxxvj s. (viij d.)
custuma v d.ob. subsidium xxij d.

Summa {
valoris xxvj s. viij d.
custume v d.ob.
subsidii xxij d.

Navis vocata Halygast de Camfer unde Fretherikus Willemson est magister exivit xxiiij die Januarii

{alienigena}

Idem pro x seldre carbonum valor xxvj s. viij d.

custuma <vj d.ob. *struck out*> iiij d. subsidium <x d. *struck out*> xvj d.

Willelmus Richerdson pro xxvj grindstones valor lxx s.

subsidium iij s. vj d.

Summa {
valoris indigene et alienigene iiij li. <vj s. *struck out*> xvj s. viij d.
valoris alienigene xxvj s. viij d.
custume <ij d.ob. *struck out*> iiij d.
subsidii iiij s.<iij d. *struck out*> x d.

Navis vocata Nicholaus de Leith unde Symon Clolk et magister exivit ultimo die Januarii

{alienigena}

Idem pro xij quarteriis brasii valor xl s.

custuma vj d. subsidium ij s.

Summa {
valoris xl s.
custume vj d.
subsidii ij s.

Navis vocata Jacob de Durdright unde Cornelius Willemson est magister exivit primo die Februarii

{alienigena}

Idem pro xlviij seldre carbonum valor iiij li.

custuma xij d. subsidium iiij s.

Idem pro xij grindstones valor x s.

custuma j d.ob. subsidium vj d.

Summa {
valoris iiij li x s.
custume xiij d.ob.
subsidii iiij s. vj d.

Navis vocata Katryn de Camfer unde Arnaldus Cornelison est magister exivit xiiij die Februari

{alienigena}

Idem pro xxxij seldre carbonum valor liij s. iiij d.

custuma viij d. subsidium ij s. viij d.

Summa {
valoris liij s. iiij d.
custume viij d.
subsidii ij s. viij d.

Navis vocata Gertrud de Seliksee unde Nicholaus Adison est magister applicuit xiiij die Februarii

{alienigena}

Idem pro xl barellis separum valor xviij s. iiij d.

custuma iij d. subsidium xj d.

Idem pro xij barellis pomorum valor x s.

custuma j d.ob. subsidium vj d.

Summa { valoris xxviij s. iiij d.
custume iiij d.ob.
subsidii xvij d.

Navis vocata James de Andwarpp unde Jacobus Johnson est magister applicuit xix die Februarii
{alienigena}
... [*50 mm. of left side damaged*]pro x last berre valor x li.
custuma xxx d. subsidium x s.
... iij pokes hop valor iij li.
custuma ix d. subsidium iij s.
.. .avelanarum valor xviij s. iiij d.
custuma ij d.ob. subsidium xj d.

Summa { valoris xiij li. xviij s. iiij d.
custume iij s. v d.ob.
subsidii xiij s. xj d.

Navis vocata Gertrude de Seliksee unde Nicholaus Adison est magister exivit xix die Februarii.
Idem pro xxviij celdris carbonum valor xlvj s. viij d.
custuma vij d. subsidium ij s. iiij d.

Summa { valoris xlvj s. viij d.
custume vij d.
subsidii ij s.iiij d.

... ultimo die Februarii
...
...
...

Summa { valoris ix li. vj s. viij d.
custuma ij s. iiij d.
subsidii ix s. iiij d.

Navis vocata James de Andwarp unde Jacobus Johnson est magister exivit vj die Marcii
{alienigena}
Idem pro iiij[xx]iiij celdris carbonum valor vij li.
custuma xxj d. subsidium vij s.
Idem pro x grindstones valor xvj s. viij d.
custuma ij d.ob. subsidium x d.

Summa { valoris vij li. xvj s. viij d.
custume xxiij d.ob.
subsidii vij s. <viij d. *struck out*> x d.

Navis vocata James de Camfer unde Jacobus Lawrensone est magister exivit xij die Marcii
{alienigena}
Idem pro xiij seldre carbonum valor xxiij s. iiij d.
custuma iij d.ob. subsidium xiiij d.

Idem pro iij grindstones valor v s.
custuma j d. subsidium iij d.
Idem pro ij pannis panni lanei stricti sine grano valor xl s.
custuma v s. vj d. subsidium ij s.

Summa {
valoris xxviij s. iiij d.
custume iiij d.ob.
subsidii xvij d.
panni ij panni sine grano
custume v s. vj d.
subsidii pannorum
alienigene ij s
}

Summa huius rotuli CCxxix li xviij s. v d.ob.q.

[*Membrane 6 face*]
Navis vocata Maudelyn de Camfer unde Petrus Symonson est magister applicuit xix die Marcii
{alienigena}
Idem pro xxx seldre frumenti valor xx li.
custuma v s. subsidium xx s.
Idem pro C waynscottes valor iij li.
custuma ix d. subsidium iij s.
Idem pro x last beer valor x li.
custuma ij s. vj d. subsidium x s.
Willelmus Blaxton pro iij doliis vini dulcis
tonnagium ix s.
Idem pro xxx seldre frumenti valor xx li.
subsidium xx s.
Idem pro iij C avelanarum valor vj s. viij d.
subsidium iiij d.
Nicholaus Haynyng pro iij seldre mixtillionis valor xl s.
subsidium ij s.
Idem pro ij doliis et dimidio vini dulcis
tonnagium vij s. vj d.

Summa {
valoris alienigene xxxiij li.
valoris indigene et alienigene lv li. xvj s. viij d.
custume viij s. iii d.
subsidii lv s. iiij d.
vini dulcis v dolio j pipe
tonnagii xvj s. vj d.
}

Navis vocata Russoyn de Stapill unde Graunt Pykard est magister exivit xix die Marcii
{alienigena}
Idem pro iiij^{xx} seldre carbonum valor vij li.
custume xxj d.ob. subsidium vij s.
Idem pro lx grindstones valor vj li. xvj s. viij d.
custuma xx d.ob. subsidium vj s. xd.

Idem pro xvij dossenis rubstones valor xx s.
custuma iij d. subsidium xij d.
Idem pro j last et di' salmonis valor xij li.
custuma iij s. subsidium xij s.
Idem pro dimidio panno panni lanei sine grano valor x s.
custuma xvj d.ob. subsidium vj d.

Summa
- valoris xxvij li. vj s. viij d.
- custume vj s. viij d.ob.
- subsidii xxvij s. <x d. *struck out*> iiij d.
- panni sine grano dimidius pannus sine grano
- custume xvij d.

Navis vocata Mary Knyght de Selyksee unde Cornelius Lark est magister applicuit xxj die Marcii
{alienigena}
Idem pro j pipe olei rape valor xl s.
custuma vj d. subsidium ij s.
Idem pro CC di' waynscotes valor iiij li.
custuma <v d. *struck out*> xij d. subsidium iiij s.
Idem pro iiij pokes hop valor iiij li. x s.
custuma xiij d.ob. subsidium iij s. vj d.
Idem pro iij seldre et di' mixtillionis valor lix s. x d.
custume ix d. subsidium iij s.

Summa
- valoris xiij li. ix s. x d.
- custume iij s. iiij d.ob.
- subsidii xiij s. vj d.

Navis vocata Cristofir de Flemyng unde Cornelius Jacobson est magister exivit xxij die Marcii
{alienigena}
Idem pro iiij^{xx} seldre carbonum valor vij li.
custuma xxj d. subsidium vij s.
Idem pro lx grindstones valor vj li. xvj s. viij d.
custuma xx d.ob. subsidium vj s. x d.
Idem pro j last et di' salmonis valor xij li.
custuma iij s. subsidium xij s.
{alienigena}
Johannes Fennyk pro v barelles et dimidio salmonis valor iij li. xiij s. iiij d.
custuma xj d.ob. subsidium iij s. viij d.

Summa
- valoris xxix li. x s.
- custume vij s. iiij d.ob.
- subsidii xxix s. vj d.

Navis vocata Katrin de Hirlame unde Johannes Gerardson est magister applicuit xxviij die Marcii
{alienigena}
Idem magister pro xij last berre valor xij li.
custuma iij s. subsidium xij s.
Idem pro xxxij seldre mixtillionis valor xvj li.
custuma iiij s. subsidium xvj s.
Summa { valoris xxviij li.
custume vij s.
subsidii xxviij s.

Navis vocata Antony de Leth unde Thomas Ramsay est magister applicuit xxix die Marcii
{alienigena}
Idem pro iij last salmonis valor xxiiij li.
custuma vj s. subsidium xxiiij s.
Idem pro j last olei valor vij li.
custuma xxj d. subsidium vij s.
Idem pro x last ostrearum valor iij li.
custuma ix d. subsidium iij s.
Idem pro j dolio vini Rochelle
tonnagium iij s.
Summa { valoris xxxiiij li.
custume viij s. vj d.
subsidii xxxiiij s.
vini j dolium
tonnagii iij s.

Navis vocata Nicholaus de Gow unde Petrus Person est magister applicuit ultimo die Marcii
{alienigena}
Idem magister pro xij last berre valor xij li.
custuma iij s. subsidium xij s.
Idem pro viij seldre frumenti valor x li.
custuma ij s. vj d. subsidium x s.
Idem pro x seldre mixtillionis valor vj li. xiij s. iiij d.
custuma xx d. subsidium vj s. viij d.
Summa { valoris xxviij li. xiij s. iiij d.
custume vij s. ij d.
subsidii xxviij s. viij d.

Navis vocata Martyn de Bulleyn unde Johannes Leonard est magister applicuit ix die Aprilis
{alienigena}
Idem magister pro xxiij seldre frumenti valor xx li.
custume v s. subsidium xx s.
Idem pro j last et ij barellis bere valor xxiij s. iiij d.
custuma iij d.ob. subsidium xiiij d.

Idem pro vij pannis panni lanei sine grano valor vij li.
custuma xix s. iij d. subsidium vij s.

Summa { valoris xxviij li. iij s. iiij d.
custume v s. iij d.ob.
subsidii xxviij s. ij d.
pannorum vij panni sine grano
custume xix s vj d.ob. }

Navis vocata heringer de Hertflew unde Gabriell de Tete est magister exivit ix die Aprilis

{alienigena}
Idem pro iiij^{xx} seldre carbonum valor vij li.
custuma xxj d. subsidium vij s.

{alienigena}
Johannes Gouerson pro j last salmonis valor viij li.
custuma ij s. subsidium viij s.
Idem pro lx grindstones valor vj li. xvj s. viij d.
custuma xx d.ob. subsidium vj s. x d.

Summa { valoris xxj li. xvj s. viij d.
custume v s. v d.ob.
subsidii xxj s. x d. }

Navis vocata George de Breele unde Fopp Willemson est magister exivit ix die Aprilis.

{alienigena}
Idem pro iiij^{xx} seldre carbonum valor vij li.
custuma xxj d. subsidium vij s.
Idem pro lxij grindstones valor vj li. xvj s. viij d.
custuma xx d.ob. subsidium vj s. x d.
Idem pro vij dossenis rubstones valor xx s.
custuma iij d. subsidium xij d.
Idem pro j last salmonis valor viij li.
custuma ij s. subsidium viij s.

Summa { valoris xxij li. xvj s. viij d.
custume v s. viij d.ob.
subsidii xxij s. x d. }

examinatur

Summa huius partis xix li. xiij s. j d.ob.

[*Membrane 6 dorse*]

{Summa totalis horum vj rotulorum}

Lane Indigenarum
xlix sacci xxv clavi
custuma xvj li. ix s. xj d.ob.
subsidium iiij^{xx}ij li. ix s. iiij d.ob.

Pelles lanute indigenarum
iiij MDCC x pelles facientes xix saccos j quarterium xxx pelles
custuma vj li. xj s. j d.ob.
subsidium xxxij li. xiiij s. v d.
Denaria Calesii xlvj s. iij d.
provenientes de iiij^{xx}iiij mercatoribus indigenis xiiij s.
Pelles lanute vocate shorlynges et lamfelles
xxxv MCj pelles facientes Ciiiij saccos dimidium xxj pelles
custuma <nihil per breve *struck out*>
subsidium
denaria Calesii } CCCCiiij li. xix s. ob.qu.
exitus coketti
Valor mercandisarum alienigarum
Diiij^{xx}x li. vj s. vj d.
custuma vij li. viij s. v d.
Panni sine grano indigenarum
xvj panni
custuma xviij s. viij d.
Panni sine grano alienigarum
xij panni xxxiij s. ob.
Vinum indigenarum
Clxxiij dolia j hogeshede
subsidium xxv li. xix s. ix d.
Valor mercandisarum indigenarum et alienigarum
Miiij C iiij^{xx}vij li. ix s. viij d.
subsidium lxxiiij li. viij s. j d. ob.

Et onerantur super compotum Cxxvj li. xiiij s. iiij d.
de residuo custume et subsidii predictorum xlix saccorum xxv clavorum lane et predictarum iiij Mvij Cx pellium lanutarum dictorum mercatorum indigenarum, videlicet, de quolibet huius sacci lane pro custuma iij s.iiij d. et pro quibuslicet CCxl pellibus lanutis iij s. iiij d., ultra vj s. viij d. de quibus superius onerant se gratis, ut reddet ad x s., et pro subsidio cuiuslicet huius sacci lane xxx iij s. iiij d. et pro quibuslicet CCxl pellibus lanutis xxxiij s. iiij d., ultra xxxiij s. iiij d. de quibus superius onerant se gratis, ut reddet ad lxvj s. viij d., iuxta formam statuti anno xx^{mo} henrici nuper de facto et non de jure regis anglie vj^{ti} inde edicti
SUMMA TOTALIS OMNIS DCCiiij^{xx}iij li. vj s. vj d.qu.

unde

Custuma lanarum et pellium lanutarum cum denariis Calesii
et exitubus coketti xxvj li. xvj d.
Subsidium lanarum et pellium lanutarum Cxv li. iij s. ix d.ob.
Custuma et subsidium pellium lanutarum vocatarum shorlynges
cum denariis calesii et exitubus coketti iiijCiiij li. xix s. ob.qu

Parva custuma x li. j d.ob.
Subsidium tonagii et pondagii C li. vij s. x d.ob.
Custuma et subsidium lanarum et pellium lanutarum de superiore Cxxvj li. xiiij s. iiij d.

6. Account of William Chauntrell, controller, from July (?) to December 1471.

E 122/162/2.

There are no enrolled accounts extant for Newcastle upon Tyne between 19 July 1469 and 30 March 1476, so this account and the one following are all the customs accounts known for this period. Unfortunately neither are well preserved. As normal with the controller's accounts no record was made of customs or subsidies paid.

The first 150 mm. of membrane 1 of this account are missing except for a strip at the left 40 mm. in width. The heading and entries relating to at least two ships are lost. The last entry is dated 9 December. We know from the heading of the following account that Chauntrell was controller from 1 January 1472, so this account probably ended on 31 December 1471. By comparing the taxable value of separate ships' cargoes with the *summa totalis* at the end of the account, it appears that the account was complete on the two membranes printed here, each 261 mm. wide, and respectively 592 mm. and 710 mm. long. The dorse of membrane 1 is blank, and the foot has been sewn to the head of membrane 2.

The proper names *Johns'* and *Adryans'* have been extended as Johnson and Adryanson.

[*Membrane 1 face*]
... [*150 mm. missing*]
Idem pro vj mattes
Idem pro viij dossenis stabellorum
Summa valoris v li. xiij s iiij d.

Navis vocata Nicholaus de Gow unde Elricus Johnson est magister applicuit x° die Augusti
{alienigena}
Idem pro DClx t... valor xxvj s. viij d.
Idem pro lx bordes vocat' deles valor xxvj s. viij d.
Summa valoris liij s. iiij d.

Navis vocata Philip et Jacob de Delff unde Johannes Mustert est magister applicuit x° die Augusti
{alienigena}

Idem pro iij M libris ferri	valor iiij li.
Idem pro ij pokes hopp	valor xv s.
Idem pro xxviij M breckstones	valor xl s.
Idem pro iiij barellis smigmatis	valor liij s. iiij d.
Idem pro v dossenis maundes	valor ij s. vj d.
Idem pro iij dossenis stabellorum	valor vj s. viij d.
Idem pro C ollis terrenis	valor vj s. viij d.
Idem pro vj barellis berre	x s.

Summa valoris [x li. xiiij s. ij d.]

Navis vocata Cristofre de Gow unde Paulus Person est magister applicuit xiij° die Augusti
{alienigena}

Idem pro xxxvij M petrarum	valor xl s.
Idem pro v barellis bituminis	valor xx s.
Idem pro vj barellis picis	valor xx s.
Idem pro C waynscottes	valor xxxiij s. iiij d.
Idem pro vj barellis berre	valor vj s. viij d.

Summa valoris vj li.

Navis vocata le Cristofre de Gow unde Jacobus Just est magister applicuit xiij° die Augusti
{alienigena}

Idem pro xxv M petrarum	valor xxvj s. viij d.
Idem pro iij barellis smigmatis	valor xl s.
Idem pro ij pokes hopp	valor xxx s.
Idem pro ij dossenis stabellorum	valor xx d.
Idem pro iij dossenis maundes	valor iij s. iiij d.

Summa valoris v li. xx d.

Navis vocata le George de Novo Castro unde Thomas Wermouth est magister exivit xiiij° die Augusti

Idem pro vj celdris carbonum	valor x s.
Richard Revet pro xvij plaustris plumbi	valor lvij li.
Idem pro vj barellis ciphorum	valor xl s.

Summa valoris lix li. x s.

[*Membrane 2 face*]
{Augusti}
Navis vocata le Mary de Novo Castro unde Reginald Johnson est magister exivit xx° die Augusti

Willelmus Brothirwyk pro CCCCxxx shorlynges	valor iij li. iij s. iiij d.
Hugo Watson pro xxx shorlynges	valor iij s. iiij d.
Johannes Lawes pro Cxx shorlynges	valor xvij s vj d.
Idem pro C lx lamfelles	valor xx s.
Johannes Brygam pro v^xx shorlynges	valor xij s. vj d.

Johannes Halyday pro CC shorlynges	valor xxx s.
Idem pro lx lamfelles	valor vj s. viij d.
Robert Hely pro Cxxx shorlynges	valor xx s.
Idem pro lx lamfelles	valor vj s. viij d.
Antonius Leishman pro v^{xx} shorlynges	valor xij s. vj d.
Rogerus Sampill pro CCC shorlynges	valor xlv s.
Ricardus Gudefello pro Cxxx shorlynges	valor xx s.
Thomas Huchon pro MC shorlynges	valor viij li. v s.
Idem pro Clxx lambfelles	valor xvj s. viij d.
Thomas Hesylden pro v^{xx}schorlynges	valor xv s.

Summa valoris xxij li. xiiij s. ij d.

Willelmus Brotherwyk pro iij quarteriis v clavis lane in ij pokes
Idem pro C pellibus lanutis
Hugo Watson pro xl pellibus lanutis
Johannes Lawes pro Cxx pellibus lanutis
Willelmus Hurlbad pro viij clavis lane in j^{o} poket
Johannes Parker pro j quarterio lane in j^{o} poke
Robertus Pykden pro j quarterio v clavis lane in j^{o} poke
Johannes Brygam pro dimidio sacco xj clavis lane in j poke
Idem pro x pellibus lanutis
Johannes Halyday pro j quarterio vj clavis lane in j poke
Idem pro xxxv pellibus lanutis
Robert Hely pro xxx pellibus lanutis
Antonius Leishman pro xx pellibus lanutis
Rogerus Sampill pro lxxx pellibus lanutis
Ricardus Gudefello pro xxx pellibus lanutis
Thomas Huchon pro iij quarteriis lane in j^{o} poke
Idem pro CC xx pellibus lanutis
Thomas Hesylden pro xv pellibus lanutis

Summa { lane iij sacci j quarterium ix clavi
pellium lanutarum ij sacci iij quarteria l pelles

{Septembris}

Navis vocata le Mary de Novo Castro unde Nicholaus Archer est magister exivit vij^{o} die Septembris

Johannes Sampill pro xviij semi peciis panni lanei largi continentibus ix pannos non grano

Idem pro iij plaustris plumbi — valor ix li.

Thomas Hanson pro xj peciis panni lanei stricti continentibus ij pannos non grano

Idem pro ij plaustris plumbi — valor vj li

Idem pro iiij barellis talowe — valor xl s.

Willelmus Davell pro ij peciis panni stricti continentibus j pannum non grano

Idem pro j pecia panni largi continente dimidium pannum non grano

Summa { pannagii xij panni et dimidius non grano
valoris xvij li.

Navis vocata le Cristofre de Selicsee unde Martyn Adryanson est magister applicuit xxij° die Septembris
{alienigena}
Idem pro xxx barellis ceparum valor xxx s.
Idem pro xvj M petris valor xvj s. viij d.
Idem pro lx bundellis allii valor v s.
Idem pro iij parvis mal*is* valor vj s. viij d.
Summa valoris lviij s iiij d.

Navis vocata le Basket de Gusse unde Johannes Cornelson est magister applicuit xxij die Septembris
{alienigena}
Idem pro xxx garbis cardonum valor xxx s.
Idem pro C ollis terrenis valor xx s.
Idem pro lxxx bundellis allii valor vj s. viij d.
Summa valoris lvj s. viij d.

{Octobris}
Navis vocata le Basket de Gusse unde Johannes Cornelson est magister exivit iiij° die Octobris
{alienigena}
Idem pro xxvj celdris carbonum valor iij li.
Summa valoris patet

Navis vocata le Cristofer de Selicsee unde Martyn Adrianson est magister exivit iiij° die Octobris
{alienigena}
Idem pro xxx celdris carbonum valor l s.
Summa valoris patet

Navis vocata le Cristofre de Novo Castro unde Nicholaus Bruke est magister exivit xvij° die Octobris
Hugo Watson pro CC shorlynges valor xxx s.
Johannes Brygam pro CCl shorlynges valor xxxvj s. viij d.
Robertus Chambre pro CCCxl shorlynges valor l s.
Robert Stokall pro CCxxv shorlynges valor xxxiijs. iiij d.
Robert Chatur pro CCCCxx shorlynges valor iij li ijs. vj d.
Nicholaus Hanyng pro CClxx shorlynges valor xxxviij s. iiij d.
Willelmus Clark pro xx grynstones valor xx s.
Georgius Carr pro j plaustro plumbi et dimidio valor iiij li. x s.
Ricardus Stephenson pro j plaustro plumbi valor iij li.
Summa valoris xxj li. x d.
Thomas Swan pro iij quarteriis lane in j poke
Hugo Watson pro xl pellibus lanutis
Johannes Brygam pro lxx pellibus lanutis
Willelmus Cristall pro j quarterio viij clavis lane in j° poke
Willelmus Fyshwik pro j quarterio viij clavis lane in j° poke
Willelmus Lange pro j quarterio viij clavis lane in j° poke

Robertus Chambre pro lxxx pellibus lanutis
Robert Stokall pro lv pellibus lanutis
Willelmus Scot pro j quarterio lane in j° poke
Robert Harden junior pro dimidio sacco lane in ju poke
Nicholaus Hanyng pro lxx pellibus lanutis
Thomas Lokwod pro dimidio sacco lane in j° poke
Robert Chatur pro Cv pellibus lanutis
Henricus Fouler pro j quarterio lane in j poke
Summa { lane iiij sacci j quarterium xj clavi
pellium lanutarum j saccus iij quarteria

Navis vocata le Gracedew de Novo Castro unde Willelmus Coke est magister exivit xxiij° die Octobris
Robertus Herryson pro lxx shorlynges valor viij s. iiij d.
Thomas Greyn pro CC shorlynges valor xxx s.
Willelmus Lange pro Clxxx shorlynges valor xxv s.
Idem pro CC lambfelles valor xx s.
Robertus Chambre pro CCCxl shorlynges valor l s.
Robert Chatur pro CCCC xx shorlynges valor iij li. ij s. vj d.
Johannes Ridesdale pro DCCCC shorlynges valor vj li. xv s.
Idem pro CCCC lamfelles valor xl s.
Johannes Bunde pro Clxxx shorlynges valor xxv s.
Ricardus Gudefello pro DClxxx shorlynges valor v li.
Robert Stokall pro CCCC shorlyinges valor iij li.
Willelmus Blaxton pro xij gryndstones valor x s.
Summa valoris xxviij li. v s. x d.
Robertus Haryson pro ij saccis et j quarterio lane in iij pokes
Thomas Greyn pro xl pellibus lanutis
Willelmus Lange pro xl pellibus lanutis
Robertus Chambre pro lxxx pellibus lanutis
Willelmus Kirklay pro j quarterio lane in j° poke
Robertus Chatur pro C pellibus lanutis
Johannes Ridesdale pro CCxl pellibus lanutis
Johannes Bunde pro xl pellibus lanutis
Idem pro viij clavis lane in j° poket
Ricardus Gudefello pro Clx pellibus lanutis
Willelmus Fyshwic pro viij clavis lane in j poket
Thomas Cudbert pro j sacco et j quarterio lane in ij pokes
Johannes Reddyng pro j sacco lane in ij pokes
[*Membrane 2 dorse*]
Willelmus Hudson pro ij saccis lane in iij pokes
Robert Stokall pro Cxx pellibus lanutis
Willelmus Bunde pro j quarterio viij clavis lane in j° poke
Robertus Brygam pro dimidio sacco et viij clavis lane in j° poke
Johannes Esyngton pro j sacco et j quarterio lane in ij pokes
Johannes Lokwod pro j sacco et dimidio lane in ij pokes
Summa { lane xj sacci dimidius et vj clavi
pellium lanutarum iij sacci j quarterium et xl pelles

{Novembris}
Navis vocata le Mary de Novo Castro unde Robertus Porter est magister exivit primo die Novembris

Robertus Harkess pro xl shorlynges	valor v s.
Georgius Carr pro CCCxl shorlynges	valor l s.
Rogerus Sampill pro Dlx shorlynges	valor iiij li. ij s. vj d.
Idem pro CC lamfelles	valor xxvj s. viij d.
Robertus Brygam pro D shorlynges	valor iij li. xv s.
Robert Hely pro Cxlv shorlynges	valor xx s.

Summa valoris xij li. xix s. ij d.

Robertus Harkes pro dimidio sacco lane in j° poke
Rolland Scot pro iij quarteriis lane in j° poke
Thomas Cudbert pro dimidio sacco viij clavis lane in j° poke
Johannes Sampill pro j sacco lane in ij pokes
Johannes Brygam pro dimidio sacco v clavis lane in j poke
Georgius Carr pro lxxx pellibus lanutis
Rogerus Sampill pro Cxx pellibus lanutis
Willelmus Bruke pro dimidio sacco lane in j° poke
Robert Herryson pro ij saccis lane in iij pokes
Robert Brygam pro Cxx pellibus lanutis
Robert Hely pro xxxv pellibus lanutis
Idem pro dimidio sacco viij clavis lane in j° poke
Willelmus Swan pro j quarterio viij clavis lane in j poke
Willelmus Kirklay pro dimidio sacco viij clavis lane in j poke
Johannes Newton pro j quarterio lane in j poke
Willelmus Scot pro dimidio sacco v clavis lane in j° poke
Robertus Harden senior pro j sacco lane in ij pokes
Thomas Stokall pro v clavis lane in j poket
Johannes Hedlem pro iij quarteriis lane in j poke
Georgius Watson pro dimidio sacco viij clavis lane in j poke
Georgius Bird pro dimidio sacco lane in j poke
Willelmus Camby pro dimidio sacco viij clavis lane in j poke

Summa { lane xij sacci xj clavi
pellium lanutarum j saccum j quarterium lv pelles

Navis vocata le Mary de Slusse unde Johannes Willemson est magister exivit xiij° die Novembris
{alienigena}

Idem pro xxiiij celdris carbonum	valor xxxvj s. viij d.

Summa valoris patet

Navis vocata le Mary de Novo Castro unde Johannes Parker est magister exivit ix° die Decembris

Robertus Hely pro CClx shorlynges	valor xxxvij s. vj d.
Willelmus Hudson pro DCClx shorlynges	valor vli. xij s. vj d.
Idem pro DClx lambfelles	valor iiij li. vj s. viij d.
Willelmus Camby pro CClx shorlynges	valor l s.
Robertus Harkes pro v[xx] shorlynges	valor xij s. vj d.

Willelmus Clark pro xxiiij gryndstones valor xx s.
Summa valoris xv li. xix s. ij d.
Robertus Hely pro lx pellibus lanutis
Johannes Sampill per iij saccis lane in iiij pokes
Thomas Davell pro ij saccis xij clavis lane in iij poke
Robertus Herryson pro iij quarteriis v clavis lane in j° poke
Rogerus Sampill pro iij quarteriis v clavis lane in j° poke
Willelmus Hudson pro iij quarteriis v clavis lane in j° poke
Idem pro Clxxx pellibus lanutis
Willelmus Camby pro dimidio sacco viij clavis lane in j poke
Idem pro lx pellibus lanutis
Robertus Hawkes pro j sacco j quarterio in ij pokes
Idem pro xx pellibus lanutis
Robertus Brygam pro dimidio sacco v clavis lane in j poke
Johannes Esyngton pro dimidio sacco x clavis lane in j poke
Willelmus Scot pro dimidio sacco viij clavis lane in j poke
Thomas Cudbert pro j sacco j quarterio lane in ij pokes
Thomas Lokwod pro j quarterio lane in j poke
Ricardus Hogeson pro dimidio sacco lane in j poke

Summa { lane xiij sacci dimidius et vj clavi
pellium lanutarum j saccus j quarterium et xx pelles

{indigena}

Summa totalis { valoris CClxxvj li. ix s. ij d.
pannagii xij panni et dimidius non grani
lane xlij sacci iij quarterius et iiij clavi
pellium lanutarum MMDC xxv continentes x saccos ij quarteria xlv pelles

{alienigena}

Summa totalis valoris xlvij li.

Memorandum quod Willelmus Chauntrell, contrarotulator, venit xxviij° die Januarii anno xj Edwardi iiij[ti] et prestitit sacrum in propria persona quod rotulus iste verus est.

7. Account of William Chauntrell, controller, for 1 January to March 1472

E 122/107/60

The three membranes, sewn Exchequer style, are each 266 mm. wide, and respectively 228 mm., 666 mm., and 190 mm. long. They are deeply creased, rubbed, and damaged. The bottom of membrane 1 is missing with the loss of entries between 24 January and 14 February. 60 mm. of the dorse are damaged at the right.

[*Membrane 1 face*]

Rotuli Willelmi Chauntrell contrarotulatoris custumarum et subsidiorum domini regis in portu ville Novi Castri super Tynam et in singulis portubus et locis eidem portui adiacentibus ... A festo circumcisionis domini ... ... quo tempore Willelmus Blaxton et Nicholaus Walker fuerunt custumarii dicti domini regis.

Navis vocata le Horse de Gow unde Laurencius Antonson est magister applicuit xiiij° die Januarii

{alienigena}

Idem magister pro xv ... paving tylle — valor xx s.
Idem pro iij coopotoriis — valor xx s.
Idem pro j maunde cum glasses — valor xx s.
Idem pro j barello smigmatis — valor x s.
Summa valoris iij li x s.

Navis vocata ... de Gow unde Fredericus Garardson est magister exivit xv° die Januarii

{alienigena}

Idem pro xxx celdris carbonum maritimorum ...
Summa valoris patet

Navis vocata le Maryknyght de Dordryght unde Symon Johnson est magister applicuit xv° die Januarii

{alienigena}

Idem magister pro ... de Ryne continentibus vij ames — valor xij li.

Idem pro xxiij M ... ...
Idem pro ... ollis terrenis valor iij s. iiij d.
Idem pro ... valor vj s. viij d.
Idem pro iij barellis smigmatis ...
Idem pro ... allecis albi ...
Idem pro iij saccis hoppe ...
Idem pro ... aughkindeles anguillarum ...
Summa valoris xvij li. xviij s.

Navis vocata le George de Dordryght unde ... est magister applicuit xviij° die Januarii
{alienigena}
Idem pro ... continentibus x ames valor xiiij li.
Idem pro xxM ... valor xx s.
Idem pro x saccis hope continentibus ... valor x s.
Idem pro ij pokes ... valor vj s. viij d.
Idem pro iij barellis smigmatis valor xxx s.
Idem pro xxvij finibus ferri valor ...
Summa valoris xviij li. v s.

Navis vocata le Horse de Gow unde Laurencius Antonson est magister exivit xx° die Januarii
{alienigena}
Idem pro xliij celdris carbonum maritimorum valor iij li. xiij s. iiij d.

... est magister applicuit xxiiij die Januarii ...

[*Foot of membrane 1 missing*]

[*Membrane 1 dorse*]
Navis vocata ... Willelmus Sage [est magister] exivit xiij° die Februarii
Idem pro xx celdris carbonum maritimorum valor xxxiij s. iiij d.
Summa valoris patet

Navis vocata Anna de Selyksee unde Johannes Pereson est magister exivit xiij° die Februarii
{alienigena}
Idem pro xxxix celdris carbonum maritimorum valor iij li
Summa valoris patet

Navis vocata le Martyn de Camfer unde Michael Pereson est magister applicuit xvij° die Februarii
{alienigena}
Idem pro dimidio C salis grossi ...
Idem pro viij barellis avelanarum ...
Idem pro vj barellis allecis ....
Idem pro lx finibus ferri continentibus M libras ...
Idem pro ij barellis osmondes ...

Idem pro ij saccis hoppe	...
Idem pro lx ollis terrenis	...
Idem pro iij dossenis stabellorum	...
Idem pro vij barellis ceparum	...
Idem pro iij barellis cum fructibus	...
Idem pro v C clapholt	...
Idem pro j dossena maundys	...
... pro vj shyffe cardonum	...
... pro iij doliis vini albi	...

Summa { valoris xij li. xiij s. iiij d.
tonnagii patet

Navis vocata le George de Brell unde Laurencius Rouse est magister applicuit xix° die Februarii
{alienigena}

Idem pro ij lastes allecis albi	valor vij li.
Idem pro vj barellis salis grossi	valor ...
Idem pro CC bundellis allii	valor vj s. viij d.
Idem pro CCCC ollis terrenis	valor ...
Idem pro iij dossenis ...	valor ...
Idem pro ij dossenis ...	valor ...
Idem pro xxiiij ulnis panni linii	valor vj s. viij d.
Idem pro xx barellis bere	valor xxvj s. viij d.
Idem pro ... parva cista	valor xx s.
... ... aghtendale anguillarum	valor ...
... pro ij dossenis mattes	...
Summa valoris xj li xiiji s iiij d.	

[*Membrane 2 face*]
{Februarii}
Navis vocata le Mary de Skedam unde Cornelius Johnson est magister applicuit xxiiij° die Februarii
{alienigena}

Idem pro j barello smigmatis	valor x s.
Summa valoris patet	
Robertus Harden pro C salis grossi	valor iiij li.
Idem pro CCxl finibus ferri continentibus ij M libras	valor iij li.
Idem pro ij barellis smigmatis	valor xxs.
Idem pro j pype cum avelanis	valor vj s. viij d.
Idem pro iij barellis allecis albi	valor xx s.
Georgius Byrd pro C salis grossi	valor iiij li.
Idem pro Clxxx finibus ferri continentibus ij M libras	valor iij li.
Idem pro v barellis smigmatis	valor l s.
Idem pro j fatte cum avelanis	valor vj s. viiij d.
Idem pro j poke mader	valor vj s. viij d.
Summa valoris xix li. x s.	

Navis vocata le Maryknyght de Selyksee unde Jacobus Pereson est magister applicuit xxvj° die Feburarii
{alienigena}
Idem pro ij lastes cinerum valor xl s.
Idem pro ij barellis salis grossi valor iij s. iiij d.
Idem pro vj dossenis maundes valor iij s. iiij d.
Idem pro j sacco hoppe valor x s.
Summa valoris lvj s. viij d.

Navis vocata le Glasse de Gow unde Johannes Walshe est magister applicuit xxvij° die Februarii
{alienigena}
Idem pro xxiv M petrarum valor xxvj s. viij d.
Idem pro ij finibus ferri continentibus M valor xxx s.
Idem pro ij barellis smigmatis valor xxvj s. viij d.
Summa valoris iiij li. iij s. iiij d.

Navis vocata le World de Gow unde Johannes Willemson est magister applicuit xxvij° die Februarii
{alienigena}
Idem pro xxxviij M petrarum valor xxx s.
Idem pro ... barellis picis valor xx s.
Summa valoris l s.

Navis vocata le World de Gowe unde Johannes Willemson est magister exivit v° die Marcii
{alienigena}
Idem pro xxxvj celdris carbonum maritimorum valor iij li.
Summa valoris patet

Navis vocata le Glasse de Gowe unde Johannes Walshe est magister exivit v° die Marcii
{alienigena}
Idem pro xxxvj celdris carbonum maritimorum valor iij li.
Summa valoris patet

Navis vocata le Martyn de Camfer unde Michael Pereson est magister exivit v° die Marcii
{alienigena}
Idem pro xx celdris carbonum maritimorum valor xxxiij s. iiij d.
Idem pro ... copertoriis lecti valor xs.
Idem pro ... dossenis rubstones valor xx d.
Idem pro ... petris plumbi continentibus dimidium plaustrum valor xxx s.
Summa valoris v li xv s.

Navis vocata le Maryknyght de Selyksee unde Jacobus Pereson est magister exivit vij° die Marcii
{alienigena}
Idem pro xxxij celdris carbonum maritimorum valor liij s. iiij d.
Summa valoris patet

Navis vocata le Cristofer de Novo Castro unde Nicholas Bruke est magister applicuit x° die Marcii
Idem magister pro iiij barellis osmondes valor xxvj s viij d.
Johannes Brygam pro lxxx finibus ferri continentibus DCCl libras valor xx s.
Idem pro j barello olei valor xiij s. iiij d.
Thomas Cudbert pro CClxv finibus ferri continentibus ijM libras valor iij li
Idem pro j pype cum sortes fructus valor xx s.
Robertus Herryson pro CCCxliij finibus ferri continentibus iiij M libras valor vj li
Robertus Chambre pro C xxxv finibus ferri continentibus M libras dimidio valor xlv s.
Willelmus Conyngame pro j barello smigmatis valor x s.
Idem pro j barello olei valor xiij s. iiij d.
Idem pro j sorte fructus valor vj s. viij d.
Idem pro j aghtendale anguillarum valor iij s. iiij d.
Idem pro j barello cum ij dossenis librarum amigdalarum valor iiij s. ij d.
Idem pro ij dossenis librarum ryse valor ...
Idem pro ij dossenis librarum onyonsede valor iij s. iiij d.
Johannes Belt pro ij barellis smigmatis valor xx s.
Idem pro j barello ... valor ...
Idem pro j aghtendale anguillarum valor iij s. iiij d.
Idem pro j sorte fructus valor ...
Idem pro di' ... dosseni librarum amigdalarum valor vj s. viij d.
Idem pro ... ...
Idem pro vj ... sede valor x d.
Idem pro j pecia linei continente xxxiij ulnas valor ...
Idem pro j pecia linei continente xxxviij ulnas valor v s.
Idem pro C xx finibus ferri continentibus ij M libras valor iij li
Robertus Brygam pro ij barellis smigmatis valor xx s.
Idem pro j barello olei valor iij s. iiij d.
Idem pro j sorte fructus valor vj s. viij d.
Willelmus Fyshwyk pro Clxxij finibus ferri continentibus ij M valor iij li.
Johannes Wynlaw pro CCiij finibus ferri continentibus iiij M valor vj li.
Idem pro dimidio barello smigmatis valor v s.

Robertus Harden pro CCClv finibus ferri continentibus iiij M libras | valor vj li
Ricardus Stephenson pro j barello allecis | valor vj s. viij d.
Willelmus Greyn pro CCxxx finibus ferri continentibus iiij M | valor vj li.
Willelmus Kyrklay pro ij barellis osmondes | valor xiij s. iiij d.
Idem pro ... finibus ferri continentibus ij M | valor iij li.
Georgius Carr pro CC xxxvij finibus ferri continentibus iiij M | valor vj li.
Alanus Carr pro j barello cum diversis speciebus | valor iij li.
Robertus Pykden pro ij barellis smigmatis | valor xx s.
Willelmus Lange pro vj barellis osmondes | valor xl s.
Idem pro xx finibus ferri continentibus ij M | valor iij li.
Summa valoris lxv li. xv s. x d.

Navis vocata le Kateryn de Bulone unde Johannes Clappholt est magister applicuit xj° die Marcii

{alienigena}
Idem pro ij saccis hoppe | valor xx s.

{alienigena}
Willelmus Spegyll pro C et j quarterio de mensura frumenti | valor xix li.
Idem pro C et j quarterio de mixtilione | valor ix li.
Summa valoris xxij li.

Navis vocata le May de Abvyle undeVincent Sancte est magister applicuit xj° die Marcii

{alienigena}
Willelmus Spegyll pro C mensuris frumenti | valor ix li.
Idem pro C mensuris mixtilionis | valor vij li.
Summa valoris xvj li.

[*Membrane 2 dorse*]

{Marcii}
Navis vocata le Michael de Stapyll in Pykardy unde Martinus Fere est magister applicuit xj° die Marcii

{alienigena}
Idem pro xx quarteriis frumenti | valor iiij li.
Idem pro xj quarteriis mixtilionis | valor xxx s.
Idem pro j dolio vini rubii
Summa { valoris v li x s. / tonagii patet

Navis vocata le Kateryn de Stapyll unde Petrus Potay est magister applicuit xj° die Marcii

{alienigena}
Idem magister pro j pype vini rubii

{alienigena}
Johannes Blykyn pro vj pypes vini rubii

Idem pro xxxvij finibus ferrii continentibus M valor xxx s.

Summa { tonnagii iij dolia et dimidium
valoris patet }

Navis vocata le John de Gowe unde Alanus Yonge est magister applicuit xj° die Marcii

{alienigena}

Idem pro xxiiij M petrarum valor xx s.
Idem pro xl finibus ferri continentibus M valor xxx s.
Summa valoris l s.

Navis vocata le Mary de Novo Castro unde Robertus Porter est magister applicuit xxj° die Marcii

Georgius Bird pro CClxxx finibus ferri continentibus iiij M valor vj li.
Johannes Newton pro Cxx finibus ferri continentibus ij M valor iij li.
Idem pro ij barellis smigmatis valor xx s.
Thomas Swan pro v barellis smigmatis valor l s.
Idem pro dimidio barello cum xx libris lini et ij peciis panni linii valor xx s.
Johannes Syd pro j barello smigmatis valor x s.
Willelmus Clark pro j poke mader valor xls.
Idem pro dimidio barello calebis valor xls.
Thomas Huchon pro ij barellis smigmatis valor xx s.
Thomas Cok pro j barello olei valor xx s.
Georgius Carr pro ij barellis smigmatis valor xxx s.
Idem pro j barello cum mercery valor v li. iiij s.
Thomas Lokwod pro ij pokes mader valor iiij li.
Idem pro dimidio barello calebis valor xl s.
Robertus Chambre pro j barello smigmatis valor x s.
Nicholaus Hanyng pro vj barellis smigmatis valor iij li.
Idem pro j poke mader valor xls.
Willelmus Hudson pro j poke mader valor xl s.
Alanus Carr pro C lxiij finibus ferri continentibus iij M valor iiij li. x s.
Idem pro ij barellis smigmatis valor xx s.
Willelmus Cristall pro ij barellis smigmatis valor xx s.
Thomas Cromer pro vj barellis smigmatis valor iij li
Idem pro j barello olei valor xx s.
Willelmus Thomson pro ij barellis smigmatis valor xx s.
Willelmus Conyngame pro j barello cum ... calapodiis et aliis mercimoniis valor iiij li.
Willelmus Camby pro Clxxj finibus ferri continentibus ij M libras valor iij li.
Robertus Stokall pro iij barellis smigmatis valor xxx s.
Idem pro j barello olei valor xx s.
Thomas Stokall pro ij barellis olei valor xl s.

Idem pro j poke mader valor xl s.
Summa valoris lxiij li. vj s. viij d.

Navis vocata le Trynyte de Novo Castro unde Henricus Dryffelde est magister applicuit xij° die Marcii
Johannes Newton pro CCC finibus ferri continentibus v M libras valor vij li. x s.
Idem pro j last picis et bituminis valor xl s.
Thomas Swan pro Cxlvj finibus ferri continentibus ij M libras valor iij li.
Thomas Cok pro xv finibus ferri continentibus di M valor xv s.
Johannes Brygam pro ij barellis smigmatis valor xx s.
Robertus Hely pro lxxxvj finibus ferri continentibus M et di' valor xlvs.
Idem pro ij barellis smigmatis valor xx s.
Willelmus Camby pro C lij finibus ferri continentibus ij M valor iij li.
Idem pro iiij barellis smigmatis valor xl s.
Thomas Stokall pro iij barellis smigmatis valor xxx s.
Idem pro j poke mader valor xl s.
Willelmus Conyngham pro j barello olei valor xiij s. iiij d.
Summa valoris xxvj li. xiij s. iiij d.

Navis vocata Mary de Novo Castro unde Johannes Parker est magister applicuit xij die Marcii
Thomas Swan pro ij barellis olei valor xxvj s. viij d.
Idem pro ij libris lini valor xxvj s. viij d.
Willelmus Hudson pro CCxx finibus ferri continentibus vM valor vij li x. s.
Idem pro j barello calebis valor iiij li.
Idem pro xij barellis smigmatis valor vj li.
Johannes Newton pro vj barellis osmondes valor xl s.
Idem pro ... valor xxxv s.
Idem pro j last picis et bituminis valor xl s.
Idem pro vj barellis osmondes valor xl s.
Robertus Herryson pro iiij barellis smigmatis valor xl s.
Idem pro lxxxviij finibus ferri continentibus M valor xxx s.
Idem pro j poke mader valor xxx s.
Robertus Hely pro lxvj finibus ferri continentibus M valor xxx s.
Idem pro j barello olei valor xx s.
Robertus Chatour pro iiij barellis osmondes valor xxvj s. viij d.
Idem pro ij barellis picis valor iij s iiij d.
Idem pro ij barellis bituminis valor iijs iiij d.
Johannes Scott pro j barello smigmatis valor x s.
Robertus Stokall pro j poke mader valor xl s.

Idem pro j barello olei	valor xx s.
Johannes Esyngton pro j poke mader	valor xl s.
Johannes Ridesdale pro j barello et dimidio smigmatis	valor xv s.
Willelmus Conyngham pro lxiiij finibus ferri continentibus M	valor xxx s.
Rogerus Sampyll pro ij barellis smigmatis	valor xx s.
Johannes Sampyll pro j barello et dimidio smigmatis	valor xx s.

Summa valoris xlvj li. xx d.

Navis vocata le Struse de Gowe und Thomas Johnson est magister applicuit xiij° die Marcii

{alienigena}

Idem pro xxx M petrarum	valor xxx s.
Idem pro j almaria	valor vj s. viij d.

Summa valoris xxxvj s. viij d.

Navis vocata le Cristofer de Gowe unde Paulus Mason est magister applicuit xiiij° die Marcii

{alienigena}

Idem pro xxiiij M petrarum	valor xxiiij s.
Idem pro iij semibarellis smigmatis	valor xv s.
Idem pro l warpe de ollis terrenis	valor v s.
Idem pro x dossenis maundes	valor iiij s.
Idem pro j dossena mattes	valor xx d.
Idem pro ij M libris ferri	valor iij li.
Idem pro j pecia panni linii continente xij ulnas	valor viij s.

Summa valoris v li. xvij s. viij d.

[*Membrane 3 face*]

Navis vocata Lilly de Gow unde Laurencius Walters est magister applicuit xiij° die Marcii

{alienigena}

Idem pro xvj M petrarum	valor xvj s.
Idem pro M pavyng tyles	valor xvj s.
Idem pro liij finibus ferri continentibus iij quarteria	valor xx s.
Idem pro j sacco hoppe	valor xiij s. iiij d.
Idem pro j dossena maundes	valor x d.
Idem pro vj mattes	valor x d.
Idem pro j hogeshede vini dulcis	

Summa {valoris iij li. vij s.
tonagii patet

Navis vocata le Maryknyght de Gow unde Henricus Samynson est magister applicuit xiij° die Marcii

{alienigena}

Idem pro j pype vini blank

Idem pro iiij barellis smigmatis valor xl s.
Idem pro xiij finibus ferri continentibus iij quarteria valor xx s.
Idem pro x M petrarum valor x s.
Idem pro ij dossenis mattes valor xx d.
Idem pro ij barellis bere valor iij s. iiij d

Summa { tonagii patet / valoris iij li. xv s.

Navis vocata George de Brell unde Laurencius Rouse est magister exivit xiiij° die Marcii
{alienigena}
Idem pro xiiij celdris carbonum maritimorum valor xxiiij s. iiij d.
Johannes Lawys pro viij gryndstones valor xl s.
Summa valoris iij li. iij s. iiij d.

Navis vocata Warld de Gow unde ... Glaser est magister exivit xvij° die Marcii
{alienigena}
Idem pro xxxviij celdris carbonum maritimorum valor iij li. iij s. iiij d.
Summa valoris patet

Navis vocata le Marie de Gow unde Adom Clayson est magister exivit xvij° die Marcii
{alienigena}
Idem pro xl celdris carbonum maritimorum valor vli. iiij s.
Summa valoris patet

[*Membrane 3 dorse*]

Summa	valoris	D ij li. vj s. iiij d.
	tonagii	vij dolia rubii et j hogeshed dulcis
	lane	iij sacci x clavis lane
	pellium lanutarum	DClxxxxv pelles lanute continentes ij saccos iij quarteria et xxxv pelles.

Hos rotulos liberavit hic (predictus) Willelmus Chauntrell xvj° die Aprilis anno duodecimo regis Edwardi iiij[ti] per manus suas proprias.

8. Account of George Bere, controller, from 12 April to 20 December 1481.

E 122/107/61

This particular account is valuable because no enrolled accounts for Newcastle upon Tyne between Michaelmas 1480 and 16 November 1486 have been preserved. Though described in the heading as *liber*, it is in fact a roll of eight membranes, 206 mm. wide, sewn Exchequer style; their lengths are 634, 279, 634, 634, 559, 508, 508 and 634 mm. The account is complete, and in good condition except for stains on membrane 4 dorse.

Of the free hands met in these accounts, this is the most individual, with more than usually idiosyncratic spelling, as, for example, *gyrndstones* and generally *seccus* for saccus. The Latin is uncertain, as is illustrated by the different case endings for the two customers' Christian names in the heading, and by the scribe's assumption that if the ablative plural of dolium is *doliis*, the singular is *dolii*. Most unusually for a controller's account, some of the custom and subsidy on wool, and the custom on cloth, was recorded. The tax paid by denizens on iron is described as *custuma*, but this was in fact the subsidy of poundage.

[*Membrane 1 face*]

Liber contrarotulamenti George Bere contrarotulatoris domini regis in portu ville Novi Castri super Tynam tam magne quam parve custume mercandisarum in portu predicto, a xij° die Aprilis anno xxj Edwardi quarti usque vicesimum diem Decembris tunc proximo sequentem.

Johannes Cartyngton
Gylberto Maners } custumariis

Navis vocata Mary de Dansk unde Laurencius Ferthland est magister applicuit xiij die Aprilis

{alienigena de Dansk}

Johannes Stornowe pro xij C wanscottes valor ix li.
xxxvj C clapholttes valor xxx s.
vj last di' bituminis valor ix li.
vij barellis picis valor xx s.
xj barellis osmondes valor iij li.
CC remesse valor xl s.
xvj C barell hedes valor xv s.
di last lini valor xl s.
j cista cum xiiij bundellis lini valor x s.
xxxviij bastis valor iij s. iiij d.
x spruce skennys valor vjs. viij d.
xij ferre burdes valor vj s. viij d.

Navis vocata the Brett de Dansk unde Henricus Ploytt est magister applicuit xiij die Aprilis.
{alienigena de Dansk}
Anton Ulson pro xiiij C wanscottes valor x li.x s.
xij C clapholttes valor x s.
ij last cineris valor xxxs.
iiij barellis osmondes valor xxx s.
xij payre tabels valor vjs. viij d.
xl kettis valor vj s. viij d.
xx[ti] trowes valor xx d.
vj payre bedes de almere valor vj s. viij d.
xxx[ti] pecis bastes valor iijs. iiij d .
{alienigena}
Henricus Ploytt pro xxx cannes valor vj s. viij d.
v barellis picis et bituminis valor xiij s. iiij d.
xx ulnas panni lewyne valor x s.

Navis vocata George de Dansk unde Barnarde Rother est magister applicuit xiij die Aprilis
{alienigena de Dansk }
Idem magister pro xviij C wanscottes valor xiij li. x s.
xl spruce delles valor xx s.
xviij C clapholttes valor xxx s.
CC remes valor xx s.
j last osmondes valor iij li.
v last picis et bituminis valor vj li.
j nest conters valor xiij iiij d
ij syngell conters valor xiij s. iiij d.
xv lin burdes valor xx d.
j cista cum xx picis wynnel valor vjs. viijd
iiij skoke trencheours valor xx d.
{alienigena}
Oytt Selmer pro ij nest conter valor xx s.
v barellis bituminis valor xiij s. iiij d.
j cista cum xiij bundellis lini valor vj s. viij d.
xv trowes valor xx d.

[*Membrane 1 dorse*]

Navis vocata Gelien de Garaunt unde Jacquet est magister applicuit ultimo die Aprilis

{alienigena}

Idem pro xiij rowles canvas	valor xx s.
CCCC libris rossyn	valor vj s. viij d.
CCC libris ferri	valor vj s. viij d.
xij payntede clothes	valor iij s. iiij d.
CCC orengis	valor xx d.

Navis vocata Mary de London unde Johannes Underwod est magister applicuit ij° die Maii

Idem magister pro vij barellis bituminis	valor xx s.

Navis vocata Jelien de Garaunt unde Jacquet est magister exivit iiij[to] die Maii

{alienigena}

Idem magister pro xxvj celdris carbonum	valor xliijs. iiij d.

Navis vocata George de Calles unde Leonardus Curson est magister exivit xj die Maii

{alienigena}

Idem pro xxxvj celdris carbonum	valor iiij li.

Navis vocata Mary de Dansk unde Laurencius Ferthland est magister exivit xiiij die Maii

{alienigena}

Idem magister pro xx celdris carbonum	valor xxxiij s. iiij d.
xx gyrndstones	valor xxxij s. vj d.
vj dossyn rubstones	valor vj s. viij d.

Navis vocata Peter de Novo Castro super Tynam unde Robertus Carter est magister applicuit xvij die Maii

Idem magister pro iij doliis vini rubii

Bartraham Yonghusband pro v doliis vini rubii

xx[xx] finis [*sic*] ferri continentibus MMMMM

custuma vij s. vj d.

MM libris rossyn valor xx s.

Johannes Brigham junior pro iij doliis vini rubii

Robertus Brigham junior pro ij doliis vini rubii

[*Membrane 2 face*]

Wilelmus Carr indigena pro iij doliis vini rubii

Robertus Harden junior pro j dolii vini rubii

Robertus Harden senior pro j dolii vini rubii

Rauffe Davell pro j pipa vini rubii

Cristofer Brigham pro j dolii vini rubii

Thomas Davel pro j dolii j pipa vini rubii

George Elwald pro j hogeshede vini rubii
CC libris rossyn valor v s.
Thomas Lokwod pro j hogeshede vini rubii
Johannes Thomson pro j dolii vini rubii
Thomas Cook pro j dolii vini rubii

[*Membrane 2 dorse*]
Navis vocata Cristofre de Novo Castro super Tynam unde Willelmus Cok est magister applicuit xvij die Maii
Idem magister pro ij doliis j hogeshede vini rubii
lxxx finis ferri continentibus M custuma xviij d.
C libris rossyn valor v s.
j pipa mell valor xx s.
Willelmus Layng pro iij pipis vini rubii
Thomas Watson pro iij pipis j hogeshede vini rubii
Thomas Swan pro iij doliis j pipa vini rubii
Robertus Watson pro ij hogeshedes vini rubii
Robertus Harden junior pro ij doliis j pipa j hogeshede vini rubii
George Elwald pro j pipa j hogeshede vini rubii
ij pipis Woode valor iij li.
Archebald Stokall pro j dolii j pipa
Robertus Harden pro ij doliis j pipa j hogeshede vini rubii
Thomas Roxsbruth pro ij doliis j pipa j hogeshede vini rubii
Peter Baxster pro ij hogeshedes vini rubii
Bartraham Yonghusband pro iij pipis vini rubii
[*Membrane 3 face*]
Thomas Davell pro iij doliis vini rubii
Johannes Cook pro iij doliis vini rubii
Ricardus Mechelson pro ij doliis j pipa vini rubii
Willelmus Hudson pro iij pipis j hogeshede vini rubii
Johannes Steyll pro j dolii vini rubii
Richard Stokall pro j pipa vini rubii
Willelmus Gaytford pro j pipa vini rubii
Robertus Chepman pro j hogeshede vini rubii
Robertus Mortymer pro j pipa j hogeshede vini rubii
Willelmus Camby pro ij hogeshedes vini rubii
Robertus Stokall pro ij doliis vini rubii
Annes Malpas pro iij hogeshedes vini rubii
Robertus Taliour pro j pipa vini rubii
Thomas Worsupp pro j pipa vini rubii
Thomas Hill pro j hogeshede vini rubii

Navis vocata Cristofre de Novo Castro super Tynam unde Nicholaus Archer est magister applicuit xxij die Maii
Idem magister pro j pipa j hogeshede vini rubii
George Elwald pro iij doliis j hogeshede vini rubii
xx pecis rossyn valor x s.
Johannes Sampoll pro vij doliis vini rubii

Thomas Lokwod pro ij doliis j pippa j hogeshede vini rubii
Robertus Pykden junior pro v doliis vini rubii
Johannes Ridesdall pro ij doliis vini rubii
Thomas Atkynson pro ij doliis vini rubii
Willelmus Cristall pro ij hogeshedes vini rubii

Navis vocata George de Dansk unde Barnard Rother est magister exivit xxiij die Maii

{alienigena}
Idem magister pro xxx celdris carbonum valor l s.
ij celdris gyrndstones valor xiij s iiij d.
ij plaustris plumbi valor viij li.xiij s. iiij d.
viij dossyn rubstones valor x s.
v C pellibus angnettorum valor xxvj s. viij d.
iiij pannis panni lanei stricti valor iiij s. vj d.
j pannis panni lanei largi valor ij s. viij d.

{alienigena}
Oytt Selmer pro iiij dossyn lam felles valor iij s. iiij d.

Navis vocata Brett de Dansk unde Henricus Ploytt est magister exivit xxiiij die Maii

{alienigena}
Idem magister pro xiij celdris carbonum valor xxxiij iiij d.
viij gyrndstones valor vj s. viij d.
x dossyn rubstones valor x. s.
xiiij petris plumbi valor v s.

[*Membrane 3 dorse*]
Navis vocata Anne de Dansk unde Martyn Howgonow est magister exivit xxiiij die Maii

{alienigena}
Idem magister pro x celdris carbonum valor xvj s. viij d.
v celdris gyrndstones valor xxxiij s. iiij d.
CCCC lamfelles valor x s.
iij pannis panni lane stricti custuma iij s. vj d.
j quarteria unius panni panni lane largi custuma vij d.

{alienigena}
Symond Rayner pro CC lamfelles valor x s.
iij gyrndstones valor v s.

{alienigena}
Johannes Stornowe pro xxxiiij petris plumbi valor xiij s. iiij d.
iij pannis panni lanei stricti custuma iij s. vj d.
j pannis panni lanei largi custuma ij s. viij d.

{alienigena}
Henricus Ploytt pro vij C lamfelles valor xl s.
ij pannis panni lanei stricti custuma ij s. iiij d.
di' pannis panni lanei largi custuma xvj d.

Navis vocata Sacre de Garaunt unde Johannes Carne est magister exivit xxv die Maii
{alienigena}
Idem magister pro xxx celdris carbonum valor l s.

Navis vocata George de Callis unde Johannes Dyrekson est magister exivit xxv die Maii
{alienigena}
Idem magister pro l celdris carbonum valor iij li. iij s. iiij d.
iiij dussenis rubstones valor v s.

Navis vocata Antone de Callis unde Pollus Johnson est magister applicuit ultimo die Maii
Richard Stark pro ij barellis saponis valor xxx s.

Navis vocata Antone de Callis unde Pollus Johnson est magister exivit iij° die Junii
Richard Stark pro xl celdris carbonum valor iij li. vj s. viij d.

Navis vocata Ternite de Garaunt unde Euon Braytan est magister applicuit vij° die Junii
{alienigena}
Idem magister pro xl finis ferri continentibus di' M valor xvj s. viij d.
Edmond Benley pro vj doliis vini rubii
viij wey grett sallt valor v li. vjs. viij d.

Navis vocata George de Callis unde Leonardus Curson est magister exivit viij die Junii
{alienigena}
Idem magister pro xxvj celdris carbonum valor iij li.

Navis vocata George de Suthwold unde Willelmus Bacarr est magister exivit xiij die Junii
Thomas Newton pro xx celdris carbonum valor xxxiij s. iiij d.
iiij celdris gryndstones valor xxvj s. viij d.

[*Membrane 4 face*]
Navis vocata Mary de Albuswik unde Willelmus Gybson est magister exivit xiij die Junii
Thomas Newton pro xxx celdris carbonum valor l s.
ij celdris gyrndstones valor xiij s. iiij d.

Navis vocata Ternite de Garaunt unde Euon Braytan est magister exivit xiiij die Junii
{alienigena}
Idem magister pro xlviij celdris carbonum valor iiij li.
iij quarteriis unius panis panni lanei stricti
custuma xxj d.

Navis vocata Larence de Thropp unde Johannes Newton est magister exivit xiiij die Junii
Willelmus Ride pro xiij celdris carbonum valor xxxiij s. iiij d.
{alienigena}
Juon de Park pro viij celdris carbonum valor xiij s. iiij d.
{alienigena}
Barnarde Foster pro ij celdris carbonum valor iij s. iiij d.

Navis vocata balenger de Holy Elland unde Johannes Dicheburn est magister applicuit xiiij die Junii
Johannes Hedlem pro vj M libris ferri valor ix li.

Navis vocata le Playtt de Dansk unde Lutt Ossman est magister applicuit xvj die Junii
{alienigena}
Idem magister pro MMCCCC clapholIt valor xvj s. viij d.
xij finis ferri valor C s.
{alienigena}
Bartholamus Rawyn pro xviij C wanscottes valor ix li.
MMCCCC clapholttes valor xvj s. viij d.
C remes valor x s.
xv barellis picis et bituminis valor xxvj s. viij d.
vj barellis cineris valor v s.
CC bowstaffes valor xx s.
lx trowes valor v s.

Navis vocata John de Callis unde Johannes Cowper est magister applicuit xxj die Junii
{alienigena}
Idem magister pro ij barellis sapponis valor xl s.
ij libris waxe custuma ij s.
j fasse bastis valor xx d.

Navis vocata Cristofre de Novo Castro super Tynam unde Nicholaus Archer est magister applicuit xxiiij die Junii
Johannes Ridesdall pro iiij barellis sapponis valor iij s. iiij d.

Navis vocata the Alvon de Garaunt unde Johannes Land est magister applicuit primo die Julii
Thomas Edwarde pro xlv doliis vini albi

Navis vocata the Playtt de Dansk unde Lut Ossman est magister exivit xxiiij die Julii
{alienigena}
Idem magister pro xl celdris carbonum valor v li.
Thomas Edward pro v coriis hirtes custum iij s. iiij d.
M lam felles valor xxvj s.

[*Membrane 4 dorse*]

Navis vocata George Sollay unde Michell Gyllison est magister applicuit ij° die Augusti

{alienigena}

Jacobus Hogonis de Camfer pro ij saccis hopp	valor xx s.
j barello sapponis	valor xiij s. iiij d.
j barello cum lini	valor vj s. viij d.
C ollis terrenis	valor vj s. viij d.
ij picis pani linii	valor x s.
Willelmus Yotson pro iij barellis sapponis	valor xl s.
Thomas Swan pro vj barellis sapponis	valor iij li.
iij barellis osmondes	valor xx s.
Willelmus Conyngham pro j last sapponis	valor viij li.
ij barellis olii trayn	valor xl s
j rondlett cum CC libris wyre	valor x s.
di' pice pani linii	valor v s.
xij libris risse	valor xx d.
xij libris comyn	valor xx d.
Robertus Brigham pro ij barellis sapponis	valor xvj s.
j mather poke	valor xx s.
Robertus Sollay pro j last ossmondes	valor iiij li.
George Carr pro v barellis sapponis	valor iij li. vjs. viij d.
j balle allom	valor xx s.
j kentall ceri	
ij balles mather	valor iiij li.
j rondlett cum iij pices fustian	valor xv s.
xl petris lini	valor xlv s.
Johannes Brigham pro iij barellis sapponis	valor xlv s.
Thomas Brown pro j rondlett cum diversis mercimoniis	valor x li
Jacobus Buk pro di' last ossmondes	valor xl v s.
di' last [ollis] terrenis	valor xx s.
Robertus Sawdon pro iij barellis sapponis	valor xl s.
di' last ossmondes	valor xl s.
Willelmus Haysande pro iiij barellis sapponis	valor ij li. xiij s. iiij d.
Johannes Ridesdall pro j cista cum diversis mercimoniis	valor xx s.
j hernes barell cum diversis mercimoniis	valor vj s. viij d.
j pice fustian alb'	valor v s.
iiij di' pices panni linii	valor iiij li.
j libra gynger	valor ij s. vj d.
Robertus Stokall pro ix barellis sapponis	valor vj li.
j last ossmondes	valor xl s
Willelmus Swan pro vj barellis sapponis	valor iiij li.
iij barellis ossmondes	valor xx s.
Johannes Bullok pro di' last sapponis	valor iiij li.

Navis vocata Jakett de Conkett unde John Johnson est magister applicuit iij° die Augusti
{alienigena}
Charlis Blak pro xij doliis j pippa vini rubii

[*Membrane 5 face*]
Navis vocata the George Swan unde Johannes Arnald est magister applicuit iiij die Augusti

Thomas Swan pro iij barellis sapponis	valor xl s.
Thomas Brown pro vj barellis sapponis	valor iiij li.
Jacobus Buk pro iij barellis sapponis	valor xl s.

Navis vocat Playtt de Dansk unde Martin Claysson est magister applicuit ultimo die Augustii
{alienigena}

George Flemyng pro xviij C wanscottes	valor xiiij li.
xlviij C clapholttes	valor xl s.
iiij last viij barellis bituminis	valor vli. xvj s. viij d.
ij last iiij barellis picis	valor lviij s. iiij d.
iiij last j barello ceneris	valor xlv s.
j petra dimidia lini	valor xx d.
xxj picis candelwyk	valor x s.
iiij payre almere bedes	valor x s.
xiij barellis picis et bituminis	valor x s.

Navis vocata George Swan de Novo Castro super Tynam unde Willelmus Robynson est magister exivit v° die Septembris

Thomas Swan pro vj celdris gyrndstonis		valor xl s.
Willelmus Yotson pro C lx Lamfelles		valor xv s.
CCCCCC xl shorlynges		valor iiij li. xv s.
CC^{m} pellibus lanutis		custuma v s. vij d.
	subsidium xxix s. x d.	
Willelmus Swan pro MCv^{xx} shorlynges		valor viij li.xvij s.vj d.
CCC^{m} pellibus lanutis		
	iij seccis lane	xxviij s iiij d.
	subsidium vij li. iiij s. ix d.	
Johannes Bullok pro vj C lvj shorlynges		valor iiij li. xvij s.
C^{m}lx pellibus lanutis		
	iij quarteriis secci lane	custuma ix s. vj d.
	subsidium xlvij s iij d.	
Thomas Davell pro vj Clx shorlynges		valor iiij li. ijs. vj d.
C^{m}lxxx pellibus lanutis		
	iij quarteriis secci lane	custuma x s.
	subsidium l s.	

Robertus Felton pro C lamfelles	valor x s.
vj Cxl shorlynges	valor iiij li. xv s.
CC pellibus lanutis	
j secco j quarterio iij	
clavis lane	custuma xiiij s. iij d.ob.
subsidium iij li. xiij s. iij d.	

[*Membrane 5 dorse*]

Willelmus Hunter pro CCC lxxxx shorlynges	valor lv s.
$C^{m}l$ pellibus lanutis	custuma iiij s. j d.ob.
subsidium xxj s x d.ob.	
Willelmus Conyngham pro xix C lamfelles	valor ix li. xs.
CCCCCC shorlynges	valor iiij li. x s.
$CC^{m}xl$ pellibus lanutis	custuma vs. viij d.
subsidium xxxv s. iiij d.ob.qu.	
Johannes Baxter pro iij quarteriis iij clavis lane	custuma vs. iiij d.ob.
subsidium xvj s. xj d.	
Archebald Stokall pro CCC lamfell	valor xxx s.
Cx shorlynges	valor xvj s. vj d.
iiij dacris di' coriorum boum hirtes	custuma xxx s.
Willelmus Scott pro iij quarteriis lane	custuma v s.
subsidium xxv s.	
Cristofer Burell pro lx shorlynges	valor vij s. viij d.
dimidio secco lane	custuma iij s. iiij d.
subsidium xvj s. viij d.	
Thomas Kirklay pro dimidio secco lane	custuma iij s. iiij d.
subsidium xvj s. viij d.	
Thomas Herryson pro j quarterio secco lane	custuma xx d.
subsidium viij s. iiij d.	
Edmonde Benley pro CCCC lxxx shorlynges	valor iij li. x s.
$C^{m}xx^{ti}$ pellibus lanutis	
dimidio secco lane	custuma vjs. viij d.
subsidium xxxiij s. viij d. qu.	
George Bird pro j quarterio viij clavis lane	custuma ijs. viij d.ob.
subsidium xiij s. v d.ob.	
Willelmus Davell pro dimidio secco lane	custuma iij s. iiij d.
subsidium xvj s. viij d.	
Willelmus Carr pro dimidio secco lane	custuma iij s. iiij d.
subsidium xvj s. viij d.	
Willelmus Hudson pro lx lamfelles	valor vs.
CCCC shorlynges	valor iij li.
$C^{m}xx^{ti}$ pellibus lanutis	
j quarterio viij clavis	
lane	custuma v s. viij d.
Jacobus Buke pro iij quarteriis viij clavis lane	custuma vj s. qu.
subsidium xxx s. j d.ob.	
Robertus Cambie pro vj C lamfelles	valor iij li.
lxx pellibus lanutis	custuma xxiij d.ob.
subsidium ix s. vj d.ob.	

[*Membrane 6 face*]

Navis vocata Jakett de Conkett unde Johannes Johnson est magister (exivit) vj^{o} die Septembris

{alienigena}

Idem magister pro xx celdris carbonum		valor xxxiij s. iiij d.
Thomas Edward pro xxxiij dacris coriorum boum (tannatorum)		valor xxix li
	xlviij petris plumbi	valor xx s.
	j quarterio unius panni panni lane stricti	custuma iij d.ob.
	v^{xx} petris cebi	valor iij li. v s.
Edwarde Rowland pro lj petris cebi		valor xxx s.

Navis vocata Marken de Novo Castro super Tynam unde Nicholaus Bruke est magister exivit viij^{o} die Septembris

Idem magister pro xx celdris gyrndstones		valor vj li. xiijs. iiij d.
Willelmus Camby pro CCC xxx shorlynges		valor xlviij s. iiij d.
	C^{m} pellibus lanutis	
	j secco j quarterio lane	custuma xij s. vj d.
	subsidium iij li. ij s. vj d.	
Willemus Yotson pro CCC shorlynges		valor iij li.
	C^{m}xx pellibus lanutis	
	j secco iij quarteriis lane	
	iij plaustris plumbi	valor xiij li. vj s. viij d.
	subsidium iij li. xiiij s.	custuma xv s.
George Bird pro M lamfelles		valor v li.
	M lxxx shorlynges	valor viij li.
	CC xl pellibus lanutis	custuma vj s. viij d.
	j pannis panni lane stricti	custuma xiiij d.
Robertus Stokall pro M CCCC shorlynges		valor x li. x s.
	CCC lxx pellibus lanutis	custuma xiij s. iiij d.
	subsidium iij li. vjs. viij d.	
Georgius Stalper pro dimidio secco viij clavis lane		custuma iij s. iiij d.ob.
	subsidium xxj s.	
Thomas Swan pro ij seccis dimidio lane		custuma xvj s. viij d.
	subsidium iiij li. xj s. iiij d.	
Johannes Baxster pro j secco j quarterio lane		custuma viij s. iiij d.
	subsidium lj s. viij d.	
Johannes Hedlem pro C lx lamfelles		valor xv s.
	vij Clxxx shorlynges	valor vli. xv s.
	CCxl pellibus lanutis	custuma vjs viij d.
	subsidium xxxiij s. iiij d.	

[*Membrane 6 dorse*]

Edmond Benley pro vj C v^{xx} shorlynges		valor vli. ijs. vj d.
	C^{m} xx^{ti} pellibus lanutis	
	ij seccis lane	custuma xvj s. viij d.
	subsidium iiij li. iij s. iiij d. qu.	

Thomas Herryson pro ij seccis lane custuma xiij s. iiij d.
subsidium iij li. vj s. viij d.
Petrus Baxter pro CC lamfelles valor xx s.
CCC shorlynges valor xlv s.
ix dacris coriorum boum tannatorum valor viij li. vj s. viij d.
ij pannis panni lanei stricti custuma ij s. iiij d.
C^m^xx pellibus lanutis
dimidio secco lane custuma vj s. viij d.ob.
subsidium xxxiij s. iiij d.qu.
Thomas Davell pro ij seccis lane custuma xiij s. iiij d.
subsidium xxxiij s. iiij d. qu.
Thomas Kerklay pro CCC lambfelles valor xxx s.
Cv^xx^x shorlynges valor xxviij s. ix d.
lx pellibus lanutis
j sacco iij quarteriis
lane custuma xiij s. iiij d.
subsidium iij li. vj s. viij d.
Willelmus Conyngham pro j secco j quarterio viij clavis lane
custuma ix s. iiij d.qu.
subsidium xlvj s. ix d. ob
Willelmus Scott pro ij seccis j quarterio viij clavis lane
custuma xvj s. qu.
subsidium iiij li. j d. ob
Johannes Buck pro j quarterio sacco viij clavis lane custuma ij s. viij d.qu.
ij pannis panni lanni stricti valor ij s. iiij d.
subsidium xiij s. j d. ob
Willelmus Davell pro CC lamfelles valor xx s.
C lxx shorlynges valor xxiiij s. iiij d.
l pellibus lanutis custuma xvij d.ob.
subsidium vj s. viij d.
Johannes Rede pro CC lamfelles valor xx s.
CC xl shorlynges valor xxxv s.
ij dacris coriorum tannatorum valor xx s.
lxxx pellibus lanutis custuma ij s. iij d.
subsidium xj s. j d.ob.
Robertus Felton pro j quarterio lane custuma xx d.
subsidium viij s. iiij d.
Willelmus Carr pro j quarterio viij clavis lane custuma ij s. viij d.qu.
subsidium xiij s. v d.ob.
Robertus Chambre pro C shorlynges valor xv s.
j quarterio viij clavis lane custuma ij s. viij d.qu.
subsidium xiij s. v d. ob.
Johannes Andreson pro x dacris coriorum boum tannatorum valor vij li.
CC pellibus shorlynges valor xxx s.

[*Membrane 7 face*]

Navis vocata Mary de Wanflett unde Johannes Ranlett est magister exivit xxiiij die Septembris

Robertus Gyssels pro xxx celdris carbonum valor iij li.
j dacra boum coriorum tannatorum valor xiij s. iiij d.

Navis vocata James de Cromer unde Johannes Palmer est magister exivit xxviij die Septembris

Johannes Howes pro v dacris coriorum boum tannatorum valor iij li.
iij dacris steklether valor xxx s.
ij barellis cebi valor xxxiij s. iiij d.

Navis vocata Playtt de Dansk unde Martin Clayson est magister exivit xiiij die Octobris

{alienigena}

Idem magister pro lx celdris carbonum valor v li.
l petris plumbi valor xxv s.

Navis vocata Cristofre de Novo Castro super Tynam unde Willelmus Cok est magister exivit xiiij die Octobris

Idem magister pro xj C lamfelles valor v li. x s.
viij clavis lane custuma xij d. qu.
ij pannis panni lanei stricti custuma ij s. iiij d.
subsidium vs. j d.ob.

Robertus Stokall pro iij celdris carbonum valor iij s. iiij d.
viij celdris gyrndstones valor liij s. iiij d.
lxxx shorlinges valor x s.
xx pellibus lanutis
iij quarteriis viij clavis lane custuma vjs. vij d.ob.
iiij coriis hirtes custuma ij s. viij d.
subsidium xxxij s. x d.ob.qu.

Thomas Davell pro iij saccis j quarterio lane custuma xx s. xx d.
subsidium v li. viij s. iiij d.

Robertus Essyngton pro CCCC lx shorlynges valor iij li. vij s. vj d.
C^m^xx pellibus lanutis
dimidio secco lane custuma vj s. viij d.
subsidium xxxiiij s. iiij d. qu.

Thomas Kerklay pro CCC lamfelles valor xxx s.
j plaustro plumbi valor iij li. vj s. viij d.
j secco j quarterio lane custuma viij s. iiij d.
subsidium xlj s. viij d.

Thomas Herryson pro Clx shorlinges valor xxij s. vj d.
j secco dimidio viij clavis lane custuma xj s.
subsidium lv s. j d.ob.

Cristofer Burell pro j quarterio viij clavis lane custuma ijs viij d.qu.
subsidium xiij s. v d.ob.

[*Membrane 7 dorse*]

Willemus Scott pro dimidio secco vj clavis lane	costuma iiijs. iiij d.qu.
subsidium xxj s. ix d.ob.	
Robertus Taylor pro viij C shorlinges	valor vj li.
CC xl pellibus lanutis	valor vj s viij d.
subsidium xxxiij s. iiij d.ob.qu.	
Willelmus Yotson pro dimidio plaustro plumbi	valor xxxiij s. iiij d.
Robertus Brigham pro viij C lamfelles	valor iiij li.
j plaustro plumbi	valor iij li. vj s. viij d.
CCCC lx shorlynges	valor iij li. vij s. vj d.
Clxxx pellibus lanutis	
dimidio secco lane	custuma viij s. iiij d.
subsidium xlj s. viij d.	
Willelmus Hudson pro v^{xx} lamfelles	valor xxvij s. vd.
v^{xx} shorlynges	iij li xvij s. vj d.
j dacra coriorum tannatorum	x s.
Cxx pellibus lanutis	
viij clavis lane	custuma iiij s. iij d.ob.qu.
subsidium xxj s. viij d. qu.	
Willelmus Camby pro CCC lamfelles	valor xxx s.
CCC xx shorlynges	valor xlij s. vj d.
Cxx pellibus lanutis	
j quarterio lane	custuma iiij s. iiij d.ob.
C coriorum boum hirtes	custuma xiij s. iiij d.
subsidium xxvj s. qu.	
Johannes Newkett pro j plaustro plumbi	valor iij li. vj s. viij d.
Annies Turuk pro C lamfelles	valor x s.
CC xl shorlynges	valor xxxv s.
lx pellibus lanutis	custuma xx d.
subsidium viij s. iiij d.	
Robertus Harden junior pro M lamfelles	valor v li. s.
iij dacris coriorum tannatorum	xl s.
Robertus Harden senior pro lxxx lamfelles	valor vj s. viij d.
CC shorlynges	valor xxx s.
lx pellibus lanutis	valor xx d.
subsidium viij s. iiij d.	
Bartram Yonghusband pro iij hogeshedes cebi	valor vj li.
j secco dimidio lane	custuma x s.
subsidium l s.	
Robertus Felton pro CC lamfelles	valor xx s.
CCC lxx shorlynges	valor lv s.
C pellibus lanutis	
dimidio secco lane	custuma vj s. viij d.
subsidium xxxiij s. iiij d.	
Cristofer Brigham pro viij C lamfelles	valor iij li.
CCClxxx shorlynges	valor lvj s. iij d.
C pellibus lanutis	iiij s. j d.ob.
subsidium xxj s. x d. ob	

[*Membrane 8 face*]

Jacobus Buk pro iij quarteriis secci lane custuma v s.
subsidium xxv s.
George Bird pro vj C lx lamfelles valor iij li. v s.
dimidio secco viij clavis lane custuma iiij s. iiij d.qu.
subsidium xxj s. ix d. ob
Thomas Atkynson pro viij clavis lane custuma xijd. qu.
subsidium v s. j d. ob
Thomas Cramlyngton pro Cv^{xx} shorlynges valor xxvij s. vj d.
lx lamfelles valor v s.
xv pellibus lanutis
dimidio secco lane custuma iijs. ix d.
subsidium xviij s. ixd.
Thomas Watson pro viij clavis lane custuma xij d qu.
Essabell Benley pro C xl shorlynges valor xx s.
C pellibus agnetorum valor x s.
viij dacris coriorum tannatorum valor v li. vj s. viij d.
xx pellibus lanutis custuma vij d.
subsidium ij s. ix d.qu.
Willelmus Davell pro dimidio secco lane custuma iij s. iiij d.
subsidium xvj s. viij d.
Johannes Hedlem pro dimidio secco viij clavis lane custuma iiij s. iiij d.qu.
subsidium xxj s. ix d.ob.
Johannes Bullok pro lxvj shorlynges valor vij s. vj d.
j pannis panni lanei stricti custuma xiiij d.
ij dacris iiij coriis boum hirtes custuma xvj s.
xv pellibus lanutis custuma v d.
subsidium ij s j d.
Johannes Andreson pro ij pipis cum iiij dacris coriorum tannatorum valor xl s.
iiij dacris coriorum (boum) hirtes custuma [*blank*]

Navis vocata Thomas de Novo Castro super Tynam unde Petrus Blak est magister exivit xxiiij die Octobris
Johannes Lynlay pro xiij celdris gyrndstones valor iiij li. vjs viij d.
xx celdris carbonum valor xxxiij s. iiij d.

Navis vocata Fle de Brell unde Cornellis Jacobson est magister applicuit primo die Decembris
Idem magister pro xij M wanscottes valor xxxvj s. vj d.
v last barell hedes valor xvj s. vj d.
xx warpp ollis terrenis valor xx d.
iij dossyn manddes valor ij s. vj d.
viij lerge mandes valor ij s. vj d.
vj mandes valor xx d.
ij dossyn mandes valor xx d.
v dossyn mattis valor v s.

iij ferdkin ellis valor x s.
xxij stollis valor iij s. iiij d.
j pice panni linii valor xx s.
dimidio barello aliciis valor v s.
iij toppes rassynges valor iij s. iiij d.
j fether bede valor v s.

[*Membrane 8 dorse*]
Navis vocata Peter de Hamsterdam unde Peter Person est magister applicuit die Deccembriis
{alienigena}
Idem magister pro diversis mercimoniis valor xij li.

Navis vocata Mary Benley de Novo Castro super Tynam unde Nicholaus Archer est magister exivit xv die Decembris
Edmund Benley pro x celdris carbonum valor x s.
xxx gyrndstones valor xxvj s. viij d.
iij dossenis rubstones valor ij s. vj d.
xij dacris coriorum tannatorum valor iiij li.
vjC lamfelles valor iij li.
CCC shorlinges valor xxx s.
lx pellibus lanutis custuma xx d.
subsidium viij s. iiij d.
Archebald Stokall pro j dacra dimidio coriorum tannatorum valor x s.
Robertus Brandlyng pro C shorlynges valor xv s.
xx pellibus lanutis custuma vij d.
subsidium ij s. ix d. qu.
Cristoffer Brigham pro ij pannis panni lanei stricti custuma ij s. iiij d.
Bartraham Yonghusband pro vj barellis cebi valor iij li.
Johannes Andreson pro j dacra coriorum boum tannatorum valor xvj s.
Esabell Benley pro vij coriis boum hirtes custuma iiij s. viij d.

Navis vocata Welcum to Husse unde Cornellis Tabertson est magister exivit xix die Decembriis
{alienigena}
Idem magister pro xviij celdris carbonum valor xxx s.

Navis vocata Alvoyn de Garaunt unde Johannes Land est magister exivit xix die Decembriis
{alienigena}
Idem magister pro lx celdris carbonum valor v li.
Thomas Edward pro M lamfelles valor xxvj s. viij d.
v coriis boum hirtes custuma iij s iiij d.

Hos octo rotulos contrarotulamenti liberavit hic predictus Georgius Bere contrarotulator per manus proprias sexto die Februarii anno xxij regis Edwardi iiij^{ti} et prestitit sacramentum etcetera.

9. Particulars of account of William Bumpsted and Robert Tempest, collectors, from 28 October 1488 to Michaelmas 1489.

E 122/108/2

The eight membranes are each 235 mm. wide. The first three are each 584 mm. in length, the last five each 559 mm. The account is in a generally good state of preservation, and material to fill gaps caused by holes has been supplied from the corresponding controller's account, E122/108/1 and E122/108/3; words taken from this source are shown in roman type in square brackets. The collectors' and controller's accounts have been collated. There are of course many differences of spelling, but very few discrepancies of fact.

Bumpsted and Tempest did not present a strictly chronological record like those in the previous accounts, but analysed their information to show petty custom and tunnage and poundage first. The wool custom and subsidy then begins on the dorse of membrane 3. At this time the merchant gild were enjoying a grant of exemption from all taxes on wool exports, and were careful to endorse their accounts accordingly. Their statement of exemption is on membrane 3 dorse. Subsequent membranes all contain *adhuc marcatores Gilde predicte* in the left margin, and *de crescencia predicta* at the right; these repeated marginal notes are not reproduced below. Whether merchants were denizen or alien was here indicated in the body of the account, rather than in the margins, and all but one of the other marginal notes are self-explanatory directions to make checking of the account totals easier. The exception consists of a character like the round form of *s*, followed by *ij da' v'*. found beside the entries for the *Mary Harden* on 24 May and the *Markyne* on 30 May; both these ships were importing wine, and a conjectural extension might be *duo dolia vini*. This, if correct, might refer to the royal prise of wine, whereby the deputy to the king's butler might purchase two tuns from each cargo of twenty tuns or more.

Because Hansards resisted paying the subsidy of tunnage and poundage, the collectors valued the pipe of wine exported on 22 January in the same way as four ames of Rhenish wine imported previously, and charged the alien custom of iijd. in the pound. The Hansards' exemption from subsidy was being called in question when this account was compiled, and the matter arose again on 31 May. Under *valor Hanse* in the final summary is entered *subsidium per processum.*

The account is printed in its form after original corrections had been made. Most of these corrections were due to the attempt to show not only that no custom or subsidy on wool was paid, but also to show what might have been paid in the absence of the grant of exemption. On wool and woolfells, the custom and subsidy due appears only in the final *Summa* where the words *nihil* were originally written. On *shorlynges, morlynges, et lambfelles* the value and the amount of poundage due from each merchant was recorded, but later expunged from the summaries in the body of the account and the words *nihil causa qua supra* inserted. The final *Summa* goes on to state the wool custom and subsidy due on these skins if they had been assessed as woolfells. This highlights the value to Newcastle merchants of the concession whereby shorlings and morlings and lambskins were subject normally to poundage. The poundage due without the grant of exemption was £11. 2s. 5d. The same fleeces considered to be wool fells attracted taxes totalling £306. 18s. 7½d.

The final Summary also contains the only instance noted in these accounts of a substantial error. The *summa totalis omnis* was shown first as £1443 6s. 1¼d., due to an error in addition earlier. There is a marginal note 'over £400 missing' and the corrected total of £1843 6s. 1¾d. was inserted.

[*Membrane 1 face*]

{Newcastell}

Particuli compoti Willelmi Bumpsted et Roberti Tempest, collectorum custumarum et subsidiorum domini regis, in portu ville de Newcastall et in singulis portubus et locis eidem portui adiacentibus, videlicet a xxviij^vo^ die Octobris anno quarto domini regis nunc Henricii vij usque festum Sancti Michaelis tunc proximo sequens.

Navis vocata le Mary Aleyn de Novo Castro unde Thomas Wode est magister applicuit ultimo die Octobris.

Willelmus Aleyn indigena pro iiij^xx^xvij quarteriis frumenti	valor xvj li. xiij s. iiij d.
Idem pro xij quarteriis frumenti	valor xl s.
Summa valoris xviij li. xiij s. iiij d.	subsidium xviij s. viij d.

Batella vocata le Margarete de Novo Castro unde Willelmus Pierson est magister exivit iij^o^ die Novembris.

Willelmus Aleyn indigena pro iij celdris carbonum	valor iij s. iiij d.

Idem pro xxx peciis plumbi continentibus v plaistra	valor xvj li. xiij s. iiij d.
Summa valoris xvj li. xvj s. viij d.	subsidium xvj s. x d.

Navis vocata le Antone unde Johannes Totil est magister exivit xvj^mo^ die Decembris.

Willelmus Aleyn indigena pro xl[1] celdris carbonum	valor xl s.
Idem pro x celdris petrarum	valor lxvj s. viij d.
Idem pro iiij dekers corriorum tannatorum	valor lx s.
Idem pro ij barellis cepi	valor xx s.
Idem pro xvj petris plumbi	valor v s.
Summa valoris ix li. xj s. viij d.	subsidium ix s. vij d.

Navis vocata le Anne de Versill in Hansa[2] unde Warner Brownson est magister applicuit xxij die Januarii

Petrus Brownsce de Hansa pro xv lastes dimidio seneris	valor xv li. x s.
Idem pro iij lastes bituminis	valor vj li.
Idem pro C waynscottes	valor xxvj s. viij d.
Idem pro C quarteriis bay salt	valor viij li. x s.
Idem pro ij last et iiij barellis litmose	valor viij li.
Idem pro iiij ame runysh wynne[3]	valor iiij li.
Idem pro CCC libris oyne sede	valor vj li.
Idem pro ij sackes di' litmose	valor vj li.
Idem pro j sacke hoppis le poise CCC libras	valor iiij li.
Idem pro xxv peciis resyns	valor lx s.
Idem pro MMM[4] garleke	valor iiij li.
Idem pro xviij barellis oynonce	valor xl s.
Idem pro iiij C clapholt	valor xx s.
Idem pro ij balis mader le poise xjC	valor xj li.
Idem pro ij boxis cum harpe stringes	valor xl s.
Summa valoris iiij^xx^ij li. vj s. viij d.	custuma xx s. vij d.

Batella vocata le Thomas de Kyncorn unde Davit Haberneth est magister applicuit xij^mo^ die Marcii.

Archebald Revers alienigena pro iiij lastes oysters	valor xxvj s. viij d.
Idem pro ix barellis allecis albi	valor lx s.
Idem pro xlviij elles panni linei	valor xiij s.iiij d.
Idem pro ij dussenis pursis ij groce poyntes ij dussenis glovis et v bokelers	valor vj s.viij d.
Summa Cvj s.viij d. custuma xvj d.	subsidium v s.iiij d.

1. *xlij* in 108/1.
2. *Wysyll in Almayn* in 108/1.
3. Above *Runysh wynn* is a cross, with another cross in the left margin, signalling the Hansards resistance to paying the subsidy, see head-note to this account.
4. The third *M* is interlined. *MM* in 108/1.

Navis vocata le Petyr de Novo Castro unde Thomas Stodard est magister applicuit xiiij° die Marcii
Willelmus Aleyn indigena pro iiij[5] last oysters   valor xiij s. iiij d.
Idem pro iiij barellis dimidio smigmatis   valor lx s.
Summa lxxiij s. iiij d.   subsidium iij s. viij d.

Batella vocata le Thomas de Kyncorn unde Davit Haberneth est magister exivit xxiiij die Marcii
Idem magister alienigena pro vij celdris carbonum   valor xj s. viij d.
Idem pro iij duodenis panni lanei stricti (sine grano)   valor xiij s. iiij d.
custuma ij s. ob.q.
Idem pro vj barellis bere   valor xiij s. iiij d.
Idem pro iij coverlites   valor viij s. iiij d.
Idem pro dimidio corrii tannati   valor xx d.
Summa valoris xlviij s. iiij d.
custuma vij d. qu.
subsidium ij s. v d.
panni iij duodene custuma ij s. ob.qu

Summa partis, videlicet

Valor marcandise unde iijd de libra.
vij li. xv s.
custuma xxiij d.qu.
Panni sine grano alienigene
iij duodene panni stricti
custuma ij s. ob.qu.
Valor unde xij d. de libra
lvj li. x s.
custuma lvj s. vj d.
Valor marcandise Hanse
iiij^{xx}ij li. vj s. viij d.
custuma xx s. vij d.
} iiij li. xiij d.

[*Membrane 1 dorse*]
Navis vocata le Anne de Vresill unde Warner Brownson est magister exivit xxvj^{to} die Marcii
Petrus Brownss de Hansa pro xlij celdris carbonum   valor lxxiij s. iij d.
Idem pro xxx stones talow   valor xxx s.
Idem pro j barello cum candelis   valor xiij s. iiij d.

5. *Tribus* in 108/1.

Idem pro viij barellis talow valor C s.
Idem pro viij stones plumbi valor iij s. iiij d.
Idem pro iiij mantilles valor xiij s. iiii d.
Idem pro ij peciis worsted simplex custuma iij d.
Idem pro iiij pannis laneis sine grano[6] custuma iiij s.
Summa valoris xj li. xiij s. iiij d. custuma ij s. xj d.
Worsted simplex ij pecie custuma iij d.
Panni sine grano iiij panni custuma iiij s.

Navis vocata le Katerine de Campe in Hansa unde Fulkard Jacobson est magister applicuit xxvij° die Marcii
Idem magister de Hansa pro xiiij last seneris valor xiiij li.
Idem pro vij last di' bituminis valor xv li.
Idem pro j poke hopis cont' CCC valor lx s.
Idem pro iij barellis smigmatis valor liij s. iiij d.
Idem pro iij pannis lineis continentibus lxxiiij[7] ulnas valor l s.
Idem pro xxx endes[8] ferri cont' vjC valor xx s.
Idem pro vjC ollis terrenis valor xxx s.
Idem pro xijC clapholt valor xl s.
Summa xlj li. xiij s. iiij d. custuma x s. v d.

Navis vocata le Jesus de Caleyn unde Willelmus King est magister exivit xxviij die Marcii
Thomas Kempe indigena pro xl celdris carbonum valor lxvj s. viij d.
subsidium iij s. iiij d.

Navis vocata le Katerine de Yermouth unde Willelmus Coke est magister exivit eodem die
Johannes Frenshe indigena pro xxxviij celdris carbonum valor lxiij s. iiij d.
subsidium iij s. ij d.

Navis vocata le Cristofer de Middilbough unde Lawrencius Johnson est magister applicuit viij[vo] die Aprilis
Idem magister alienigena pro l quarteriis salis grocii valor vj li. xiij. iiijd
Idem pro j last seneris valor xx s.
Idem pro x barellis bituminis valor xxvj s. viij d.
Idem pro ij barellis smigmatis valor xxxiij s. iiij d.

---

6. 108/3 adds *largis et strictis*, indicating that the collectors here followed a common practice of aggregating assorted cloths to express their quantity in the fiscal unit of the cloth of assize.
7. *lxxv* in 108/3.
8. *xxiv peciis ferri* in 108/3.

Idem pro iij last hering barelles[9] valor x s..
Summa xj li. iij s. iiij d.
custuma ij s. ix d. ob
subsidium xj s. ij d.

Navis vocata le Cristofer de Hampsterdham unde Johannes Artsom est magister applicuit xv° die Aprilis

Idem magister alienigena pro vC waynscotes	valor vj li. xiij s. iiij d.
Idem pro xxxij last seneris	valor xx li.
Idem pro iij last bituminis	valor iiij li.
Idem pro iij M clapholt	valor lx s.
Idem pro CCCC bowstavis	valor iiij li.
Idem pro Ciiij orys	valor lx s.
Idem pro C smale bumkyns	valor xx s.
Idem pro vj barellis trane	valor iiij li.
Idem pro viij milstons parv'	valor xiij s. iiij d.

Summa xlvj li. vj s. viij d.
custuma xj s. vij d.
subsidium xlvj s. iiij d.

Navis vocata le Cristofer de Hamsterdham unde Petrus Claison est magister applicuit eodem die
Idem magister alienigena pro vj peciis linei continentibus Clx ulnas valor iiij li.
custuma xij d. subsidium iiij s.

Navis vocata le Cristofer de Dansk in Hansa unde Lutekyn Couste est magister applicuit xxij[do] die Aprilis.

Simon Skould de Hansa pro x last iiij barellis bituminis Idem pro dimidio last picis	valor xvj li. xiij s. iiij d.
Idem pro ixC waynscotes	valor xv li.
Idem pro iijM clapholt	valor lx s.
Idem pro iij last di' seneris	valor lx s.
Idem pro iiij nest counters	valor iiij li.

Summa xlj li. xiij s. iiij d.
custuma x s. v d.

Summa partis videlicet

9. *iij last emptie barelles* in 108/3.

Valor unde iijd etc.
lxj li. x s.
custuma xv s. iiij d.ob.
[*Membrane 2 face*]
Valor unde xij d. etc.
lxviij li.
subsidium lxviij s.
Wursted simpl' Hanse
ij pecie
custuma iij d.
Panni sine grano Hanse
iiij panni
custuma iiij s.
Valor marcandise Hanse
iiij^{xx}xv li.
custuma xxiij s. ix d.

} Cxj s. iiij d.ob.

Navis vocata le Cristofer de Middilbught unde Lawrencius Johnson est magister exivit eodem die
Idem magister alienigena pro xxix celdris carbonum — valor xlviij s. iiij d.
Idem pro ij duodenis panni lanei stricti sine grano — valor x s.
custuma xvj d.ob.
Summa lviij s. iiij d. custuma vij d. qu.
subsidium ij s. xj d.

Navis vocata le Katryne de Campe in Hansa unde Fulkard Jacobson est magister exivit xxiij^{cio} die Aprilis
Idem magister de Hansa pro iiij^{xx} xiiij celdris carbonum — valor vij li. xvj s. viij d.
Idem pro vjC libris plumbi — valor xxvj s. viij d.
Idem pro xij duodenis et dimidia panni lanei stricti sine grano
custuma iij s. j d.ob.
Idem pro x virgis panni lanei largi sine grano
custuma v d.
Summa ix li. iij s. iiij d.
custuma[10] ij s. iij d.ob.

Navis vocata le Brodhenric de Dansk in Hansa unde Thomas Yotkyn est magister applicuit vj^{to} die Maii
Idem magister de Hansa pro CC waynscottes — valor liij s. iiij d.
Idem pro j counter — valor vj s. viij d.
Idem pro ij last seneris — valor xl s.
Idem pro iij cofers cum v skok trenchers — valor vj s. viij d.
Idem pro x barellis bituminis — valor xxvj s. viij d.

10. Followed by *xviij d.ob.*, struck out.

Idem pro j coffer cum iiij bundellis lini valor vj s. viij d.
Summa vij li. xxj d.
Hans Lawrence de Hansa pro viij lastes et xlv bundellis lini valor xlviij li.
Idem pro iiij lastes ix barellis bituminis et xxj barellis picis valor viij li.
Idem pro viij lastes ix barellis seneris[11] valor viij li.
Idem pro viij nest counters valor viij li.
pro j pecia lawen continente lv ulnas valor xiij s. iiij d.
Idem pro j barello cum glasses et lxxv treyes valor xiij s. iiij d.
Idem pro vC waynscottes valor vj li.
Idem pro iiij M Clapholt valor iiij li.
Summa iiij^{xx}iij li. vj s. viij d. custuma xx s. x d.

Navis vocata le Cristofer de Dansk in Hansa unde Lutekyn Cowse est magister exivit viij^{vo} die Maii
Simon Skould de Hansa pro x celdris carbonum valor xvj s. viij d.
Idem pro ij celdris gryndstonis valor xx s.
Idem pro xiij peciis plumbi continentibus ij foderas[12] iij quarteria valor xj li. xvj s. viij d.
Idem pro xx duodenis rubstonis valor xx s.
Idem pro j panno[13] sine grano custuma xij d.
Summa xiiij li. xiij s. iiij d.
custuma iij s. viij d.

Navis vocata le Anne de Dansk in Hansa unde Thomas Kempe est magister applicuit ix^{no} die Marcii
Idem magister de Hansa pro iiij last viij barellis picis et vj lastes ix barellis bituminis valor xvij li.
Idem pro CCxxx orys valor lxvj s. viij d.
Idem pro CC waynscottes valor liij s. iiij d.
Idem pro iiij scok wynnow valor xxvj s. viij d.
Idem pro iiij^{xx}xvj fir delys valor xl s.
Idem pro iijMvjC clapholt valor lx s.
Idem pro viijCxvj bowstavis valor x li.
Idem pro xxx peciis bast ropis valor vj s. viij d.
Idem pro xx bundellis lini valor xx s.
Idem pro ij nest counters valor xl s.
Idem pro xiiij barellis litmose valor lx s.

11. *smigmatis* in 108/3. The collectors' entry of *seneris* is more likely to be correct because the shipment is by a Hansard merchant: Hansards regularly imported wood-ash.
12. *ij plaustra* in 108/3.
13. *xxiiij virgis panni lanei largi* in 108/3. These are the standard dimensions of one cloth of assize.

Idem pro xxx ollis line
ix scok trenchoures
v paires tablis[14]
xxx peperquernis
v grates valor xxvj s. viij d.
Summa xlvij li. custuma xj s. ix d.
Hans Leevyn de Hansa pro xj last viij barellis bituminis
vj barellis picis valor xvj li.
Idem pro iiij barellis osmondes valor xxvj s. viij d.
Idem pro ij last lini valor xij li.
Summa xxix li. vj s. viij d. custuma vij s. iiij d.

Summa partis videlicet

Pannis sine grano Hanse
iiij panni dimidius j virga
custuma iiij s. vj d.ob.
Valor Hanse
Ciiij^{xx}x li. x s.
custuma xlvij s. vij d.ob.
Valor unde iijd etc.
xlviij s. iiij d.
custuma vij d. qu. } lvij s. ob.qu.
Panni sine grano alienigene
ij duodene stricte
custuma xvj d.ob.
Valor unde xij d. etc.
lviij s. iiij d.
subsidium ij s. xj d.

[*Membrane 2 dorse*]
Navis vocata le Cristofer de Hamsterdham unde Johannes Artson est magister exivit xiij° die Maii
Idem magister alienigena pro lxvj celdris carbonum valor Cvj s. viij d.
Idem pro viij duodenis panni stricti sine grano valor xl s.
custuma v s. vj d. subsidium ij s.
Summa Cvj s. viij d. custuma xvj d. subsidium v s. iiij d.

Navis vocata le Anne de Dansk unde Thomas Kempe est magister exivit xxij^{do} die Maii
Idem magister de Hanse pro x celdris carbonum valor xvj s. viij d.
Idem pro xx duodenis rubstonis valor xx s.
Idem pro xxviij peciis plumbi continentibus vij foderas valor [xxij li. x s.]

14. 108/3 omits *xxx peperquernis* and *v grates.*

Idem pro xviij virgis panni lanei sine grano
custuma ix d.
Summa xxxiij li. vj s. viij d. custuma viij s. iiij d.
Simon Skould de Hansa pro ix peciis plumbi continentibus iij foderas
valor xiij li. xiij s. iiij d. custuma iij s. v d.

Navis vocata le Cristofer de Hamsterdham unde Petrus Claison est magister exivit eodem die
Idem magister alienigena pro ij duodenis panni lanei stricti sine grano valor x s.
Custuma xvj d.ob. subsidium vj d.
Thomas Lokwod indigena pro v^xx celdris carbonum valor C s.
subsidium v s.

Navis vocata le Mary Harden unde Johannes Mortymer est magister applicuit xxiiij^to die Maii
Robertus Harden indigena pro j dolio vini
subsidium iij s.
Idem pro viij balettes wode cont' viij mesuras valor liij s. iiij d.
subsidium ij s. viij d.
Willelmus Heth indigena pro viij doliis vini
subsidium xxiiij s.
Idem pro x peciis rosyn continentibus j carte valor xiij s. iiij d.
Idem pro iiij balettes wode cont' iiij mesuras valor xxvj s. viij d.
Idem pro x^xx xv finis ferri continentibus ij dolia dimidium valor vj li. xiij s. iiij d.
Summa viij li. xiij s. iiij d. subsidium viij s. viij d.
Thomas Ilderton indigena pro xiij doliis vini subsidium xxix s.
Bartram Yonghusband indigena pro v doliis vini subsidium xv s.
Idem pro ij pipis wode valor iiij li. x s.
Idem pro x peciis rosyn[15] valor x s.
summa c s.
subsidium v s.
Thomas Andrwson indigena pro iiij doliis vini
subsidium xij s.
Alicia Harden indigena pro iiij doliis vini
subsidium xij s.
Cristoferus Bringham indigena pro v doliis j (hogeshede) vini
subsidium xv s. ix d.
Willelmus Selbi indigena pro iij doliis vini
subsidium ix s.
Ricardus Hebborn indigena pro iij pipis vini
subsidium iiij s. vj d.
Willelmus Davell indigena pro iiij doliis vini
subsidium xij s.

15. 108/3 adds *continentibus j carte.*

Thomas Haden indigena pro ij doliis vini
subsidium vj s.
Walterus Frodyngham indigena pro j dolio pipa hogeshede vini
subsidium v s. iij d.
Willelmus Harden indigena pro ij doliis pipa hogeshede vini
subsidium viij s. iij d.
Cristoferus Borell indigena pro j hogeshede
subsidium ix d.
Willelmus Chevernus indigenapro j pipa vini
subsidium xviij d.
Willellmus Carver indigena pro j hogeshede vini
subsidium ix d.

Navis vocata le Markyne unde Willelmus Marbotel est magister applicuit xxx die Maii
Robertus Saunderson indigena pro v doliis vini
subsidium xv s.
Idem magister indigena pro ij doliis vini[16]
subsidium vj s.
Cristoferus Brigham indigena pro x doliis vini
subsidium[17] xxx s.
Idem pro iiij^{xx}x finis ferri continentibus j dolium[18] valor liij s. iiij d.
subsidium ij s. viij d.
Idem pro j cart rosyn valor xiij s. iiij d.
subsidium viij d.
Willelmus Davell indigena pro vj doliis pipa
subsidium xix s. vj d.
Bartram Yonghusband indigena pro vj doliis pipa vini
subsidium xix s. vj d.
Georgius Selby indigena pro iij doliis vini
subsidium ix s.
Robertus Hely indigena pro iij doliis vini
subsidium ix s.
Georgius Eryngton indigena pro j dolio vini
subsidium iij s.
Georgius Bird indigena pro xvj doliis vini
subsidium xlviij s.

Summa partis videlicet

16. 108/3 adds *rubei de gaskonia*.
17. Followed by *xs*, struck out.
18. *j carte* in 108/3.

Valor unde iij d. de libra
cvj s. viij d.
custuma xvj d.
Panni sine grano alienigene
ij panni dimidio
custuma vj s. x d.ob.
Valor unde xij d. etc.
xxxij li. x s.
subsidium xxxij s. vj d.
Vinum indigenarum
Cix doliis j hogeshed
subsidium xvj li. vij s. ix d.
Valor Hanse
xlvij li.
custuma xj s. ix d.
Pannis sine grano
xviij virge
custuma ix d.

} xix li. xj d.ob.

[*Membrane 3 face*]
Johannes Blakston indigena pro iij doliis vini
subsidium ix s.
Ricardus Hebborn indigena pro v doliis vini
subsidium xv s.
Johannes Paschley indigena pro j dolio vini
subsidium iij s.
Johannes Eltham indigena pro ij doliis j hogeshede vini
subsidium vj s. ix d.
Thomas Harop indigena pro iij doliis vini
subsidium ix s.
Robertus Brigham indigena pro iiij doliis pipa hogeshede vini
subsidium xiij s. iij d.
Georgius Carr indigena pro vij doliis vini
subsidium xxj s.
Willelmus Velxdale indigena pro ij doliis vini
subsidium vj s.
Willelmus Tomson indigena pro iiij doliis vini
subsidium xij s.
Thomas Ilderton indigena pro ij doliis vini
subsidium vj s.
Johannes Hedle indigena pro j pipa vini
subsidium xviij d.
Edwardus Lilborn indigena pro j pipa vini
subsidium xviij d.
Cristoforus Borell indigena pro vij doliis j hogeshede vini
subsidium xxj s. ix d.
Willelmus Hanyng indigena pro viij doliis j pipa
subsidium xxv s. vj d.

Willelmus Camby indigena pro xv doliis vini
subsidium xlv s.
Georgius Stalper indigena pro vij doliis vini
subsidium xxj s.
Edmondus Gerveys indigena pro ij doliis vini
subsidium vj s.
Henricus Bidnell indigena pro ij doliis vini
subsidium vj s.
Cristoferus Davell indigena pro ij doliis vini
subsidium vj s.
Thomas Lokwod indigena pro ij doliis j hogeshede vini
subsidium vj s. ix d.
Johannes Harle indigena pro ij doliis vini
subsidium vj s.
Rogerus Raw indigena pro j dolio j hogeshede vini
subsidium iij s. ix d.
Jacobus Blak indigena pro j pipa vini
subsidium xviij d.
Willelmus Hurlbat indigena pro j pipa vini
subsidium xviij d.

Navis vocata le Brodhenrik de Dansk unde Thomas Yetkyn est magister exivit ultimo die Maii
Idem magister de Hansa pro xx celdris [carbonum] valor xxxiij s. iiij d.
Idem pro xij duodenis rubstonis valor x s.
Idem pro xxj peciis plumbi ponderantibus iij foderas valor xiij li. vj s. viij d.
Idem pro xvj virgis panni stricti sine grano facientibus iiij virgas panni assise
custuma ij d.
{vinum Hanse}
Idem pro j pipa vini
custuma xijd pro alienigena custuma ut supra pro dicta custuma valev' iiij li. et sic oneratur etc postea.[19]
Summa xv li. x s. custuma iij s. x d.ob.
Hans Lawrence de Hansa pro x peciis plumbi ponderantibus ij plaistra valor viij li. xiij s. iiij d.
custuma ij s. ij d.
Cristoferus Bier de Hansa pro xvij peciis plumbi ponderantibus iij plaistra valor xiij li.
custuma iij s. iij d.

19. This explanation by the collectors concerns the Hansards' exemption from subsidy and refers to the precedent established earlier, and signalled by the marking of an entry on 22 January, see note 3 above, and also head-note to this account.

Hans Leven de Hansa pro xxvj peciis plumbi ponderantibus j plaistrum valor iiij li. xiij s. iiij d.
custuma xiiij d.

Navis vocata le Anne de Versill unde Warner Brounson est magister applicuit xvij° die Junii

Idem magister de Hansa pro [xiiij^{C} brike] valor xxxiij s. iiij d.
Idem pro xijC clapholt valor xx s.
Idem pro CC ollis terrenis valor xiij s. iiij d.
Idem pro iiij shive tasilles valor iij s. iiij d.
Idem pro dimidio barello melle valor x s.
Idem pro ij balis mader pond' viij^{C} valor vj li.
Summa x li. custuma ij s. vj d.

Navis vocata le Anne de Versil unde Warner Brounson est magister exivit xiij° die Julii

Idem magister de Hansa pro xxx celdris carbonum valor l s.
custuma vij d.ob.

Summa huius partis videlicet

Vinum indigenarum
iiij^{xx} dolia j hogeshed
subsidium xij li. xv s. ix d.
Panni sine grano Hanse
custuma ij d.
Valor Hanse
lviij li. vj s. viij d.
xiiij s. vij d.

} xiij li. x s. vj d.

[*Membrane 3 dorse*]

Navis vocata le [Nicholaus de Novo Castro unde Nicholaus] Bentbowe est magister exivit xxij^{do} die [Aprilis anno regis Henriici vij quarto]

{Marcatores infrascripti sunt gubernatores et marcatores gilde marcatorie ville regis Novi Castri super Tynam.}

{De crescencia comitatuum Northumbrie, Cumbrie, Westmorlandie, et episcopatus Dunelmensis necnon comitatuum de Allerton et Rychemond}

Thomas Grene indigena pro ix saccis j quarterio viij clavis in iij sarpleris
Idem pro Dxl pellibus lanutis
Thomas Riddale indigena pro iiij saccis iij quarteriis vij clavis
Idem pro CCCxl pellibus lanutis
Edwardus Borell indigena pro DCCCClx pellibus lanutis
Willelmus Selby indigena pro Dxx pellibus lanutis
Rolandus Harrison indigena pro DClxxij pellibus lanutis
Johannes Bewick indigena pro CClx pellibus lanutis
Willelmus Hunter indigena pro dimidio sacco viij clavis in j poke

Idem pro Ciiij^{xx}xxij pellibus lanutis
Edwardus Lilborn indigena pro CCCC^{xx} pellibus lanutis
Christoferus Brigham indigena pro iiij saccis in j sarplera
Idem pro Dxx pellibus lanutis
Georgius Eryngton indigena pro CCCxiiij pellibus lanutis
Willelmus Scott indigena pro v saccis in j sarplera
Christoferus Borell indigena pro CCC pellibus lanutis
Georgius Selby indigena pro iiij saccis iij quarteriis in j sarplera
Idem pro Ciiij^{xx} pellibus lanutis
Henricus Bidnell indigena pro CCCxvij pellibus lanutis
Willelmus Yotson indigena pro CCClx pellibus lanutis
Robertus Hely indigena pro CCCCiiij^{xx} pellibus lanutis
Thomas Camby indigena pro iiij saccis j quarterio in j sarplera
Idem pro Ciiij^{xx} pellibus lanutis
Willelmus Wardell indigena pro CCCxx pellibus lanutis
Johannes Passhley indigena pro ij saccis iij quarteriis viij clavis in j sarplera
Idem pro iiij^{xx}xij pellibus lanutis
Ricardus Hebborn indigena pro Ciiij^{xx}viij pellibus lanutis
Georgius Conyngham indigena pro DC pellibus lanutis
Thomas Andresson indigena pro CCClx pellibus lanutis
Willelmus Swan indigena pro CCxl pellibus lanutis
Robertus Harden indigena pro iij saccis in j sarplera
Idem pro lij pellibus lanutis

Summa partis videlicet

Sacci lane xxxviij sacci iij quarteriis v clavi
custuma nihil subsidium nihil
Pelles lanute viijMDvij pelles facientes xxx saccos
j quarterium xlvij pelles
} gratis quia postea in pede

[*Membrane 4 face*]

Thomas Grene indigena pro xx celdris carbonum valor xx s.
subsidium xij d.
Idem pro CClx pellibus vocatis shorlynges et morlynges xxxvij s. vj d.
subsidium xxij d.ob.
Idem pro C pellibus angnetorum valor x s.
subsidium vj d.
Thomas Riddale indigena pro iiij^{xx} pellibus
shorlynges et morlynges valor x s.
subsidium vj d.
Idem pro CC pellibus angnetorum valor xx s.
subsidium xij d.
Edwardus Borell indigena pro iiijCxxx pellibus
shorlynges et morlynges valor lxv s.
subsidium iij s. iij d.

Idem pro CC pellibus angnetorum valor xx s.
subsidium xij d.

Willelmus Selby indigena pro iiij^{xx} pellibus
shorlynges et morlynges valor x s.
subsidium vj d.

Idem pro DCCC pellibus angnetorum valor iiij li.
subsidium iiij s.

Rouland Harryson indigena pro Cxxx pellibus
shorlynges et morlynges valor xviij s. iiij d.
subsidium xj d.

Willelmus Wardel indigena pro C pellibus
shorlynges et morlynges valor xv s.
subsidium ix d.

Idem pro D pellibus angnetorum valor l s.
subsidium ij s. vj d.

Johannes Bewik indigena pro CCCCxxx
pellibus shorlynges et morlynges valor lxiij s. iiij d.
subsidium iij s. ij d.

Willelmus Hunter indigena pro Clx pellibus
shorlynges et morlynges valor xxij s. vj d.
subsidium xiij d.ob.

Edwardus Lilborn indigena pro CC pellibus
shorlynges et morlynges valor xxx s.
subsidium xviij d.

Cristoferus Brigham indigena pro CCCv^{xx}
pellibus shorlynges et morlynges valor lx s.
subsidium iij s.

Georgius Eryngton indigena pro CCv^{xx}
pellibus shorlynges et morlynges valor xlij s. vj d.
subsidium ij s. j d.ob.

Idem pro CCxxx pellibus angnetorum valor xxij s. vj d.
subsidium xiij d.ob.

Cristoferus Borell indigena pro C pellibus
shorlynges et morlynges valor xv s.
subsidium ix d.

Idem pro CCxl pellibus angnetorum valor xxiiij s. iiij d.
subsidium xiiij d.

Georgius Selby indigena pro CClx pellibus
shorlynges et morlynges valor xxxvij s. vj d.
subsidium xxij d.ob.

Henricus Bidnel indigena pro CC pellibus
shorlynges et morlynges valor xxx s.
subsidium xviij d.

Willelmus Yotson indigena pro CClxxij
pellibus shorlynges et morlynges valor xl s.
subsidium ij s.

Robertus Hely indigena pro Cxx pellibus
shorlynges et morlynges valor xviij s. iiij d.
subsidium xj s.
Ricardus Hebborn indigena pro lx pellibus
shorlynges et morlynges valor vij s. vj d.
subsidium iiij d.ob.
Idem pro Clx pellibus angnetorum valor xv s.
subsidium ix d.
Thomas Andreson indigena pro CCiiij^{xx}
pellibus shorlynges et morlynges valor xxxvij s. vj d.
subsidium xxij d.ob.
Idem pro Cxxx pellibus angnetorum valor xij s. vj d.
subsidium vij d.ob.
Willelmus Swan indigena pro C pellibus
shorlynges et morlynges valor xv s.
subsidium ix d.
Thomas Lokwod indigena pro iiijMiiijC pellibus
angnetorum valor xxj li.
subsidium xxj s.
Johannes Passhley indigena pro Cxx pellibus
shorlynges et morlynges valor xvij s. vj d.
subsidium x d.ob.
Thomas Camby indigena pro CCC pellibus
shorlynges et morlynges valor xlv s.
subsidium ij s. iij d.
Idem pro lx pellibus angnetorum valor v s.
subsidium iij d.
Summa pellium vocatarum shorlynges et morlynges et lambfelles
xjMCCxxij pelles facientes lxv li. xv s. x d.
subsidium[20] gratis quia postea in pede

Navis vocata le Mary Huberd de Novo Castro super Tynam unde
Johannes Mortimer est magister exivit eodem die
Thomas Swan indigena pro x saccis dimidio ix clavis in iij sarpleris
Idem pro CCCC pellibus lanutis
Willelmus Selby indigena pro v saccis in ij sarpleris
Idem pro CCxl pellibus lanutis
Ricardus Hebborn indigena pro iiij saccis j quarterio in j sarplera
Idem pro CCClx pellibus lanutis
Willelmus Camby indigena pro iiij saccis j quarterio viij clavis
Idem pro DC pellibus lanutis
Robertus Stokall indigena pro iiij saccis dimidio viij clavis in iij sarpleris
Alicia Harden indigena pro ij saccis iij quarteriis in j sarplera
Idem pro CCC pellibus lanutis
[*Membrane 4 dorse*]
Robertus Baxster indigena pro Mxxx pellibus lanutis

---

20. Followed by *lxvs. ix d.ob.*, struck out.

Johannes Baxster indigena pro j sacco iij quarteriis in j poke
Idem pro DCxlij pellibus lanutis
Robertus Bryngham indigena pro ij saccis j quarterio iiij clavis in j sarplera
Idem pro DCxl pellibus lanutis
Henricus Bidnell indigena pro ij saccis in j sarplera
Idem pro D pellibus lanutis
Thomas Harrison indigena pro iij saccis dimidio viij clavis in j sarplera
Idem pro DC pellibus lanutis
Georgius Conyngham indigena pro ij saccis dimidio in j sarplera
Willelmus Davell indigena pro iiij saccis j quarterio in j sarplera
Willelmus Scott indigena pro iiij saccis j quarterio v clavis in j sarplera
Johannes Pashely indigena pro v saccis xij clavis in ij sarpleris
Idem pro CCCCiiij^{xx} pellibus lanutis
Georgius Carr indigena pro iij saccis dimidio viij clavis in j sarplera
Willelmus Tomson indigena pro iij quarteriis de sacco in j poke.
Robertus Harden indigena pro ij saccis iij quarteriis iiij clavis in j sarplera
Idem pro DCCCClx pellibus lanutis
Georgius Eryngton indigena pro ij saccis iij quarteriis viij clavis in j sarplera
Robertus Hely indigena pro ij saccis iij quarteriis viij clavis in j sarplera
Johannes Witwang indigena pro ij saccis in j sarplera
Thomas Grene indigena pro iiij saccis j quarterio viij clavis in j sarplera
Willelmus Heryngton indigena pro CCC pellibus lanutis
Georgius Bird indigena pro iij saccis iij quarteriis j clavo in j sarplera et j poke
Johannes Batemason indigena pro Cxxxvj pellibus lanutis
Thomas Papede indigena pro lx pellibus lanutis
Willelmus Stokall indigena pro iij quarteriis de sacco in j poke
Idem pro Cx pellibus lanutis
Johannes Willy indigena pro CC pellibus lanutis
Thomas Molle indigena pro dimidio sacco in j poke

Sacci lane iiij^{xx}ij sacci xiij clavi custuma nihil subsidium nihil Pelles lanute vijMDlviij pelles facientes xxxj saccos j quarterium custuma nihil subsidium nihil	causa qua supra

Thomas Papede indigena pro viij celdris carbonum valor viij s. iiij d.
subsidium v d.
Idem pro x celdris petrarum molarum valor lxvj s. viij d.
subsidium iij s. iiij d.
Roulond Sothern indigena pro ix celdris molarum valor lx s.
subsidium iij s.

Thomas Swan indigena pro DCCCxxx pellibus
agnetorum valor iiij li. ij s. vj d.
subsidium iiij s. j d.ob.
Willelmus Selby indigena pro DC pellibus
angnetorum valor lx s.
subsidium iij s.
Ricardus Hebborn indigena pro lxviij pellibus
shorlynges et morlynges valor viij s. iiij d.
subsidium v d.
Idem pro CCCC pellibus angnetorum valor xl s.
subsidium ij s.
[*Membrane 5 face*]
Willelmus Camby indigena pro Clx pellibus
shorlynges et morlynges valor xxij s. vj d.
subsidium xiij d.ob.
Idem pro DC xxx pellibus angnetorum valor lxij s. vj d.
subsidium iij s. j d.ob.
Alicia Harden indigena pro iiij^{xx}iiij pellibus
shorlynges et morlynges valor x s.
subsidium vj d.
Johannes Baxster indigena pro xlij pellibus
shorlynges et morlynges valor v s.
subsidium iij d.
Robertus Brigham indigena pro iiij^{xx} pellibus
shorlynges et morlynges valor x s.
subsidium vj d.
Henricus Bidnell indigena pro CC pellibus
angnetorum valor xx s.
subsidium xij d.
Thomas Papede indigena pro iiij^{xx} pellibus
shorlynges et morlynges valor x s.
subsidium vj d.
Willelmus Heryngton indigena pro C pellibus
shorlynges et morlynges valor xv s.
subsidium ix d.
Willelmus Stokal indigena pro l pellibus
shorlynges et morlynges valor vj s. viij d.
subsidium iiij d.
Johannes Willy indigena pro CC pellibus
shorlynges et morlynges valor xxx s.
subsidium xviij d.
Edmundus Benly indigena pro CCC pellibus
shorlynges et morlynges valor xlv s.
subsidium ij s. iij d.

Pelles vocate shorlynges etc. iijMDCCxliiij pelles facientes xxj li. vij s. vj d.
subsidium[21] nihil causa qua supra

---

21. Followed by *xxj s. iiij d.ob.*, struck out.

Navis vocata le Anne de Lyn unde Thomas Bowsey est magister exivit eodem die
Thomas Harryson indigena pro iij saccis in j sarplera
Idem pro CCxl pellibus lanutis
Bertram Yonghusband indigena pro iiij saccis dimidio iij clavis in j sarplera
Cristoferus Brigham indigena pro v saccis dimidio ij clavis in ij sarplera
Georgius Coningham indigena pro iij saccis viij clavis in j sarplera
Thomas Swan indigena pro iij saccis iiij clavis in j sarplera
Willelmus Scott indigena pro ij saccis iij quarteriis in j sarplera
Willelmus Wardell indigena pro DCxx pellibus lanutis
Emery Scott indigena pro iij saccis dimidio iij clavis in j sarplera
Idem pro CCClx pellibus lanutis
Alexander Creswell indigena pro Diiij^{xx} pellibus lanutis
Thomas Morpath indigena pro CCCCxx pellibus lanutis
Georgius Selby indigena pro CCCCiiij^{xx} pellibus lanutis
Willelmus Hunter indigena pro CClxx pellibus lanutis
Johannes Witwang indigena pro iij saccis j quarterio viij clavis in j sarplera
Idem pro C pellibus lanutis
Georgius Bird indigena pro vj saccis iij quarteriis x clavis in ij sarpleris
Robertus Harden indigena pro ij saccis iij quarteriis viij clavis in j sarplera
Willelmus Haning indigena pro ij saccis vj clavis in j sarplera
Georgius Stalper indigena pro iij saccis iij quarteriis viij clavis in j sarplera
Petrus Bewyk indigena pro vij saccis iij clavis in ij sarpleris
Idem pro CCxl pellibus lanutis
Roulond Harryson indigena pro iiij saccis dimidio in j sarplera
Georgius Carre indigena pro ij saccis iij quarteriis in j sarplera
Roulonde Swynborn indigena pro xxviij pellibus lanutis
Georgius Eryngton indigena pro [CCC pellibus lanutis]
[*Membrane 5 dorse*]
Johannes Baxter indigena pro ij saccis in j sarplera
Robertus Brigham indigena pro iij saccis dimidio vij clavis in j sarplera
Idem pro Ciiij^{xx} pellibus lanutis
Thomas Lokwod indigena pro CCC pellibus lanutis
Johannes Thikpenny indigena pro iij saccis in j sarplera
Johannes Parsirley indigena pro iij quarteriis de sacco vj clavis in j poke

Sacci lane
lxviij sacci j quarterium xxiij clavi
custuma nihil
subsidium nihil
Pelles lanute
iiijMCxviij pelles facientes xvij saccos xxxviij pelles
custuma nihil
subsidium nihil
} causa qua supra

Thomas Bowsey indigena pro vj celdris carbonum	valor x s.
subsidium vj d.	
Idem pro xvj celdris petrarum molarum	valor vj li.
subsidium vj s.	
Idem pro xj duodenis rubstones	valor x s.
subsidium vj d.	
Thomas Harison indigena pro Dlx pellibus angnetorum	valor lv s.
subsidium ij s. ix d.	
Emery Scott indigena pro Clx pellibus shorlynges et morlynges	valor xxij s. vj d.
subsidium xiij d.ob.	
Alexander Creswell indigena pro Ciiij[xx]xij pellibus shorlynges et morlynges	valor xxvj s. viij d.
subsidium xvj d.	
Idem pro CCC pellibus angnetorum	valor xxx s.
subsidium xviij d.	
Thomas Morpath indigena pro lx pellibus shorlynges et morlynges	valor vij s. vj d.
subsidium iiij d.ob.	
Idem pro lx pellibus angnetorum	valor v s..
subsidium iij d.	
Willelmus Hunter indigena pro iiij[xx]viij pellibus shorlynges et morlynges	valor xj s. viij d.
subsidium vij d.	
Idem pro CCC pellibus angnetorum	valor xxx s.
subsidium xviij d.	
Georgius Selby indigena pro C pellibus shorlynges et morlynges	valor xv s.
subsidium ix d.	
Johannes Witwang indigena pro C pellibus shorlynges et morlynges	valor xv s.
subsidium ix d.	
Idem pro l pellibus angnetorum	valor v s.
subsidium iij d.	
Petrus Bewyk indigena pro CCxxx pellibus shorlynges et morlynges	valor xxxv s.
subsidium xxj d.	
Roulond Swynborn indigena pro lx pellibus shorlynges et morlynges	valor vij s. vj d.
subsidium iiij d.ob.	
Georgius Eryngton indigena pro lx pellibus shorlynges et morlynges	valor vij s. vj d.
subsidium iiij d.ob.	
Robertus Brigham indigena pro CC pellibus shorlynges et morlynges	valor xxx s.
subsidium xviij d.	

Thomas Lokwode indigena pro C iiij^{xx}xv pellibus shorlynges et morlynges valor xxviij s. iiij d.
subsidium xvij d.
Pelles vocate shorlynges etc MMDv^{xx}xv pelles facientes xvj. li. xj s. viij d.
subsidium[22] nihil causa qua supra

Navis vocata le George de Novo Castro unde Johannes Totill est magister exivit eodem die
William Wardell indigena pro DCvj pellibus lanutis
Thomas Morpath indigena pro CCCxl pellibus lanutis
Johannes Bullok indigena pro Cxl pellibus lanutis
Robertus Solley indigena pro xj saccis j quarterio ix clavis in iij sarpleris
Idem pro CCCCxx pellibus lanutis
Robertus Gray indigena pro iij saccis dimidio viij clavis in j sarplera
Robertus Wade indigena pro CCCCviij pellibus lanutis
Emery Scotte indigena pro v saccis iij quarteriis v clavis in ij sarpleris
Willelmus Scot indigena pro vj saccis iij quarteriis in ij sarpleris
Idem pro CCCiiij^{xx} pellibus lanutis
Edwardus Lilborn indigena pro ij saccis dimidio iiij clavis in j sarplera
Idem pro Ciiij^{xx} pellibus lanutis
Johannes Snow indigena pro ij saccis viij clavis in j sarplera
Idem pro Cxl pellibus lanutis
Johannes Witwang indigena pro iij saccis dimidio viij clavis in j sarplera
[*Membrane 6 face*]
Cristoferus Borell indigena pro iij saccis viij clavis in j sarplera
Idem pro Cxx pellibus lanutis
Thomas Swan indigena pro vj saccis j quarterio viij clavis in j sarplera
Johannes Baxster indigena pro ij saccis dimidio in j sarplera
Willelmus Swan indigena pro ij saccis dimidio in j sarplera
Willelmus Davell indigena pro ij saccis iij quarteriis in j sarplera
Radulfus Brown indigena pro iiij^{xx}xvj pellibus lanutis
Thomas Harryson indigena pro iiij saccis j quarterio v clavis in j sarplera
Thomas Baxster indigena pro lx pellibus lanutis
Willelmus Yotson indigena pro ij saccis iij quarteriis viij clavis in j sarplera
Idem pro CCClx pellibus lanutis
Georgius Car indigena pro CCxl pellibus lanutis
Bartram Yonghusbond pro v saccis in j sarplera
Jacobus Bokk[23] indigena pro iij saccis j quarterio viij clavis in j sarplera
Georgius Bird indigena pro j sacco iij quarteriis viij clavis in j poke
Johannes Trott indigena pro iij quarteriis de sacco in j poke
Willelmus Sele indigena pro iij^{xx} pellibus lanutis

---

22. Followed by *xvj s. vij d.* struck out.
23. *Blak* in 108/3.

Sacci lane
lxxj dimidius ix clavi
custuma nihil
subsidium nihil
Pelles lanute
MMMDlxx facientes xiiij saccos dimidium xxx pelles
custuma nihil
subsidium nihil
} causa qua supra

Radulfus Bikar indigena pro iiij celdris carbonum valor v s.
subsidium iij d.
Idem pro xij celdris grendstonis valor iiij li.
subsidium iiij s.
Idem pro xj duodenis rubstonis valor x s.
subsidium vj d.
Thomas Morpath indigena pro xl pellibus
shorlynges et morlynges valor v s.
subsidium iij d.
Johannes Bullok indigena pro Ciiij^{xx} pellibus
shorlynges et morlynges valor xxv s.
subsidium xv d.
Robertus Solley indigena pro Clx pellibus
shorlynges et morlynges valor xxij s. vj d.
subsidium xiij d.ob.
Robertus Wade indigena pro lxxij pellibus
shorlynges et morlynges valor x s.
subsidium vj d.
Willelmus Scott indigena pro C pellibus
shorlynges et morlynges valor xv s.
subsidium ix d.
Idem pro CCiiij^{xx} pellibus angnetorum valor xxvj s. viij d.
subsidium xvj d.
Edward Lilborn indigena pro Cxxvj pellibus
shorlynges et morlynges valor xx s.
subsidium xij d.
Cristoforus Borell indigena pro CC pellibus
shorlynges et morlynges valor xxx s.
subsidium xviij d.
Radulfus Brown indigena pro CC pellibus
shorlynges et morlynges valor xxx s.
subsidium xviij d.
Thomas Baxster indigena pro lxxj pellibus
shorlynges et morlynges valor x s.
subsidium vj d.
Willelmus Yotson indigena pro CC pellibus
shorlynges et morlynges valor xxx s.
subsidium xviij d.

Georgius Carr indigena pro DC pellibus
shorlynges et morlynges valor iiij li. x s.
subsidium iiij s. vj d.
Idem pro M pellibus angnellorum valor C s.
subsidium v s.
Willelmus Sele indigena pro CC pellibus
shorlynges et morlynges valor xxx s.
subsidium xviij d.

Pelles vocata shorlynges etc. MMMCCClxix pelles facientes xxij li. iij s. ij d.
subsidium[24] xxij s. ij d.ob.

Navis vocata le Mary Harden de Novo Castro unde Lewys Sothern est magister exivit eodem die
Robert Harden indigena pro vj saccis iij quarteriis iij clavis in ij sarpleris
Idem pro CCxl pellibus lanutis in j sarplera
Ricardus Hebborn indigena pro ij saccis in j sarplera
Idem pro xxvj pellibus lanutis
Willelmus Selby indigena pro iiij saccis v clavis in ij sarpleris
Idem pro xx pellibus lanutis
Bartram Yonghusbond indigena pro [iiij saccis dimidio v clavis in j sarplera]
Idem pro [CCxl pellibus lanutis]
[*Membrane 6 dorse*]
Thomas Riddale indigena pro [iiij saccis viij clavis in j sarplera]
Alicia Harden indigena pro [v saccis iij quarteriis xij clavis in iij sarpleris][25]
Robertus Hely indigena pro vj saccis viij clavis in ij sarpleris
Jacobus Buk indigena pro vij saccis dimidio vij clavis
Thomas Harryson indigena pro CCCxxv pellibus lanutis
Willelmus Camby indigena pro iiij saccis dimidio in j sarplera
Idem pro CCCC pellibus lanutis
Cristoferus Brigham indigena pro iij saccis iij quarteriis in j sarplera
Willelmus Davell indigena pro iij saccis in j sarplera
Rogerus Raw indigena pro j sacco dimidio iiij clavis in j poke
Idem pro C pellibus lanutis
Robertus Baxster indigena pro iiij saccis j quarterio viij clavis in ij pokes
Thomas Swan indigena pro iij saccis dimidio in j sarplera
Johannes Passhley indigena pro ij saccis dimidio in j sarplera
Willelmus Tomson indigena pro j sacco vj clavis in j poke
Willelmus Scot indigena pro ij saccis iiij clavis in j sarplera
Willelmus Hanyng indigena pro ij saccis dimidio viij clavis in j sarplera

---

24. Here the scribe omitted to erase the subsidy and write *Nihil.*
25. 108/3 adds *Idem pro Diiij^{xx} pellibus lanutis*, and the discrepancy appears to have passed the Exchequer's scrutiny of both collectors' and controller's rolls noted in the last marginal note before the final summary.

Jacobus Blak indigena pro ij saccis j quarterio iiij clavis in j sarplera
Idem pro Cxx pellibus lanutis
Johannes Harle indigena pro ij saccis iij quarteriis in j sarplera
Idem pro lx pellibus lanutis
Henricus Bidnell indigena pro ij saccis iij quarteriis in j sarplera
Georgius Bird indigena pro v saccis iij quarteriis viij clavis in ij sarpleris
Petrus Bewik indigena pro iij saccis dimidio viij clavis in j sarplera
Johannes Blakston indigena pro j sacco j quarterio viij clavis in j sarplera
Robertus Solley indigena pro ij saccis in j sarplera

Sacci lane
iiij^{xx}xj sacci iij quarteria ij clavi
custuma nihil
subsidium nihil
Pelles lanute
MDxxxvj pelles facientes vj saccos j quarterium xxxvj pelles
custuma nihil
subsidium nihil
} causa qua supra

Robertus Harden indigena pro vj celdris grinstonis valor xl s.
subsidium ij s.
Idem pro iij duodenis rubstonis valor iij s. iiij d.
subsidium ij d.
Idem pro xiijCiiij^{xx} pellibus angnetorum valor vj li. xvj s. viij d.
subsidium vjs x d.
Idem pro vijCv^{xx} pellibus shorlynges et morlynges valor Cxvij s. v d.ob.
subsidium v s. x d.ob.
Ricardus Hebborn indigena pro lx[26] pellibus angnetorum valor v s.
subsidium iij d.
Willelmus Selby indigena pro D pellibus angnetorum valor l s.
subsidium ij s. vj d.
Idem pro C pellibus shorlynges et morlynges valor xv s.
subsidium ix d.
Bartram Yonghusbond indigena pro CCCiiij^{xx} pellibus angnetorum valor xxxvj s. viij d.
subsidium xxij d.
Idem pro CCxxx pellibus shorlynges et morlynges valor xxxiij s. iiij d.
subsidium xx d.
Alicia Harden indigena pro Dlx pellibus angnetorum valor lv s.
subsidium ij s. ix d.

26. C in 108/3.

[*Membrane 7 face*]

Idem pro CCCCv^{xx} pellibus shorlynges et morlynges valor lvij s. vj d.
subsidium ij s. x d.ob.

Willelmus Camby indigena pro CClx pellibus angnetorum valor xxv s.
subsidium xv d.

Idem pro Ciiij^{xx} pellibus shorlynges et morlynges valor xxv s.
subsidium xv d.

Rogerus Raw pro xl pellibus shorlinges et morlinges valor v s.
subsidium iij d.

Jacobus Blak indigena pro CC pellibus shorlinges et morlinges valor xxx s.
subsidium xviij d.

Johannes Harl indigena pro xlviij pellibus shorlinges et morlinges valor vj s. viij d.
subsidium iiij d.

Johannes Branlyng indigena pro C pellibus shorlinges et morlinges valor xv s.
subsidium ix d.

Idem pro xx pellibus angnetorum valor xx d.
subsidium j d.

Robertus Solley indigena pro v^{xx} pellibus shorlinges et morlinges valor xiij s. iiij d.
subsidium viij d.

Idem pro C pellibus angnetorum valor x s.
subsidium vj d.

Willelmus Yotson pro viij peciis plumbi continentibus ij plaustra valor vj li.
subsidium vj s.

Thomas Harryson indigena pro CCC pellibus shorlinges et morlinges valor xlv s.
subsidium ij s. iij d.

Petrus Bewik indigena pro iij peciis plumbi continentibus j plaustrum valor lx s.
subsidium iij s.

Pelles vocate shorlynges etc. centum per vj^{xx}
vMvjCxvij pelles facientes valorem xxxiiij li. iij s. iiij d.
subsidium[27] nihil causa qua supra

Navis vocata le Markyn de Novo Castro unde Willelmus Marbotell est magister exivit eodem die

Willelmus Camby indigena pro xj saccis dimidio viij clavis in iij sarpleris

27. Followed by *xxxiiij s. ij d.*, struck out.

Idem pro DCCCClx pellibus lanutis
Robertus Brigham pro xiij saccis vij clavis in iiij sarpleris
Idem pro CCClx pellibus lanutis
Thomas Swan indigena pro x saccis iij quarteriis viij clavis in iij sarpleris
Idem pro Dxl pellibus lanutis
Ricardus Watson indigena pro iij quarteriis de sacco in j poke
Willelmus Scott indigena pro xij saccis dimidio vij clavis in iij sarpleris
Roulonde Harrison indigena pro viij saccis j quarterio in ij sarpleris
Petrus Bewik indigena pro xiij saccis j clavo in iij sarpleris
Idem pro DCCxx pellibus lanutis
Cristoforus Brigham indigena pro x saccis j quarterio x clavis in iij sarpleris
Alicia Harden indigena pro Cxxviij pellibus lanutis
Willelmus Davell indigena pro v saccis iij quarteriis ix clavis in ij sarpleris
Idem pro CCCCiiij^xx^xij pellibus lanutis
Georgius Bird indigena pro viij saccis j quarterio in ij sarpleris
Idem pro CCCCl pellibus lanutis
Georgius Selby indigena pro iiij saccis j quarterio v clavis in j sarplera
Willelmus Selby indigena pro iij saccis iij quarteriis viij clavis in j sarplera
Georgius Car indigena pro iiij saccis in j sarplera
Idem pro DC pellibus lanutis
Johannes Passhley indigena pro iij saccis j quarterio viij clavis in j sarplera
Willelmus Swan indigena pro iij saccis dimidio in j sarplera
Willelmus Carr indigena pro vij saccis j quarterio iiij clavis in ij sarpleris
Johannes Penrith indigena pro iij quarteriis de sacco in j poke
Johannes Baxster indigena pro j sacco iij quarteriis iiij clavis
Idem pro iiij^xx^xv pellibus lanutis
Robertus Clerk indigena pro iiij saccis dimidio in j sarplera et j poke
[*Membrane 7 dorse*]
Rogerus Raw indigena pro ij saccis iij quarteriis x clavis in j sarplera
Jacobus Buk indigena pro ix saccis iij quarteriis x clavis in iij sarpleris
Emery Scott indigena pro vj saccis in ij sarpleris
Thomas Harryson indigena pro viij saccis j quarterio vj clavis in ij sarpleris
Thomas Riddale indigena pro iiij saccis j quarterio vj clavis in j sarplera
Robertus Baxster indigena pro ij saccis dimidio in j sarplera
Robertus Harden indigena pro viij saccis j quarterio v clavis in iij sarpleris
Idem pro DCCCC pellibus lanutis
Johannes Thikpenny indigena pro CCCxx pellibus lanutis
Ricardus Hebborn indigena pro CCC pellibus lanutis
Thomas Coke indigena pro CCClx pellibus lanutis
Robertus Stokal indigena pro iij saccis iij quarteriis in j sarplera
Willelmus Hurlbatt indigena pro iij quarteriis de sacco in j poke

Sacci lane Clxxv sacci j quarterium xij clavi custuma nihil subsidium nihil Pelles lanute vjMCCx pelles facientes xxv saccis iij quarteriis xxx pelles custuma nihil subsidium nihil	causa qua supra

Willelmus Camby indigena pro Cxxxij pellibus shorlynges et morlynges	valor xx s.
subsidium xij d.	
Idem pro Cxxx pellibus angnetorum	valor xij s. vj d.
subsidium vij d.ob.	
Robertus Brygham indigena pro CClxviij pellibus shorlynges et morlynges	valor xxxviij s. iiij d.
subsidium xxiij d.	
Thomas Swan indigena pro iijClx pellibus shorlynges et morlynges	valor liij s. iiij d.
subsidium ij s. viij d.	
Petrus Bewik indigena pro CCC pellibus shorlynges et morlynges	valor xlv s.
subsidium ij s. iij d.	
Willelmus Davell indigena pro CC pellibus shorlynges et morlynges	valor xxx s.
subsidium xviij d.	
Idem pro CC pellibus angnetorum	valor xx s.
subsidium xij d.	
Georgius Bird indigena pro l pellibus shorlynges et morlynges	valor vj s. viij d.
subsidium iiij d.	
Georgius Carr indigena pro CCCClx pellibus shorlynges et morlynges	valor lxvij s. vj d.
subsidium iij s. iiij d.ob.	
Idem pro DCCC pellibus angnetorum	valor iiij li.
subsidium iiij s.	
Johannes Baxster indigena pro xl pellibus shorlynges et morlynges	valor v s.
subsidium iij d.	
Idem pro CC pellibus angnetorum	valor xx s.
subsidium xij d.	
Robertus Harden indigena pro CClx pellibus shorlynges et morlynges	valor xxxvij s. vj d.
subsidium xxij d.ob.	
Johannes Thikpenny indigena pro Clx pellibus angneti	valor xv s.
subsidium ix d.	
Idem pro Cxx pellibus shorlinges et morlinges	valor xvij s. vj d.
subsidium x d.ob.	

Ricardus Hebborn indigena pro CCC pellibus
shorlinges et morlinges valor xlv s.
subsidium ij s. iij d.
Willelmus Pikden indigena pro CCxiij pellibus
shorlinges et morlinges valor xxxj s. viij d.
subsidium xix d.
Idem pro CC pellibus agnetorum valor xx s.
subsidium xij d.
Thomas Coke indigena pro CCxx pellibus
shorlynges et morlynges valor xxxiij s. iiij d.
subsidium xx d.

{Summa} pellium vocatorum shorlynges etc. centum ut supra
iiijMvCxxxiij pelles facientes valorem xxix li. xviij s. iiij d.
subsidium[28] nihil causa qua supra

Navis vocata le Mari Aleyn de Novo Castro unde Willelmus Bull est magister exivit eodem die.
Willelmus Aleyn indigena pro iij quarteriis viij clavis in j poke
Idem pro CCxx pellibus lanutis
Georgius Stalper indigena pro iiij saccis iij quarteriis xij clavis in ij sarpleris
Idem pro iiij^{xx} pellibus lanutis
Jacobus Buk indigena pro iij saccis viij clavis in j sarplera
Thomas Coke indigena pro CCiiij^{xx}x pellibus lanutis
Robertus Brigham indigena pro iij saccis in j sarplera
Idem pro Cxx pellibus lanutis
[*Membrane 8 face*]
Georgius Bird indigena pro v saccis dimidio viij clavis in ij sarpleris
Idem pro lx pellibus lanutis
Thomas Harryson indigena pro ij saccis j quarterio in j sarplera
Idem pro Cxx pellibus lanutis
Johannes Blakston indigena pro v saccis dimidio in ij sarpleris
Bartram Yonghusband indigena pro iij saccis dimidio in j sarplera
Idem pro iiij^{xx} pellibus lanutis
Thomas Swan indigena pro iij saccis dimidio in j sarplera
Thomas Smyth indigena pro Cxx pellibus lanutis

Sacci lane
xxxij sacci j quarterium x clavi
custuma nihil
subsidium nihil
Pelles lanute
MCCx pelles facientes v saccos x pelles
custuma nihil
subsidium nihil
} causa qua supra

28. Followed by *xxix s. xj d.*, struck out.

William Aleyn indigena pro iiij celdris carbonum valor v s.
subsidium iij d.
Idem pro iij celdris petrarum valor xx s.
subsidium xij d.
Idem pro CCC pellibus shorlynges et morlynges valor xlv s.
subsidium ij s. iij d.
Georgius Stalper indigena pro C pellibus angnetorum valor x s.
subsidium vj d.
Idem pro xxv pellibus shorlynges et morlynges valor iij s. iiij d.
subsidium ij d.
Thomas Coke indigena pro C iiij^{xx}x pellibus shorlinges et morlynges valor xxvj s. viij d.
subsidium xvj d.
Robertus Brigham indigena pro Cxviij pellibus shorlynges et morlynges valor xvj s. viij d.
subsidium x d.
Georgius Bird indigena pro Diiij^{xx}x pellibus shorlynges et morlynges valor iiij li. v s.
subsidium iiij s. iij d.
Thomas Harryson indigena pro lx pellibus shorlynges et morlynges valor vij s. vj d.
subsidium iiij d.ob.
Idem pro Cxxx pellibus angnetorum valor xij s. vj d.
subsidium vij d.ob.
Bartram Yonghusband indigena pro iiij^{xx} pellibus shorlynges et morlynges valor x s.
subsidium vj d.
Idem pro Cxl pellibus angnetorum valor xiij s. iiij d.
subsidium viij d.
Thomas Smyth indigena pro C pellibus shorlynges et morlynges valor xv s.
subsidium ix d.
Robertus Harden indigena pro DCCiiij^{xx} pellibus angnetorum valor lxxvj s. viij d.
subsidium iij s. x d.
{Summa} pellium vocatarum shorlinges etc. centum ut supra MMDxxxiij pelles facientes valorem xvj li. xx d.
subsidium[29] nihil causa qua supra

Navis vocata le George Galaunt de Novo Castro unde Johannes Arnot est magister exivit eodem die
Robertus Stokal indigena pro iij saccis iij quarteriis iiij clavis in j sarplera et j poke
Idem pro C pellibus lanutis
Robertus Wade indigena pro iiij^{xx} pellibus lanutis

29. Followed by *xvj s. j d.*, struck out.

Jacobus Buk indigena pro ij saccis dimidio iiij clavis in j sarplera
Idem pro CCClx pellibus lanutis
Thomas Andreson indigena pro xl pellibus lanutis
Thomas Hanson indigena pro lx pellibus lanutis
Willelmus Carr indigena pro DCCxx pellibus lanutis
Johannes Pashley indigena pro lx pellibus lanutis
Willelmus Hanyng indigena pro CCxl pellibus lanutis
Thomas Watson indigena pro ij saccis dimidio in j sarplera
Robertus Baxster indigena pro j sacco in j poke
Johannes Penryth indigena pro ix saccis in iij sarpleris
Idem pro CCCxx pellibus lanutis
Thomas Camby indigena pro C pellibus lanutis
Robertus Patenson indigena pro Cxx pellibus lanutis
Willelmus Pygden indigena pro dimidio sacco in j poke
Georgius Baxster indigena pro iij quarteriis de sacco in j poke
Edwardus Conyngham indigena pro iiij saccis in j sarplera et j poke

Sacci lane
xxv sacci viij clavi
custuma nihil
subsidium nihil
Pelles lanute
MMCC pelles facientes iix saccos xl pelles
custuma nihil
subsidium nihil

Johannes Arnot indigena pro iiij celdris carbonum valor v s.
subsidium iij d.
Idem pro iij celdris petrarum valor xx s.
subsidium xij d.
Robertus Stokal indigena pro xl pellibus shorlynges et morlynges valor v s.
subsidium iij d.
Idem pro C pellibus angnetorum valor x s.
subsidium vj d.
Robert Wade indigena pro lx pellibus angnetorum valor v s.
subsidium iij d.
Jacobus Buk indigena pro CCCl pellibus shorlynges et morlynges valor [lij s. viij d.]
subsidium ij s. vij d.
Thomas Andreson indigena pro iiij^{xx} pellibus shorlynges et morlynges valor x s.
subsidium vj d.
Idem pro C pellibus angnetorum valor x s.
subsidium vj d.

Thomas Hanson indigena pro lx pellibus shorlynges et morlynges valor vij s. vj d.
subsidium iiij d.ob.
Idem pro lx pellibus angnetorum valor v s.
subsidium iij d.
Willelmus Carr indigena pro CCCiiij^{xx} pellibus shorlynges et morlynges valor lv s.
subsidium ij s. ix d.
Idem pro CCCC pellibus angnetorum valor xl s.
subsidium ij s.
Johannes Paschley pro C pellibus shorlinges et morlinges valor xv s.
subsidium ix d.
Idem pro vj peciis plumbi continentibus CC libras valor vj s. viij d.
subsidium iiij d.
Willelmus Hanyng pro CC pellibus shorlynges et morlinges valor xxx s.
subsidium xviij d.
Idem pro Ciiij^{xx} pellibus angnetorum valor xvj s. viij d.
subsidium x d.
Archibold Stokal indigena pro C pellibus shorlynges et morlynges valor xv s.
subsidium ix d.
Idem pro v^{xx} pellibus agnetorum valor viij s. iiij d.
subsidium v d.
Robertus Baxster indigena pro C pellibus shorlinges et morlinges valor xv s.
subsidium ix d.
Idem pro lx pellibus agnetorum valor v s.
subsidium iij d.
Thomas Camby indigena pro lxvj pellibus shorlinges et morlinges valor viij s. iiij d.
subsidium v d.
Robertus Patenson indigena pro xlvj pellibus shorlinges et morlinges valor vj s. viij d.
subsidium iiij d.
Idem pro iiij^{xx} pellibus agnetorum valor vj s. viij d.
subsidium iiij d.
Idem pro ij dacris coriorum tannatorum valor xxvj s. viij d.
subsidium xvj d.

Pelles vocata shorlynges etc. Centum ut supra MMDxxij pelles facientes valorem xvj li. v s. x d.
subsidium[30] nihil causa qua supra

30. Followed by *xvj s. iij d.ob.*, struck out.

{Examinantur cum rotulis Roberti Colyngwod}

{MClxxij li. xiiij s. x d.qu.}

{per breve} [*Bracketed to include* exitus sigilli regis *below*]
Sacci lane Thome Grene, Thome Riddalle, Edwardi Borell, et aliorum marcatorum existentium gubernatorum Gilde marcatorie ville regis Novi Castri super Tinam [indigenarum] de crescencia comitatuum Northumbrie, Cumbrie, Westmorlandie ac episcopatus Dunelmensis, necnon comitatuum de Allerton et Richmond

Diiij^xx sacci, j quarterium, v clavi

{custuma[31] Ciiij^xx xv li. viij s. xj d.ob.qu.
subsidium[32] ixClxxvij li. iiij s. x d.ob.

Pellium[33] lanutarum predictorum marcatorum et gubernatorum[34] de crescencia predicta

xxxiiijMixCix pelles facientes Cxlv sacci j quarterium xlix pelles

{custuma[35] xlviij li. ix s. viij d.ob.
subsidium[36] CCxlij li. viij s. v d.ob.

Denaria Calesii xxiiij li. vij s. x d.ob.

Exitus sigilli regis quod dicitur cokettus
provenientes de Ciiij^xx xj marcatoribus[37] xxxj s. x d.

Summa[38] MCCCCiiij^xx ix li. xj s. viij d.ob.qu.[39]

Valor marcatorum alienigarum unde iij d. de libra
lxxvij li.
custuma xix s. iij d.
Panni sine grano alienigarum
iiij panni dimidius vj virge
custuma x s. iij d.ob } xxix s. vj d.ob.

Valor marcatorum indigenarum et alienigarum unde xij d. de libra
Ciiij^xx xiiij li. xv s.
subsidium ix li. xiiij s. ix d.
Vina indigenarum
Ciiij^xx xiiij dolia ij pipa
subsidium xxix li. iij s. vj. d. } xxxviij li. xviij s. iij d.

Panni sine grano hanse
ix panni xj virge
custuma ix s. v d.ob. vj li. viij s.

---

31. Followed by *nihil*, struck out.
32. Followed by *nihil*, struck out.
33. *Pellm'* in MS.
34. *et gubernatorum* is interlined.
35. Followed by *nihil*, struck out.
36. Followed by *nihil*, struck out.
37. Followed by *nihil*, struck out.
38. Followed by *Miiij^xx ix li. vij d.ob.qu.*, struck out.
39. The same total is also entered at the left.

Valor Hanse

CCCClxiij li. iij s. iiij d. custuma Cxviij s. iij d.ob.
subsidium per processum
Worsted simplex hanse ij pecie iij d.

{per breve} [*Bracketed to include* exitus coketti *below*]

Pelles predictorum Thome, Thome, ac Edwardi, ac aliorum marcatorum gubernatorum gilde predicte, de crescencia predicta vocat' shorlynges et morlynges et lambfelles

xxxvjMv^{xx}xvj pelles facientes Cl saccos j quarterium xl pelles

Valor[40]
Subsidium[41]
Custuma[42] l li. vij s.
Subsidium[43] CCl li. xiij s. x d.ob.
Denaria Calesii[44] C s. iij d.

Exitus coketti provenientes de Cv marcatoribus[45] xvij s. vj d.

} CCCvj li. xviij s. vij d.ob.

{deest denarium supra CCCC li.}

SUMMA TOTALIS OMNIS[46] MDCCCxliij li. vj s. j d. ob.qu.

40. Followed by *CCxxij li. vij s. iiij d.*, struck out.
41. Followed by *xj li. ij s. v d.*, struck out.
42. Followed by *nihil*, struck out.
43. Followed by *nihil*, struck out.
44. Followed by *nihil*, struck out.
45. Followed by *nihil*, struck out.
46. Followed by *MCCCCxliij li. vj s. j d.qu.* struck out.

10. Particulars of account of Robert Colyngwod, controller, from 28 October 1488 to Michaelmas 1489.

E 122 108/1 and E 122 108/3

Despite the two piece-numbers, the two rolls are complementary, and together make up the complete account. 108/1 is 215 mm. wide and 520 mm. long; 108/2 is made up of eleven membranes, sewn head to tail, ranging in width from 210 mm. to 225 mm., and measuring in all 6160 mm. The condition is good.

The account follows that of the collectors, no. 9 above, very closely; differences of substance are recorded in the footnotes to that account. The only original material is the heading of the account, and the note of its receipt at the Exchequer; these are given below. Robert Colyngwod had died during, or immediately after, his term of office as controller, and his account was presented at the Exchequer by his executor.

[*Heading to Robert Colyngwod's account, E 122/108/1 m. 1*]

{Novum Castrum}

Contrarotulamentum Roberti Colyngwod, contrarotulatoris regis custumarum et subsidiorum in portu ville Novum Castrum super Tynam et in singulis portubus et locis eidem portui adiacentibus, videlicet a xxvii^{mo} die Octobris anno quarto domini regis nunc Henrici vij usque festum Sancti Michaelis tunc proximo sequens.

[*At the end of the account is the Exchequer clerk's acknowledgment of delivery, E 122/108/3 m. 11*]

Hunc rotulum continentem xj pecias liberavit hic Johannes Collingwode executor et testator predicti Roberti Collingwode, defuncti, per manus suas proprias xxvj^{to} die Octobris anno quinto [domini regis nunc Henrici vij.]

11. Particulars of account of William Baxter, controller, from Michaelmas 1494 to Michaelmas 1495.

E 122/108/8

The five membranes are 260 mm. wide, and 838, 864, 787, 787 and 720 mm. long respectively. All have been damaged at the left for between 90 and 180 mm. with staining and holes. Membrane 5 is also heavily rubbed. Some portions of the damaged areas cannot be read under ultra-violet light, and in consequence a number of merchants' names are missing from the text below.

No attempt was made by the clerk to total the value for each ship, although the words *Summa valoris* with a ruled line were entered in readiness.

[*Membrane 1 face*]

Rotulus Willelmi Baxter contrarotulatoris domini nunc regis in portu ville Novo Castri super Tinam et in singulis portubus et locis eidem portui adiacentibus, a festo Sancti Michaelis archangeli anno regis Henrici septimi decimo, usque idem festum videlicet per unum annum integrum.

Navis vocata le Julian de Novo Castro super Tinam unde Johannes Arnald est magister exivit viij die Octobris anno regis Henrici septimi decimo

Idem magister indigena pro j barrelle sepi valor x s.
Willelmus Scott indigena pro ij plaustris plumbi valor vj li.
Idem pro xl pellibus tannatis vaccorum sutis valor xl s.
Idem pro ij dussenis ulnarum panni lanei stricti continentibus dimidium pannum
Jacobus Buk indigena per ij plaustris et dimidio plumbi valor vij li. x s.
Idem pro xl pellibus vaccarum tannatis sutis valor xl s.
Idem pro iij barelles sepi valor xxx s.
Edwardus Baxter indigena pro xxv pellibus tannatis valor xxv s.
Idem pro xvj barrelles allecis albi valor xxxiij s. iiij d.

Rogerus Raw indigena pro dimidio plaustro
plumbi valor xxx s.
Idem pro xv pellibus tannatis sutis valor xv s.
Idem pro ij dussenis panni lanei stricti continentibus dimidium pannum
Cristoferus Burrell indigena pro xx pellibus
tannatis sutis valor xx s.
Edwardus Conyngham indigena pro iiij^{xx}xv pellibus vaccarum tannatis valor lxxxxv s.
Bartramus Yonghusband indigena pro ij plaustris
et dimidio plumbi valor vij li. x s.
Idem pro vj dussenis ulnarum panni lanei stricti continentibus j pannum et dimidium
Johannes Penreth indigena pro viij dussenis panni lanei stricti continentibus ij pannis
Johannes Harll indigena pro vj dussenis panni lanei stricti continentibus j pannum et dimidium
Georgius Car senior indigena
pro iij plaustris et dimidio plumbi valor x li. x s.
Idem pro xl pellibus vaccarum tannatis valor xl s.
Summa valoris [*blank*]

Navis vocata le George de Novo Castro unde Willelmus Marbotell est magister exivit eodem die et anno
... Swan indigena pro xxx pellibus tannatis sutis summa valoris xxx s.
Idem pro j plaustro plumbi valor lx s.
... Brigham indigena pro xv plaustris plumbi valor xlv li.
Idem pro xxvj dussenis panni lanei stricti continentibus vj pannos et dimidium
... indigena pro xxx pellibus tannatis vaccarum valor xxx s.
... indigena pro ij barrelles et di' sepi valor xxv s.
... pro iiij dussenis panni lanei stricti
... pro vj dussenis panni lanei stricti
... pro xl pellibus vaccarum tannatis valor xl s.
... pro xviij dussenis panni lanei stricti
... pro v barrelles sepi valor l s.
... pro xl pellibus vaccarum tannatis valor xl s.
... pro iij dussenis panni lanei stricti
... ... pellibus tannatis vaccarum valor xv s.
... pro vj^{xx}x pellibus vaccarum tannatis valor lxx s.
... pro viij dussenis panni lanei stricti
... pro l pellibus vaccarum tannatis valor l s.
... pro x pellibus vaccarum tannatis valor x s.
... pro j barrelle sepi valor x s.
Summa valoris [*blank*]

... de Camfer unde Witell est magister exivit xiiij^{o} die Octobris anno regis Henrici vij^{mi} decimo
... pro x cheldris carbonum valor xvj s. viij d.
... pro ij cheldris petrarum valor xvj s. viij d.
... pro x pellibus vaccarum tannatis valor x s.
Summa valoris [*blank*]

Navis vocata le Nicolas de Leyth unde Willelmus Mirremont est magister applicuit xvij^{o} die Octobris anno x^{mo} regis Henrici vij^{mi}
... ... barrelles salmonis valor iij li. xiij s. iiij d.
... pro ij laste allecis albi salsi valor l s.
... ... barrelles trane olei valor xxx s.
... pro di' C libris mader valor vj s. viij d.
Summa valoris [*blank*]

Navis vocata le Gabrielle de Danske under Hanse Laurence est magister applicuit xxiiij^{o} die Octobris anno x^{mo} Henrici vij^{mi}
Idem magister de Hanse pro iij M waynskottes valor xiij li.
Idem pro xxiiij C clapholt valor xx s.
Idem pro j last osmondes valor xl s.
Hans Stole alienigena de Hanse pro ij nestes cownters valor xxvj s. viij d.
Idem pro xxiiij C clapholt valor xiij s. iiij d.
Idem pro xviij balles flax valor xiij s. iiij d.
Idem pro lx parv' trowes valor vj s. viij d.
Idem pro j barrelle vitrorum ad potandum valor iij s. iiij d.
Idem pro iij bonches blodii fili valor xx d.
Idem pro ij cistis continentibus xiij balles flax valor x s.
Idem pro iij balles flax et ij parv' mastes valor iij s. iiij d.
Idem pro j parva pecia cere continente j quarterium quintalli
Summa valoris [*blank*]

Batella vocata le Martyn de Disert unde Alexander Brown est magister applicuit ultimo die Octobris anno x^{mo} Henrici vij^{mi}
Johannes Beteson alienigena pro vj wey salis albi valor xxx s.
Idem pro vj barelles allecis albi salsi valor xx s.
Idem pro ij barrelles grilse fisch valor xiij s. iiij d.
Summa valoris [*blank*]

The Nicolas de Leyth unde Willelmus Mirremont est magister exivit iij^{o} die Novembris anno x^{mo} Henrici vij^{mi}
Idem magister alienigena pro iij dacris pellium vaccarum tannatorum valor xxx s.
Georgius Birde pro j plaustro plumbi valor lx s.
Summa valoris [*blank*]

The James de Novo Castro super Tinam unde Robertus Hebburn est magister exivit iiij^{o} die Novembris anno x^{mo} Henrici vij^{mi}

Willelmus Allan indigena pro xiiij cheldris carbonum valor xv s.

Idem pro viij cheldris gryndstonys valor liij s. iij d.

Idem pro iij dossenis rubstonys valor xx d.

Summa valoris [*blank*]

[*Membrane 1 dorse*]

The Mare de Novo Castro super Tinam unde Thomas Wode est magister exivit vj^{o} die Novembris anno x^{mo} Henrici vij^{mi}

Idem magister indigena pro xx cheldris carbonum valor xx s.

Idem pro iiij cheldris petrarum valor xx s.

Summa valoris [*blank*]

The Mare de Sunderland unde Rous Huker est magister applicuit penultimo die Novembris anno x^{mo} Henrici vij^{mi}

Radulphus Wycleff indigena pro xx barrelles salmonis valor x li.

Idem pro j last viij barrelles allecis albi valor iij li. vj s. viij d.

Summa valoris [*blank*]

The Saint Ive de Groy unde Alanus Elleyn est magister applicuit iiij^{mo} die Decembris anno x^{mi} Henrici vij^{mi}

Willelmus Rob indigena pro lx doliis vini non dulcis

Summa tonagii [*blank*]

The Ive de Groy unde Alanus Elleyn est magister exivit x^{mo} die Decembris anno x^{mo} Henrici vij^{mi}

Idem magister alienigena pro xl cheldris carbonum valor lxvj s. viij d.

Idem pro xx peciis plumbi valor vj s. viij d.

Idem pro ij dussenis panni lanei stricti valor x s.

Summa valoris [*blank*]

The Anne de Novo Castro unde Johannes Tutyll est magister applicuit xiij^{o} die Januarii anno x^{mo} Henrici vij^{mi}

Georgius Stalper indigena pro xxxj finibus ferri ponderantiibus D valor xv s.

Idem pro vij doliis j pyp et un' hogeshede vini non dulcis

Jacobus Blak indigena pro xxxj finibus ferri ponderantibus D valor xv s.

Idem pro iij doliis et j hogeshede vini non dulcis

Willelmus Haynyng indigena pro ij doliis et un' pyp vini non dulcis

Johannes Passeley indigena pro iij doliis et un'hogeshede vini gasconii

Ricardus Hebburn indigena pro iiij doliis et un'hogeshede vini gasconii

Johannes Baxter indigena pro j hogeshede ferri valor xiij s. iiij d.

Idem pro viij doliis vini non dulcis

Ricardus Wrangwysh indigena pro iij doliis et un' pyp vini non dulcis
Willelmus Car indigena pro ij doliis vini non dulcis
Willelmus Allan indigena pro ix^{xx} finibus ferri ponderantibus iij M valor iiij li. x s.
Idem pro ij pypes cane wade valor liij s. iiij d.
Idem pro iij cartes rossen valor xxx s.
Idem pro vij doliis et un' pyp vini non dulcis
Johannes Allan indigena pro lx finibus ferri ponderantibus M
valor xxx s.
Idem pro ij doliis vini gasconii
Johannes Blaxton indigena pro j dolio vini gasconii
... indigena pro iij doliis vini non dulcis
... indigena apro j dolio et un' hogeshede vini non dulcis
Willelmus Byrde pro j hogeshede vini gasconii
Summa valoris [*blank*]
tonnagii [*blank*]

The Katrin de Depe unde Peronet est magister applicuit iij^{o} die Februarii anno x^{mo} Henrici vij^{mi}
Idem magister alienigena pro xxx peciis fructus valor xl s.
Idem pro v barrelles et di'avelanarum valor xiij s. iiij d.
Idem pro lxxx libris clavorum valor vj s. viij d.
... pro ij doliis vini
... ... parv' barrelle olei valor vj s. viij d.
... ...peciis fructus valor vj s. viij d.
... ...parv' clavis valor vj s. viij d.
... ...vj libris suger valor vj s. viij d.
... ... un' hogeshede vini
Summa valoris [*blank*]
tonnagii [*blank*]

Le Gabriell de Danske unde Hanse Laurence est magister exivit iiij^{o} die Februarii anno x^{mo} Henrici vij^{mi}
... ... xl celdris carbonum valor lxvj s. viij d.
... ... plaustris plumbi valor xvj li.
... alienigena de Hanse pro ij pannis panni lanei largi sine grano
... alienigena de Hanse pro ij plaustris et dimidio plumbi valor x li.
Summa valoris [*blank*]

The Tresoier de Depe unde Gilliaume Clerk est magister applicuit vj^{o} die Februarii anno x^{mo} Henrici vij^{mi}
Oliverus de Pound alienigena pro ij pypes et di' fructus valor xl s.
Idem pro xiiij ores valor iij s. iiij d.
Idem pro ij barrelles ceparum valor xx d.
Idem pro j dussena pare cardes valor iij s. iiij d.
Idem pro vj ulnis panni linei valor xx d.

Idem pro ij M clavis valor iij s. iiij d.
Idem pro lxxxj finibus ferri ponderantibus M valor xxxiij s. iiij d.
Idem pro v doliis vini non dulcis
Summa valoris [*blank*]
tonnagii [*blank*]

The Katren de Depe und Petir Revnot est magister exivit xij die Februarii anno x^{mo} Henrici vij^{mi}
Idem magister alienigena pro xviij cheldris carbonum valor xxvj s. viij d.
Idem pro iij cheldris gryndstonys valor xxvj s. viij d.
Idem pro ij dacris corriorum tannatorum vaccarum valor xxxiij s. iiij d.
Summa valoris [*blank*]

The Tresoier de Depe unde Gilliaume Clerk est magister exivit xiij die Februarii anno x^{mo} Henrici vij^{mi}
Willelmus Riddall alienigena pro xxij cheldris carbonum valor xxvj s. viij d.
Idem pro ij dacris pellium vaccarum tannatorum valor xl s.
Idem pro ij dussenis ulnarum panni lanei stricti valor v s.
Summa valoris [*blank*]

The George de Novo Castro unde Willelmus Marbotell est magister applicuit xviij die Februarii anno x^{mo} Henrici vij^{mi}
Thomas Swan indigena pro j pyp vini non dulcis
Idem pro j carte rosen valor x s.
Willelmus Harden indigena pro v doliis vini non dulcis
Robertus Harden indigena pro v doliis et j pype vini non dulcis
Georgius Shell pro j hogeshed vini non dulcis
Johannes Taylour indigena pro j pype vini non dulcis
Gilbertus Whyte indigena pro j pype vini non dulcis
Henricus Barrow indigena pro j pyp vini
Georgius Car indigena pro ij doliis et un' hogeshede vini non dulcis
Willelmus Camby indigena pro j cart rossen valor x s.
Idem pro vij doliis vini non dulcis
Thomas Camby indigena pro iiij doliis et j pype vini
Cristoferus Brigham indigena pro v doliis et j hogeshed vini
Willelmus Davell indigena pro iij doliis vini non dulcis
[*Membrane 2 face*]
Willelmus Selbye indigena pro j dolio vini non dulcis
Georgius Bird indigena pro j cart rossen valor x s.
Idem pro vij doliis et j pype vini
Bartramus Yonghusband indigena pro iiij peciis rossen valor vj s. viij d.
Georgius Selby indigena pro j pype et un' hogeshede vini
Rogerus Haynyng indigena pro j pype vini non dulcis
Summa valoris [*blank*]
tonnagii [*blank*]

The Julyan de Novo Castro unde Johannes Arnald est magister applicuit xviij^{o} die Februarii anno x^{mo} Henrici vij^{mi}
Idem magister pro lxxx finibus ferri valor xxx s.
Idem pro j pype vini
Cristoferus Burrell indigena pro iiij^{xx} xiij finibus ferri valor xl s.
Idem pro j cart rossen valor x s.
Willclmus Scott indigena pro iij^{xx}xix finibus ferri valor xxx s.
Idem pro v doliis et j pype vini
Edwardus Conyngham indigena pro x^{xx} finibus lukes ferri valor iiij li. x s.
Idem pro v doliis vini
Johannes Penreth indigena pro vij^{xx}ix finibus ferri valor lxvj s. viij d.
Idem pro di' carte rosen valor v s.
Idem pro ij doliis et j pype vini
Johannes Harll indigena pro iij doliis vini
Rogerus Raw indigena pro di' cart rossen valor v s.
Idem pro iij doliis vini
Georgius Car indigena pro iij doliis et un' pype vini
Bartramus Yonghusband indigena pro iij doliis vini
Willelmus Harden indigena pro j pype vini
Jacobus Buk indigena pro iiij^{xx} xv finibus ferri valor xl s.
Idem pro ij pypes cane wade valor lx s.
Idem pro iij doliis vini
Johannes Thomson indigena pro j pype vini
Robertus Mirreman indigena pro j pype et un' hogeshed vini
Summa valoris [*blank*]
tonnagii [*blank*]

The Bonaventure de Abveyll unde Johannes Dere est magister applicuit xxij^{mo} die Februari anne x^{mo} Henrici vij^{mi}
Idem magister alienigena pro lx finibus ferri ponderantibus M valor xxx s.
Idem pro iij panyers vitri valor xx s.
Idem pro vj bunches corke valor vj s. viij d.
Idem pro j ponshon vinagre valor vj s. viij d.
Idem pro xviij ores valor vj s. viij d.
Summa valoris [*blank*]

... Abveyll unde Johannes Pym est magister exivit xxij die Februarii anno x^{mo} Henrici vij^{mi}
... ... cheldris carbonum valor xxiij s. iiij d.
... ... dimidia cheldra grindstonys valor v s.
Summa valoris [*blank*]

... Jenett de Bullon unde Johannes de John est magister exivit ultimo die Februarii anno x^mo^ Henrici vij^mi^
Idem magister alienigena ... cheldris carbonum valor xiij s. iiij d.
... cheldris petrarum valor viij s. iiij d.
Summa valoris [*blank*]

... Bullon unde Johannes Catenyey est magister exivit ultimo die Februarii anno x^mo^ Henrici vij^mi^
Idem magister alienigena pro xvj cheldris carbonum valor xxvj s. viij d.
Idem pro j cheldra gryndstonys valor viij s. iiij d.
Idem pro viij rubstonys valor xx d.
Summa valoris [*blank*]

The Jakett de Bullon unde Thomas Richerd est magister exivit ultimo die Februarii anno x^mo^ Henrici vij^mi^
Idem magister alienigena pro xv cheldris carbonum valor xxv s.
Idem pro di' cheldra petrarum et xij rubstonys valor v s.
Summa valoris [*blank*]

The Bonaventure de Abveyll unde Johannes Dere est magister exivit ij^o^ die Marcii anno x^mo^ Henrici vij^mi^
Idem magister alienigena pro xxiiij cheldris carbonum valor xl s.
Summa valoris [*blank*]

The Anne de Novo Castro unde Johannes Tutyll est magister exivit xv^o^ die Marcii anno x^mo^ Henricii vij^mi^
Robertus Baxter indigena pro CCxx pellibus lanutis continentibus iij quarteria xl pelles
Bartramus Yonghusband indigena pro j sarplera lane ponderante ij saccos
Idem pro lx pellibus lanutis continentibus j quarterium
Thomas Anderson indigena pro iiij sarpleris lane ponderantibus viij saccos
Thomas Cambye indigena pro j sarplera lane ponderante ij saccos et dimidium
Idem pro lx pellibus lanutis continentibus j quarterium
Willelmus Swan indigena pro j sarplera lane ponderante ij saccos
Thomas Grene indigena pro j sarplera lane ponderante ij saccos dimidium vij clavos
Willelmus Selbye indigena pro CC xvj pellibus lanutis continentibus iij quarteria xxxvj pelles
Willelmus Allan indigena pro ij sarpleris lane ponderantibus iij saccos iij quarteria
Idem pro CCCCxx pellibus lanutis continentibus j saccum iij quarteria
Maurus Mawer indigena pro j sarplera lane ponderante j saccum j quarterium
Idem pro lxxxx pellibus lanutis continentibus j quarterium xxx pelles

Ricardus Hebburn indigena pro j sarplera lane ponderante j saccum iiij clavos
Idem pro iiij^{xx}x pellibus lanutis continentibus j quarterium xxx pelles
Robertus Harden indigena pro j sarplera lane ponderante j saccum iij quarteria
Idem per C iiij^{xx} pellibus lanutis continentibus iij quarteria
Johannes Batemanson indigena pro lx pellibus lanutis continentibus j quarterium
Georgius Car indigena pro j sarplera lane ponderante j saccum iij quarteria iiij clavos
Idem pro C iiij^{xx} pellibus lanutis continentibus iij quarteria
Georgius Stalper indigena pro ij sarpleris lane continentibus ij saccos iij quarteria ij clavos
Willelmus Hayning indigena pro j sarplera lane ponderante j saccum et dimidium
Idem pro iij^{xx}xv pellibus lanutis continentibus j quarterium xv pelles
Willelmus Car indigena pro j sarplera lane ponderante ij saccos
Thomas Cook indigena pro j sarplera lane ponderante j saccum
Johannes Blaxton indigena pro j sarplera lane ponderante ij saccos dimidium iij clavos
Georgius Birde indigena pro j pokett lane ponderante iij quarteria
Willelmus Birde indigena pro j sarplera lane ponderante j saccum

Sequitur pondagium in eadem nave

Robertus Baxter indigena pro CClx pellibus shorlynges et morlynges valor xxxvij s. vj d.
Bartramus Yonghusband indigena pro iij plaustris plumbi valor ix li.
Idem pro Clx pellibus shorlynges et morlynges valor xxij s. vj d.
[*Membrane 2 dorse*]
Willemus Selbye indigena pro Cxxx pellibus agnellorum valor xix s. ij d.
Willelmus Allan indigena pro x cheldris carbonum valor x s.
Idem pro ij cheldris gryndstonys valor x s.
Idem pro CCC iiij^{xx}vj pellibus shorlynges valor lxx s. x d.
Maurus Mawer indigena pro CC pellibus shorlynges et morlynges valor xxvij s. vj d.
Ricardus Hebburn indigena pro Cxj pellibus morlynges valor xvj s. viij d.
Idem pro v^{xx}vij pellibus agnellorum valor viij s. iiij d.
Robertus Harden indigena pro Clx pellibus shorlynges et morlynges valor xxij s. vj d.
Johannes Batemanson indigena pro Clx pellibus shorlynges et morlynges valor xxij s. vj d.
Georgius Car indigena pro ij dacris corriorum tannatorum aridorum valor x s.
Idem pro j hogeshede sepi valor x s.
Idem pro C xv pellibus shorlynges valor xvj s. viij d.

Willelmus Haynyng indigena pro v^{xx}x pellibus shorlynges et morlynges valor xiij s. iiij d.
Willelmus Car indigena pro lx pellibus shorlynges valor vij s. vj d.
Georgius Birde indigena pro CCCliiij pellibus shorlynges et morlynges valor lxvj s. viij d.
Summa valoris [*blank*]

The Mare Hayrbred de Novo Castro unde Johannes Happ est magister exivit xv^{o} die Marcii anno x^{mo} Henrici septimi
Johannes Brandlyng indigena pro Ciiij^{xx} pellibus lanutis continentibus iij quarteria
Thomas Grene indigena pro j sarplera lane ponderante ij saccos viij clavos
Idem pro Ciiij^{xx} pellibus lanutis continentibus iij quarteria
Thomas Camby indigena pro j sarplera lane ponderante j saccum
Idem pro CCxl pellibus lanutis continentibus j saccum
Willelmus Davell indigena pro j sarplera lane ponderante j saccum et dimidium
Idem pro Ciiij^{xx} pellibus lanutis continentibus iij quarteria
Thomas Ridall indigena pro j sarplera lane ponderante ij saccos j quarterium iiij clavos
Idem pro Ciiij^{xx} pellibus lanutis continentibus iij quarteria
Willelmus Selbye indigena pro Cxx pellibus lanutis continentibus dimidium saccum
Ricardus Conynyham indigena pro CCxvj pellibus lanutis continentibus iij quarteria xxxvj pelles
Robertus Gray indigena pro ij sarpleris lane ponderantibus v saccos
Idem pro iiij^{xx} x pellibus lanutis continentibus j quarterium xxx pelles
Cristoferus Brigham indigena pro Cxx pellibus lanutis continentibus dimidium saccum
Georgius Selbye indigena pro iiij^{xx}x pellibus lanutis continentibus j quarterium xxx pelles
Willelmus Draver indigena pro CCxxx pellibus lanutis continentibus iij quarteria l pelles
Robertus Baxter indigena pro CCxx pellibus lanutis continentibus iij quarteria xl pelles
Willelmus Pykden indigena pro xxx pellibus lanutis continentibus dimidium quarterium
Robertus Harden indigena pro j sarplera lane ponderante ij saccos
... indigena pro j pokett continente j quarterium iij clavos
... pro j sarplera lane ponderante j saccum et dimidium
... pro j sarplera lane ponderante j saccum iij quarteria
... pro j sarplera lane ponderante iij saccos
Sequitur pondagium in eadem nave
... ... cheldris gryndstonys valor xxvj s. viij d.
... pro CCv^{xx} pellibus shorlynges et morlynges valor xlij s. vj d.
... pro CClx pellibus agnellorum valor xxv s.
... pro CC pellibus shorlynges et morlynges valor xxx s.

... pro Ciiij^{xx} pellibus shorlynges et morlynges	valor xxv s.
... pro j plaustro plumbi	valor lx s.
... pro CClx pellibus shorlynges et morlynges	valor xxvij s. vj d.
... pro Ciiij^{xx} pellibus shortynges et morlynges	valor xxxv s.
... pro Ciiij^{xx} pellibus shortynges et morlynges	valor xxxv s.
... pro Ciij^{xx} pellibus shorlynges et morlynges	valor xxij s. vj d.
... ... pellibus shorlynges et morlynges	valor xxv s.
... ... CCC pellibus shorlynges et morlynges	valor xxxvij s. vj d.
... ... pellibus agnellorum	valor xxx s.
... ... pellibus shorlynges et morlynges	valor xxvij s. vj d.
... ... pellibus agnellorum	valor xxv s.
... ... pellibus shorlynges et morlynges	valor xxv s.
... pro CCCx pellibus agnellorum	valor xxxiij s. iiij d.
... pro CC xxx pellibus shorlynges and morlynges	valor xlviij s. iiij d.
... ... pellibus shorlynges et morlynges	valor xviij s. iiij d.
Summa valoris [*blank*]	

The Mare James de Novo Castro unde Nicolaus Blak est magister exivit xv die Marcii anno x^{mo} Henrici vij^{mi}

Willelmus Herryson indigena pro j sarplera lane ponderante v saccos j quarterium vj clavos

Willelmus Harden indigena pro j sarplera lane ponderante j saccum iij quarteria

Henricus Bednall indigena pro j sarplera lane ponderante j saccum j quarterium

Idem pro xxx pellibus lanutis continentibus dimidium quarterium

Ricardus Conyngham indigena pro ij sarpleris lane ponderantibus iij saccos et dimidium

Idem pro lxxx pellibus lanutis continentibus j quarterium xxx pelles

Thomas Riddall indigena pro j sarplera lane ponderante ij saccos

Idem pro Cxx pellibus lanutis continentibus dimidium saccum

Willelmus Felton indigena pro ij sarpleris lane ponderantibus iiij saccos vij clavos

Idem pro Cxx pellibus lanutis continentibus dimidium saccum

Robertus Hely indigena pro j sarplera lane ponderante j saccum dimidium v clavos

Idem pro xl pellibus lanutis continentibus dimidium quarterium x pelles

Georgius Stalper indigena pro j sarplera lane ponderante j saccum dimidium

Rolandus Herryson indigena pro CCC pellibus lanutis continentibus j saccum et j quarterium

Thomas Harden indigena pro j sarplera lane ponderante ij saccos j quarterium ix clavos

Thomas Moll indigena pro lx pellibus lanutis continentibus j quarterium

Ricardus Hebburn indigena pro j sarplera lane ponderante j saccum

Willelmus Swan indigena pro j sarplera lane ponderante j saccum dimidium iiij clavos

Willelmus Camby indigena pro j sarplera lane ponderante j saccum j quarterium
Idem pro C pellibus lanutis continentibus j quarterium xl pelles
Georgius Selby indigena pro j pokett lane ponderante j quarterium
Sequitur pondagium in eadem nave
Radulphus Biker indigena pro viij cheldris carbonum valor vj s. viij d.
Idem pro ij cheldris grinstonys valor x s.
Henricus Bednall indigena pro Clxij pellibus shorlynges et morlynges valor xxij s. vj d.
Ricardus Conyngham indigena pro Cl pellibus shorlynges et morlynges valor xxj s. viij d.
Thomas Riddall indigena pro C pellibus shorlynges valor xv s.
Willelmus Felton indigena pro Cvj pellibus shorlynge et morlynges valor xv s. x d.
Robertus Hely indigena pro v^{xx} pellibus shorlynes et morlynges valor xij s. vj d.
Rolandus Herryson indigena pro CCiiij^{xx} pellibus shorlynges et morlynges valor xl s.
Georgius Conyngham indigena pro C pellibus shorlynges et morlynges valor xv s.
Thomas Moll indigena pro iiij^{xx}vij pellibus shorlynges et morlynges valor x s. x d.
Willelmus Camby indigena pro Cxx pellibus shorlynges et morlynges valor xvij s. vj d.
Summa valoris [*blank*]

The botte of Qweenes ferrie unde Donkan Andresen est magister applicuit xj^{o} die Aprilis anno x^{mo} Henrici vij^{mi}
Robertus Barton alienigena pro v barrelles smigmatis valor l s.
Idem pro vj barrelles allecis albi salsi
Idem pro j barrelle salmonis valor xiij s. iiij d.
Idem per ij barrelles trane olei valor xxx s.
[*Membrane 3 face*]
Idem pro ij last cinerum valor xl s.
Idem pro ij pokes canabi valor xl s.
Idem pro v parv' fulles kettylles valor x s.
Idem pro lx libris patellis eneis valor xv s.
Idem pro C libris suger valor xx s.
Idem pro j coper kettylle gravus valor x s.
Idem pro iiij peciis panni linei continentibus iiij^{xx}x elle valor xl s.
Summa valoris [*blank*]

The Nicolas de Depe unde Georgius Roundey est magister exivit xiiij^{o} die Aprilis anno x^{mo} Henrici vij^{mi}
Giles Irake alienigena pro xiiij cheldris carbonum valor xxiij s. iiij d.
Idem pro ij cheldris gryndstones valor xvjs. viij d.
Idem pro j quarterio unius plaustri plumbi valor xlvj s. viij d.

Idem pro j dussena virgarum panni lanei stricti valor v s.
Summa valoris [*blank*]

The Katren de Depe unde Petir Revnott est magister exivit xiiij° die Aprilis anno x^{mo} Henrici vij^{mi}
Idem magister alienigena pro xxiiij cheldris carbonum valor xl s.
Idem pro ij barrelles bituminis valor vj s. viij d.
Idem pro j plaustro et uno quarterio plumbi valor lxx s.
Summa valoris [*blank*]

The botte de Qwhenes ferrie unde Donkan Andreson est magister exivit xxiij° die Aprilis anno x Henrici vij^{mi}
Robertus Barton alienigena pro vij cheldris ordei valor xlvj s. viij d.
Idem pro j dacra et dimidia corriorum tannatorum aridorum valor xx s.
Summa valoris [*blank*]

The Margret de Novo Castro unde Willelmus Tutyll est magister applicuit ii° die Maii anno x^{mo} Henrici vij^{mi}
... pro x last cinerum valor iiij li. x s.
... pro j ballet mader pond' D valor xxxiij s. iiij d.
... ... ij credylles vitri valor xx s.
... ... vj barrelles smigmatis valor iiij li.
Summa valoris [*blank*]

The Antone de Cales unde Willelmus Mateson est magister applicuit xvij° die Maii anno x^{mo} Henrici vij^{mi}
... ... schyff tasylles valor xlvj s. viij d.
... ... last bituminis valor xxvj s. viij d.
... ... barrelles smigmatis valor lxx s.
... ... ores valor x s.
... ... peccis panni linei continentibus xx virgas valor vj s. viij d.
... ... pair qweschens valor vj s. viij d.
... ... last emptie barrelles valor v s.
... ... pokes hoppe valor lv s.
... ... hogeshed vini non dulcis
Summa valoris [*blank*]

... de Novo Castro unde Johannes Smyth est magister exivit xix° die Maii anno x^{mo} Henrici vij^{mi}
... pro xij cheldris carbonum valor x s.
... pro viij cheldris le gryndstones valor xxx s.
... ... cepi valor xj s. viij d.
... ... dussenis virgarum panni lanei stricti
... ... pellibus agnellorum valor xxx s.
Summa valoris [*blank*]

The Cristofer de Depe unde Cristoferus Meisther est magister exivit xix^{o} die Maii anno x^{mo} Henrici vij^{mi}

... pro xxiiij cheldris carbonum valor xl s.
... pro iiij dacris corriorum pellium tannatorum valor iiij li.
... pro vij virgis panni lanei stricti valor ij s. vj d.
Summa valoris [*blank*]

The Breger de Bullon unde Girrum Kanney est magister exivit xx^{o} die Maii anno x^{mo} Henrici vij^{mi}

Idem magister alienigena pro xviij cheldris carbonum valor xxx s.
... pro ij cheldris le gryndstonys valor xvj s. viij d.
... pro ij dacris et dimidio pellium tannatarum aridarum valor xxxiij s. iiij d.
... pro vij dussenis virgarum panni lanei stricti valor xxx s.
Summa valoris [*blank*]

The Cronew de Depe unde Gilliaume Allen est magister exivit xxj^{o} die Maii anno x Henrici vij^{mi}

Johannes de Santt Malow alienigena pro j plaustro plumbi valor lxvj s. viij d.
Idem pro xxx cheldris carbonum valor l s.
Idem pro ij cheldris petrarum valor xvj s. viij d.
Idem pro vij dussenis virgarum panni lanei stricti valor xxxv s.
Summa valoris [*blank*]

The Katren de Bullon unde Collen Lobbey est magister exivit $xxij^{o}$ die Maii anno x^{mo} Henrici vij^{mi}

Idem magister alienigena pro xxiij cheldris carbonum valor xxxviij s. iiij d.
Idem pro ij dussenis rubstonys valor xx d.
Summa valoris [*blank*]

The Antone de Cales unde Willelmus Mateson est magister exivit ij^{o} die Junii anno x^{mo} Henrici vij^{mi}

Idem magister indigena pro xx cheldris carbonum valor xxxiij s. iiij d.
Idem pro xv cheldris petrarum valor v li. x s.
Idem pro vj dussenis virgarum panni lanei stricti
Summa valoris [*blank*]

The Cristofer de Cales unde Johannes Halewell est magister applicuit iij^{o} die Junii anno x^{mo} Henrici vij^{mi}

Willelmus Johnson indigena de Cales pro iij pokettes hoppe valor iiij li.
Summa valoris [*blank*]

The Katren de Depe unde Petir Revnott est magister exivit iiij^{o} die Junii anno x^{mo} Henrici vij^{mi}
Idem magister alienigena pro xx cheldris carbonum valor xxxiij s. iiij d.
Willelmus Swan indigena pro j plaustro plumbi valor lx s.
Summa valoris [*blank*]

[*Membrane 3 dorse*]
The Cristofer de Cales unde Johannes Halowell est magister exivit vij^{o} die Junii anno x^{mo} Henrici vij^{mi}
Willelmus Johnson indigena pro xvj cheldris carbonum valor xxvj s. viij d.
Idem pro xv cheldris gryndstonys valor vj li.
Summa valoris [*blank*]

The Mare James de Novo Castro unde Nicholaus Blak est magister applicuit xvj die Junii anno x^{mo} Henrici vij^{mi}
Bartramus Yonghusband indigena pro lxvij finibus ferri ponderantibus M valor xxx s.
Willelmus Felton indigena pro xv^{xx} parvis finibus lukes ferri ponderantibus ij dolia valor vj li.
Georgius Conyngham pro iij^{xx}x finibus ferri ponderantibus M valor xxx s.
Henricus Bednall indigena pro vj^{xx} finibus ferri ponderantibus MD valor xl s.
Thomas Harden indigena pro ix^{xx} parvis finibus lukes ferri ponderantibus M valor lx s.
Robertus Harden indigena pro lx parvis finibus lukes ferri ponderantibus D valor xv s.
Thomas Riddall indigena pro xvj^{xx} peciis ferri ponderantibus iij M valor iiij li. x s.
Maurus Mawer indigena pro j hogeshed xj parv' ballet cane wade valor xiij s. iiij d.
Idem pro xxxvij finibus ferri ponderantibus CCCC valor xiij s. iiij d.
Thomas Moll indigena pro j poke canabi valor xx s.
Rolandus Herryson indigena pro xviij^{xx} parvis finibus ferri ponderantibus ij dolia valor vj li.
Ricardus Hebburn pro iij pypys tasylles valor xx s.
Idem pro j barrelle verguce valor vj s. viij d.
Idem pro j barrelle cum pannis valor xxvj s. viij d.
Idem pro xiij^{xx} finibus ferri ponderantibus iij M valor iiij li. x s.
Idem pro j stodye ferri pro fabro valor vj s. viij d.
Willelmus Swan indigena pro v^{xx} parvis finibus ponderantibus M valor xxxvj s. viij d.
Summa valoris [*blank*]

The Cristofer de Kessynglond unde Thomas Percy est magister exivit xvij die Junii anno x^mo^ Henrici vij^mi^

Willelmus Canmeld indigena pro xx cheldris carbonum	valor xxvj s. viij d.
Idem pro j cheldra et dimidia petrarum	valor x s.
Summa valoris [*blank*]	

The George Byker de Novo Castro unde Willelmus Cheverous est magister applicuit xxij^o^ die Junii anno x^mo^ Henrici vij^mi^

Robertus Gray indigena pro x barrelles smigmatis	valor C s.
Idem pro j pype cum C libris canabi Idem pro j gros spinctrorum Idem pro ij gros wyvurn lases Idem pro j libra fili	valor v li. vj s. viij d.
... pro vj peciis holand panni linei continentibus vij^xx^ virgas	valor v li. vj s. viij d.
Wilelmus Draver indigena pro ij barrelles smigmatis	valor xx s.
Idem pro j pok canabi	valor xx s.
Idem pro CC warpe crusis	valor vj s. viij d.
Rolandus Herryson indigena pro iiij barrelles smigmatis	valor xl s.
Georgius Stalper indigena pro v cast crusis	valor xiij s. iiij d.
Idem pro iij barrelles smigmatis	valor xxx s.
Robertus Baxter pro iij barrelles smigmatis	valor xl s.
Thomas Camby ... balletts mader pond' CCCC	valor xxvj s. viij d.
Idem ... barrelles smigmatis	valor xx s.
... ... barrelles smigmatis	valor l s.
Idem ... ballet mader pond' CCCC	valor xxvj s. viij d.
Georgius Car indigena ... barrelles smigmatis	valor xx s.
Summa valoris [*blank*]	

The Mare Hayrbred de Novo Castro unde Johannes Happ est magister applicuit xxvj^o^ die Junii anno x^mo^ Henrici vij^mi^

... ... parvis pokettis mader ponderantibus CCCC	valor xxvj s. viij d.
... pro j poke canabi	valor xx s.
... pro ij barrelles smigmatis	valor xx s.
... ... ij pokes canabi	valor xl s.
... ... barelle steyll	valor xxvj s. viij d.
... ... pokett mader pond' D	valor xxvj s. viij d.
... ... maund cont' xvj rim alb'paupire ... ... rym nigr' paupire	valor xx s.
... ... finibus lukes ferri	valor xxx s.
... ... barrelles smigmatis	valor xl s.
... ... mader	valor xxvj s. viij d.

... ... poke canabi	valor xx s.
... ... j cista suger	valor xxvj s. viij d.
... ... parvis kettylles	valor x s.
... ... balett mader pond' D	valor xxvj s. viij d.
... ... iij barrelles smigmatis	valor xxx s.
... ... j poke canabi	valor xx s.
... ... j balett mader	valor xxvj s. viij d.
... ... j poke canabi	valor xx s.
... ... iiij barrelles smigmatis	valor xl s.
... ... pro j balett mader	valor xxvj s. viij d.
... pro ij barrelles smigmatis	valor xx s.
Thomas Conyngham indigena ro iiij barrelles smigmatis	valor xl s.
Idem pro j poke canabi	valor xx s.
Thomas Riddall indigena pro di'barrelle steyll	valor xxvj s. viij d.
Idem pro j balett mader pond' D	valor xxvj s. viij d.
Idem pro j parv' barrelle wyer	valor xx s.
Bartramus Yonghusband indigena pro di' barrell steyll	valor xxvj s. viij d.
Idem pro j cista continente xij pecias panni linei continentibus CC lx elles	valor vij li. x s.
Willelmus Allan indigena pro di' barrelle steyll	valor xxvj s. viij d.
Thomas Camby indigena pro di' barrelle steyll	valor xxvj s. viij d.
Idem pro ij barrelles smigmatis	valor xx s.
Willelmus Draver indigena pro j barrelle smigmatis	valor x s.
Henricus Bednall indigena pro iiij barrelles smigmatis	valor xl s.
Thomas Cook indigena pro iij barrelles smigmatis	valor xxx s.
Summa valoris [*blank*]	

The Jakett de Bullon unde Thomas Richerd est magister exivit xxvij die Juneii anno x^{mo} Henrici vij^{mi}

Idem magister alienigena pro xv cheldris carbonum	valor xxv s.
Idem pro vj parv' gryndstonys	valor xx d.
Summa valoris [*blank*]	

The Grace de Dew de Bullon unde Johannes Cattanyey est magister exivit xxvij die Junii anno x^{mo} Henrici vij^{mi}

Idem magister alienigena pro xxx cheldris carbonum	valor l s.
Idem pro ij parv' gryndstonys	valor xx d.
Idem pro vj virgis panni lanei stricti	valor iij s. iiij d.
Summa valoris [*blank*]	

[*Membrane 4 face*]
The Barbara de Bullon unde Onerey Goddert est magister exivit xxvij die Junii anno x Henrici vij^{mi}
Anton Benwysse alienigena pro xvij cheldris carbonum valor xxx s.
Idem pro dimidia cheldra petrarum valor iij s. iiij d.
Summa valoris [*blank*]

The Jenett de Bullon unde Johannes de John est magister exivit penultimo die Junii anno x^{mo} Henrici vij^{mi}
Idem magister alienigena pro x cheldris carbonum valor xvj s. viij d.
Idem pro vj cheldris petrarum valor l s.
Summa valoris [*blank*]

The Katren de Berwyk unde Robertus Huker est magister exivit vj^{o} die Julii anno x^{mo} Henrici vij^{mi}
Willelmus Selby indigena pro M pellibus agnellorum valor C s.
Georgius Car indigena pro DC pellibus agnellorum valor lx s.

The Nicolas de Leyth unde Willelmus Mirremonte est magister applicuit xvj die Julii anno x^{mo} Henrici vij^{mi}
Robert Barton alienigena pro CCCC mode fisch valor liij s. iiij d.
Idem pro v barrelles salmonis valor l s.
Summa valoris [*blank*]

The Nicolas de Leyth unde Willelmus Mirremonte est magister exivit xxij^{o} die Julii anno x Henrici vij
Robert Barton alienigena pro j dacra pellium vaccarum tannatarum valor xiij s. iiij d.
Georgius Birde indigena pro iij plaustris plumbi valor ix li.
Idem pro ij doliis vini
Summa valoris [*blank*]

The neffe de Bullon unde Reynold Pottage est magister applicuit xvj die Augusti anno x Henrici vij
Idem magister alienigena pro l ores valor xiij s. iiij d.
... pro j wey salis grossi valor xiij s. iiij d.
summa valoris [*blank*]

... de Abbevyll unde Johannes de Mirre est magister applicuit xviij^{o} die Augusti anno x^{mo} Henrici vij^{mi}
... ... finibus ferri valor xxvj s. viij d.
Summa valoris [*blank*]

The Cristofer de Cales unde Johannes Hogeson est magister applicuit xx^{o} die Augusti anno x Henrici vij^{mi}
... ... parv' pokes hoppe valor iiij li.
... ... M cast crusis valor xxx s.
... ... vj barrelles smigmatis valor iij li.

... ... pokes fethers valor xxvj s. viij d.
... ... vjC bonches corke
... ... j parv' tabyll image valor iij s. iiij d.
... ... paving tylde valor x s.
... ... barelle cum lasis et poyntes threyde valor xx s.
... ... dussenis virgis parvarum peciarum panni linei valor vj s. viij d.
Summa valoris [*blank*]

The Antone de Cales unde Willelmus Mateson est magister applicuit xxiiij° die Augusti anno xj^{mo} Henrici vij^{mi}
... pro xij M breke valor xiij s. iiij d.
... pro xiij barrelles bituminis valor xxx s.
... ... xij ores valor v s.
... ... iij barrelles smigmatis valor xxx s.
... ... schyffe tassylles vj s. viij d.
... ... Clx bonches onyons vjs. viij d.
... ... iij parv' pokes hoppe valor xl s.
... ... ix virgis panni linei valor iij s. iiij d.
... ... x fether bede tykkes valor xx s.
Summa valoris [*blank*]

The Fransoce de Stapilles unde Tossen Peryngall est magister exivit xxiiij° die Augusti anno xj^{mo} Henrici vij
Idem magister alienigena pro xvj cheldris carbonum valor xxvj s. viij d.
Summa valoris [*blank*]

The Nicolas de Depe unde Willelmus Rowdin est magister applicuit xxv° die Augusti anno xj^{mo} Henrici vij^{mi}
Idem magister alienigena pro iiij^{xx} finibus ferri ponderantibus M valor xxx s.
Summa valoris [*blank*]

The Jossett de Bullon unde Reynold Pottage est magister exivit xxv° die Augusti anno xi^{mo} Henrici vij^{mi}
Idem magister alienigena pro xx cheldris carbonum valor xxxiij s. iiij d.
Idem pro xviij petris sepi valor x s.
Summa valoris [*blank*]

The Jakett de Bullon unde Johannes Mirres est magister exivit xxv die Augusti anno xj^{mo} Henrici vij^{mi}
Idem magister alienigena pro xviij cheldris carbonum valor xxx s.
Summa valoris [*blank*]

The Margret de Stapilles unde Johannes Spanyez est magister exivit xxv° die Augusti anno xj° Henrici vij^{mi}
Idem magister alienigena pro xxvj cheldris carbonum valor xliij s. iiij d.
Summa valoris [*blank*]

The Gabrielle de Stapilles unde Johannes Pottez est magister exivit xxv^{o} die Augusti anno xj^{mo} Henrici vij
Idem magister alienigena pro xx cheldris carbonum valor xxxiij s. iiij d.
Idem pro dimidia cheldra petrarum valor iij s. iiij d.
Summa valoris [*blank*]

The Jakett de Bullon unde Thomas Richerd est magister exivit xxv^{o} die Augusti anno xj^{mo} Henrici vij^{mi}
Idem magister alienigena pro xiij cheldris carbonum valor xxiij s. iiij d.
Summa valoris [*blank*]

[*Membrane 4 dorse*]
The Pete Savorey de Abveyll unde Johannes Mirr est magister exivit xxv^{o} die Augusti anno xj Henrici vij^{mi}
Idem magister alienigena pro xx cheldris carbonum valor xxxiij s. iiij d.
Summa valoris [*blank*]

The Mare de Abveyll unde Willelmus Charles est magister exivit xxv^{o} die Augusti anno xj^{mo} Henrici vij^{mi}
Idem magister alienigena pro xxxij cheldris carbonum valor liij s. iiij d.
Summa valoris [*blank*]

The Nicolas de Depe unde Willelmus Rowdyn est magister exivit xxviij die Augusti anno xj^{mo} Henrici vij^{mi}
Idem magister alienigena pro xx cheldris carbonum valor xxxij s. iiij d.
Summa valoris [*blank*]

The Barbara de Bullon unde Onerey Goddert est magister <exivit *struck out*> applicuit ultimo die Augusti anno xj^{mo} Henrici vij^{mi}
Idem magister alienigena pro lxxx botte ores valor xx s.
Summa valoris [*blank*]

The Barbara de Bullon unde Onerey Goddert est magister exivit primo die Septembris anno xj^{mo} Henrici vij^{mi}
Idem magister alienigena pro xx cheldris carbonum valor xxxiij s. iiij d.
Summa valoris [*blank*]

The Margaret de Novo Castro unde Johannes Smyth est magister exivit x^{mo} die Septembris anno xj^{mo} Henrici vij^{mi}
Thomas Sanderson indigena pro viij cheldris carbonum valor viij s. iiij d.
Idem pro x cheldris petrarum valor l s.
Idem pro CC pellibus agnellorum valor xx s.
Thomas Cambye indigena pro MC pellibus agnellorum valor v li. x s.
Robertus Baxter indigena pro MCC pellibus agnellorum valor vj li.
Idem pro xlvij pellibus shorlinges valor vj s. viij d.
Georgius Selby indigena pro CCxl pellibus agnellorum valor xxiij s. iiij d.

Georgius Birde indigena pro DCC pellibus agnellorum valor iij li. x s.
Willelmus Davell indigena pro DC pellibus agnellorum valor iij li.
Georgius Stalper indigena pro CCC xxx pellibus agnellorum valor xxxij s. vj d.
Robertus Harden indigena pro D pellibus agnellorum valor l s.
Cristoferus Brigham indigena pro DCC pellibus agnellorum valor iij li. x s.
Idem pro xxx pellibus shorlinges valor iij s. iiij d.
Willelmus Haynyng indigena pro CC pellibus agnellorum valor xx s.
Katerina Burrell indigena pro Clx pellibus agnellorum valor xv s.
Henricus Bednall indigena pro CCC pellibus agnellorum valor xxx s.
Willelmus Conynghame indigena pro CC xl pellibus agnellorum valor xxiij s. iiij d.
Summa valoris [*blank*]

The Antone de Cales unde Willelmus Mateson est magister exivit xij° die Septembris anno xj° Henrici vij^{mi}
... pro xviij cheldris carbonum valor xlvj s. viij d.
... pro viij cheldris petrarum valor viij s. iiij d.
Summa valoris [*blank*]

... unde Johannes Dine est magister exivit xiiij° die Septembris anno xj^{mo} Henrici vij^{mi}
... pro xxx cheldris carbonum valor l s.
... pro iij dacris corriorum tannatorum valor l s.
... pro ij dussenis virgarum panni lanei stricti valor x s.
Summa valoris [*blank*]

The Cristofer de Cales unde Johannes Hogston est magister exivit xv° die Septembris anno xi° Henrici vij^{mi}
... ... xxviij cheldris carbonum valor xlvj s. viij d.
... ... iij cheldris petrarum valor xxvj s. viij d.
... ... j dacra corriorum tannatorum valor xvj s. viij d.
... ... l libris throms valor v s.
Summa valoris [*blank*]

... de Novo Castro unde Lodvicus Sothern est magister exivit xvj° die Septembris anno xj° Henrici vij^{mi}
... Brigham pro viij sarpleris lane ponderantibus xiij saccos
Idem pro iiij^{xx} pellibus lanutis continentibus j quarterium et dimidium
... pro vj sarpleris lane ponderantibus x saccos j quarterium vij clavos
... pro j sarplera lane ponderante j saccum iij quarteria iij clavos
... pro lx pellibus lanutis continentibus j quarterium

... pro j sarplera lane ponderante v saccos v clavos
... pro j sarplera lane ponderante j saccum j quarterium v clavos
Willelmus Davell indigena pro iij sarpleris lane ponderantibus iiij saccos iij clavos
Robertus Harden indigena pro j sarplera lane ponderante j saccum dimidium iij clavos
Idem pro Cxx pellibus lanutis continentibus dimidium saccum
Georgius Birde indigena pro ij sarpleris lane ponderantibus iij saccos iiij clavos
Idem pro Cxx pellibus lanutis continentibus dimidium saccum
Johannes Passeley indigena pro iiij^{xx}x pellibus lanutis continentibus j quarterium et dimidium
Georgius Stalper indigena pro j sarplera lane ponderante j saccum iij quarteria

Sequitur pondagium in eadem nave

Cristoferus Brigham indigena pro iij plaustris plumbi valor ix li.
Idem pro iiij^{xx} pellibus shorlynges valor x s.
Willelmus Harden indigena pro v^{xx}v pellibus shorlynges et morlynges valor xiij s. iiij d.
Johannes Blaxton indigena pro Cxv pellibus shorlynges et morlynges valor xvj s. viij d.
Robertus Harden indigena pro CC pellibus shorlynges et morlynges valor xxx s.
Georgius Birde indigena pro lx pellibus shorlynges valor vij s. vj d.
Johannes Passeley indigena pro C xxxiiij pellibus shorlynges valor xx s.
Georgius Stalper indigena pro C iiij^{xx} pellibus shorlynges valor xxv s.

Summa valoris [*blank*]

The George de Novo Castro unde Johannes Arnold est magister exivit xvj° die Septembris anno xj° Henrici vij^{mi}
Thomas Swan indigena pro iij sarpleris lane ponderantibus ij saccos et dimidium
Robertus Harden indigena pro ij sarpleris lane ponderantibus iij saccos vij clavos
Idem pro iiij^{xx} pellibus lanutis continentibus j quarterium xxx pelles
[*Membrane 5 face*]
Georgius Birde indigena pro iij sarpleris lane ponderantibus iiij saccos j quarterium iiij clavos
Idem pro xlv pellibus lanutis continentibus dimidium quarterium xv pelles
Maurus Mawer indigena pro j sarplera lane ponderante j saccum iij quarteria
Jacobus Buk indigena pro ij sarpleris lane ponderantibus iij saccos
Ricardus Wrangwish indigena pro j sarplera ponderante j saccum j quarterium
Johannes Passelely indigena pro ij sarpleris lane ponderantibus iij saccos j quarterium vij clavos

Willelmus Swan indigena pro iij sarpleris lane ponderantibus iij saccos j quarterium
Georgius Selby indigena pro ij sarpleris lane ponderantibus ij saccos x clavos
Idem pro xxx pellibus lanutis continentibus dimidium quarterium
Robertus Baxter indigena pro j sarplera lane ponderante j saccum j quarterium
Idem pro CC xxv pellibus lanutis continentibus iij quarteria et xlv pelles
Johannes Baxter indigena pro ij sarpleris lane ponderantibus iij saccos j quarterium
Johannes Brandlyng indigena pro j sarplera lane ponderante ij saccos j quarterium
Bartramus Yonghusband indigena pro ij sarpleris lane ponderantibus ij saccos j quarterium v clavos
Willelmus Hayning indigena pro j sarplera lane ponderante j saccum v clavos
Cristoferus Brigham indigena pro iij sarpleris lane ponderantibus iiij saccos iij quarteria v clavos
Willelmus Felton indigena pro ij sarpleris lane ponderantibus iij saccos iiij clavos
Thomas Moll indigena pro j sarplera lane ponderante j saccum j quarterium
Idem pro xl pellibus lanutis continentibus xl pelles
... Conyngham indigena pro iij sarpleris lane ponderantibus iiij saccos j quarterium v clavos
Willelmus Davell indigena pro j sarplera lane ponderante j saccum iij quarteria viij clavos
Rogerus Raw indigena pro ij sarpleris lane ponderantibus ij saccos j quarterium vj clavos
... indigena pro j sarplera lane ponderante j saccum j quarterium
... indigena pro j sarplera lane ponderante j saccum dimidum
... indigena pro j sarplera lane ponderante iij quarteriis iij clavos
... indigena pro j sarplera lane ponderante j saccum j quarterium

Sequitur pondagium in eadem nave

... ... grindstons	valor vij s. vj d.
... ... cheldris carbonum	valor ij s. vj d.
... pro vj cheldris petrarum	valor xx s.
... pro ij barrelles sepi	valor xx s.
... Harden indigena pro CC pellibus shorlynges et morlynges	valor xv s.
... pro vj dossenis virgarum panni lanei stricti	
... ... shorlynges et morlynges	valor xij s. vj d.
... ... plaustris plumbi	
... ... pellibus shorlinges and morlinges	valor vj s. viij d.
... ... pellibus shorlinges and morlinges	valor xxxvij s. vj d.
... ... pellibus shorlinges	valor x s.
... ... pellibus agnellorum	valor vj s. viij d.

... ... barrelles cepi	valor xxvj s. viij d.
... ... pellibus agnellorum	valor v s.
... ... pellibus morlinges	valor vij s. vj d.
... ... virgarum panni lanei stricti	
... ... pellibus shorlinges and morlinges	valor vij s. vj d.
... ... pellibus shorlinges and morlinges	valor xiij s. vj d.
... ... dussenis virgarum panni lanei stricti	
Summa valoris [*blank*]	

The Anne de Novo Castro unde Johannes Tutyll est magister exivit xvj die Septembris anno xj° Henrici vij^{mi}

... indigena pro iiij parvis sarpleris ponderantibus iiij saccos iij quarteria v clavos

... indigena pro iij sarpleris lane ponderantibus vj saccos

Johannes Passeley indigena pro j sarplera lane ponderante j saccum j quarterium

Idem pro Cxx pellibus lanutis continentibus dimidium saccum

Willelmus Scott indigena pro ij sarpleris lane ponderante iij saccos dimidium

Idem pro lx pellibus lanutis continentibus j quarterium

Johannes Baxter indigena pro iij sarpleris lane ponderantibus iij saccos

Johannes Bewyk indigena pro j sarplera lane ponderante j saccum j quarterium

Idem pro lx pellibus lanutis continentibus j quarterium

Georgius Stalper indigena pro iij sarpleris lane ponderantibus iij saccos iij quarteria

Willelmus Haynyng indigena pro ij sarpleris lane ponderantibus iij saccos

Idem pro xxx pellibus lanutis continentibus dimidium quarterium

Thomas Horseley indigena pro xv pellibus lanutis continentibus xv pelles

Rogerus Raw indigena pro j sarplera lane ponderante j saccum dimidium

Idem pro xxx pellibus lanutis continentibus xxx pelles

Ricardus Wrangwish indigena pro j sarplera lane ponderante j saccum iij quarteria

Willelmus Harden indigena pro j sarplera lane ponderante ij saccos

Maurus Mawer indigena pro ij sarpleris lane ponderantibus ij saccos iij quarteria

Idem pro Cxx pellibus lanutis continentibus dimidium saccum

Johannes Blaxton indigena pro ij sarpleris lane ponderantibus iij saccos

Willelmus Davell indigena pro j sarplera lane ponderante ij saccos

Thomas Conyngham indigena pro ij sarpleris lane ponderantibus iij saccos v clavos

Georgius Birde indigena pro j sarplera lane ponderante j saccum dimidium

Jacobus Blak indigena pro j sarplera lane ponderante j saccum dimidium

Johannes Penreth indigena pro j sarplera lane ponderante j saccum iij quarteria
Idem pro CCx pellibus lanutis continentibus iij quarteria xxx pelles
Cristoferus Davell indigena pro j sarplera lane ponderante j saccum j quarterium vj clavos
Willelmus Felton indigena pro j sarplera lane ponderante j saccum dimidium viij clavos
Sequitur pondagium in eadem nave
Johannes Tutyll indigena pro dimidio plaustro plumbi valor xxx s.
Idem pro lxxiiij pellibus shorlinges valor viij s. iiij d.
[*Membrane 5 dorse*]
Robertus Allen indigena pro x cheldris carbonum valor viij s. iiij d.
Idem pro iiij cheldris gryndstonys valor xx s.
Idem pro iij dussenis rubstonys valor v s.
Idem pro Cxxx pellibus shorlynges et morlynges valor xviij s. iiij d.
Johannes Passeley pro CCCxx shorlynges et morlynges valor xlvij s. vj d.
Willelmo Scott indigena pro Cxxviij shorlynges valor xviij s. iiij d.
Idem pro C xx pellibus agnellorum valor xj s. viij d.
Johannes Bewyk indigena pro CC xliij pellibus shorlynges et morlynges valor xxv s.
Idem pro lxxx pellibus agnellorum valor vj s. viij d.
Willelmus Haynyng indigena pro xxx pellibus shorlynges valor iij s. iiij d.
Thomas Horseley indigena pro j plaustro et iij quarteriis plumbi valor v li. v s.
Idem pro xxj pellibus lanutis valor ij s. vj d.
Rogerus Raw indigena pro ij plaustris et j quarterio plumbi valor vj li. xv s.
Idem pro lxxxviij pellibus shorlynges valor xj s. viij d.
Maurus Mawer indigena pro Clxxvj pellibus shorlynges et morlynges valor xxiij s. vj d.
Idem pro ij dussenis panni lanei stricti
Willelmus Davell indigena pro ij dussenis panni lanei stricti
Johannes Penreth indigena pro Cl pellibus shorlinges et morlinges valor xxj s. vj d.
Summa valoris [*blank*]

The Mare Grace de Novo Castro unde Willelmus Marbotell est magister exivit xvj die Septembris anno xj° Henrici vij^mi^
Ricardus Benett indigena pro j sarplera lane ponderante j saccum
Georgius Birde indigena pro iiij sarpleris lane ponderantibus vj saccos j quarterium viij clavos
Willelmus Birde indigena pro j sarplera lane ponderante j saccum iij quarteria viij clavos
Johannes Blaxton indigena pro ij sarpleris lane ponderantibus ij saccos dimidium v clavos

Johannes Passeley indigena pro j sarplera lane ponderante j saccum
Willelmus Selby indigena pro j parv' pokett lane ponderante dimidium saccum viij clavos
Willelmus Allen indigena pro j sarplera lane ponderante j saccum
... Swan indigena pro j sarplera lane ponderante j saccum

Sequitur pondagium in eadem nave

... pro xx cheldris carbonum	valor xx s.
... pro iij quarteriis unius plaustri plumbi	valor xlv s.
... pro vij dussenis panni lanei stricti	
... pro v dacris pellium tannatarum aridarum	valor l s.
... pro vj dussenis panni lanei stricti	
... pro ij barellis sepi	valor xiij s. iiij d.
... pro iij dacris pellium tannatarum aridarum	valor xxx s.

Summa valoris [*blank*]

... rotulos liberavit predictus contrarotulator xj die Novembris anno xj regis Henrici septimi.

12. Particulars of account of Humphrey Metcalf and Bartram Mitford, collectors, from Michaelmas 1499 to Michaelmas 1500.

E 122/108/4

The account consists of fifteen membranes: 1, 673 mm. long x 267 mm. wide; 2, 686 x 270 mm.; 3, 699 x 279 mm.; 4, 679 x 270 mm.; 5, 689 x 279 mm.; 6, 689 x 281 mm.; 7, 689 x 281 mm.; 8, 686 x 279 mm.; 9, 699 x 281 mm.; 10, 696 x 279 mm.; 11, 670 x 263 mm.; 12, 689 x 263 mm.; 13, 749 x 180 mm.; 14, 77 x 222 mm.; and 15, 63 x 247 mm. Membranes 1–12 form the collectors' account. Membrane 13 is a schedule listing goods shipped free of subsidy because equivalent quantities had earlier been lost at sea. Membranes 14 and 15 each contain a letter certifying membership of the Teutonic Hanse in London.

All the information in the collectors' account is presented in the text below, but a few amounts of custom and subsidy, shown by ..., are missing due to damage. Passages in square brackets in roman type have been supplied from the controller's account, E 122/108/5; this has also been compared with the collectors' account, and the few instances where it differs in wording have been noted.

There were many interlineations, in a different hand from that of the principal scribe, resulting from the need to remove any doubts about either the status of exporters or the place of origin of the wool they shipped. To qualify for the privileges granted by the king to the merchant gild of Newcastle upon Tyne, membership of the gild had to be made abundantly clear. That the wool exported was grown in Northumberland, Westmorland, Cumberland, the bishopric of Durham and in the counties of Richmond and Allerton had also to be stated without ambiguity, since it was only to wool from these areas that the gilds' privileges applied. In addition to an old-established exemption of inferior woolfells – shorlings, morlings and lambfells – from the wool custom and subsidy, the gild members in the period of this account were excused all but one quarter of the normal rate of duty on fleece wool and on first quality woolfells, *pelles lanute*.

The final summary of account shows that out of £3,006. 14 s. 2½ d. chargeable, only £358. 13 s. 11¼ d. was due from the collectors at Newcastle after these exemptions and privileges had been applied.

[*Membrane 1 face*]

{Novum Castrum}
Particule compoti Umfridi Metcalf et Bartrami Mitford collectorum custumarum et subsidiorum domini regis lanarum coriorum et pellium lanutarum, ac parve custume, necnon subsidiorum tonagii et pondagii regis, in portu ville Novi Castri super Tinam et in singulis portubus et locis eidem portui adiacentibus, a festo Sancti Michaelis anno xv^{mo} usque idem festum tunc proximo sequens, scilicet, per unum annum integrum, per visum et testimonium Willelmi Baxter contrarotulatoris eorundem ibidem per idem tempus.

Navis vocata le Edwarde de Novo Castro unde Willelmus Kervour est magister exivit decima die Octobris anno regni regis Henrici vij^{mi} xv^{mo}
de Edwardo Baxter indigena (mercatore Gilde Novi Castri de crescencia infrascripta) pro iiij^{xx} pellibus tannatis siccis
subsidium nichil quia allocatur per breve domini regis super bona deperdita. valor xl s.
de Johanne Brandlyng indigena pro xj dossenis pellium vitulorum tannatarum siccarum valor xl s.
subsidium ij s.
de Thoma Harden indigena pro xj dossenis pellium vitulorum tannatarum siccarum valor xl s.
subsidium ij s.
et de eodem pro[1] xx dossenis virgarum panni lanei stricti
pannagium v s. x d.
de Roberto Bartraham indigena pro ij barrelles sepi valor x s.
et de eodem pro iiij dossenis virgarum panni lanei stricti
pannagium xiiij d.
de Edwardo Conyngham indigena (marcatore Gilde subscripte de crescencia subscripta) pro lxxxx pellibus
tannatis siccis valor iiij li. x s.
subsidium nichil quia allocatur per breve regis predictum
et de eodem pro ij dossenis virgarum panni lanei stricti
pannagium vij d.
de Thoma Welden indigena pro viij dossenis pellium vitulorum tannatarum siccarum valor xxx s.
subsidium xviij d.

Navis vocata le James de Novo Castro unde Lodvicus Sothern [est magister exivit x die Novembris] (cum lanis et pellibus lanutis de crescencia comitatuum Northumbrie, Westmorlandie, episcopatus Dunelmensis et comitatuum Richmond et Allerton)
de Johanne Snow mercatore societatis Gilde de Novo Castro pro una sarplera lane ponderante ij saccos dimidium vj clavos
custuma iiij s. iiij d.ob. subsidium xxj s. x d.

1. Followed by *v dossenis*, struck out.

de Willelmo Camby mercatore eiusdem Gilde pro ij sarpleris lane ponderantibus iiij saccos
custuma vj s. viij d. subsidium nichil quia allocatur per breve
et de eodem pro ij sarpleris lane ponderantibus iij saccos viij clavis
et pro lx pellibus lanutis continentibus j quarterium
Summa iij sacci j quarterium viij clavi
custuma v s. viij d.qu. }
subsidium xxvij s. v d. } xxxij s. j d.qu.
de Roberto Baxter mercatore ibidem pro iiij sarpleris lane ponderantibus viij saccos dimidium vj clavos
et de eodem pro lx pellibus lanutis continentibus j quarterium
Summa viij sacci iij quarteria vj clavi
custuma xiiij s. ix d.ob. }
subsidium lxxiij s. xj d. } iiij li. viij s. viij d.ob.
de Thoma Herryson nuper mercatore eiusdem Gilde per Willelmum Bird executorem suum pro lx pellibus lanutis continentibus j quarterium
Summa v sacci
custuma viij s. iiij d. subsidium nichil quia allocatur per breve
et de eodem Willelmo Bird pro xx pellibus lanutis
custuma }
subsidium } x d.
de Cristofero Brigham mercatore ibidem pro iij sarpleris lane ponderantibus vij saccos j quarterium
custuma xij s. j d. subsidium ...
de Willelmo Davell mercatore ibidem pro iij sarpleris lane ponderantibus [v saccos]
de Johanne Passheley mercatore ibidem pro j sarplera lane ponderante j saccum [iij quarteria viij clavos]
et de eodem pro lx pellibus lanutis continentibus [j quarterium]
[Summa ij sacci viij clavi]
de Cristofero Raw mercatore ibidem pro iij sarpleris lane ponderantibus v saccos iij quarteria iij clavos
custuma viij s. j d. subsidium xl s. v d.
de Willelmo Car mercatore ibidem pro j sarplera lane ponderante ij saccos j quarterium
custuma iij s. ix d. subsidium xviij s. ix d.
de Georgio Hebburn mercatore ibidem pro j sarplera lane ponderante ij saccos dimidium
custuma iiij s. ij d. subsidium xx s. x d.
de Bartramo Yonghusband mercatore ibidem pro iiij sarpleris lane ponderantibus viij saccos dimidium vj clavos
custuma xiiij s. iiij d.ob. subsidium lxxj s. x d.

de Edwardo Baxter mercatore ibidem pro ij sarpleris lane ponderantibus iij saccos iij quarteria iij clavos
custuma vj s. iiij d.qu. subsidium xxxj s. ix d.
de Jacobo Tennaund mercatore ibidem pro j sarplera lane ponderante j saccum j quarterium
et de eodem pro lx pellibus lanutis continentibus j quarterium
Summa j saccus dimidius
custuma ij s. vj d. subsidium xij s. vj d.
de Rolando Herryson mercatore ibidem pro ij sarpleris lane ponderantibus iij saccos dimidium iij clavos
custuma v s. xj d.qu. subsidium nichil quia allocatur per breve
de Lodvico Sothern mercatore ibidem pro ij pokettes lane ponderantibus j saccum iij quarteria
custuma ij s. xj d. subsidium xiiij s. vij d.
de Ricardo Conyngham mercatore ibidem pro j sarplera lane ponderante j saccum iij quarteria
custuma ij s. xj d. subsidium xiiij s. vij d.
de Willelmo Haynyng mercatore ibidem pro j sarplera lane ponderante ij saccos v clavos
et de eodem pro Cxx pellibus lanutis continentibus dimidium saccum
Summa ij saccos dimidium v clavos
Custuma iiij s. iiij d. subsidium nichil quia allocatur per breve
et de eodem pro vij clavis lane
custuma iij d. ob } xix d.
subsidium xv d. ob }
de Thoma Cooke mercatore ibidem pro j sarplera lane ponderante ij saccos j quarterium
custuma iij s. ix d. subsidium xviij s. ix d.
de Thoma Laton mercatore ibidem pro j sarplera lane ponderante iij quarteria vj clavos
custuma } viij s. viij d.
subsidium }
de Johanne Baxter mercatore ibidem pro ij sarpleris lane ponderantibus ij saccos vj clavos

Examinatur
Summa partis xxxiij li. vij s. ij d.ob.qu.
Sequitur pondagium predicte navis [cum aliis pellibus vocatis shorlinges et morlinges et agnellis de crescencia predicta]
[*Membrane 1 dorse*]

[de Johanne Snaw indigena pro iiij celdris carbonum	iij s. iiij d.
vj celdris petrarum	xxx s.
Summa totalis valoris	xxxiij s. iiij d.]

... ...

[de Willelmo Camby indigena mercatore societatis Gilde predicte pro C pellibus shorlinges et morlinges xv s.
et CCiiij^{xx} pellibus agnellorum xxvj s. viij d.
Summa totalis valoris lj s. viij d.]

... ...

[de Willelmo Birde indigena mercatore societatis Gilde predicte pro v^{xx} pellibus agnellorum xviij s. iiij d.]

[de Thoma Haryson indigena mercatore societatis Gilde predicte per dictum Willelmum Birde executorem suum pro C pellibus agnellorum valor x s.
subsidium nichil quia allocatur per breve]

de Johanne Paslew indigena (mercatore societatis Gilde predicte) pro Clx pellibus shorlinges et morlinges valor xxiij s. vj d.

de Cristofero Raw indigena (mercatore ibidem) pro Cv^{xx} pellibus shorlinges et morlinges valor xxvij s. vj d.
subsidium xvj d.ob.

de Jacobo Tennaund indigena (mercatore ibidem) pro Clx pellibus shorlinges et morlinges valor xxij s. vj d.
subsidium xiij d.ob.

de Willelmo Haynyng indigena (mercatore ibidem) pro lx pellibus shorlinges et morlinges vij s. vj d.
Cxl pellibus agnellorum xiij s. iiij d.
Summa valoris xx s. x d
subsidium nichil quia allocatur per breve

de Thoma Cook indigena (mercatore ibidem) pro xl pellibus morlinges valor v s.
subsidium iij d.

de Andrea Bewyk indigena (mercatore ibidem) pro v^{xx} pellibus shorlinges valor xij s. vj d.
subsidium vij d.ob.

Navis vocata le George de Novo Castro unde Willelmus Michelson est magister exivit decimo die Novembris anno xv^{mo} (cum lanis et pellibus lanutis de crescencia predicta)

de Bartramo Yonghusband mercatore ibidem pro ij sarpleris lane ponderantibus iiij saccos j quarterium

et de eodem pro Cxx pellibus lanutis continentibus dimidium saccum
Summa iiij sacci iij quarteria
custuma vij s. xj d. subsidium xxxix s. vij d.

de Cristofero Brigham mercatore ibidem pro iij sarpleris lane ponderantibus vj saccos j quarterium xij clavos
custuma x s. x d. subsidium liiij s. ij d.

de Thoma Gibson mercatore ibidem per Cristoferum Brigham attornatum suum
custuma x s. subsidium nichil quia allocatur per breve

de Thoma Weltden mercatore ibidem pro iij sarpleris lane ponderantibus v saccos vj clavos

...

de Thoma Swan mercatore ibidem pro j sarplera lane ponderante j saccum j quarterium v clavos

custuma ij s. ij d. subsidium nichil quia allocatur per breve

et de eodem pro ij sarpleris lane ponderantibus iij saccos dimidium j clavum

...

de Thoma Camby nuper mercatore ibidem per Willelmum Birde executorem suum pro j sarplera lane ponderante j saccum dimidium vij clavos

custuma ij s. viij d. subsidium nichil quia allocatur per breve

et de dicto Willelmo Birde mercatore ibidem pro vj clavis lane

custuma ij d.ob. subsidium nichil quia allocatur per breve

de Georgio Car seniore mercatore ibidem pro ij sarpleris lane ponderantibus ij saccos iij quarteria

et de eodem pro CCClx pellibus lanutis continentibus j saccum dimidium

Summa iiij sacci j quarterium

custuma vij s. j d. subsidium xxxvs. v d.

de Roberto Baxter mercatore ibidem pro ij sarpleris lane ponderantibus iij saccos iij quarteria vj clavos

custuma vj s. v d.ob. subsidium xxxijs. iij d.

de Georgio Birde juniore mercatore ibidem pro j poket lane ponderante dimidium saccum

custuma x d.
subsidium iiij s. ij d. } v s.

de Johanne Blaxton mercatore ibidem pro ij sarpleris lane ponderante v saccos

custuma viij s. iiij d. subsidium xlj s.[2] viij d.

de Willelmo Davell mercatore ibidem pro ij sarpleris lane ponderantibus iiij saccos iij quarteria

custuma vij s. xj d. subsidium xxxix s. vij d.

de Rogero Raw mercatore ibidem pro ij sarpleris lane et un' poket lane ponderantibus iij saccos iij quarteria iij clavos

custuma vj s. iiij d. subsidium xxxj s. viij d.

de Jacobo Tennaund mercatore ibidem pro j sarplera lane ponderante j saccum dimidium iij clavos

...

de Roberto Brigham mercatore ibidem pro ij sarpleris lane ponderantibus iij saccos dimidium iij clavos

...

de Roberto Bartram mercatore ibidem pro j sarplera lane ponderante j saccum iij quarteria

custuma ij s. xj d. subsidium xiiij s. vij d.

de Antonio Rede mercatore ibidem pro j sarplera lane ponderante j saccum j quarterium

custuma ij s. j d. subsidium x s. v d.

2. Followed by *iiij d.*, struck out.

de Roberto Wilkinson mercatore ibidem pro j poket ponderante dimidium saccum
custuma et subsidium } v s.

Sequitur pondagium eiusdem navis (cum aliis pellibus vocatis shorlinges morlinges de crescencia predicta)
de Roberto Cromer indigena pro iij quarteriis (plaustrati) plumbi valor xlv s.
subsidium ij s. ij d.
de Bartramo Yonghusband indigena (mercatore gilde predicte) pro vj cheldris molarum xxx s.
uno plaustrato plumbi lx s.
valor iiij li. x s.
subsidium iiij s. vj d.
et de eodem CCC^ma^ pellibus shorlinges et morlinges xlvij s. vj d.
CCC^ma^iiij^xx^ pellibus agnellorum xxxvj s. viij d.
Summa iiij li. iiij s. ij d.
subsidium iiij s. ij d.ob.
de Thoma Weltden indigena (mercatore dicte gilde) pro lx pellibus shorlinges valor vij s. vj d.
subsidium iiij d.ob.
de Willelmo Birde indigena (mercatore predicte gilde) pro j plaustrato plumbi valor lx s.
subsidium iij s.
de Georgio Car seniore indigena (mercatore predicte gilde) pro CClx pellibus shorlinges et morlinges xxxvij s. vj d.
DCv^xx^ pellibus agnellorum lxviij s. iiij d.
Summa valoris Cv s. x d.
subsidium v s. iij d.ob.
de Rogero Raw indigena (mercatore predicte Gilde) pro xl pellibus shorlinges et morlinges valor v s.
subsidium iij d.
de Jacobo Tennaund indigena (mercatore predicte Gilde) pro j plaustrato plumbi valor lx s.
subsidium iij s.

Examinatur Probatur Summa partis xxvij li. xiiij s. vj d.ob.

[*Membrane 2 face*]
Navis vocata le Antonye de Novo Castro unde Nicholaus Blak est magister exivit decimo die Novembris anno xv^mo^ (cum lanis et pellibus lanutis de crescencia predicta.)
de Cristofero Brigham mercatore ibidem pro ij sarpleris lane ponderantibus v saccos vj clavos.
custuma vij s. vj d.ob. subsidium xlij s. viij d.

de Roberto Baxter mercatore ibidem pro iij sarpleris lane ponderantibus vij saccos
et de eodem pro lx pellibus lanutis continentibus j quarterium
Summa vij sacci j quarterium
custuma xij s. j d. subsidium lx s. v d.
de Willelmo Camby mercatore ibidem pro iij sarpleris lane ponderantibus v saccos dimidium iij clavos
et de eodem pro iiij^{xx} pellibus lanutis continentibus j quarterium xx pelles
Summa v sacci iij quarteria iij clavi xx pelles
custuma ix s[3]. x d. subsidium xlix s. j d.qu.
de Willelmo Davell mercatore ibidem pro iij sarpleris lane ponderantibus vj saccos vj saccos j quarterium v clavos
et de eodem pro xl pellibus lanutis
Summa vj sacci j quarterium v clavi xl pelles
custuma x s. x d.ob.qu. subsidium liiij s. iij d.ob.
de Bartramo Yonghusband mercatore ibidem pro iiij sarpleris lane ponderantibus ix saccos dimidium vij clavos
custuma xvj s. j d.ob. subsidium iiij li. iij d.ob.
de Georgio Car seniore mercatore ibidem executore testamenti Thome Herryson nuper mercatore ibidem pro j sarplera lane ponderante j saccum dimidium xiij clavos
custuma ij s. ix d. subsidium nichil quia allocatur per breve
et de eodem Georgio Car pro iij sarpleris lane ponderantibus vij saccos dimidium vj clavos
custuma xij s. viij d.ob. subsidium lxiij s. vj d.
de Johanne Blaxton mercatore ibidem pro ij sarpleris lane ponderantibus iiij saccos dimidium
custuma vij s. vj d. subsidium xxxvij s. vj d.
de Thoma Swan mercatore ibidem pro ij sarpleris lane ponderantibus iij saccos
custuma v s. subsidium xxv s.
de Willelmo Car mercatore ibidem pro ij sarpleris lane ponderantibus ij saccos iij quarteria iij clavos
custuma iiij s. viij d.qu. subsidium xxiij s. v d.
de Roberto Herryson mercatore ibidem pro ij sarpleris lane ponderantibus iiij saccos j quarterium
et de eodem pro lx pellibus lanutis continentibus j quarterium
Summa iiij saccos dimidium
custuma vij s. vj d. subsidium xxxvij s. vj d.
de Rolando Herryson mercatore ibidem pro j sarplera lane ponderante ij saccos j quarterium x clavos
custuma iiij s. j d. subsidium nichil quia allocatur per breve
et de eodem Rolando pro j sarplera lane ponderante j saccum dimidium iiij clavos
custuma ij s. vij d.qu. subsidium xiij s.

3. Followed by *ix d.*, struck out.

de Hugone Eryngton mercatore ibidem pro j sarplera lane ponderante ij saccos dimidium vj clavos
custuma iiij s. iiij d.ob. subsidium xxj s. x d.
de Johanne Baxter mercatore ibidem pro j sarplera lane ponderante ij saccos
custuma iij s. iiij d. subsidium xvj s. viij d.
de Georgio Baxter mercatore ibidem pro j sarplera lane ponderante ij saccos iij clavos
custuma iij s. v d.qu. subsidium xvij s. ij d.
de Thoma Hill mercatore ibidem pro C xx pellibus lanutis continentibus dimidium saccum
custuma } v s.
subsidium }
de Johanne Brigham mercatore ibidem pro ij sarpleris lane ponderantibus ij saccos j quarterium
custuma iij s. ix d. subsidium xviij s. ix d.
de Willelmo Draver mercatore ibidem pro ij sarpleris lane ponderantibus iij saccos dimidium vj clavos
custuma vj s. subsidium xxx s. ij d.
de Henrico Bednall mercatore ibidem pro ij sarpleris lane ponderantibus j saccum dimidium j quarterium vj clavos
et de eodem pro iiij^{xx}x pellibus lanutis continentibus j quarterium et dimidium quarterium
Summa ij sacci dimidium quarterium vj clavi
custuma iij s. vij d. subsidium xvij s. xj d.
de Rogero Raw mercatore ibidem pro j sarplera lane ponderante j saccum j quarterium iij clavos
custuma ij s. ij d. subsidium nichil quia allocatur per breve
de Nicholao Blak mercatore ibidem pro j sarplera lane ponderante j saccum
custuma } x s.
subsidium }
de Johanne Thomson mercatore ibidem pro j balett lane ponderante j quarterium
custuma } ij s. vj d.
subsidium }
de Georgio Bird seniore mercatore ibidem pro Cxx pellibus lanutis continentibus dimidium saccum
custuma x d. subsidium nichil quia allocatur per breve
xxxviij li. ix s. vj d.ob.
ix s. x d.qu.
Sequitur pondagium eodem navis (cum aliis pellibus vocatis shorlinges et morlinges et agnellis de crescencia predicta)
de Willelmo Steyll indigena pro vj cheldris
gryndstonys valor xxx s.
subsidium ij s. vj d.

de Cristofero Brigham indigena (mercatore societatis Gilde predicte) pro CC libris plumbi x s.
iij cheldris gryndstonis xv s.
Summa valoris xxv s.
subsidium xv d.

de Roberto Baxter indigena (mercatore ibidem) pro C pellibus shorlinges et morlinges valor xv s.
subsidium ix d.

de Willelmo Camby indigena (mercatore ibidem) pro Cxl pellibus shorlinges et morlinges valor xx s.
subsidium nichil quia allocatur per breve

de eodem Willelmo pro Cxliij pellibus shorlinges et morlinges xx s.
lx pellibus agnellorum v s.
Summa valoris xxv s.
subsidium xv d.

de Willelmo Davell indigena (mercatore ibidem) pro iiij^{xx}x pellibus shorlinges et morlinges xj s. viij d.
Clx pellibus agnellorum xv s.
Summa valoris xxvj s. viij d.
subsidium xvj d.

de Bartramo Yonghusband indigena (mercatore ibidem) pro ij plaustratis plumbi valor vj li.
subsidium vj s.

de Georgio Birde juniore indigena (mercatore ibidem) pro iiij^{xx} pellibus shorlinges et morlinges x s.
Clx pellibus agnellorum xv s.
Summa valoris xxv s.
subsidium xv d.

de Thoma Herryson indigena (nuper mercatore ibidem) per Georgium Car indigenam (mercatorem ibidem) executorem suum pro iiij^{xx} pellibus shorlinges et morlinges valor x s.
subsidium nichil quia allocatur per breve

de dicto Georgio Car (mercatore ibidem) pro Cxl pellibus shorlinges et morlinges valor xx s.
subsidium xij d.

de Roberto Herryson indigena (mercatore ibidem) pro Cl pellibus shorlinges et morlinges valor xx s.
subsidium xij d.

de Rolando Herryson indigena (mercatore ibidem) pro C pellibus shorlinges et morlinges xv s.
lx pellibus agnellorum v s.
valor xxs.
subsidium xij d.

de Hugene Eryngton indigena (mercatore ibidem) pro iiij^{xx} pellibus shorlinges et morlinges valor xv s.
subsidium lx d.

de Georgio Baxter indigena (mercatore ibidem) pro Cxl pellibus shorlinges et morlinges valor xx s.
subsidium xij d.
de Thoma Hyll indigena pro C pellibus shorlinges et morlinges xv s.
CC pellibus agnellorum xx s.
Summa valoris xxxv s.
subsidium xxj d.
de Willelmo Draver indigena pro xxx pellibus shorlinges et morlinges valor iij s. iiij d.
subsidium ij d.
de Henrico Bednall indigena pro Clx pellibus shorlinges et morlinges xxij s. vj d.
Cl pellibus agnellorum xiij s. iiij d.
Summa valoris xxxv s. x d.
subsidium xxj d.ob.
de Georgio Bird seniore indigena pro CCv^{xx} pellibus agnellorum valor xxviij s. iiij d
subsidium nichil quia allocatur per breve
et de eodem pro Dc pellibus shorlinges et morlinges iiij li. x s.
CCCxx pellibus agnellorum xxxj s. viij d.
Summa valoris vj li. xx d.

Examinatur

xxxixli.vijs.ob.qu.

[*Membrane 2 dorse*]
Navis vocata [le Mary Harebred de Novo Castro unde Johannes Harper est magister exivit x die Novembris cum lane et pellibus lanutis de crescencia predicta etc.]
de Johanne Huddiswell mercatore societatis Gilde predicte [pro una sarplera lane ponderante ij saccos dimidium]
custuma iiij s. ij d. subsidium xx s. x d.
de Johanne Brandlyng mercatore ibidem [pro Cxx pellibus lanutis continentibus dimidium saccum]
custuma, subsidium } xv s.
de Bartramo Yonghusband mercatore ibidem [pro iij sarpleris lane ponderantibus vj saccos dimidium]
custuma x s. x d. subsidium liiij s. ij d.
de Johanne Baxter mercatore ibidem [pro ij sarpleris lane ponderantibus iij saccos iij quarteria iij clavos]
custuma vj s. iiij d. subsidium xxxjs. ix d.
de Edwardo Baxter mercatore ibidem pro j sarplera lane ponderante ij saccos j quarterium
custuma iij s. ix d. subsidium xvij s. x d.

de Cristofero Brigham mercatore ibidem pro iiij sarpleris lane ponderantibus viij saccos dimidium
et de eodem pro iiij^{xx} pellibus lanutis continentibus j quarterium xx pelles
viij sacci iij quarteria xx pelles
custuma xiiij s. ix d. subsidium lxxiij s. vij d.ob.
de Georgio Car seniore mercatore ibidem pro iij sarpleris lane ponderantibus vij saccos ix clavos
custuma xj s. xj d.ob. subsidium lix s. x d.
de Willelmo Camby mercatore ibidem pro iij sarpleris lane ponderantibus iiij saccos j quarterium
custuma vij s. j d. subsidium xxxv s. v d.
de Georgio Hebburn mercatore ibidem pro ij sarpleris lane ponderantibus iiij saccos iij quarteria
custuma vij s. xj d. subsidium xxxix s. vij d.
de Willelmo Selby mercatore ibidem pro Cxx pellibus lanutis continentibus dimidium saccum
custuma } v s.
subsidium }
de Thoma Herryson mercatore ibidem pro j sarplera lane ponderante ij saccos j quarterium
custuma iij s. ix d. subsidium xviij s. ix d.
de Thoma Molle mercatore ibidem pro ij sarpleris lane ponderantibus iij saccos iij quarterium viij clavos
custuma vj s. vj d.qu. subsidium xxxij s. vij d.
de Johanne Blaxton mercatore ibidem pro j sarplera lane ponderante ij saccos j quarterium
custuma iij s. ix d. subsidium xviij s. ix d.
de Willelmo Draver mercatore ibidem pro ij sarpleris lane ponderantibus ij saccos dimidium viij clavos
custuma iiij s. v d.qu. subsidium xxij s. ij d.
de Johanne Bewyk mercatore ibidem pro ij sarpleris lane ponderantibus iiij saccos j quarterium vj clavos
custuma vij s.[4] iij d.ob. subsidium[5] xxxvj s. iiij d.ob.
de Georgio Selby mercatore ibidem pro j quarterio lane
custuma v d. subsidium nichil quia allocatur per breve
et de eodem Georgio pro j sarplera lane ponderante ij saccos dimidium
et pro iiij^{xx} pellibus lanutis continentibus j quarterium xx pelles
ij saccos iij quarteria xx pelles
...
de Ricardo Conyngham mercatore ibidem pro ij sarpleris lane ponderantibus iiij saccos iij quarteria
...

4. Followed by *ij d.*, struck out.
5. Followed by *xxvj s. xj d.*, struck out.

de Willelmo Wilkinson mercatore ibidem [pro ij pokettes lane ponder' j saccum j quarterium viij clavos]

...

de Willelmo Car mercatore ibidem pro j sarplera lane ponderante ij saccos
custuma iij s. iiij d. subsidium xvj s. viij d.
de Georgio Birde seniore mercatore ibidem pro CCxl pellibus lanutis continentibus j saccum
custuma xx d. subsidium nichil quia allocatur per breve
de Willelmo Saunderson mercatore ibidem pro j sarplera lane ponderante ij saccos
custuma iij s. iiij d. subsidium xvj s. viij d.
xxxiiij li. x s. j d.ob.qu.
ij s. j d.

Sequitur pondagium eiusdem navis (cum aliis pellibus vocatis shorlinges et morlinges et agnellis de crescencia predicta)

de Willelmo Hayrbred indigena pro viij cheldris molarum valor xl s.
subsidium ij s.

de Johanne Brandlyng indigena (mercatore Gilde predicte) pro Dxl pellibus shorlinges et morlinges iiij li.
CC pellibus agnellorum xx s.
Summa valoris C s.
subsidium v s.

de Cristofero Brigham indigena (mercatore ibidem) pro Clx pellibus shorlinges et morlinges xxij s. vj d.
Dxxxvj pellibus agnellorum liij s. iiij d.
Summa valoris lxxv s x d.
subsidium iij s. ix d.ob.

de Willelmo Selby indigena (mercatore ibidem) pro CCC iiij^{xx} pellibus shorlinges et morlinges lv s.
DCCC pellibus agnellorum iiij li.
Summa valoris vj li. xv s.
subsidium vj s. ix d.

de Georgio Selbye indigena (mercatore ibidem) pro Ciiij^{xx} pellibus shorlinges et morlinges xxvj s. viij d.
CCCClx pellibus agnellorum xlv s.
Summa valoris lxxj s. viij d.
subsidium iij s. vij d.

de Georgio Bird seniore indigena (mercatore ibidem) pro DCCC pellibus shorlinges et morlinges vj li.
DCCC pellibus agnellorum iiij li.
Summa valoris x li.
subsidium xxs.

de Thoma Laton indigena (mercatore ibidem) pro C^{ma} pellibus shorlinges et morlinges valor xv s.
custuma ix d.

xxxj s. x d.ob.

Navis vocata le Margret de Brikelsay unde Jacobus Goldaker est magister exivit decimo die Novembris anno xv[ma] (cum lanis et pellibus lanutis de crescencia predicta)

de Cristofero Brigham mercatore ibidem pro ij sarpleris lane ponderantibus iiij saccos dimidium
custuma vij s. vjd. subsidium xxxvij s. vj d.

de Willelmo Selby mercatore ibidem pro j sarplera lane ponderante ij saccos et de eodem pro Cxl pellibus lanutis continentibus dimidium saccum xx pelles ij sacci dimidius xx pelles
custuma iiij s. iiij d. subsidium xxj s. vj d.ob.

de Bartramo Yonghusband mercatore ibidem pro ij sarpleris lane ponderantibus iiij saccos j quarterium
custuma vij s. j d. subsidium xxxv s. v d.

de Georgio Birde seniore mercatore ibidem pro DC pellibus lanutis continentibus ij saccos dimidium
custuma iiij s. ij d. subsidium nichil quia allocatur per breve.

de Georgio Conyngham mercatore ibidem pro una sarplera lane ponderante j saccum iij quarteria j clavum
custuma ij s. xj d.ob. subsidium nichil quia allocatur per breve

et de eodem pro una sarplera lane ponderante j saccum iij quarteria xij clavos
custuma iij s. iij d.ob.qu. subsidium xvj s. viij d.

de Ricardo Rumney mercatore ibidem pro una sarplera lane ponderante j saccum iij clavos
custuma } x s. vij d.
subsidium }

de Thoma Molle mercatore ibidem pro ij sarpleris lane ponderantibus iij saccos dimidium iij clavos
custuma vij s. vij d. subsidium xxxviij s.

de Henrico Bednall pro j sarplera lane ponderante j saccum iij quarteria vj clavos
custuma iij s. j d. subsidium xv s. vij d.

de Georgio Hebburn mercatore ibidem pro ij sarpleris lane ponderantibus ij saccos
custuma iij s. iiij d. subsidium xvj s. viij d.

de Georgio Selby mercatore ibidem pro j sarplera lane ponderante ij saccos iij clavos
custuma iij s. v d.qu. subsidium nichil quia allocatur per breve.

Summa partis xlviij li. ij s. xj d.

Examinatur

[*Membrane 3 face*]

de Cristofero Raw mercatore ibidem pro j sarplera lane ponderante j saccum dimidium
custuma ij s. vj d. subsidium xij s. vj d.

de Thoma Herrison nuper mercatore ibidem per Georgium Car executorem suum pro j sarplera lane ponderante j saccum iij quarteria iij clavos
custuma iij s. qu. subsidium nichil quia allocatur per breve.
de Thoma Riddall mercatore ibidem pro lx pellibus lanutis continentibus j quarterium
custuma }
subsidium } ij s. vj d.

Sequitur pondagium in eadem nave (cum aliis pellibus vocatis shorlinges et morlinges et agnellis.)
de Jacobo Goldaker indigena pro ij cheldris molarum
valor xs. subsidium vj d.
de Cristofero Brigham indigena pro iij cheldris molarum valor xv s.
subsidium ix d.
de Willelmo Selby indigena (mercatore Gilde predicte) pro CCCiiij^{xx}xiiij pellibus shorlinges et morlinges valor lvj s. viij d.
subsidium ij s. x d.
de Georgio Bird seniore indigena (mercatore ibidem) pro CC pellibus shorlinges et morlinges xxx s.
DCCC pellibus agnellorum iiij li.
valor cx s.
subsidium nichil quia allocatur per breve
de Ricardo Rumney indigena (mercatore ibidem) pro iiij^{xx} pellibus shorlinges et morlinges valor x s.
subsidium vj d.
de Thoma Riddall indigena (mercatore ibidem) pro Clx pellibus shorlinges et morlinges valor xxij s. vj d.
subsidium xiij d.ob.

Navis vocata le Anne de Novo Castro unde Thomas Harrop est magister exivit decimo die Novembris anno xv^{mo} (cum lanis et pellibus lanutis de crescencia predicta.)
de Bartramo Yonghusband mercatore ibidem pro iij sarpleris lane ponderantibus iiij saccos j quarterium iij clavos
custuma vij s. ij d.qu. subsidium xxxv s. xj d.
de Johanne Huddiswell mercatore ibidem pro iij sarpleris lane ponderantibus vj saccos dimidium
custuma x s. x d. subsidium liiij s. ij d.
de Roberto Harden mercatore ibidem pro j sarplera lane ponderante j saccum iij quarteria ix clavos
custuma iij s. iij d. subsidium nichil quia allocatur per breve.
de Willelmo Harden mercatore ibidem pro dimidio sacco et x clavis
custuma xiiij d. subsidium nichil quia allocatur per breve
et de eodem pro ij sarpleris lane ponderantibus iij saccos ix clavos
custuma v s. ij d.ob. subsidium xxvj s. vj d.
de Johanne Passhely mercatore ibidem pro j poket lane pond' dimidium saccum iij clavos
... ...

de Mauro Mawer mercatore ibidem pro j sarplera lane ponderante j saccum iij quarteria iij clavos

custuma iij s. qu. subsidium xv s. j d.

de Thoma Hanson mercatore ibidem pro un' poket lane pond' j quarterium iij clavos

custuma vj d.qu.
subsidium ij s. vj d.ob.qu. } iij s. j d.

Sequitur pondagium eiusdem navis (cum aliis pellibus vocatis shorlinges et morlinges et agnellis de crescencia predicta.)

de Bartramo Yonghusband indigena pro iij plaustratis plumbi valor ix li.

subsidium ix s.

et de eodem pro xvij dossenis pellium vitulorum tannatarum siccarum

Summa valoris iij li. x s.

subsidium iij s. vj d.

de Johanne Huddiswell indigena (mercatore predicte gilde) pro CCC pellibus shorlinges et morlinges xlv s.

lx pellibus agnellorum v s.

Summa valoris l s.

subsidium ij s. vj d.

de Roberto Harden indigena (mercatore ibidem) pro CCCxl pellibus shorlinges et morlinges valor l s.

subsidium ij s. vj d.

de Johanne Passheley indigena (mercatore ibidem) pro lx pellibus morlinges valor vij s. vj d.

subsidium iiij d.ob.

de Willelmo Selby indigena (mercatore ibidem) pro Clx pellibus shorlinges et morlinges valor xxij s. vj d.

subsidium xiij d.ob.

de Mauro Mawer indigena (mercatore ibidem) pro iij dossenis pellium vitulorum tannatarum siccarum valor x s.

subsidium vj d.

et de eodem pro Clx pellibus shorlinges et morlinges valor xxij s. vj d.

subsidium xiij d.ob.

de Thoma Hanson indigena (mercatore ibidem) pro xxxvj dossenis pellium vitulorum tannatarum siccarum valor vj li. x s.

subsidium vj s. vj d.

et de eodem pro v^{xx} pellibus shorlinges et morlinges valor xij s. vj d.

subsidium vij d.ob.

Navis vocata Mare Allen de Novo Castro unde Walterus Plous est magister exivit decimo die Novembris anno xv^{mo} (cum lanis et pellibus lanutis de crescencia predicta)

de Willelmo Allen nuper mercatore ibidem per Johannem Allen executorem suum pro iiij sarpleris lane ponderantibus x saccos v clavos

custuma xvj s. x d. subsidium nichil quia allocatur per breve

de dicto Johanne Allen mercatore ibidem pro ij sarpleris lane ponderantibus iiij saccos j quarterium
custuma vij s. j d. subsidium nichil quia allocatur per breve
et de predicto Johanne Allen mercatore ibidem pro iij sarpleris lane ponderantibus iiij saccos iij quarteria iij clavos
custuma viij s. ij d. subsidium xl s. j d.
de Roberto Brigham mercatore ibidem pro ij sarpleris lane ponderantibus ij saccos j quarterium
custuma iij s. ix d. subsidium xviij s. ix d.
et de dicto Roberto pro j pokett lane pond' iij quarteria
custuma xv d. subsidium nichil quia allocatur per breve
de Roberto Harden mercatore ibidem pro ij sarpleris lane ponderantibus iij saccos dimidium iiij clavos
custuma v s. xj d.ob.qu. subsidium xxix s. xj d.
et de eodem Roberto Harden pro j poket lane pond' ix clavos
custuma iij d.ob. subsidium nichil quia allocatur per breve
de Cristofero Brigham mercatore ibidem pro j balet lane pond' j quarterium
custuma } ij s. vj d.
subsidium }
de Ricardo Conyngham mercatore ibidem pro j sarplera lane ponderante ij saccos
custuma iij s. iiij d. subsidium xvj s. viij d.
de Thoma Herryson nuper mercatore ibidem per Georgium Car executorem suum pro j sarplera lane ponderante j saccum dimidium vj clavos
custuma ij s. viij d.ob. subsidium nichil quia allocatur per breve.
de Jacobo Tennaund mercatore ibidem pro j sarplera lane ponderante j saccum j quarterium
custuma ij s. j d. subsidium x s. v d.
de Johanne Blaxton mercatore ibidem pro j sarplera lane ponderante v saccos dimidium
custuma ix s. ij d. subsidium xlv s. x d.
de Thoma Welden mercatore ibidem pro ij sarpleris lane ponderantibus j saccum j quarterium
custuma ij s. j d. subsidium x s. v d.
de Georgio Stalper mercatore ibidem pro ij sarpleris lane ponderantibus iij saccos dimidium
custuma v s. x d. subsidium nichil quia allocatur per breve
de Ricardo Wrangwyssh mercatore ibidem pro ij sarpleris lane ponderantibus ij saccos dimidium vj clavos
custuma iiij s. iiij d. subsidium xxj s. x d.
de Willelmo Pykden mercatore ibidem pro j sarplera lane ponderante j saccum iij quarteria
custuma ij s. xj d. subsidium xiiij s. vij d.

Summa partis vij li. xvij s. ix d.qu.

Examinatur

[*Membrane 3 dorse*]

de Roberto Bartram mercatore ibidem pro una sarplera lane ponderante j saccum dimidium vj clavos

... ...

de Willelmo Selby mercatore ibidem pro una sarplera lane ponderante ij saccos iij clavos

... ...

de Adomaro Scott mercatore ibidem pro un' poket lane pond' iij quarteria

custuma } vij s. vj d.
subsidium

de Georgio Birde seniore mercatore ibidem pro iiij^{xx} pellibus lanutis continentibus j quarterium xx pelles

custuma } iij s. iiij d.
subsidium

xlvij s. vij d.

Sequitur pondagium in eodem nave (cum aliis pellibus vocatis shorlinges et morlinges et agnellis de crescencia predicta)

de Willelmo Allen indigena (nuper mercatore Gilde predicte) per Johannem Allen executorem suum pro iij dossenis virgarum panni lanei stricti continentibus unum pannum

pannagium nichil quia allocatur per breve

et de eodem Willelmo (mercatore ibidem) pro Clx pellibus shorlinges et morlinges

subsidium nichil quia allocatur per breve

et de eodem Johanne (mercatore ibidem) pro CCCC pellibus shorlinges et morlinges valor lx s.

subsidium iij s.

de Roberto Brigham indigena (mercatore ibidem) pro v^{xx} pellibus shorlinges et morlinges valor xij s. vj d.

subsidium vij d.ob.

de Cristofero Brigham indigena (mercatore ibidem) pro xl pellibus tannatis siccis mortlinges et stiklinges valor xxxiij s.iiijd.

subsidium xx d.

et de eodem pro Clx pellibus agnellorum valor xv s.

subsidium ix d.

de Johanne Blaxton indigena (mercatore ibidem) pro Clx pellibus shorlinges et morlinges valor xxij s. vj d.

subsidium xiij d.ob.

de Georgio Birde seniore indigena (mercatore ibidem) pro Ciiij^{xx} pellibus shorlinges et morlinges valor xxv s.

subsidium xv d.

ix s. vij d.

Navis vocata le Dave de Novo Castro unde Robertus Meryman est magister exivit decimo die Novembris anno xv^{mo} (cum lanis et pellibus lanutis de crescencia predicta)

de Thoma Saunderson mercatore ibidem pro iiij sarpleris lane ponderantibus vj saccos iij quarteria iij clavos
custuma xj s. iiij d.qu. subsidium lvj s. ix d.
de Ricardo Wrangwysssh mercatore ibidem pro ij sarpleris lane ponderantibus iij saccos dimidium iij clavos
custuma v s. xj d.qu. subsidium xxix s. vij d.
de Roberto Merryman mercatore ibidem pro j pokett lane pond' j quarterium
custuma } ij s. vj d.
subsidium }
de Jacobo Buke mercatore ibidem er Willelmum Swan attornatum suum pro iij sarpleris lane ponderantibus iij saccos viij clavos
custuma v s. iij d.qu. subsidium nichil quia allocatur per breve
de Willelmo Swan mercatore ibidem pro j balett lane pond' j quarterium ij clavos
custuma v d.ob. subsidium nichil quia allocatur per breve
et de dicto Willelmo pro vj clavis lane
custuma } xiiij d.qu.
subsidium }
de Johanne Bewyk mercatore ibidem pro una sarplera lane ponderante j saccum j quarterium vj clavos
custuma ij s. iij d.ob. subsidium xj s. v d.
de Roberto Herryson mercatore ibidem pro una sarplera lane ponderante j saccum dimidium vj clavos
custuma ij s. viij d.ob. subsidium xiij s. vj d.
de Willelmo Harden mercatore ibidem pro una sarplera lane ponderante j saccum j quarterium
custuma ij s. j d. subsidium x s. v d.
de Roberto Bartram mercatore ibidem pro una sarplera lane ponderante j saccum iij quarteria vj clavos
custuma iij s. j d. subsidium xv s. vij d.
de Willelmo Scott mercatore ibidem pro una sarplera lane ponderante j saccum dimidium
custuma ij s. vj d. subsidium xij s. vj d.

ix li. ij s. vj d.qu.
v s. ix d.

Sequitur pondagium eiusdem navis (cum aliis pellibus vocatis shorlinges et morlinges et agnellis de crescencia predicta).
de Thoma Saunderson indigena (mercatore ibidem) pro iij cheldris molarum xv s.
Clx pellibus shorlinges et morlinges xxij s. vj d.
Summa valoris xxxvij s. vj d.
subsidium xxij d.ob.
de Ricardo Wrangwyssh indigena mercatore ibidem pro xxx pellibus tannatis siccis mortlinges et stiklinges valor xx s.
subsidium xij d.

de Roberto Herryson indigena (mercatore ibidem) pro xl pellibus shorlinges et morlinges v s.
C^ma^ pellibus agnellorum x s.
Summa valoris xv s.
subsidium ix d.
de Willelmo Scott indigena (mercatore ibidem) pro Cxx pellibus shorlinges et morlinges valor xvij s. vj d.
subsidium x d.ob.

iiij s. vj d.

Navis vocata le Trinite de Novo Castro unde Willelmus Cheverous est magister exivit decimo die Novembris anno xv^mo^ (cum lanis et pellibus lanutis de crescencia predicta etc.)
de Mauro Mawer mercatore ibidem pro una sarplera lane ponderante j saccum j quarterium
custuma ij s. j d. subsidium x s. v d.
de Willelmo Hayning mercatore ibidem pro un' poket lane pond' iij quarteria
custuma xv d.
subsidium vj s. iij d. } vij s. vj d.
de Thoma Hyll mercatore ibidem pro una sarplera lane ponderante ij saccos
custuma iij s. iiij d. subsidium xvj s. viij d.
de Johanne Bewyk mercatore ibidem pro una sarplera lane ponderante j saccum dimidium vj clavos
custuma ij s. viij d.ob. subsidium xiij s. vj d.
de Ricardo Conyngham mercatore ibidem pro una sarplera lane ponderante ij saccos
custuma iij s. iiij d. subsidium xvj s. viij d.
de Roberto Baxter mercatore ibidem pro una sarplera lane ponderante j saccum
custuma
subsidium } x s.
de Willelmo Scott mercatore ibidem pro una sarplera lane ponderante ij saccos j quarterium
custuma iij s. ix d. subsidium xviij s. ix d.
de Georgio Eryngton mercatore ibidem pro una sarplera lane ponderante j saccum dimidium
custuma ij s. vj d. subsidium xij s. vj d.
de Georgio Stalper mercatore ibidem pro una sarplera lane ponderante j saccum j quarterium
custuma ij s. j d. subsidium nichil quia allocatur per breve
de Thoma Gybson mercatore ibidem pro ij sarpleris lane ponderantibus iij saccos j quarterium
custuma v s. v d. subsidium xxvij s. j d.
de Henrico Barrow mercatore ibidem pro una sarplera lane ponderante j saccum dimidium
custuma ij s. vj d. subsidium xij s. vj d.

de Roberto Bartram mercatore ibidem pro una sarplera lane ponderante j saccum j quarterium
custuma ij s. j d. subsidium x s. v d.
de Willelmo Pykden mercatore ibidem pro una sarplera lane ponderante j saccum
custuma } x s.
subsidium }

Examinatur Probatur
Summa partis xxij li. vj s. ix d.ob.
ix li. xiij s. viij d.ob.
ij s. j d.

Sequitur pondagium eiusdem navis (cum aliis pellibus vocatis shorlynges et morlinges de crescencia predicta)
[*Membrane 4 face*]
de Willelmo Swan indigena (mercatore Gilde predicte) pro iiij cheldris molarum valor xx s.
subsidium xij d.
de Johanne Bewyk indigena (mercatore ibidem) pro v^{xx} pellibus shorlinges et morlinges valor xij s. vj d.
subsidium vij d.ob.
de Ricardo Conyngham indigena (mercatore ibidem) pro Clx pellibus shorlinges et morlinges valor xxij s. vj d.
subsidium xiij d.ob.
de Thoma Gybson indigena (mercatore ibidem) pro CC pellibus shorlinges et morlinges valor xxx s.
subsidium xviij d.
de Willelmo Pykden indigena (mercatore ibidem) pro lx pellibus shorlinges et morlinges valor vij s. vj d.
subsidium iiij d.ob.

Navis vocata le Antonye de Novo Castro unde Nicholaus Blak est magister applicuit xiiij^{o} die Januarii anno xv^{mo}
de Willelmo Steyll indigena pro uno dolio ferri lx s.
xij barrelles smigmatis vj li.
Summa valoris ix li.
subsidium ix s.
de Hugone Eryngton indigena pro ij doliis ferri vj li.
j hogeshed fructus x s.
Summa valoris vj li. x s.
subsidium vj s. vj d.
de Johanne Thomson indigena pro j barrelle smigmatis x s.
un' poke canabi xx s.
Summa valoris xxx s.
subsidium xviij d.
de Roberto Harden indigena pro j barrelle smigmatis valor x s.
subsidium vj d.

de Cristofero Brigham indigena pro j pype revylles flax valor xiij s. iiij d.
subsidium viij d.
de Georgio Bird seniore indigena pro iij pypes ferri valor iiij li. x s.
subsidium iiij s. vj d.
de Georgio Bird juniore indigena pro D libris ferri valor xv s.
subsidium ix d.
de Johanne Allen indigena pro iij barrelles smigmatis valor xxx s.
subsidium xviij d.

Navis vocata le James de Novo Castro unde Lodvicus Sothern est magister applicuit xx° die Jannuarii anno xv^{mo}

de Willelmo Car indigena pro j pyp fructus	xx s.
j pype avelanarum	x s.
un' name vini renensis	xx s.
Summa valoris	l s.
[subsidium ij s. vj d.]	
et de eodem pro duobus doliis vini gasconii	
tonnagium vj s.	
de Johanne Passheley indigena pro j pyp fructus	xx s.
un' pokett mather	xxvj s. viij d.
un' barrelle cum un' rym papyr[6]	xx d.
uno quarterio canabi	xx d.
j grosse spinctrum	xx d.
x libris gallys	xx d.
Summa valoris	liij s. iiij d.
subsidium ij s. viij d.	
de Johanne Brigham indigena pro di' barrelle calebis	xxvj s. viij d.
lx pannis depictis	iij s. iiij d.
Summa valoris	xxx s.
subsidium xviij d.	
de Willelmo Camby indigena pro j fulle kettylles	xiij s. iiij d.
j pyp avelanarum	x s.
xx bonches[7] wispes steyll	x s.
un' balet alome	vj s. viij d.
j hogeshed cum viij ollis eneis	xvj s. viij d.
di' C battrey[8]	x s.
C libris canabi	vj s. viij d.
j barelle cum di' pece boutell	xx d.
ij dossenis librarum piperis	xxvj s. viij d.
ij libris gynger[9]	xx d.
iij di' pece dornykes	x s.
dimidia libra rawe sylk	xx d.

6. The corresponding controller's account, 108/5, has *papir alb'*.
7. 108/5 has *xx peces*.
8. 108/5 has *battrey pannes*.
9. 108/5 has *gynger sicc'*.

xv libris fili blodii[10]	ij s. iiij d.
Summa valoris	v li. xvij s. iiij d.
subsidium v s. xj d.	
de Thoma Moll indigena pro ij barrelles smigmatis	valor xx s.
subsidium xij d.	
de Roberto Baxter indigena pro j pype avelanarum	x s.
j hogeshed rasyng corens	x s.
j fulle kettylles	xiij s. iiij d.
j poke mather	xxvj s. viij d.
j hogeshed fructus	x s.
j pipe cum ij dossenis wyer	xiij s. iiij d.
v ollis eneis	x s.
lx libris canabi	iij s. iiij d.
ij grosse spinctrum	iij s. iiij d.
Summa valoris	C s.
subsidium v s.	
de Edward Baxter indigena pro iij pipes ferri	valor lxxxx s.
subsidium iiij s. vj d.	
de Willelmo Scott indigena pro j pipe fructus	xx s.
ij barrelles smigmatis	xx s.
j fulle kettylles	xiij s. iiij d.
j barrelle rasenes[11]	vj s. viij d.
Summa valoris	lx s.
subsidium iij s.	
de Cristofero Brigham indigena pro un' hogeshed fructus	x s.
j parv' pokett onyon seide	vj s. viij d.
xxx wispes steyll	x s.
j parva cista pectenum[12]	x s.
di' barrelle calebis	xxvj s. viij d.
Summa valoris	lxiij s. iiij d.
subsidium iij s. ij d.	
de Cristofero Raw indigena pro iij barrelles smigmatis	xxx s.
j pipe avelanarum	x s.
j poke canabi	xx s.
ij pipes fructus	xl s.
j dolio ferri	lx s.
j barrelle revylles flax	x s.
Summa valoris	viij li. x s.
subsidium viij s. vj d.	
de Georgio Birde seniore indigena pro j pipe fructus	xx s.
j poke canabi	xx s.
una cista suger	xxvj s. viij d.
xij balys course woode	vj li.
j fulle kettylles	xiij s. iiij d.
Summa valoris	x li.
subsidium x s.	

10. 108/5 has *blew threid.*
11. 108/5 has *graunt rasenes.*
12. The MS. has *pecten'* throughout.

de Georgio Car seniore indigena pro j pipe ferri	xxx s.
vj bales[13] wode course	lx s.
C libris alome	vj s. viij d.
Summa valoris	iiij li. xvj s. viij d.
subsidium iiij s. x d.	
de Roberto Sallay indigena pro j barrelle smigmatis	valor x s.
subsidium vj d.	
de Willelmo Davell indigena pro ij bales[14] madre	valor liij s. iiij d.
subsidium ij s. viij d.	
de Johanne Snow indigena pro j pipe ferri	xxx s.
j fulle kettylles	xiij s. iiij d.
Summa valoris	xliij s. iiij d.
subsidium ij s. ij d.	
de Willelmo Swan indigena pro iij barrelles smigmatis	valor xxx s.
subsidium xviij d.	
de Willelmo Draver indigena pro j fulle kettylles	xiij s. iiij d.
un' maunde cont' ij dossenis tyn belles	xx d.
ij dossenis belles lede	xx d.
iij di' peces fustean	x s.
j dossena librarum galles	xx d.
di' pece boutell	xx d.
un' grosse spinctrum	xx d.
iiij ollis eneis	vj s. viij d.
xij parv' pannes	vj s. viij d.
Summa valoris	xlv s.
subsidium ij s. iij d.	
de Henrico Bednall indigena pro cista pectenum	x s.
j pok madre	xxvj s. viij d.
j fulle kettylles	xiij s. iiij d.
j barrelle mellis	x s.
un' maund cont' x gold skynnys	iij s. iiij d.
j dossena colourd skynnys	xx d.
j grosse lases wyvourn	vj s. viij d.
M nedylles	xx d.
iiij dacres cultellorum	iij s .iiij d.
di' pece boutell	xx d.
j dossena coffers	iij s. iiij d.
j rym papir[15]	xx d.
j dossena libris comyn	xx d.
vj proose pellibus	xx d.
viij ollis eneis	xvj s. viij d.
vj long sawes	vj s. viij d.
Summa valoris	v li. x s.
subsidium v s. vj d.	

13. 108/5 has *balettes*.
14. 108/5 has *balettes*.
15. 108/5 has *alb' papir*.

de Henrico Barrow indigena pro j dolio ferri	lx s.
j barrelle sope	x s.
Summa valoris	lxx s.
subsidium iij s. vj d.	
de Willelmo Birde indigena pro j barrelle smigmatis	x s.
j hogeshed fructus	x s.
Summa valoris	xx s.
subsidium xij d.	
Summa partis	Cvij s. ij d.ob.

Examinatur Probatur

[*Membrane 4 dorse*]

Navis vocata le George de Novo Castro unde Willelmus Hamond est magister applicuit xx^{o} die Januarii anno xv^{mo}.

de Willelmo Selby indigena pro un' roundlett cont' iij C libris canabi	xx s.
xij ollis eneis	xxx s.
di' C libris battrey	xx s.
Summa Valoris	lxx s.
subsidium iij s. vj d.	
de Willelmo Shaldfurth indigena pro j pipe ferri	xxx s.
v barrelles smigmatis	l s.
Summa valoris	iiij li.
subsidium iiij s.	
de Willelmo Camby indigena pro iiij barrelles smigmatis	xl s.
j pokkett canabi	xx s.
Summa valoris	lx s.
subsidium iij s.	
de Thoma Moll indigena pro di' last allecis albi	xx s.
xl wispes steyll	xiij s. iiij d.
Summa valoris	xxxiij s. iiij d.
subsidium xx d.	
de Roberto Herryson indigena pro j fulle kettylles	xiij s. iiij d.
un' barrell cum ij dossenis bagges	x s.
iij di' peces dornykes	x s.
di' grosse wivorn lases	xx d.
j gross hatt bandes	xx d.
xx peces crole ribben	iij s. iiij d.
dimidia dossena coffers	xx d.
ij dossenis librarum onyon sede	v s.
Idem un' parv' maund cont' lx libris canabi	iij s. iiij d.
xviij coffers	v s.
di' grosse spinctrum	xx d.
di' grosse cultellorum	xx d.
C libris battrey	xx s.
Summa valoris	lxxviij s. iiij d.
subsidium iij s. xj d.	

de Roberto Baxter indigena pro iiij balettes cane woode	xl s.
j poke canabi	xx s.
j pip ferri	xxx s.
Summa valoris	iiij li. x s.
subsidium iiij s. vj d.	
de Johanne Blaxton indigena pro x bales woode	x li.
j last bituminis	xx s.
j pipe ferri	xxx s.
x ollis eneis	xx s.
iij barrelles smigmatis[16]	xxx s.
Summa valoris	xv li.
subsidium xv s.	
de Cristofero Brigham indigena pro ij di' barrelles calebis	liij s. iiij d.
xx wispes steyll	vj s. viij d.
j pok onyon sede	xx s.
iij parv' barrelles trane olei	xxx s.
iij balettes canewoode	xxx s.
j dolio ferri	lx s..
un' parv' barrelle cum iij grosse spinctrum	v s.
j grosse bedes	xx d.
viij bagges	iij s. iiij d.
Summa valoris	x li. x s.
subsidium x s. vj d.	
de Roberto Bartram indigena pro j fulle kettylles	valor xiij s. iiij d.
subsidium viij d.	
de Cristofero Raw indigena pro j dolio ferri	lx s.
j pipe avelanarum	l s.
iij barrelles smigmatis	xxx s.
Summa valoris	C s.
subsidium v s.	
de Rogero Raw indigena pro vj barrelles smigmatis	valor lx s.
subsidium iij s.	
Idem pro un' butte malvesy[17]	
tonnagium xviij d.	
de Willelmo Car indigena pro iij barrelles sope	valor xxx s.
subsidium xviij d.	
de Hugone Eryngton indigena pro iiij barrelles smigmatis	valor xl s.
subsidium ij s.	
de Willelmo Davell indigena pro j pipe fructus	xx s.
j bale madre	xxvj s. viij d.
j pipe revylles flax	xiij s. iiij d.
Summa valoris	lx s.
subsidium iij s.	

16. 108/5 has *sope.*
17. 108/5 has *un' butte vini dulcis.*

de Johanne Baxter indigena pro un' barrelle mellis	x s.
j hogeshede fructus	x s.
Summa valoris	xx s.
subsidium xij d.	
de Willelmo Draver indigena pro j barrelle sope	valor x s.
subsidium vj d.	
de Johanne Bewyk indigena pro j barrelle smigmatis[18]	v s.
j hogeshede avelanarum	v s.
j barrelle fructus	v s.
C libris canabi	Cj s. viij d.
viij bagges	iij s. iiij d.
ij parv' grosse spinctrum	iij s. iiij d.
summa valoris	xxxiij s. iiij d.
subsidium xx d.	
de Bartramo Yonghusband indigena pro di' barrelle calebis	xxvj s. viij d.
ij doliis ferri	vj li.
Summa valoris	vij li. vj s. viij d.
subsidium vij s. iiij d.	
de Antonio Rede indigena pro ij barrelles sope'	xx s.
iiij swerdes	vj s. viij d.
Summa valoris	xxvj s. viij d.
subsidium xvj d.	
de Georgio Car indigena pro j fulle kettylles	xiij s. iiij d.
j poke madre	xxvj s. viij d.
Summa valoris	xl s.
subsidium ij s.	
de Thoma Riddall indigena pro j fulle kettylles	xiij s. iiij d.
C libris canabi	vj s. viij d.
Summa valoris	xx s.
subsidium xij d.	
de Thoma Welden indigena pro un' barrelle rape olei	valor x s.
subsidium vj d.	
de Mauro Mawer indigena pro j pipe fructus	valor xx s.
subsidium xij d.	
de Jacobo Tennand indigena pro j pipe fructus	valor xx s.
subsidium xij d.	
de Willelmo Scott indigena pro j pipe ferri	xxx s.
j hogeshede fructus	x s.
Summa valoris	xl s.
subsidium ij s.	

18. 108/5 has *smigmatis*. The reversal of nomenclature by the controller in notes 16 and 18 indicates that no distinction between *smigm'* and *sope* was made. Subsequent reversals are not noted.

Navis vocata le Anne de Novo Castro unde Thomas Harrop est magister applicuit xxij° die Januarii anno xv^{mo}.

de Johanne Passheley indigena pro ij barrelles

avelanarum	iij s. iiij d.
iiij C libris ferri	x s.
Summa valoris	xiij s. iiij d.

subsidium viij d.

et de eodem pro un' hogeshede vini gasconii

tonnagium ix d.

de Willelmo Davell indigena pro j barrelle rape olei valor x s.

subsidium vj d.

de Bartramo Yonghusband indigena pro uno dolio ferri	lx s.
et un' pipe cum xij bagges	v s.
j grosse tree bedes	xx d.
un' grosse glasces	xx d.
dimidia pecia vustian	iij s. iiij d.
un' grosse graunt comes	xx d.
j grosse crokes	xx d.
ij paperes bonettes	vj s. viij d.
ij M bulyons	xx d.
ix saddilles	xx s.
ij peces bukrame	v s.
iiij par tallor sheres	iij s. iiij d.
vj women purses	iij s. iiij d.
j grosse cultellorum	xx d.
C virgis canvas	x s.
Summa valoris	vj li. vj s. viij d.

subsidium vj s. viij d.

Idem pro ij doliis vini gasconii

tonnagium vj s.

de Johanne Huddiswell indigena pro ij barrelles

avelanarum	iij s. iiij d.
CCCC libris ferri	xv s.
et j pipe cont' vj libras onyon sede	xx d.
j dossena parv' purses	v s.
j dossena bagges	vj s. viij d.
di' grosse cultellorum	ij s. vj d.
j grosse tyn brochus	xx d.
iiij dossenis comis[19]	iij s. iiij d.
ij dossenis glasces[20]	iij s. iiij d.
j rym papir	xx d.
ij dossenis broschis	xx d.
v dossenis tree bedes	xx d.
j grosse poyntes	x d.
j grosse crokes[21]	xx d.

---

19. 108/5 has *graunt comes*.
20. 108/5 has *merroures*.
21. 108/5 has *dawg crokes*.

di' grosse tyn rynges	x d.
di' pece vustian	xx d.
di' grosse lutestringes	x d.
j grosse bulyons	xx d.
Summa valoris	lv s.
subsidium ij s. ix d.	
de Roberto Harden indigena pro D libris ferri	Valor xv s.
subsidium ix d.	
Idem pro uno dolio vini gasconii	
tonnagium iij s.	
de Mauro Mawer indigena pro v peces rosen	x s.
j pipe course woode	xl s.
j barrelle avelanarum	xx d.
M libris ferri	xxx s.
Summa valoris	iiij li. xx d.
subsidium iiij s. j d.	
et de eodem pro un' pipe vini gasconii	
tonnagium xviij d.	
de Thoma Hanson indigena pro M ferri	valor xxx s.
subsidium xviij d.	
et de eodem pro un' pipe vini gasconii	
tonnagium xviij d.	

Summa partis Cxj s. v d.

Examinatur

[*Membrane 5 face*]

de Willelmo Harden indigena pro v bales course woode	l s.
iiij barellis avelanarum	vj s. viij d.
Summa valoris	lvj s. viij d.
subsidium ij s. x d.	
et de eodem pro j dolio et un' pipe vini gasconii	
tonnagium iiij s. vj d.	
de Edwardo Baxter indigena pro vj bales cane woode	valor xxvj s. viij d.
subsidium iij s. iiij d.	
de Roberto Bertram indigena pro uno parvo fardello	
cum v saddilles	x s.
ij dossenis parv' balances	iij s. iiij d.
D sadler naylles	xx d.
v bagges	xx d.
ij dossenis cultellorum	iij s. iiij d.
j dossena yalow skynnys	iij s. iiij d.
v par tabylles[22]	xx d.
iij dossenis comis	xx d.
Summa valoris	xxvj s. viij d.
subsidium xvj d.	

22. 108/5 has *playing tabylles*.

de Willelmo Selby indigena pro j cista parvorum pectenum x s.
j barelle avelanarum xx d.
j barrelle olei x s.
Summa valoris xxj s. viij d.
subsidium xiij d.
de Johanne Allen indigena pro DC libris ferri valor xx s.
subsidium xij d.

Navis vocata le Mare Allen de Novo Castro unde Walter [Plous] est magister applicuit xxiiij° die Januarii anno xv^{mo}
de Johanne Allen indigena pro iij doliis ferri ix li.
j last et di' allecis albi C s.
ij pipes avelanarum xx s.
j pipe fructus xx s.
j pokett onyon sede xx s.
C libris alome vj s. viij d.
ij barrelles smigmatis xx s.
j barrelle rape olei x s.
j pokett canabi xx s.
ij dossenis compas vj s. viij d.
Summa valoris xx li. iij s. iiij d.
subsidium xx s. ij d.
de Edwardo Baxter indigena pro j hogeshed fructus x s.
vj saddylles xiij s. iiij d.
j barrelle smigmatis x s.
Summa valoris xxxiij s. iiij d.
subsidium xx d.
de Thoma Moll indigena pro MMM libris ferri[23] vij li. x s.
xx boge skynnys iij s. iiij d.
ij bounches corke xx d.
Summa valoris vij li. xv s.
subsidium vij s. ix d.
de Willelmo Camby indigena pro j barrelle fructus x s.
j barrelle rape olei x s.
Summa valoris xx s.
subsidium xij d.
de Willelmo Scott indigena pro iiij barrelles sope valor xl s.
subsidium ij s.
de Johanne Passheley indigena pro ij barrelles smigmatis valor xx s.
subsidium xij d.
de Henrico Bednall indigena pro un' pokett canabi xx s.
vj barrelles bituminis x s.
Summa valoris xxx s.
subsidium xviij d.

23. 108/5 has iij *pipes ferri*.

de Johanne Baxter indigena pro ij pipes avelanarum	x s.
j pyp et un' hogeshede fructus	xxx s.
j dolio ferri	lx s.
xl libris onyon sede	vj s. viij d.
Summa valoris	Cvj s. viij d.
subsidium v s. iiij d.	
de Cristofero Brigham indigena pro j barrelle smigmatis	x s.
j cista suger	xxvj s. viij d.
Summa valoris	xxxvj s. viij d.
subsidium xxij d.	
de Georgio Hebburn indigena pro iij doliis ferri	ix li.
j pipe fructus	xx s.
Summa valoris	x li.
subsidium x s.	
de Georgio Car indigena pro ij doliis ferri	vj li
iij bales wode	lx s.
Summa valoris	ix li.
subsidium lx s.	
de Willelmo Davell indigena pro ij barrelles smigmatis	xxs.
j dolio ferri	lx s.
Summa valoris	lxxx s.
subsidium iiij s.	
de Mauro Mawer indigena pro j dolio ferri	valor lx s.
subsidium iij s.	
de Johanne Blaxton indigena pro iiij balettes cane wode[24]	valor xl s.
subsidium ij s.	

Navis vocata le Dave de Novo Castro unde Robertus Meryman est magister applicuit xxvj° die Januarii anno xv^{mo}.

de Thoma Saunderson indigena pro ij doliis ferri	valor vj li.
subsidium vj s.	
et de eodem pro un' hogeshede vini	
tonnagium xviij d.	
de Ricardo Wrangwyssh indigena pro iij doliis ferri	vj li.
iij barrelles smigmatis	xxx s.
Summa valoris	vij li. x s.
subsidium vij s. vj d.	
et de eodem pro uno dolio vini non dulcis	
tonnagium iij s.	
de Willelmo Scott indigena pro ij pipes avelanarum	xx s.
un' ame renysshe wyne	xx s.
Summa valoris	xl s.
subsidium ij s.	

24. 108/5 has *iij balettes wode course*. Subsequent similar qualifications of description are not noted.

de Rolando Herryson indigena pro vj barrelles smigmatis	lx s.
ij fulle kettylles	xxvj s. viij d.
j pipe cum iij dossenis coffers	vj s. viij d.
di' grosse lasces	xx d.
di' grosse spinctrum	x d.
di' grosse cultellorum	x d.
lx libris canabi	iij s. iiij d.
Summa valoris	C s.
subsidium v s.	
de Willelmo Steyll indigena pro iij barrelles sope	valor xxx s.
subsidium xviij d.	
de Willelmo Davell indigena pro j pipe fructus	valor xx s.
subsidium xij d.	
de Thoma Moll indigena pro j hogeshede fructus	valor x s.
subsidium vj d.	
de Roberto Meryman indigena pro D libris ferri	xv s.
j barrelle sope	x s.
Summa valoris	xxv s.
subsidium xv d.	
de Henrico Bednall indigena pro j barrelle sope	valor x s.
subsidium vj d.	
de Roberto Baxter indigena pro j barrelle sope	valor x s.
subsidium vj d.	
de Georgio Selby indigena pro j fulle kettylles	valor xiij s. iij d.
subsidium viij d.	

Navis vocata le Trinite de Novo Castro unde Willelmus Chevorous est magister applicuit v° die Februarii anno xv^mo^.

de Willelmo Swan indigena pro ij doliis ferri	vj li.
j last bituminis	xx s.
j pipe fructus	xx s.
Summa valoris	viij li.
subsidium viij s.	
et de eodem pro j pipe vini non dulcis	
tonnagium xviij d.	
de Thoma Swan indigena pro ij doliis ferri	valor vj li.
subsidium vj s.	
et de eodem pro un' hogeshede vini gasconii	
tonnagium ix d.	

Examinatur

Probatur

Summa partis	vj li. xj s. ix d.

[*(Membrane 5 dorse*]

de Willelmo Davell indigena pro j hogeshede fructus	valor x s.
subsidium vj d.	

de Ricardo Conyngham indigena pro v doliis ferri valor xv li.
subsidium xv s.
de Edwardo Baxter indigena pro j pipe revylles flax valor xx s.
subsidium xij d.
et de eodem pro uno dolio vini gasconii
tonnagium iij s.
de Johanne Pasheley indigena pro un' hogeshed fructus valor x s.
subsidium vj d.
de Willelmo Scott indigena pro M libris ferri xxx s.
ij barellis bituminis iij s. iiij d.
Summa valoris xxxij s. iiij d.
subsidium xx d.
de Willelmo Draver indigena pro j barrelle fructus valor vj s. viij d.
subsidium iiij d.
de Willelmo Birde indigena pro j barrelle rape olei valor x s.
subsidium vj d.
de Georgio Stalper indigena pro DCC libris ferri xx s.
j barrelle sope x s.
j hogeshed fructus x s.
Summa valoris xl s.
subsidium ij s.
et de eodem pro ij doliis vini gasconii
tonnagium vj s.
de Georgio Car indigena pro M libris ferri valor xxx s.
subsidium xviij d.
de Mauro Mawer indigena pro j pipe fructus xx s.
iij barrelles smigmatis xxx s.
M libris ferri xxx s.
Summa valoris iiij li.
subsidium iiij s.
de Willelmo Pykden indigena pro j hogeshed fructus valor x s.
subsidium vj d.
de Willelmo Selby indigena pro j hogeshede fructus valor x s.
subsidium vj d.
de Henrico Fenkill indigena pro j hogeshed vini gasconii
tonnagium ix d.
de Roberto Harden indigena pro j hogeshed vini gasconii
tonnagium ix d.

The Nicholas de Depe unde Peryn Loure est magister applicuit viij^{o} die Februarii anno xv^{mo}.
de eodem magistro alienigena pro vj barelles avelanarum valor ij s. viij d.
custuma j d. subsidium iiij d.
de Georgio Birde seniore indigena pro j pipe vini gasconii
tonnagium xviij d.

de Bartramo Yonghusband indigena pro v barelles olei l s.
xij barelles avelanarum xv s.
D libris ferri xv s.
Summa valoris iiij li.
subsidium iiij s.
de Mauro Mawer indigena pro ij barrelles olei valor xx s.
subsidium xij d.
de Johanne Huddiswell indigena pro iiij barrelles oleivalor xl s.
subsidium ij s.
de Johanne Allen indigena pro D libris ferri xv s.
v pecis rossen x s.
Summa valoris xxvs.
subsidium xv d.

The Nicholas predicta exivit xv° die Februarii anno xv^{mo}
de eodem magistro alienigena pro xx cheldris carbonum valor xxxiij s. iiij d.
custuma v d. subsidium xx d.

The Margaret de Bullan unde Ranold Potage est magister applicuit xvj die Februarii anno xv^{mo}.
de eodem magistro alienigena pro j barelle avelanarum xiij s. iiij d.
j wey salis grossi vj s. viij d.
Summa valoris xx s.
custuma iij d. subsidium xij d.

The Mare de Maldon unde Stephanus Brandreth est magister applicuit xvij die Februarii anno xv^{mo}.
de Johanne Gren indigena Londonii pro xlij doliis vini gasconii
tonnagium vj li. vj s.
et de eodem pro x bales woode valor vj li. vj s. viij d.
subsidium vj s. viij d.

The Poshell de Treporte unde Thomas Greyll est magister applicuit xx° die Februarii anno xv^{mo}.
de eodem magistro alienigena pro lx barrelles pomorum valor xxvj s. viij d.
custuma iiij d. subsidium xvj d.

The Poshell predicta exivit xxij die Februarii anno xv^{mo}.
de Edwardo Baxter indigena pro xx cheldris carbonum xx s.
dimidio plaustrato plumbi xxx s.
Summa valoris l s.
subsidium ij s. vj d.

The Margret de Bullon unde Ranold Potage est magister exivit xxiiij^{mo} Februarii anno xv^{mo}
de eodem magistro alienigena pro xxviij cheldris carbonum valor xlvj s. viij d.
custuma vj d. subsidium ij s. iiij d.

The Julian de Leyth unde Johannes Lentourn est magister applicuit xxv die Februarii anno xv^{mo}.
de Johanne Elys alienigena pro iiij barrelles allecis albi valor xiij s. iiij d.
customa ij d. subsidium viij d.

The Petir de Leyth unde Robertus Penman est magister applicuit eodem die et anno.
de Willelmo Symson alienigena pro vj barrelles allecis albi valor xx s.
custuma iij d. subsidium xij d.

Examinatur
Summa partis ix li. xiij s. iiij d.

[*Membrane 6 face*]
The Cristofer de Wyk unde Cornelius Hugetson est magister applicuit xxv^{o} die Februarii anno xv^{mo}.

de eodem magistro alienigena pro xx barrelles pomorum	xx s.
ij last emptie barrelles	x s.
xl libris canabi	iij s. iiij d.
lx virgis panni linei course	xx s.
Summa valoris[25]	liij s. iiij d.

custuma[26] viij d. subsidium[27] ij s. viij d.

The Katren de Depe unde Johannes Bartyn est magister applicuit xxv^{o} die Februarii anno xv^{mo}

de Petro Jewey alienigena pro xxv quarteriis ordii	l s.
xvj barrelles farini	xxiij s. iiij d.
CCC libris ferri	xxs.
Summa valoris	iiij li. xiij s. iiij d.

custuma xiiij d. subsidium iiij s. viij d.

The Julian de Leyth unde Johannes Lentourn est magister exivit xxvij^{o} die Februarii anno xv^{mo}

de Johanne Elys alienigena pro iij C libris ferri	x s.
iij cheldris carbonum	iij s. iiij d.
Summa valoris	xiij s. iiij d.

custuma ij d. subsidium viij d.

25. Followed by *xliij s. iiij d*, struck out.
26. Followed by *vj d.ob.*, struck out.
27. Followed by *ij s. ij d.*, struck out.

The Josset de Bullon unde Colyn Sarlote est magister exivit xxvij die Februarii anno xv^{mo}.
de eodem magistro alienigena pro xviij cheldris carbonum valor xxx s.
custuma iiij d.ob. subsidium xviij d.

The Mynyon de Bullon under Hareot Peare est magister exivit xxxvij die Februarii anno xv^{mo}.
de eodem magistro alienigena pro xviij cheldris carbonum valor xxxs.
custuma iiij d.ob. subsidium xviij d.

The Grace de Dew de Bullon unde Johannes Catanyey est magister exivit xxvij die Februarii anno xv^{mo}.
de eodem magistro alienigena pro xxxvj cheldris carbonum valor lx s.
custuma lx d. subsidium iij s.

Navicula de Leyth (vocata le Petir) unde Robertus Penman est magister exivit ultimo die Februarii
de Willelmo Symson alienigena pro vij C libris ferri valor xx s.
custuma iij d. subsidium xij d.

The Margret de Bullon unde Olyver Gerard est magister exivit ultimo die Februarii
de eodem magistro alienigena pro xx cheldris carbonum valor xxxiij s. iiij d
custuma v d. subsidium xx d.

The Jakket de Bullon unde Garryn de Cauen est magister exivit ultimo die Februarii
de eodem magistro alienigena pro xx cheldris carbonum valor xxxij s. iiij d.
custuma v d. subsidium xx d.

The Katren de Depe unde Johannes Bertyn est magister exivit vij^{o} die Marcii anno xv^{mo}.
de Petro Jewey alienigena pro xij cheldris carbonum valor xx s.
custuma iij d. subsidium xij d.

The Cristofer de Wyk in Holand unde Cornelius Hugetson est magister exivit xij^{o} die Marcii
de eodem magistro alienigena pro x cheldris carbonum xvj s. viij d.
dimidia cheldra petrarum iij s. iiij d.
Summa valoris xx s.
custuma iij d. subsidium xij d.

et de eodem pro ij dossenis virgarum panni lanei stricti course continentibus dimidium panni valor x s.
pannagium xvj d.ob. subsidium panni vj d.

Navis vocata le Edward de Novo Castro unde [William Carver est magister applicuit xvj° die Marcii anno xvmo]
de Thoma Weltden indigena pro ij doliis j pipe vini gasconii
tonnagium vij s. vj d.
de Roberto Harden indigena pro ij doliis j pipe vini gasconii
tonnagium vij s. vj d.
et de eodem pro ij bales woode valor xxvj s. viij d.
subsidium xvj d.
de Johanne Brandlyng indigena pro iij pipes vini gasconii
tonnagium iiij s. vj d.
de Thoma Harden indigena pro iij pipes vini gasconii
tonnagium iiij s. vj d.
de Jacobo Tennaund indigena pro j pipe vini gasconii
tonnagium xviij d.
de Willelmo Harden indigena pro j pipe un' hogeshed vini gasconii
tonnagium ij s. iij d.
de Georgio Baxter indigena pro j pipe vini gasconii
tonnagium xviij d.
de Edwardo Conyngham indigena pro v balettes wode valor lx s.
subsidium iij s.
et de eodem pro ij doliis j pipe vini gasconii
tonnagium vij s. vj d.
de Thoma Laton indigena pro j pipe vini gasconii
tonnagium xviij d.
de Roberto Bartram indigena pro ij doliis j pipe vini gasconii
tonnagium vij s. vj d.
de Thoma Horseley indigena pro iij doliis vini gasconii
tonnagium ix s.
de Thoma Hanson indigena pro ij doliis vini gasconii
tonnagium vj s.
de Georgio Conyngham indigena pro j pipe et un' hogeshed vini gasconii
tonnagium ij s. iij d.
de Willelmo Swan indigena pro j pipe j hogeshed vini gasconii
tonnagium ij s. iij d.

The Vallerey de Abevyll unde Janin Byssherd est magister exivit xix° die Marcii anno xvmo
de Gylliam de Wyse[28] alienigena pro xij cheldris
carbonum xx s.
dimidia cheldra molarum iij s. iiij d.
ij plaustratis plumbi vj li. xiij s. iiij d.
Summa valoris vij li. xvj s. viij d.
custuma xxiij d.ob. subsidium vij s. x d.

28. 108/5 has *de eodem magistro.*

Examinatur

Summa Partis Cvj s. viij d.

[*Membrane 6 dorse*]

The Pete Colwin de Stapill unde Robertus [Clement] est magister exivit ultimo die Marcii anno xv^mo^.

de eodem magistro alienigena pro xvj cheldris carbonum valor xxvj s. viij d

custuma iiij d. subsidium xvj d.

The Michaell de Humflew unde Rogerus Breyley est magister exivit ultimo die Marcii anno xv^mo^.

de eodem magistro alienigena pro xvj cheldris carbonum valor xxvj s. viij d

una cheldra petrarum vj s. viij d.

Summa valoris xxxiij s. iiij d.

custuma v d. subsidium xx d.

The Nicholas de Depe unde Harry de [Loyt'] est magister exivit iij^o^ die Aprilis anno xv^mo^.

de eodem magistro alienigena pro x cheldris carbonum xvj s. viij d.

v cheldris petrarum xxij s. iiij d.

Summa valoris l s.

custuma vij d.ob. subsidium ij s. vj d.

The Michaell de Bullon und Edmund Hagvarde est magister exivit vij^o^ die Aprilis anno xv^mo^.

de eodem magistro alienigena pro xx cheldris carbonum xxxiij s. iiij d.

custuma v d. subsidium xx d.

The Marie de Harflew unde Gilliam Jakes est magister exivit xiiij^o^ die Aprilis anno xv^mo^.

de Arnold Delegrate alienigena pro xviij cheldris carbonum valor xx s.

custuma iiij d.ob. subsidium xviij d.

The Nicholas de Depe unde Peryn Lour est magister exivit xvij^o^ die Aprilis anno xv^mo^.

de eodem magistro alienigena pro xxj cheldris carbonum [xxxv s.]

Idem pro ij cheldris petrarum [xiij s. iiij d.]

Summa valoris [xlviij s. iiij d.]

custuma vij d.qu. subsidium ij s. vj d.

The Cristofer de Dansk unde Thomas Holdehesse est magister applicuit [xxvj die Aprilis]
de eodem magistro mercatore de Hansa

pro vij last picis et bituminis	vij li.
v last cinerum	C s.
xiiij barrelles osmundes	lx s.
x nest counteres	vj li. xiij s. iiij d.
MCClx waynskottes	xvj li.
MMCCCC clapholt	xxvj s. viij d.
CClx ores	liij s. iiij d.
xxxvij bales flex	xxxiiij s. iiij d.[29]
di' skoke playing tabylles	xiij s. iiij d.
vij dossenis wode cannes	v s.
xx skoke trenshours	v s.
iiij skoke trowes	xx s.
iij skoke parv' trowes	iij s. iiij d.
j nest cistarum	v s.
x dakre russ skynnys	xx s.
j skoke et dimidio drynking glasses	v s.
j libra awmer bedes	xiij s. iiij d.
Summa valoris	xlvij li. xvj s. viij d

custuma xj s xj d.ob. subsidium nichil quia de Hansa

The Antonie de Novo Castro unde Johannes Passheley est magister exivit xxviij° die Aprilis anno xv^mo^.
de Bartramo Yonghusband indigena pro xlviij petris plumbi — xvj s. viij d.

xij wey salis albi[30]	iiij li.
ij boltes oleron canvas	xx s.
Summa valoris	v li. xvj s. viij d.

subsidium v s. x d.
et de eodem pro iij integris pannis lanei strictis
pannagium iij s. vj d.
et pro uno dolio vini gasconii
tonnagium iij s.
de Johanne Passhely indigena pro uno plaustrato plumbi — iij li.
subsidium iij s.
et de eodem pro ij dossenis virgarum panni lanei stricti continentibus dimidium pannum
pannagium vij d.
et pro un' hogeshede vini
tonnagium ix d.
de Peter Chartor indigena pro xl peces plumbi — valor xiij s. iiij d.

---

29. There is a cross by *xxxiiij s. iiij d.*, and a cross in the margin. To agree with the *Summa* the value should be *xxxiij s. iiij d.*
30. 108/5 has *salis grossi.*

subsidium viij d.
de eodem pro una dossena virgarum panni lanei stricti continente j quarterium panni
pannagium iij d.ob.
de Johanne Steyll indigena pro viij cheldris carbonum valor viij s. iiij d.
subsidium v d.
de Roberto Cromer indigena mercatore societatis Gilde predicte pro ij plaustratis plumbi valor vj li.
subsidium vj s.
de eodem Roberto pro CC pellibus agnellorum valor xx s.
subsidium xij d.
de eodem pro iiij dossenis virgarum panni lanei stricti continentibus unum pannum
pannagium xiiij d.
de Roberto Harden indigena pro dimidio panno lanei stricto
pannagium vij d.
de Thoma Horsley indigena mercatore Gilde predicte pro ij plaustratis plumbi valor vj li.
subsidium vj s.
de eodem pro CCC pellibus agnellorum valor xxx s.
subsidium xviij d.
et de eodem pro viij dossenis virgarum panni lanei stricti continentibus ij pannos
pannagium ij s. iiij d.
de Willelmo Davell indigena pro j plaustrato et iij quarteriis plumbi C s.
un' wey salis grossi x s.
Summa valoris v li. x s.
subsidium v s. vj d.
et de eodem pro iiij dossenis virgarum panni lanei stricti continentibus unum pannum
pannagium xiiij d.
de Thoma Saunderson indigena pro lx petris plumbi xx s.
j wey et di' salis grossi xv s.
j pipe vinagre x s.
Summa valoris xlv s.
subsidium ij s. iij d.
de Willelmo Wilkinson indigena mercatore Gilde predicte pro ij wey salis albi valor xiij s. iiij d.
subsidium viij d.
et de eodem pro CCC pellibus agnellorum valor xxx s.
subsidium xviij d.
et de eodem pro vj dossenis virgarum panni lanei stricti continentibus unum pannum et dimidium
pannagium xxj d.
de Willelmo Harden indigena pro dimidio panno lanei stricto
pannagium vij d.
de Willelmo Swan indigena pro un' hogeshed vini

tonnagium ix d.
de Cristofero Brigham indigena pro xij dossenis virgarum panni lanei stricti continentibus iij pannos integros
pannagium iij s. vj d.
de Willelmo Car indigena mercatore predicte Gilde pro lxx pellibus agnellorum valor v s. x d.
subsidium iij d.ob.
et de eodem Willelmo pro v dossenis virgarum panni lanei stricti continentibus unum pannum et j quarterium
pannagium xvij d.ob.

The Edwarde de Novo Castro unde Willelmus Kervour est magister exivit xxviij° die Aprilis anno xv^{mo} [cum lanis et pellibus lanutis de crescencia predicta etc.]
de Willelmo Swan mercatore ibidem pro ij sarpleris lane ponderantibus iij saccos j quarterium iij clavos
custuma v s. vij d. subsidium xxvij s. vj d.ob.qu.
de Georgio Car mercatore ibidem pro ij sarpleris lane ponderantibus iij saccos iij quarteria
custuma vj s. iij d. subsidium xxj s. iij d.
de Thoma Riddall mercatore ibidem pro iij sarpleris lane ponderantibus vj saccos iij quarteria vj clavos
custuma xj s. v d. subsidium lvij s. iij d.
de Johanne Brandling mercatore ibidem pro iij sarpleris lane ponderantibus v saccos dimidium viij clavos
custuma ix s. v d.qu. subsidium xlvij s. ij d.

Examinatur
Summa Partis xiij li. xvij s. x d.ob.qu.

[*Membrane 7 face*]
de Rogero Raw mercatore ibidem pro una sarplera lane ponderante ij saccos
custuma iij s. iiij d. subsidium xvj s. viij d.
de Bartramo Yonghusband mercatore ibidem pro una sarplera lane ponderante j saccum iij quarteria
custuma ij s. ix d. subsidium xiiij s. vij d.
de Thomas Hanson mercatore ibidem pro iij sarpleris lane ponderantibus v saccos iij quarteria
custuma ix s. vij d. subsidium xlvij s. xj d.
de Cristofero Raw mercatore ibidem pro una sarplera lane ponderante j saccum iij quarteria
custuma ij s. xj d. subsidium xiiij s. vij d.
de Cristofero Brigham mercatore ibidem pro un' pokett lane pond' j quarterium
custuma } ij s. vj d.
subsidium }
de Willelmo Birde mercatore ibidem pro una sarplera lane ponderante

ij saccos j quarterium
custuma iij s. ix d. subsidium xviij s. ix d.
de Willelmo Davell mercatore ibidem pro una sarplera lane ponderante j saccum dimidium iij clavos
custuma ij s. vij d.qu. subsidium xiij s.
de Edwardo Baxter mercatore ibidem pro una sarplera lane ponderante j saccum iij quarteria
custuma ij s. xj d. subsidium xiiij s. vij d.
de Alano Elder mercatore ibidem pro Cxx pellibus lanutis continentibus dimidium saccum
custuma } v s.
subsidium }

Sequitur pondagium eiusdem navis (cum pellibus vocatis shorlinges morlinges et agnellis de crescencia predicta)
de Willelmo Swan indigena (mercatore Gilde predicte) pro CCiiij^{xx} pellibus shorlinges et morlinges valor xl s.
subsidium ij s.
de Georgio Car indigena (mercatore ibidem) pro XV pellibus tannatis siccis mortlinges et stiklinges valor xx s.
subsidium xij d.
de Johanne Brandlyng indigena (mercatore ibidem) pro CClx pellibus shorlinges et morlinges valor xxxvij s. vj d
subsidium xxij d.ob.
de Bartramo Yonghusband indigena (mercatore ibidem) pro ij dacres corriorum salsorum
custuma xvj d. subsidium vj s. viij d.
denaria Calesii j d.ob.qu. cokettum ij d.
et de eodem (mercatore ibidem) pro CCxxx pellibus shorlinges et morlinges valor xxxiij s. iiij d
subsidium xx d.
et de eodem (mercatore ibidem) pro ij plaustratis plumbi valor vj li.
subsidium vj s.
de Thoma Hanson indigena (mercatore ibidem) pro CCiiij^{xx} pellibus shorlinges et morlinges valor xl s.
subsidium ij s.
de Willelmo Harden indigena (mercatore ibidem) pro CCCC iiij^{xx} pellibus shorlinges et morlinges valor lv s.
subsidium ij s. ix d.
de Willelmo Davell indigena (mercatore ibidem) pro C pellibus shorlinges et morlinges valor xv s.
subsidium ix d.
de Alano Elder indigena (mercatore ibidem) pro CCCxx pellibus shorlinges et morlinges valor xlvij s. vj d.
subsidium ij s. iiij d.ob.

The James de Novo Castro unde Lodvicus Sothern est magister exivit xxviij die Aprilis anno xv (cum lanis et pellibus lanutis de crescentia predicta etc)

de Willelmo Swan mercatore ibidem pro una sarplera lane ponderante j saccum iij quarteria

custuma ij s. xj d. subsidium xiiij s. vij d.

de Thoma Gren mercatore ibidem pro iij sarpleris lane ponderantibus v saccos dimidium

et de eodem pro lx pellibus lanutis continentibus j quarterium v sacci iij quarteria

custuma ix s. vij d. subsidium xlvij s. xj d.

de Thoma Riddall mercatore ibidem pro una sarplera lane ponderante ij saccos

et de eodem pro CCC pellibus lanutis continentibus j saccum j quarterium iij sacci j quarterium

custuma v s. v d. subsidium xxvij s. j d.

de Johanne Brandlyng mercatore ibidem pro una sarplera lane ponderante ij saccos vj clavos

custuma iij s. vj d.ob. subsidium xxvij s. viij d.

de Cristofero Raw mercatore ibidem pro ij sarpleris lane ponderantibus iij saccos dimidium

custuma v s. x d. subsidium xxix s. ij d.

de Rogero Raw mercatore ibidem pro j sarplera lane ponderante j saccum iij quarteria

et de eodem pro lx pellibus lanutis continentibus j quarterium ij saccos

custuma iij s. iiij d. subsidium xvj s. viij d.

de Georgio Car mercatore ibidem pro Ciiij^{xx} pellibus lanutis continentibus iij quarteria

custuma }
subsidium } vij s. vj d.

de Lodvico Sothern mercatore ibidem pro una sarplera lane ponderante j saccum

custuma }
subsidium } x s.

de Johanne Passheley mercatore ibidem pro Ciiij^{xx} pellibus lanutis continentibus iij quarteria

custuma }
subsidium } vij s. vj d.

de Roberto Baxter mercatore ibidem pro Cxx pellibus lanutis continentibus dimidium saccum

custuma }
subsidium } v s.

de Roberto Harden mercatore ibidem pro una sarplera lane ponderante j saccum j quarterium iij clavos

et de eodem pro Ciiij^{xx} pellibus lanutis continentibus j quarterium ij sacci iij clavi

custuma iij s. v d.qu. subsidium xvij s. ij d.

de Willelmo Bird (mercatore ibidem) pro [Ciiij^{xx} pellibus lanutis continentibus iij quarteria]
custuma } subsidium } vij s. vj d.
de Willelmo Haynyng (mercatore ibidem) pro j sarplera [lane ponderante ij saccos]
et de eodem pro Cxx pellibus lanutis continentibus dimidium saccum ij sacci dimidius
custuma iiij s. ij d. subsidium xx s. x d.
de Willelmo Selby mercatore ibidem pro lx pellibus lanutis continentibus j quarterium
custuma } subsidium } ij s. vj d.
de Willelmo Camby mercatore ibidem pro Cxx pellibus lanutis continentibus dimidium saccum
custuma } subsidium } v s.
de Georgio Bird seniore mercatore ibidem pro lx pellibus lanutis continentibus j quarterium
custuma } subsidium } ij s. vj d.
de Thoma Laton mercatore ibidem pro j sarplera lane ponderante j saccum dimidium
custuma ij s. vj d. subsidium xij s. vj d.

Sequitur pondagium eiusdem navis cum aliis pellibus vocatis shorlinges et morlinges et agnellis de crescencia predicta
de Thoma Gren indigena (mercatore gilde predicte) pro CCCCxl pellibus shorlinges et morlinges valor lxv s.
subsidium iij s. iij d.
de Thoma Riddall indigena (mercatore ibidem) pro Mxx pellibus shorlinges et morlinges vij li. xij s. vj d.
CCCClx pellibus agnellorum xlv s.
Summa valoris ix li. xvij s. vj d.
subsidium ix s. x d.ob.
de Cristofero Raw indigena (mercatore ibidem) pro C^{ma}xxvj pellibus shorlinges et morlinges valor xviij s. iiij d.
subsidium xj d.
de Rogero Raw indigena (mercatore ibidem) pro CCv^{xx} shorlinges et morlinges valor xlij s. vj d.
subsidium ij s. j d.ob.
de Georgio Car indigena (mercatore ibidem) pro iiijCxl pellibus shorlinges et morlinges valor lxv s.
subsidium iij s. iij d.
de Johanne Passheley indigena (mercatore ibidem) pro iiijClx pellibus shorlinges et morlinges valor lxvij s. vj d.
subsidium iij s. iiij d.ob.

de Roberto Baxter indigena (mercatore ibidem) pro Dlx pellibus shorlinges et morlinges valor iiij li. ij s. vj d.
subsidium iiij s. j d.ob.
de Roberto Harden indigena (mercatore ibidem) pro CCxx pellibus shorlinges et morlinges valor xxxij s. vj d.
subsidium xix d.ob.
de Willelmo Birde indigena (mercatore ibidem) pro CCCv^xx pellibus shorlinges et morlinges valor lvij s. vj d.
subsidium ij s. x d.ob.

Summa partis xxvj li. vij s. vj d.ob.qu.

[*Membrane 7 dorse*]
de Johanne Batemanson indigena (mercatore Gilde predicte) pro Clx pellibus shorlinges et morlinges valor xxij s. vj d.
subsidium xiij d.ob.
de Willelmo Haynyng indigena (mercatore ibidem) pro CCCCxx pellibus shorlinges et morlinges valor lxij s. vj d.
subsidium iij s. j d.ob.
de Willelmo Selby indigena (mercatore ibidem) pro D pellibus shorlinges et morlinges valor lxxv s.
subsidium iij s. ix d.
de Willelmo Camby indigena (mercatore ibidem) pro CCC pellibus shorlinges et morlinges valor xlv s.
subsidium ij s. iij d.
de Georgio Bird seniore indigena (mercatore ibidem) pro CCCClx pellibus shorlinges et morlinges valor lxvij s. vj d.
subsidium iij s. iiij d.ob.
de Johanne Huddiswell indigena (mercatore ibidem) pro Clxx pellibus shorlinges et morlinges valor xxiij s. iiij d.
subsidium xiiij d.
de Thoma Laton indigena (mercatore ibidem) pro Cxl pellibus shorlinges et morlinges valor xx s.
subsidium xij d.

xv s. ix d.ob.

Navis vocata le Katren de Novo Castro unde Robertus Lighton est magister exivit eodem die anno xv^mo (cum lanis et pellibus lanutis de crescencia predicta.)
de Thoma Riddall mercatore ibidem pro ij sarpleris lane ponderantibus iij saccos j quarterium
et de eodem pro CCC pellibus lanutis continentibus j saccum j quarterium iiij sacci dimidius
custuma vij s. vj d. subsidium xxxvij s. vj d.
de Thoma Gren mercatore ibidem pro iij sarpleris lane ponderantibus v saccos dimidium vj clavos

et de eodem pro lx pellibus lanutis continentibus j quarterium v sacci iij quarteria vj clavis
custuma ix s. ix d.ob. subsidium xlviij s. xj d.
de Roberto Baxter mercatore ibidem pro iiij^{xx}x pellibus lanutis continentibus j quarterium dimidio quarterium
custuma } iij s.
subsidium }
de Cristofero Raw mercatore ibidem pro una sarplera lane ponderante j saccum j quarterium iij clavos
custuma ij s. ij d. subsidium x s. ij d.
de Johanne Bewyk mercatore ibidem pro ij sarpleris lane ponderantibus iij saccos iij quarteria xij clavos
custuma vj s. vij d.ob.qu. subsidium xxxiij s. iij d.
de Johanne Brandlyng mercatore ibidem pro lx pellibus lanutis continentibus j quarterium
custuma } ij s. vj d.
subsidium }
de Thoma Hyll mercatore ibidem pro xxx pellibus lanutis continentibus dimidium quarterium
custuma } xv d.
subsidium }
de Roberto Herryson mercatore ibidem pro [j sarplera lane ponderante j saccum iij quarteria vj clavos
et de eodem pro lx pellibus lanutis continentibus j quarterium]
Summa ij sacci vj clavi
custuma iij s. vj d.ob. subsidium xvij s. viij d.
de Willelmo Camby mercatore ibidem pro j balett lane pond' iij quarteria
et de eodem pro Cx pellibus lanutis continentibus j quarterium dimidium quarterium xx pelles
Summa j saccus dimidium quarterium xx pelles
custuma ij s. qu. subsidium x s. j d.
de Willelmo Selby mercatore ibidem pro una sarplera lane ponderante j saccum j quarterium iij clavos
custuma ij s. ij d.qu. subsidium x s. xj d.
de Mauro Mawer mercatore ibidem pro una sarplera lane ponderante ij saccos viij clavos
custuma iij s. vij d.qu. subsidium xviij s.
de Jacobo Tennaund mercatore ibidem pro una sarplera lane ponderante j saccum j quarterium
custuma ij s. j d. subsidium x s. v d.
xij li. iiij s. viij d.ob.qu.

Sequitur pondagium eiusdem navis cum aliis pellibus vocatis shorlinges et morlinges et agnellis de crescencia predicta
de Thoma Riddall indigena (mercatore predicte Gilde) pro D pellibus shorlinges et morlinges valor lxxvs.
subsidium iij s. ix d.

et de eodem pro uno plaustrato plumbi valor lx s.
subsidium iij s.
de Thoma Gren indigena (mercatore ibidem) pro CClxxiiij pellibus shorlinges et morlinges xxxix s. ij d.
Clx pellibus agnellorum lv s.
Summa valoris liiij s. ij d.
subsidium ij s. viij d.ob.
de Thoma Weltden indigena (mercatore ibidem) pro j plaustrato plumbi valor lx s.
subsidium iij s.
de Roberto Baxter indigena (mercatore ibidem) pro CCCCxx pellibus shorlinges et morlinges valor lxij s. vj d.
subsidium iij s. j d.ob.
de Johanne Passheley indigena (mercatore ibidem) pro C pellibus shorlinges et morlinges valor xv s.
subsidium iij d.
de Johanne Brandlyng indigena (mercatore ibidem) pro CC pellibus shorlinges et morlinges valor xxx s.
subsidium xviij d.
de Thoma Hyll indigena mercatore ibidem pro Cxl pellibus shorlinges et morlinges valor xx s.
subsidium xij d.
de Roberto Herryson indigena (mercatore ibidem) pro D pellibus shorlinges et morlinges valor lxxv s.
subsidium iij s. ix d.
de Willelmo Camby indigena (mercatore ibidem) pro CClxx pellibus shorlinges et morlinges valor xxxviij s. iiij d.
subsidium xxiij d.
de Jacobo Tennaund indigena (mercatore ibidem) pro lxxiij pellibus shorlinges et morlinges valor viij s. iiij d.
subsidium v d.

xviij s. iij d.

Navis vocata le Dave de Novo Castro unde Jacobus Robynson est magister exivit eodem die anno xv^mo (cum lanis et pellibus lanutis de crescencia predicta etc)
de Georgio Conyngham mercatore ibidem pro j sarplera lane ponderante j saccum dimidium vj clavos
et de eodem pro lx pellibus lanutis continentibus j quarterium j saccus iij quarteria vj clavi
custuma iij s. j d.ob. subsidium xv s. vij d.
de Thoma Cooke mercatore ibidem pro ij sarpleris lane ponderantibus iiij saccos
custuma vj s. viij d. subsidium xxxiij s. iiij d.
de Ricardo Wrangwyssh mercatore ibidem pro iij sarpleris lane ponderantibus iiij saccos iij quarteria iiij clavos
custuma viij s. j d. subsidium xl s. iij d.

de Roberto Bartram mercatore ibidem pro ij sarpleris lane ponderantibus iij saccos j quarterium
custuma v s. v d. subsidium xxvij s. j d.
de Ricardo Conyngham mercatore ibidem pro ij sarpleris lane ponderantibus iij saccos iij quarteria viij clavos
custuma vj s. vj d.qu. subsidium xxxij s. vij d.
de Roberto Harden mercatore ibidem pro j sarplera lane ponderante ij saccos
custuma iij s. iiij d. subsidium xvj s. viij d.
de Thoma Saunderson mercatore ibidem pro j sarplera lane ponderante ij saccos viij clavos
custuma iij s. vij d.qu. subsidium xviij s.
de Johanne Huddiswell mercatore ibidem pro j sarplera lane ponderante ij saccos iij quarteria
custuma iiij s. vij d. subsidium xxij s. xj d.
xij li. vij s. ix d.

Sequitur pondagium eiusdem navis (cum aliis pellibus vocatis shorlinges et morlinges et agnellis de crescencia predicta)
de Georgio Conyngham indigena (mercatore gilde predicte) pro ij dakers coriorum salsorum
custuma xvj d. subsidium vjs. viij d. denaria calesii ij d. cokettus ij d.
et de eodem pro CClx pellibus shorlinges et morlinges
valor xlij s. vj d.
subsidium ij s. j d.ob.

Summa partis xxvij li. iij s. vij d.ob.qu.

[*Membrane 8 face*]
de Thoma Cook indigena (mercatore ibidem) pro CCC pellibus shorlinges et morlinges valor xlv s.
subsidium ij s. iij d.
de Johanne Brandlyng indigena (mercatore ibidem) pro v dossenis pellium vitulorum tannatarum siccarum valor xx s.
subsidium xij d.
de Ricardo Wrangwyssh indigena (mercatore ibidem) pro v^{xx} pellibus shorlinges et morlinges valor xij s. vj d.
subsidium vij d.ob.
et pro un' barrelle sepi valor x s.
subsidium vj d.
de Roberto Bartram indigena (mercatore ibidem) pro CCiiij^{xx}xij pellibus shorlinges et morlinges valor xlj s. viij d.
subsidium ij s. j d.
de Johanne Huddiswell indigena mercatore ibidem pro Cxl pellibus shorlinges et morlinges valor xx s.
subsidium xij d.

Navis vocata le George de Novo Castro unde Johannes Elyson est magister exivit eodem die et anno (cum lanis et pellibus lanutis de crescencia predicta etc.)

de Willelmo Selby mercatore ibidem pro iiij^{xx}x pellibus lanutis continentibus j quarterium et dimidium

custuma } iij s. ix d.
subsidium }

de Henrico Bednall mercatore ibidem pro Cx pellibus lanutis continentibus j quarterium dimidium xx pelles

custuma } iiij s. vij d.
subsidium }

de Georgio Selby mercatore ibidem pro lx pellibus lanutis continentibus j quarterium

custuma } ij s. vj d.
subsidium }

de Johanne Morpath mercatore ibidem pro j sarplera lane ponderante j saccum j quarterium iij clavos

et de eodem pro Ciiij^{xx} pellibus lanutis continentibus iij quarteria ij sacci iij clavi

custuma iij s. v d.qu. subsidium xvij s. ij d.

de Georgio Birde mercatore ibidem pro iiij^{xx}x pellibus lanutis continentibus j quarterium et dimidium

custuma } iij s. ix d.
subsidium }

de Willelmo Birde mercatore ibidem pro Clx pellibus lanutis continentibus j quarterium

custuma } ij s. vj d.
subsidium }

de Willelmo Pykden mercatore ibidem pro una sarplera lane ponderante j saccum iij quarteria

et de eodem pro lx pellibus lanutis continentibus j quarterium ij saccos

custuma iij s. iiij d. subsidium xvj s. viij d.

de Mauro Mawer mercatore ibidem pro una sarplera lane ponderante ij saccos

custuma iij s. iiij d. subsidium xvj s. viij d.

de Johanne Bewyk mercatore ibidem pro iij sarpleris lane ponderantibus iij saccos j quarterium

custuma v s. v d. subsidium[31] xxvij s. j d.

de Andrea Bewyk mercatore ibidem pro un' poket lane pond' dimidium saccum

custuma } v s.
subsidium }

de Georgio Eryngton mercatore ibidem pro Cxx pellibus lanutis continentibus dimidium saccum

custuma } v s.
subsidium }

de Willelmo Hayning mercatore ibidem pro un' pokett lane pond' j quarterium vij clavos
custuma } iij s. x d.qu.
subsidium }
de Ricardo Conyngham mercatore ibidem pro ij sarpleris lane ponderantibus iij saccos iij clavos
custuma v s. j d.qu. subsidium xxv s. vj d.
de Georgio [Clarkeson] mercatore ibidem pro Cxx pellibus lanutis continentibus dimidium saccum
custuma } v s.
subsidium }
de Roberto Hely mercatore ibidem pro una sarplera lane ponderante j saccum
... ...
de Roberto Brigham mercatore ibidem pro un' pokett lane pond' j quarterium
... ...
Sequitur pondagium eiusdem navis (cum aliis pellibus vocatis shorlinges et morlinges et agnellis de crescencia predicta.)
de Willelmo Shaldfurth indigena pro iij cheldris

petrarum	xv s.
iiij cheldris carbonum	v s.
Summa valoris	xx s.

subsidium xij d.
de Willelmo Selby indigena (mercatore Gilde predicte) pro CCC iiij[xx] pellibus shorlinges et morlinges valor lxx s.
subsidium iij s. vj d.
de Henrico Bednall indigena (mercatore ibidem) pro Cl pellibus shorlinges et morlinges valor xxj s. viij d.
subsidium xiij d.
de Georgio Selby indigena (mercatore ibidem) pro CCiiij[xx]xij pellibus shorlinges et morlinges valor xlj s. viij d.
subsidium ij s. j d.
de Johanne Morpath indigena (mercatore ibidem) pro CCxxvj pellibus

shorlinges et morlinges	xxxiij s. iiij d.
CC pellibus agnellorum	xx s.
Summa valoris	liij s. iiij d.

subsidium ij s. viij d.
de Georgio Bird seniore indigena mercatore ibidem pro D pellibus shorlinges et morlinges valor lxxv s.
subsidium iij s. ix d.
de Willelmo Bird indigena (mercatore ibidem) pro Cxl pellibus

shorlinges et morlinges	xx s.
Clx pellibus agnellorum	xv s.
Summa valoris	xxxv s.

subsidium xxj d.

---

31. Followed by *xvij s. j d.*, struck out.

de Willelmo Pykden indigena (mercatore ibidem) pro CC pellibus shorlinges et morlinges xxx s.
xl pellibus agnellorum iij s. iiij d.
Summa valoris xxxiij s. iiij d.
subsidium xx d.
de Georgio Bird juniore indigena (mercatore ibidem) pro Ciiij^xx pellibus shorlinges et morlinges valor xxv s.
subsidium xv d.
de Roberto Brigham indigena (mercatore ibidem) pro CC pellibus shorlinges et morlinges valor xxx s.
subsidium xviij d.
de Mauro Mawer indigena (mercatore ibidem) pro CCiiij^xx pellibus shorlinges et morlinges valor xl s.
subsidium ij s.
de Johanne Bewyk indigena (mercatore ibidem) pro CC pellibus shorlinges et morlinges valor xxx s.
subsidium xviij d.
de Andrea Bewyk indigena (mercatore ibidem) pro C pellibus shorlinges et morlinges valor xv s.
subsidium ix d.
de Georgio Eryngton indigena (mercatore ibidem) pro CCCC lx pellibus shorlinges et morlinges valor lxvij s. vj d.
subsidium iij s. iiij d.ob.
de Georgio Clerkson indigena (mercatore ibidem) pro CCC pellibus shorlinges et morlinges valor xlv s.
subsidium ij s. iij d.
de Alano Car indigena (mercatore ibidem) pro v^xxxij pellibus shorlinges et morlinges valor xiij s. iiij d.
subsidium viij d.

Navis vocata le Mare de Lee unde Johannes Bowles est magister exivit eodem die et anno (cum lanis et pellibus lanutis mercatorum gilde predicte de crescencia predicta etc.)
de Bartramo Yonghusband mercatore ibidem pro v parvis sarpleris ponderantibus vj saccos dimidium et iij clavos
et de eodem pro lx pellibus lanutis continentibus j quarterium vj sacci iij quarteria iij clavi
custuma xj s. iiij d. subsidium lvj s. viij d.
de Johanne Baxter mercatore ibidem pro lx pellibus lanutis continentibus j quarterium
custuma } ij s. vj d.
subsidium }

Sequitur pondagium eiusdem navis (cum aliis pellibus vocatis shorlinges et morlinges de crescencia predicta)
de Bartramo Yonghusband indigena (mercatore gilde predicte) pro CCCCiiij^xx pellibus shorlinges et morlinges valor lxx s.
subsidium iij s. vj d.

de Johanne Baxter (mercatore ibidem) pro CCCCiiij^{xx} pellibus shorlinges et morlinges valor lxx s.
subsidium iij s. vj d.
et de eodem pro iiij dossenis virgarum panni lanei stricti continentibus j pannum
pannagium xiiij d.
de Willelmo Swan indigena (mercatore ibidem) pro iiij cheldris carbonum v s.
iiij cheldris petrarum xx s.
Summa valoris xxv s.
subsidium xv d.
de Edwardo Baxter indigena (mercatore ibidem) pro iiij cheldris carbonum v s.
iiij cheldris petrarum xx s.
Summa valoris xxv s.
subsidium xv d.
Examinatur
Summa partis xiij li. xj s. viij d.ob.

[*Membrane 8 dorse*]
Navis vocata le Margret de Novo Castro unde Willelmus Hamond est magister exivit eodem die et anno.
de Thoma Saunderson mercatore ibidem pro una sarplera lane ponderante ij saccos
custuma iij s. iiij d. subsidium xvj s. viij d.
de eodem Thoma indigena pro xvj cheldris carbonum xvj s. viij d.
viij cheldris petrarum xl s.
Summa valoris lvj s. viij d.
subsidium ij s. x d.

The Nicholas de Depe unde Peryn Lowre est magister exivit eodem die et anno
de Georgio Bird seniore mercatore ibidem pro una sarplera lane ponderante ij saccos viij clavos
custuma iij s. viij d. subsidium xviij s.
de Jacobo Tennaund mercatore ibidem pro un pokett lane pond' j quarterium x clavos
custuma } iiij s. v d.qu.
subsidium }

The Julian de Leyth unde David Lyell est magister applicuit xj° die Maii anno xv^{mo}.
de Johanne Elys alienigena pro CCC mode fisch valor xl s.
custuma vj d. subsidium ij s.

The Michaell de Depe unde Gerard Fever est magister exivit xij° die Maii anno xv^{mo}.
de eodem magister alienigena pro xx cheldris carbonum valor xxxiij s. iiij d.
custuma v d. subsidium xx d.

The Barbara de Gow unde Adrianus [Laurence est magister exivit xiij° die Maii anno xv]
de eodem magistro alienigena pro xxvj cheldris [carbonum valor xliij s. iiij d.]
... ...

The Bonaventure de Depe [unde John de Rone est magister exivit xvj° die Maii] anno xv^{mo}
de eodem magistro alienigena pro xx [cheldris carbonum valor xxxiij s. iiij d.]
custuma v d. subsidium xx d.

The Julian de Leyth unde David Lyell est magister exivit xvj ° die Maii anno xv^{mo}.
de Johanne Elys alienigena pro iiij cheldris frumenti valor liij s. iiij d.
custuma viij d. subsidium ij s. viij d.

The George de Wismere unde Johan Smyth est magister applicuit xviij° die Maii anno xv^{mo}.

de Johan Resse mercatore de Hansa pro v last cinerum	C s.
xvC waynskottes	xv li.
MMMMCCCC clapholt	liij s. iiij d.
xlv last et di' bituminis	xlv li.
iiij^{xx} pellibus ovium tannatis siccis	xxvj s. viij d.
xv daker russe skynnys	lx s.
xxxiiij pellibus vaccarum tannatis siccis	xxiij s. iiij d.
xxj peces wyer graunt	xxxiij s. iiij d.
Summa valoris	lxxv li. vj s. viij d.

custuma xviij s. x d. subsidium nichil quia de Hansa

de Herwino wan de Mole mercatore de Hansa pro un' pak lewyn	viij li.
iiij parv' pipes coperus veridis	vij li.
Summa valoris	xv li.

custuma iij s. ix d.

de Georgio Lyndenberch mercatore de Hansa pro v
last bituminis C s.
xx peces bastes vj s. viij d.
Summa valoris Cvj s. viij d.
custuma xvj d.
pro uno quintallo cere
custuma xij d.

The James de Cales unde Walterus Cortes est magister applicuit [xxj° Maii anno xv^{mo} Henrici vij^{mi}]
de Ranold Carpenter indigena Calesii pro j pipe vini gasconii
tonnagium xviij d.
de eodem pro ij hogesheds[32] vinagre valor xx s.
subsidium xij d.

The Cristofer de Dansk unde Thomas Holdhesse est magister exivit xxiiij° die Maii anno xv^{mo}.
de eodem magistro mercatore de Hansa pro x cheldris
carbonum xvj s. viij d.
vj cheldris gryndstones xl s.
dossenis rubstonis viij s. iiij d.
xij wey salis albi vj li.
ij plaustratis iij quarteriis xxij petris plumbi ix li. x s.
Summa valoris xviij li. xv s.
custuma iiij s. viij d.ob. subsidium nichil
et de eodem pro iij fardellis panni lanei stricti et largi sine grano continentibus inter se xj integros pannos
pannagium xj s. vj d.
de Bartramo Yonghusband indigena pro iij wey salis albi[33] valor xx s.
subsidium xij d.

The Katren de Wellys unde Thomas Sothern est magister exivit eodem die et anno.
de Thoma Weltden indigena pro j dolio et un hogeshede vini
tonnagium iij s. ix d.
et de eodem pro xij dossenis virgarum panni lanei stricti course continentibus iij pannos
pannagium iij s. vj d.
et de eodem pro dimidia cheldra brasii valor v s.
subsidium iij d.
de Georgio Birde seniore indigena pro j dolio et j hogeshed vini
tonnagium iij s. ix d.
et de eodem pro xij dossenis virgarum panni lanei stricti course continentibus iij pannos
pannagium iij s. vj d.

---

32. 108/5 has *ij ponshons.*
33. 108/5 has *salis grossi.*

The Cristofer de Gowe unde Hugett Willemson est magister applicuit xv die Maii

de eodem magistro alienigena pro xvM breykstones xiij s. iiij d.
iij last cinerum xl s.
D gyrth staffes iij s. iiij d.
lx warpe ollis terrenis xx d.
iij barrelles bituminis iij s. iiij d.
vj barrelles sope lx s.
Summa valoris vj li. xx d.
custuma xviij d.qu. subsidium vj s. j d.

Summa partis vj li. viij s. vij d.ob.
Examinatur

[*Membrane 9 face*]

The George de Tonesburgh unde Toure Halwardson est magister applicuit xxv° die Maii anno xv^{mo}.

de eodem magistro alienigena pro M single sparres xiij s. iiij d.
vj bomkyns iii s. iiij d.
DC raffters xx s.
Summa valoris xxxviij s. iiij d.[34]
custuma v d.ob.qu. subsidium xxiij d.
de Johanne Henryk alienigena pro MDCCC raffters xlvj s. viij d.
MM hasylle roddes iij s. iiij d.
CC bylle shaftes iij s. iiij d.
Summa valoris liij s. iiij d.
custuma viij d. subsidium ij s. viij d.
et de eodem pro un hogeshed vini non dulcis
tonnagium ix d.

The Blythe de Donwyche unde Nicholaus Baldwyn est magister exivit xxvj° die Maii anno xv^{mo}.

de Alexander Fethirstanehalgh indigena pro xvj cheldris petrarum valor xvj s. viij d.
subsidium x d.

The James de Cales unde Walter Cortes est magister exivit xxvj° die Maii anno xv^{mo}.

de Ranold Carpenter indigena Calesii pro xxx cheldris carbonum valor l s.
subsidium ij s. vj d.

The Cristofer de Wyk unde Cornelius Hugettson est magister exivit xxix° die Maii anno xv^{mo}.

de eodem magistro alienigena pro vj cheldris petrarum valor xl s.
custuma vj d. subsidium ij s.

---

34. The correct total is *xxxvj s. viij d.*

The Barbara de Depe unde Johannes Englisch est magister exivit penultimo die Maii anno xv^{mo}.

de eodem magistro alienigena pro xx cheldris carbonum	xxxiij s. iiij d.
uno plaustrato et dimidio plumbi	vj li.
Summa valoris	vij li. xiij s. iiij d.
custuma xxiij d. subsidium vij s. viij d.	

The Fransose de Depe unde Gillian van Ere est magister exivit penultimo die Maii anno xv^{mo}.

de eodem magistro alienigena pro xx cheldris carbonum	xxxiij s. iiij d.
uno plaustrato et dimidio plumbi	vj li.
Summa valoris	vj li. xiij s. iiij d.
custuma xxiij d. subsidium vij s. viij d.	

The Katren de Novo Castro unde Robertus Lighton est magister applicuit primo die Junii anno xv^{mo}.

de Roberto Herryson indigena pro ij fulles kettylles	xxvj s. viij d.
ij barrelles smigmatis	xx s.
iiij^{xx} elles panni linii course	xl s.
C caste croses	iij s. iiij d.
ij grosse rede lasces	vj s. viij d.
xij libris greyne gynger	iij s. iiij d.
un' boxe aulittes	xx d.
ij ketylles et iiij candelabris	vj s. viij d.
vj ollis eneis	xxv s.
Summa valoris	vj li. xiij s. iiij d.
subsidium vj s. viij d.	
de Georgio Car indigena pro xij bales wode	xij li.
j pok canabi	xx s.
ij doliis ferri	vj li.
Summa valoris	xix li.
subsidium xix s.	
de Roberto Baxter indigena pro iij last cinerum	xl s.
j balett madre	xxvj s. viij d.
iij bales woode	lxxx s.
j barrelle corke	iij s. iiij d.
j barrell cont' xj peces bukrams	xl s.
lx libris comyn	vj s. viij d.
ij di' peces fustean	vj s. viij d.
Summa valoris	x li. iij s. iiij d.
subsidium x s. ij d.	
de Johanne Bewyk indigena pro una cista continente iij di' peces fustean	x s.
di' pece saten de Sipres	v s.
C elles panni linei course	l s.
vij par shuttylles	xx d.
xij lyn shuttylles	xx d.

ij dossenis slayes	xx d.
j barrelle smigmatis	x s.
j poke canabi	xx s.
xij bagges	v s.
Summa valoris	cv s.
subsidium v s. iij d.	
de Johanne Passheley indigena pro j poke mader	xxvj s. viij d.
C libris canabi	vj s. viij d.
j ryme alb' papire	xx s.
Summa valoris	xxxv s.
subsidium xxj d.	
de Thoma Greyn indigena pro ij fulles kettylles	xxvj s. viij d.
j poke canabi	xx s.
j poke madre	xxvj s. viij d.
j pipe cum dimidia dossena librarum fili blodii	ij s. vj d.
j dossena double plate[35]	xx d.
iij dossenis wyre	vj s. viij d.
di' pece fustean	iij s. iiij d.
vj rolles latton plate	vj s. viij d.
iij rymes papire alb'	v s.
j dossena bonettes	xiij s. iiij d.
iij grosse rede lasces	vj s. viij d.
j parv' pece[36] lyne cloth	x s.
Summa valoris	vj li. ix s. iij d.
subsidium vj s. v d.ob.	
et pro uno quarterio quintalli cere	valor x s.
subsidium vj d.	
de Antonio Rede indigena pro iij barrelles sope	xxx s.
j fulle kettylles	xiij s. iiij d.
vj honde sawys	vj s. viij d.
Summa valoris	l s.
subsidium ij s. vj d.	
de Henrico Bednall indigena pro [ij barrelles sope	valor xx s.]
subsidium xij d.	
de Alexander Baxter indigena pro [iij pipes ferri	iiij li. x s.]
v barrelles sope	l s.
j fulle kettylles	xiij s. iiij d.
Summa valoris	vij li. xiij s. iiij d.
subsidium vij s. viij d.	

The Margret de Novo Castro unde Willelmus [Hamond] est magister applicuit iiij° die Junii anno xv^mo

de Willelmo Hanyng indigena pro viij doliis vini gasconii	
tonnagium xxiiij s.	
et de eodem vj bonche corke	valor iij s. iiij d.
subsidium ij d.	

35. 108/5 has *white plate.*
36. 108/5 has *j remnant.*

de Roberto Sothern indigena pro ij di' peces fusteane vj s. viij d.
xx virgis panni lanei course x s.
Summa valoris xvj s. viij d.
subsidium x d.

The Cristofer de Gow unde Hugett Willemson est magister exivit vij° die Junii anno xv^{mo}
de eodem magistro alienigena pro xxxij cheldris carbonum liij s. iiij d.
ij cheldris petrarum xiij s. iiij d.
iiij dossenis rubstones iij s. iiij d.
Summa valoris lxxx s.
custuma x d.ob. subsidium iij s. vj d.

The Dukler de Andwarp unde Coppyn van Lare est magister exivit eodem die et anno.
de eodem magistro alienigena pro iij cheldris carbonum vj s. viij d.
xj cheldris petrarum iiij li.
xij dossenis rubstons xiij s. iiij d.
Summa valoris C s.
custuma xv d. subsidium v s.

Examinatur
Summa partis vj li.viij s. ob.qu.

[*Membrane 9 dorse*]
The George de Novo Castro unde Johannes Elyson est magister applicuit xj° die Junii anno xv^{mo}.
de Willelmo Shaldfurth indigena pro j dolio ferri lx s.
ij pokettes hoppes xxx s.
ij barrelles smigmatis xx s.
Summa valoris v li. x s.
subsidium v s. vj d.
de Lodvico Sothern indigena pro j hogeshede vini gasconii
tonnagium ix d.
de Roberto Baxter indigena pro CC libris alome xiij s. iiij d.
x bales wood x li.
Summa valoris x li. xiij s. iiij d.
subsidium x s.[37] viij d.
de Johanne Bewyk indigena pro iij pipes vini gasconii
tonnagium iiij s. vj d.
de Thoma Riddall indigena pro ij fulles kettylles xxvj s. viij d.
vij peces bukram xx s.
Summa valoris xlvj s. viij d.
subsidium ij s. iiij d.

37. Followed by *vj d.*, struck out.

de Thoma Greyn indigena pro C alome	vj s. viij d.
ij barrelles smigmatis	xx s.
Summa valoris	xxvj s. viij d.
subsidium xvj d.	
de Cristofero Brigham indigena pro j pipe ferri	valor xxx s.
subsidium xviij d.	
de Willelmo Selby indigena pro ij barrelles sope	xx s.
j hogeshed cont' ij peces fustean	xiij s. iiij d.
iiij di' pece boutell	v s.
iij peces revylles flax	iij s. iiij d.
j rym papur alb'	xx d.
Summa valoris	xliij s. iiij d.
subsidium ij s. ij d.	
de Georgio Selby indigena pro di' barrelle sope	valor v s.
subsidium iij d.	
de Henrico Fenkyll indigenapro di' barrelle sope	valor v s.
subsidium iij d.	
de Johanne Batmanson indigena pro j fulle kettylles	xiij s. iiij d.
un' maund cont' j pece holand cloth course	xiij s. iiij d.
ij rym alb' papire	iij s. iiij d.
iij grosse di' pectenum	xx d.
di' grosse playing cardes	v s.
di' grosse girdylles	xx d.
j dossena purses	v s.
Summa valoris	xliij s. iiij d.
subsidium ij s. ij d.	
de Johanne Huddiswell indigena pro j barrelle et di' smigmatis	xv s.
j barrelle et di' graunt spinctrum	xx d.
[j dossena parv' premes	v s.][38]
di' grosse beltes	xx d.
j grosse poyntes	xx d.
j grosse bedes	xx d.
j grosse lasces	xx d.
j grosse wyvorn lasces	iij s. iiij d.
j grosse whistylles	iij s. iiij d.
j some nedylles	iij s. iiij d.
iij dossenis rasurs	iij s. iiij d.
vjC parv' comis	iij s. iiij d.
ij di' peces dornykes	vj s. viij d.
j dossena white plate	xx d.
j dossena knyves	xx d.
xij peciis taysis[39]	xx d.

38. *j dossena parv' premes v s.* is omitted in the collectors' account, but must be included if the *Summa* is to be correct.

39. 108/5 has *faysis.*

ij di' cloutes nedylles	xx d.
Summa valoris	lviij s. iiij d.
subsidium ij s. xj d.	
de Georgio Eryngton indigena pro ij fulles kettylles	xiij s. iiij d.
un' hogeshed cont' viij bras pottes	xx s.
xviij candylstykkes	vj s. viij d.
iiij^xx flax[40]	vj s. viij d.
Summa valoris	xlvj s. viij d.
subsidium ij s. iiij d.	
de Georgio Bird seniore indigena pro j laste bituminis	xx s.
x bales woode	x li.
Summa valoris	xj li.
subsidium xj s.	
de Georgio Car seniore indigena pro j balett madre	xxvj s. viij d.
j pokett alome cont' C	vj s. viij d.
Summa valoris	xxxiij s. iiij d.
subsidium xx d.	
de Willelmo Davell indigena pro j poke hemp	valor xx s.
subsidium xij d.	
de Willelmo Swan indigena pro j pipe un' hogeshed vini non dulcis	
tonnagium ij s. iij d.	
de Willelmo Harden indigena pro j bale madre	xxvj s. viij d.
j pok hoppes	xx s.
Summa valoris	xlvj s. viij d.
subsidium ij s. iiij d.	
et de eodem pro j hogeshed vini non dulcis	
tonnagium ix d.	
de Johanne Allan indigena pro j maund cont' MM trenshers	valor x s.
subsidium vj d.	
de Willelmo Bird indigena pro ij fulles kettylles	xxvj s. viij d.
un maund cont' ij couched beddes[41]	xx s.
CCC hemp	xx s.
j pece et di' fustiane	x s.
ij dossenis baggis	viij s. iiij d.
vj grosse pointes	x s.
ix libris aulettes	v s.
j grosse pynnes	xx d.
j dossena cofers	vj s. viij d.
ix brasse pottes	xxvj s. viij d.
ij peces chamlett	xxxiij s. iiij d.
Summa	viij li. viij s. iiij d.
subsidium viij s. v d.	
de Willelmo Camby indigena pro ij fulles kettylles	xxvj s. viij d.
C libris lini	x s.
j ferkyn racenes corens	vj s. viij d.

40. 108/5 has *iiij^xx*xij libris lini.
41. 108/5 has *ij beddes tapstre.*

Summa valoris xliij s. iiij d.
subsidium ij s. ij d.
de Willelmo Haynyng indigena pro ij pokes hemp xl s.
CC^ma cruses vj s. viij d.
ij dossenis cofers[42] viij s. iiij d.
lx libris revylles flax[43] v s.
Summa valoris lx s.
subsidium iij s.
de Roberto Sothern indigena pro j poke hemp xx s.
j barrelle sope x s.
Summa valoris xxx s.
subsidium xviij d.

The Dave de Novo Castro unde Jacobus Robinson est magister applicuit xij^o die Junii xv^mo
de Thoma Saunderson indigena pro uno dolio vini
tonnagium iij s.
de Georgio Conyngham indigena pro v doliis vini non dulcis
tonnagium xv s.
de Johanne Brandlyng indigena pro ij doliis vini non dulcis
tonnagium vj s.
et de eodem pro x peces rosen valor xiij s. iiij d.
subsidium viij d.
de Johanne Huddiswell indigena pro j barrelle smigmatis valor x s.
subsidium vj d.
de Thoma Cooke indigena pro j hogeshed vini non dulcis
tonnagium ix d.
de Jacobo Robynson indigena pro j hogeshede vini non dulcis
tonnagium ix d.

The Mare de Abvill unde Johannes Dere est magister exivit xiij^o die Junii anno xv^mo
de eodem magistro alienigena pro x cheldris carbonum xvj s. viij d.
ij cheldris petrarum xiij s. viij d.
Summa valoris xxx s.
custuma iiij d.ob. subsidium xviij d.

The George de Tonesburgh unde Toure Halwartson est magister exivit eodem die et anno
de eodem magister alienigena pro xij virgis panni lanei stricti course continentibus j quarterium valor vj s. viij d.
pannagium viij d.qu. subsidium panni iiij d.

Examinatur
Summa partis C s. ix d.ob.qu.

42. Followed by *vj s. viij d.* struck out.
43. 108/5 has *C libris lini.*

[*Membrane 10 face*]
The Jakett de Depe unde Johannes Fokkett est magister exivit xvj° die Junii anno xv^{mo}
de eodem magistro alienigena pro xx cheldris carbonum valor xxxiij s. iiij d.
custuma v d. subsidium xx d.
et de eodem pro ij dossenis panni lanei stricti course valor x s.
pannagium xvj d.ob. subsidium panni vj d.

The Rame de Gow unde Henrik Johnson est magister applicuit xviij° die Junii anno xv^{mo}
de eodem magistro alienigena pro j pokett hoppes cont' CCCC^{ma} valor xiij s. iiij d.
custuma ij d. subsidium viij d.

The Margret de Depe unde Willelmus Russell est magister applicuit xxj° die Junii anno xv^{mo}
de eodem magistro alienigena pro vij balettes woode de amyas valor xxx s.
custuma iiij d.ob. subsidium xviij d.

The Margret de Depe unde Willelmus Russell est magister exivit xxij° die Junii anno xv^{mo}
de Jacobo Burrell indigena pro xvj cheldris carbonum xx s.
v cheldris molarum xxx s. iiij d.
Summa valoris liij s. iiij d.
subsidium ij s. viij d.
de Georgio Birde indigena pro di' daker coriorum salsorum valor xxxiij s. iiij d.
custuma iiij d. subsidium xx d.
de eodem pro v dosssenis pellium vitulorum tannatarum siccarum valor xvj s. viij d.
subsidium x d.

The Edwarde de Novo Castro unde Willelmus Kervour est magister applicuit xxiiij° die Junii anno xv^{mo}
de Edwardo Baxter indigena pro xx^{ti} peti pokes cane wode valor vj li. xiij s. iiij d.
subsidium vj s. viij d.
et de eodem pro j pipe j hogeshed vini non dulcis
tonnagium ij s. iij d.
de Roberto Harden indigena pro un' pipe ferri valor xxx s.
subsidium xviij d.

et de eodem pro uno dolio et j hogeshed vini
tonnagium iij s. ix d.
de Bartramo Yonghusband indigena pro ij doliis ferri valor vj li.
subsidium vj s.
de Ricardo Wrangwysh indigena pro j pipe ferri valor xxx s.
subsidium xviij d.
de Thoma Hanson indigena pro ij doliis vini non dulcis
tonnagium vj s.
et de eodem pro ij pipes cane wode course valor iiij li.
subsidium iiij s.
de Georgio Car indigena pro ij doliis ferri valor vj li.
subsidium vj s.
et de eodem pro vj pety balettes Frensh wode valor xl s.
subsidium ij s.
de Thoma Riddall indigena pro iij doliis ferri valor lx li.
subsidium ix s.
de Thoma Swan indigena pro j pipe ferri valor xxx s.
subsidium xviij d.
de Willelmo Harden indigena pro j pipe ferri valor xxx s.
subsidium xviij d.
et de eodem pro uno dolio vini non dulcis
tonnagium iij s.
de Johanne Brandlyng indigena pro ij doliis et un' pipe vini gasconii
tonnagium vij s. vj d.

de Alano Elder indigena pro j pece holand course	xiij s. iiij d.
j dossena parv' bagges	iij s. iiij d.
di' grosse playing cardes	v s.
vj purcez	xx d.
ij di' peces bultell	ij s. vj d.
ij rym papur[44]	iij s. iiij d.
j grosse bedes	xx d.
j grosse di' comes	iij s. iiij d.
j dossena purcez	iij s. iiij d.
Summa valoris	xxxvij s. vj d.

subsidium xxij d.ob.

de Johanne Batmanson indigena pro j pece holandes course	xiij s. iiij d.
ij rymes papur alb'	ij s. iiij d.
iij grosse comis	xx d.
di' grosse playing cardes	v s.
di' grosse gyrdylles	xx d.
j dossena purces course	v s.
Summa valoris	xxx s.

subsidium xviij d.

44. 108/5 has *papur alb'*.

de Georgio Conyngham indigena pro ij peces
fustian xiij s. iiij d.
xxx elles canvas vj s. viij d.
j grosse playing cardes xiij s. iiij d.
vj rymes papur alb' x s.
j grosse comis[45] iij s. iiij d.
a some bolions cont' M vj s. viij d.
Summa valoris liij s. iiij d.
subsidium ij s. viij d.

The Dave de Novo Castro unde Jacobus Robynson est magister exivit xxvj° die Junii anno xv^{mo}
de Thoma Saunderson indigena pro xij cheldris
carbonum valor xiij s. iiij d.
et de eodem pro vj cheldris molarum[46] valor xl s.
Summa valoris liij s. iiij d.
subsidium ij s. viij d.

The George de Wyssemere unde Hanse Smythe est magister exivit xxvj° die Junii anno xv^{mo}
de Hanse Resse mercatore de Hansa pro xiiij plaustratis plumbi et iij quarteriis lvj li.
xl cheldris carbonum lxvj s. viij d.
v wey salis albi xl s.
Summa valoris lxj li. vj s. viij d.
custuma xv s. iiij d.
de Georgio Lyndenberch mercatore de Hansa pro j
plaustrato plumbi valor iiij li.
custuma xij d.

The Rame de Gowe in Holande unde Henricus Johnson est magister exivit xxvij° die Junii anno xv^{mo}
de eodem magistro alienigena pro xliiij cheldris
carbonum valor iij li. xiij s. iiij d.
custuma xj d. subsidium iij s. viij d.

The Michaell de Depe unde Gerard Fever est magister applicuit penultimo die Junii anno xv^{mo}
de eodem magistro alienigena pro iiij^{xx} quarteriis
ordii valor vj li. xiij s. iiij d.
custuma xx d. subsidium vj s. viij d.

The Katren de Depe unde Peryn Loure est magister applicuit penultimo die Junii anno xv

---

45. 108/5 has *comis large.*
46. 108/5 has *vj cheldris petrarum.*

de Bartramo Yonghusband indigena pro xxvj [quarteriis] ordii humidi corrupti valor xiij s. iiij d.
subsidium viij d.
et de eodem pro uno dolio ferri valor iij li.
subsidium iij s.
Examinatur
Summa partis Cxvj s. ij d.ob.

[*Membrane 10 dorse*]
The Mare de Lee unde Johannes Bolles est magister applicuit iij° die Julii anno xv^mo^
de Edwardo Baxter indigena pro xl quarteriis ordii valor iij li. vj s. viij d.
subsidium iij s. iiij d.
de Willelmo Swan indigena pro xl quarteriis ordii valor iij li. vj s. viij d.
subsidium iij s. iiij d.

The Michaell de Depe unde Gerard Fever est magister exivit x° die Julii anno xv^mo^
de eodem magistro alienigena pro xxiiij cheldris carbonum xl s.
j cheldra molarum vj s. viij d.
Summa valoris xlvj s. viij d.
custuma vij d. subsidium ij s. iiij d.

The Katren de Depe unde Peryn Loure est magister exivit xj° die Julii anno xv^mo^
de eodem magistro alienigena pro xx cheldris carbonum valor xxxiij s. iiij d.
custuma v d. subsidium xx d.

The Cristofer de Depe unde Johannes Saveroy est magister applicuit xj° die Julii anno xv^mo^
de eodem magistro alienigena pro vjC libris gualde[47] valor xl s.
custuma vj d. subsidium xxiiij d.

The Cristofer predicta exivit xiiij° die Julii anno xv^mo^
de eodem magistro alienigena pro xvij cheldris carbonum xxiij s. iiij d.
x cheldris molarum lxvj s. viij d.
uno plaustrato plumbi iij li. xj s. viij d.
ij dossenis rubstones xx d.
Summa valoris viij li. iij s. iiij d.
custuma ij s. ob. subsidium viij s. ij d.

47. 108/5 has *gualde course.*

The Mare de Lee unde Johannes Bolles est magister exivit xxij° die Julii anno xv^{mo}

de eodem magistro indigena pro iiij cheldris carbonum valor vj s. viij d.
subsidium iiij d.

de Edwardo Baxter indigena pro viij quarteriis ordii valor xiij s. iiij d.
subsidium viij d.

de Willelmo Swan indigena pro viij quarteriis ordii valor xiij s. iiij d.
subsidium viij d.

de Willelmo Scott indigena pro xv plaustratis plumbi valor xlv li.
subsidium xlv s.

The Cristofer de Gow unde Hugett Willemson est magister applicuit xxij° die Julii anno xv^{mo}

de eodem magistro alienigena pro vij C hoppes valor xxvj s. viij d.
custuma iiij d. subsidium xvj d.

Navis vocata le James de Novo Castro unde Lodvicus Sothern est magister applicuit xxvij° die Julii anno xv^{mo}

de Georgio Conyngham indigena pro x^{cem} bales gualde	lx li.
et pro j barrelle smigmatis	xv s.
Summa valoris	ix li. xv s.
subsidium ix s. ix d.	
de Johanne Morpath indigena pro j hogeshede cont' j dossena piperis	xx s.
iij peces fusteane	xx s.
j pece bulesy[48]	iij s. iiij d.
j dossena greyne coperus	iij s. iiij d.
di' grosse lasces	xx d.
vj libris suger cande	iij s. iiij d.
iij dossenis whistelles	xx d.
Summa valoris	liij s. iiij d.
subsidium ij s. viij d.	
de Willelmo Selby indigena pro j pok madre	xxvj s. viij d.
j bale alome	xiij s. iiij d.
iiij barrelles smigmatis	xlj s. viij d.
viij kettylles	x s.
Item a maund cont' ij dossenis cofres	vj s. viij d.
ix ollis eneis	xx s.
j dossena frying pannes	v s.
un rym papur alb'	vj s. viij d.

48. 108/5 has *j pece bukram.*

iij dossenis librarum wyre	iij s. iiij d.
ij tykes fethirbeddes course	vj s. viij d.
j dossena candylstykkes	vj s. viij d.
C hemp	vj s. viij d.
ij dossenis bagges	vj s. viij d.
iij M nedilles	v s.
di' grosse lasces et pointes	iij s. iiij d.
ij peces holande	xxvj s. viij d.
j pece fusteans	vj s. viij d.
j dossena comyn	xx d.
iij peces bucrams	x s.
ij di' peces bultelli	iij s. iiij d.
Summa valoris x li. xv s.	
subsidium x s. ix d.	
de Alano Car indigena pro ij hogeshedes vini gasconii	
tonnagium xviij d.	
de Rogero Raw indigena pro v barrelles smigmatis	valor l s.
subsidium ij s. vj d.	
et de eodem pro ij hogeshedes vini gasconii	
tonnagium xviij d.	
de Georgio Eryngton indigena pro ij bales madre	liij s. iiij d.
x barrelles smigmatis	v li.
Summa valoris	vij li. xiij s. iiij d.
subsidium vij s. viij d.	
de Johanne Snow indigena pro ij lastes picis et bituminis	xl s.
et de eodem pro iiij barrelles smigmatis	xl s.
Summa valoris	iiij li.
subsidium iiij s.	
de Willelmo Pykden indigena pro ij dossenis cofres	vj s. viij d.
lx libris canabi	iij s. iiij d.
iij dossenis bagges	x s.
di' C libris candilstykkes	xiij s. iiij d.
vj dossenis cultellorum	v s.
iij peces bukrams	x s.
j grosse wivurn gyrdilles	v s.
j grosse rede lases	x d.
ij dossenis smalle glasses[49]	x d.
vj di' peces dornykes	xx s.
di' grosse pynnys	xx d.
iiij chaffoures[50]	v s.
j rym papur alb'	xx d.
Summa valoris	iiij li. iij s. iiij d.
subsidium iiij s. ij d.	

49. 108/5 has *smalle merroues.*
50. 108/5 has *fyre chaffoures.*

de Georgio Selby indigena pro j bale alome	xiij s. iiij d.
ij barrelles sope	xx s.
Item un maunde cont' C^ma^ hemp	vj s. viij d.
x ollis eneis	xx s.
viij frying pannes[51]	v s.
ij rymes papur alb'	iij s. iiij d.
ij dossenis cofres	vj s. viij d.
v^c^ trenshors	xx d.
iij peces holandes course	xxxiij s. iiij d.
j pece fustean	vj s. viij d.
ij di' peces boutell	iij s. iiij d.
ij peces bukrames	x s.
ij dossenis bagges parv'	vj s. viij d.
j grosse spinctrum	xx d.
di' grosse wivurnes lasces	xx d.
iij libris fili	xij d.
ij dossenis libris brinstone	viij d.
xxv libris hemp	xx d.
ij dossenis white plate	xx d.
Summa valoris vij li. v s.	
subsidium vij s. iij d.	
de Ricardo Blaxton indigena pro ij barrelles smigmatis	valor xx s.
subsidium xij d.	
de Johanne Brandlyng indigena pro j balet madre	xxvj s. viij d.
j poke alome	xiij s. iiij d.
j pok canabi	xx s.
iiij barelles sope	xl s.
ij fulles kettylles	xxx s.
vj parvis ollis eneis	xiij s. iiij d.
lx libris hemp	iij s. iiij d.
j graunt kettylle	iij s. iiij d.
lx loves suger	viij s. iiij d.
viij libris comfettes	iij s. iiij d.
un grosse lasces	xx d.
j gross di' pynnis	iij s. iiij d.
di' grosse cultellorum	xx d.
j dossena comyn	x d.
j dossena ryse et	x d.
pro j hogeshede cum iij dossenis wolcardes	viij s. iiij d.
ij di' peces dornykes	vj s. viij d.
ij di' peces holande	xv s.
j pece canvas	v s.
j dossena pety bagges	xx d.

51. 108/5 has *yron pannes*.

vj libris galles	xx d.
j grosse spinctrum	xx d.
iij dossenis playing cardes et	xx d.
pro x patellis	x s.
Summa valoris	xj li. xx d.
subsidium xj s. j d.	
et de eodem pro ij hogeshedes vini	
tonnagium xviij d.	

Summa partis vj li. xvj s. ob.

Examinatur

[*Membrane 11 face*]

de Thoma Saunderson indigena pro vj barrelles smigmatis	iij li.
j dolio ferri	iij li.
viij ollis eneis	xv s.
Clx libris hemp	x s.
Summa valoris	vij li. v s.
subsidium vij s. iij d.	
de Ricardo Conyngham indigena pro j pok hemp	xx s.
ij barelles sope	xx s.
iij pannes	xx d.
di' barrelle litmose	iij s. iiij d.
xv balettes gualde cane	vij li. x s.
ij fulles kettylles	xxvj s. viij d.
lx libris coperus	x s.
lx libris canabi	iij s. iiij d.
ij rymes papur alb'	iij s. iiij d.
j pece dornykes	vj s. viij d.
j pece bultelli	xx d.
di' pece fusteane	iij s. iiij d.
Summa valoris	xij li. x s.
subsidium xij s. vj d.	
et de eodem pro uno dolio vini gasconii	
tonnagium iij s.	
de Willelmo Bird indigena pro j bag[52] alome	xiij s. iiij d.
vj barrelles sope	iij li.
ij fulles kettylles	xxvj s. viij d.
j balett madre	xx s.
Summa valoris	vj li.
subsidium vj s.	
et de eodem pro j hogeshed vini rubii	
tonnagium ix d.	

52. 108/5 has *CC alome*.

de Willelmo Swan indigena pro xij balettes gualde cane	valor vj li.
subsidium vj s.	
et de eodem pro j pipe et j hogeshede vini non dulcis	
tonnagium ij s. iij d.	
de Bartramo Yonghusband indigena pro ij pokes hemp	valor xl s.
subsidium ij s.	
de Johanne Lermonth indigena pro di' barrelle smigmatis	valor v s.
subsidium iij d.	
de Thoma Riddall indigena pro j bale alome	xiij s. iiij d.
j poke madre	xxvj s. viij d.
di' barrelle stelle	xl s.
iiij fulles kettylles	liij s. iiij d.
iiij peces donce papur	iij s. iiij d.
xvj brasse pottes	xxxiij s. iiij d.
j pok canabi	xx s.
j barrelle smigmatis	x s.
ij dossenis swordes course	xiij s. iiij d.
ij peces holande	xxv s.
ij di' peces fusteane	vj s. viij d.
ij brasse pottes	xv s.
j grosse cultellorum	x s.
di' grosse rede lasces	xx d.
Item una cista continente ij dossenis cofres	vj s. viij d.
xv brass pottes	xxxiij s. iiij d.
vj grosse pynnes	x s.
viij dossenis white plate	vj s. viij d.
di' grosse playing cardes	v s.
ij rym papur alb'	iij s. iiij d.
di' grosse beltes	xx d.
Summa valoris	xvj li. xviij s. iiij d.
subsidium xvj s. xj d.	
de Henrico Barrow indigena pro un' barrelle smigmatis	valor x s.
subsidium vj d.	
de Roberto Brigham indigena pro un parv' pece cere cont' dimidium quintallum	
{vide breve custumarum}	
custuma cere vj d.[53] xij d.	
et de eodem pro di' C weght ketylles	valor x s.
subsidium vj d.	
de Thoma Cook indigena pro iiij beddes tapstre	valor xxxiij s. iiij d.
subsidium xx d.	

53. There is a cross after *vj d.*

de Georgio Bird seniore indigena pro ij pipes flax corupt'[54]	xx s.
xij brass pottes	xxvj s. viij d.
C hemp	vj s. viij d.
iij C libris ferri	x s.
Summa valoris	iij li. iij s. iiij d.
subsidium iij s. ij d.	
de Johanne Huddiswell indigena pro ij dossenis galles	v s.
ij dossenis comes	v s.
ij dossenis coperous	v s.
ij dossenis rasurs	xx d.
j grosse knyvys	iij s. iiij d.
j dossena parv' bagges	iij s. iiij d.
j dossena cruell beltes	iij s. iiij d.
j grosse great pynnes	iij s. iiij d.
Summa valoris	xxx s.
subsidium xviij d.	
de Cristofero Raw indigena pro ij dossenis cofres	vj s. viij d.
C hemp	vj s. viij d.
vij bras pottes	xv s.
C^ma^ weght pannes	xx s.
di' C hemp	iij s. iiij d.
ij dossenis comyn	ij s. vj d.
ij di' pece fustean	vj s. viij d.
iiij peces bukrams	xiij s. iiij d.
di' grosse rede lasces	xx d.
di' grosse wivurn lasces	xx d.
j grosse cultellorum	iij s. iiij d.
di' grosse spinctrum	xx d.
di'grosse parvorum spinctrum	x d.
Summa valoris	iiij li. iij s. iiij d.
subsidium iiij s. ij d.	
de Henrico Fenkill indigena pro iiij^xx^xij peces holandes	valor xxxiij s. iiij d.
subsidium xx d.	
de Thoma Gren indigena pro j dolio et iij C libris ferri	valor iij li. x s.
subsidium iij s. vj d.	
de Cristofero Brigham indigena pro vj libris piperis	x s.
ij peces bukrams	vj s. viij d.
x brasse pottes	xx s.
C Hemp	vj s. viij d.
vj libris threde	xx d.

54. 108/5 has *ij pipes revylles flax.*

j grosse rede lasces iij s. iiij d.
vj lofes suger vj s. viij d.
Summa valoris lv s.
subsidium ij s. ix d.
de Mauro Mawer indigena pro j barrelle litmosse valor vj s. viij d.
subsidium iij d.
de Roberto Conyngham indigena pro ij barrelles smigmatis valor xx s.
subsidium xij d.
de Ricardo Ruminy indigena pro j balett madre cont' iijC valor xiij s. iiij d.
subsidium viij d.

The Nicholas de Stapilles unde Mariott Pottey est magister applicuit xxviij° die Julii anno xv^mo^
de eodem magistro alienigena pro vijC libris ferri valor xx s.
custuma iij d. subsidium xij d.

The Nicholas predicta exivit xxix° die Julii anno xv^mo^
de supradicto Maryott Pottey alienigena pro xl cheldris carbonum valor xl s.
custuma vj d. subsidium ij s.

The Margret de Stapilles unde Guillyam de Hoy est magister applicuit xxix° die Julii anno xv^mo^
de eodem magistro alienigena pro vjC libris ferri valor xx s.
custuma iij d. subsidium xij d.

The Margret predicta exivit penultimo die Julii anno xv^mo^
de predicto Guillyame de Hoy alienigena pro xvj cheldris carbonum valor xxvj s. viij d.
custuma iiij d. subsidium xvj d.

The Marie de Abvile unde Johannes Dere est magister exivit ultimo die Julii anno xv^mo^
de eodem magistro alienigena pro xvij cheldris carbonum xxviij s. iiij d.
j cheldris petrarum viij s. iiij d.
Summa valoris xxxvj s. viij d.
custuma v d.ob. subsidium xxij d.

The Barbara de Gow unde Adrian Laurence est magister exivit primo die Augusti anno xv^mo^
de eodem magistro alienigena pro xx cheldris carbonum xxxiij s. iiij d.
vj cheldris petrarum xl s.
Summa valoris iij li. xiij s. iiij d.
custuma xj d. subsidium iij s. viij d.

The Jakett de Rone unde Guillam le Quertey est magister exivit primo die Augusti anno xv^{mo}
de eodem magistro alienigena pro xx cheldris carbonum
valor xxxiij s. iiij d.
custuma v d. subsidium xx d.

examinatur
Summa partis iiij li. xv s.

[*Membrane 11 dorse*]
The Cristofer de Gow unde Hugat Willemson est magister exivit primo die Augusti anno xv^{mo}
de eodem magistro alienigena pro xxx cheldris carbonum

	l s.
ij cheldris petrarum	xiij s. iiij d.
vj dossenis rubstons	iij s. iiij d.
Summa valoris	iij li. vj s. viij d.

custuma x d. subsidium iij s. iiij d.

The Marie de Amyas unde Ricardus Cowehm est magister exivit iiij° die Augusti anno xv^{mo}
de eodem magistro alienigena pro xl cheldris carbonum
valor iij li. vj s. viij d.
custuma x d. subsidium iij s. iiij d.

The Martyn de Andwarp unde Petrus Meus est magister exivit xviij° die Augusti anno xv^{mo}
de eodem magistro alienigena pro xxx cheldris carbonum
valor l s.
custuma vij d.ob. subsidium ij s. vj d.

The James de Andwarp unde Claes Northost est magister exivit xviij die Augusti anno xv^{mo}
de eodem magistro alienigena pro xxx cheldris carbonum
valor l s.
custuma vij d.ob. subsidium ij s. vj d.

The Anne de Gowe unde Jacobus van Brekenbergh est magister applicuit xxv die Augusti anno xvj^{mo}
de eodem magistro alienigena pro xxviij quarteriis [frumenti]

	iij li. x s.
xv parv' paynted clothes	x s.
xx^{ti} ores	viij s. iiij d.
Summa valoris	iiij li. viij s. iiij d.

custuma xiij d.qu. subsidium iiij s. v d.
et de eodem pro j pipe et un' hogeshed vini rubii
tonnagium ij s. iij d.

The Anne predicta exivit secundo die Septembris anno xvj^{mo}
de eodem Jacobo van Brekenberghe alienigena pro xl cheldris carbonum iij li. vj s. viij d.
vj cheldris molarum xl s.
Summa valoris v li. vj s. viij d.
custuma xvj d. subsidium v s. iiij d.

The Katren de Wellys unde Johannes Thomson est magister applicuit v^{to} die Septembris anno xvj^{mo}
de Thoma Welden indigena pro ij last trane olei iiij li.
ij barelles litmosse iij s. iiij d.
Summa valoris iiij li. iij s. iiij d.
subsidium iiij s. ij d.
de Georgio Bird seniore indigena pro j last et di' trane olei valor lx s.
subsidium iij s.

Navis vocata le Mare Gallant de Depe unde Rollyn Babyn est magister applicuit vj^{to} die Septembris anno xvj^{mo}
de Jacobo Kawshes alienigena pro xxxvj balettes cane wode xviij li.
iij parv' ponshons cane wode lx s.
MMM libris ferri iiij li. x s.
viij virgis damask xl s.
vj virgis velvet xl s.
Summa valoris xxix li. x s.
custuma vij s. iiij d.ob. subsidium xxix s. vj d.
de Matheo Doublet alienigena pro xx balettes cane wode valor x li.
custuma ij s. vj d. subsidium x s.
de Rolando Babyn alienigena pro viij balettes cane wode valor iiij li.
custuma xij d. subsidium iiij s.
de Rolando Valere alienigena pro M ferri xxx s.
vj barelles ferri xiij s. iiij d.
Summa valoris xliij s. iiij d.
custuma vj d.ob. subsidium ij s. j d.
de Colard Broges alienigena pro D libris ferri valor xv s.
custuma ij d.qu. subsidium ix d.

Navis vocata le Antony de Novo Castro unde Johannes Passheley est magister applicuit ix^{o} die Septembris anno xvj^{mo}
de Willelmo Harden indigena pro j last et di' flax vj li.
di' last osmondes xx. s.
j nest counteres xiij s. iiij d.
Summa valoris vij li. xiij s. iiij d.
subsidium vij s. viij d.

de Johanne Passheley indigena pro j last osmondes	xl s.
j last picis	xvj s. viij d.
iiij nest counters	liij s. iiij d.
j last di' flax	vj li.
lx waynskottes	x s.
Summa valoris	xij li.
subsidium xij s.	
de Roberto Harden indigena pro di' last osmondes	valor xx s.
subsidium xij d.	
de Cristofero Brigham indigena pro vj barelles osmondes	
	xx s.
j last cinerum	x s.
j last flax	iiij li.
ij nest counters	xxvj s. viij d.
Summa valoris	vj li. xvj s. viij d.
subsidium vj s. x d.	
de Roberto Yonghusband indigena pro di' last osmondes	
	xx s.
di' last flax	xl s.
un' nest counteres	xiij s. iiij d.
Summa valoris lxxiij s. iiij d.	
subsidium iij s. viij d.	
de Willelmo Davell indigena pro j last flax	iiij li.
di' last osmondes	xx s.
ij nest counters	xxvj s. viij d.
Summa valoris	vj li. vj s. viij d.
subsidium vj s. iiij d.	
de Thoma Horssley indigena pro j last osmondes	xl s.
j last et di' flax	vj li.
xiiij barrelles cinerum	xiij s. iiij d.
iij nest counters	liij s. iiij d.
Summa valoris	xj li. vj s. viij d.
subsidium xj s. iiij d.	

The James de Tonysburgh unde Hanse Eylma est magister applicuit xvj° die Novembris anno xvj^mo^

de eodem magistro alienigena pro m girth stovres	iij s. iiij d.
M parv' raffters	xl s.
iiij dossenis oke sparres	vj s. viij d.
Summa valoris	l s.
custuma vij d.ob. subsidium ij s. vj d.	

Examinatur

Summa partis vij li. vj s. ij d.

[*Membrane 12 face. This contains returns from the outports of Newcastle on Tyne. Losses in it through damage cannot be recovered from the controller's account as this does not cover the outports.*]

The Nicholas de Depe unde Peryn Ranold est magister exivit de Hartylpoll viij die Februarii anno xv^{mo}
de Roberto Fewler indigena pro v dacres coriorum salsorum
custuma iij s. iiij d. subsidium xvj s. viij d. denaria calesii iiij d.
cokettes ij d.

The Katren de Thynburgh unde Andreas ... ... Septembris anno xvj^{mo}
de eodem magistro alienigena pro xijC oke sparres
valor v li. vj s. viij d.
... ...

Dicta navis exivit xxviij die Septembris anno xvj^{mo}
de dicto magistro alienigena pro xij dossenis virgarum panni lanei stricti continentibus iij pannos integros valor lxv s.
subsidium panni iij s. iij d. pannagium viij s. iij d.

The Egle de Depe unde Johannes du Gardeyn est magister applicuit ... ... Witbe ... ... Augusti anno xvj^{mo}
de Edwardo Baxter indigena pro xx^{ti} wey salis grossi ...
de eodem magistro alienigen pro iij wey salis grossi ...

The Nicholas de Kyngcorn unde David Lyell est magister exivit de Sunderland xxviij die Septembris anno xvj^{mo}
de eodem magistro alienigen pro xxx quarteriis frumenti
valor v li.
custuma xv d. subsidium v s.

Hos xij rotulos liberavit hic infrascriptus Humfridus Metcalf xxix die Januarii anno xvj regis Henrici septimi per manus suas proprias et prestitit sacramentum

Summa partis lvj s. ij d.
xxxvj s. ij d.

Examinatur cum rotulis contrarotulatoris custumarum et subsidiorum regis ibidem per tempus predictum.

adhuc

Summa predictorum xij rotulorum

Lane et pelles lanute de crescencia comitatuum Northumbrie, Cumbrie, Westmorlandie ac episcopatus Dunelmensis necnon comitatuum de Allerton et Richemond, quorundam Cristoferi Brigham, Johannes Snawe, Roberti Baxter et aliorum mercatorum societatis Gilde mercatorie ville Novi Castrii super Tinam, indigenarum, in portu predicto ad diversas vices intra tempus predictum custumate et abinde versus partes exteras traducte

CCCiiij^{xx}xij sacci, dimidius, iiij clavi lane

custuma
subsidio
et denariis Calesii } onerantur MDCCCCiiij li. xvj s.iiij d.[56]

vMCCCiiij^{xx}x pelles lanute facientes xxij saccos quarterium, dimidium quarterium et xx pelles

custuma
subsidio
et denariis Calesii } onerantur iiij^{xx}vj li. xiiij s.[57]

Pelles vocate shorlyng et morlyng ac pelles agnellorum de crescencia predicta, quorundam Willelmi Camby, Roberti Baxter et aliorum mercatorum societatis Gilde predicte, indigenarum, in portu predicto ad predictas vices intra tempus predictum custumate et abinde versus partes exteras traducte

xxxijMxlviij pelles facientes Clx saccos xlviij pelles

Valor CCxxj li. xiij s. iiij d.

Subsidium gratis xj li. xx d.

Custuma, subsidio et denariis Calesii predictarum xxijMxlviij pellium vocatarum shorlyng et morlyng ac pellium agnellorum prout mercatores indigene solvere tenentur

onerantur DCviij li. vij s. xj d.

Exitus coketti provenientes de CClxxv mercatoribus lanarum et pellium predictarum eskippatarum

Custuma onerantur xlv s. x d.

[*Membrane 12 dorse. Column headings,* li. s. d., *occur at three points on this membrane.*]

Lane et pelles lanute de crescencia predicta quorundam Willelmi Camby, Rolandi Herryson et aliorum mercatorum Gilde predicte,

56. Beneath *MDCCCCiiij li. xvj s. iiij d.* is written *gratis CCxlvj li. ix s. v d.qu.*, struck out.

57. Beneath *iiij^{xx}vj li. xiiij s.* is written *gratis xj li. iiij s.*, struck out.

indigenarum, in portu predicto intra tempus predictum, custumate et abinde versus portes exteras traducte, pro tantis lanis et pellibus lanutis in diversis vicibus periclitatis et deperditis; quorum quidem mercatorum nomina cum seperalibus parcellis lanarum et pellium lanutarum per ipsos sic eskippatarum, in quadam cedula recitantur; hii parcelli annexati seperatim, particulariter et nominatim specificantur et ostenduntur

lxij sacci j quarterium xj clavi
custuma gratis Ciiij s. iiij d.qu.
subsidio onerantur xxvj li. vj d.qu.

MCxl pelles lanute facientes iiij saccos iij quarteria
custuma gratis vij s. xj d.
subsidio onerantur xxxix s. vij d.

Residuo custume et subsidii cum denariis Calesii predictorum lxij saccorum j quarterii xj clavorum et predictarum MCxl pellium facientium iiij saccos iij quarteria, prout mercatores indigene solvere tenentur
onerantur CCxxvj li. v s. vij d.qu.

Pelles vocate shorlyng et morlyng ac pelles agnellorum de crescencia predicta quorundam Willelmi Camby, Rolandi Herryson et aliorum mercatorum Gilde predicte indigenarum in portu predicto intra tempus predictum, custumate et abinde versus partes exteras traducte, pro tantis pellibus alia vice super mare periclitatis et deperditis; quorum quidem mercatorum nomina cum seperalibus parcellis dictarum pellium per ipsos sic eskippatarum in predicta cedula recitantur; hii parcelli annexati seperatim, particulariter et nominatim specificantur et ostenduntur

DCCCClx pelles vocate shorlyng et morlyng C^ma^ per vj^xx^ facientes iiij saccos iij quarteria
Valor vij li.
subsidium vij s.

MCCxx pelles agnellorum C per vj^xx^ facientes vj saccos dimidium xx pelles
Valor vj li. xj s. viij d.
subsidium vj s. vij d.

Residuo subsidii cum custuma et denariis Calesii earundem ixClx pellium vocatarum shorlyng et morlyng et predictarum MCCCxx pellium agnellorum prout mercatores indigene solvere tenentur
onerantur xliij li. iij s. iij d.

Exitus sigilli regis quod dicitur coketti provenientes de xxxix mercatoribus
custuma onerantur vj s. vj d.

Valor $iiij^{xx}$ pellium tannatarum siccarum Edwardi Baxter mercatoris Gilde predicte indigene in portu predicto eskippatarum et versus partes exteras traductarum pro tantis pellibus tannatis siccis alia vice periclitatis et deperditis

iiij li.

subsidio onerantur iiij s.

Residuo subsidii et custume cum denariis Calesii earundem $iiij^{xx}$ pellium facientium viij dacras pellium sive coriorum prout mercatores indigene solvere tenentur

onerantur xxviij s. viij d.

Cokettus ij d.

Valor $iiij^{xx}$ pellium tannatarum siccarum Edwardi Conyngham mercatoris Gilde predicte, indigene in portu predicto custumatarum et abinde versus partes exteras traductarum pro tantis pellibus tannatis siccis alia vice periclitatis et deperditis

iiij li. x s.

subsidio onerantur iiij s. vj d.

Residuo subsidii et custuma cum denariis Calesii earundem $iiij^{x}x$ pellium facientium ix dacras pellium sive coriorum prout mercatores indigene solvere tenentur

onerantur xxxij s. ij d.

cokettus

coketto onerantur ij d.

Examinatur

Valor $xxx^{xx\ s.}$ pellium tannatarum siccarum vocatarum mortlyng et stiklyng cuiusdam Ricardi Wrangwysh mercatoris Gilde predicte indigene, $xl^{xxxiijs.\ iiij\ d.}$ pellium tannatarum siccarum vocatarum mortlyng et stiklyng cuiusdam Cristoferi Brigham mercatoris Gilde predicte, et $xv^{xx\ s.}$ pellium vocatarum mortlyng et stiklyng cuiusdam Georgii Carr mercatoris Gilde predicte; in toto, $iiij^{xx}v$ pellium facientium viij dacras dimidiam

lxxiij s. iiij d.

subsidio onerantur iij s. viij d.

Residuo subsidii cum custume et denariis Calesii predictarum $iiij^{xx}v$ pellium facientium viij dacras dimidiam prout mercatores mercatores indigene pro corriis solvere tenentur

onerantur xxxj s.

coketto onerantur vj d.

Corria salsa diversorum mercatorum indigenarum in portu predicto custumata et abinde versus partes exteras traducta

ix dacra dimidia	
custuma	vj s.
subsidium	xxxij s.
denaria Calesii	viij d.ob.qu.
coketti	viij d.

Valor alienigarum unde iij d. de libra

CCxix li. xj s. viij d.	
custuma	liiij s. x d.ob.qu.

Valor diversorum Hanse unde iij d. de libra

CCxxvij li. xj s. viij d.	
custuma	lvj s. xj d.

Panni sine grano

Indigene xxix panni	
custuma	xxxiij s. x d.
Alienigene iiij panni vj virge	
custuma	xj s. viij d.qu.
Hanse xj panni dimidius	
custuma	xj s. vj d.

Cere Hanse

j quintallus	
custuma	xij d.

Valor mercandisarum diversorum mercatorum indigenarum et alienigenarum unde xij d. de libra

MCxxxj li. xiij s. iiij d.	
subsidium	lvj li. xj s. x d.

Vinum indigenarum

Cxij dolia pipa hogeshede	
tonnagium	xvj li. xviij s. iij d.

Vinum alienigene non dulcis

j dolium	
tonnagium	iij s.

SUMMA TOTALIS OMNIS	MMMvj li. xiiij s. ij d.ob.
unde { gratis	iijClviij li. xiij s.xj d.qu.
{ onerantur	ijMDCxlviij li. iij d.qu.

[*Membrane 13 face*]

Noticie diversarum personarum mercatorum Gilde Novi Castri, indigenarum, cum diversis parcellis lanarum, pellium lanutarum ac pellium vocatarum shorlyng et morlyng ac pellium agnellorum, necnon pellium tannatarum siccarum in portu predicto, pro tantis lanis, pellibus lanutis, pellibus vocatis shorlyng et morlyng ac pellibus agnellorum et pellibus tannatis siccis alia vice super mare periclitatis et deperditis, absque aliquo subsidio proinde soluto iuxta formam cuiusdem actus inde editi, provisionaliter eskippatis, manifeste particulariter et separatim, prout in hiis particulis poterit apparere inferius, specificantur et declarantur.

Edwardus Baxter mercator Gilde predicte indigena
    iiij^{xx} pelles tannate sicce   valor iiij li.
Edwardus Conyngham mercator Gilde predicte indigena
    iiij^{xx}x pelles tannate sicce   valor iiij li. x s.
Willelmus Camby mercator Gilde predicte indigena
    iiij sacci lane
    iiijCv^{xx} pelles vocate shorlynges et morlynges   valor lxxij s. vj d.
Thomas Herrison mercator Gilde predicte indigena per Willelmum Bird executorem suum
    iiij sacci iij quarteria lane
    lx pelles lanute
    C pelles agnellorum   valor x s.
Thomas Herrison nuper mercator Gilde predicte indigena per Georgium Car indigenam mercatorem ibidem executorem suum
    iij sacci j quarterium ix clavi lane
    iiij^{xx} pelles shorlynges et morlynges   valor x s.
Willelmus Hanyng mercator Gilde predicte indigena
    ij sacci v clavi lane
    Cxx pelles lanute
    lx pelles shorlinges et morlinges   valor vij s. vj d.
    Cxl pelles agnellorum   valor xiij s. iiij d.
Rouland Herryson mercator Gilde predicte indigena
    vj sacci lane
Thomas Gibson mercator Gilde predicte indigena per Cristoferum Brigham attornatum suum
    vj sacci lane
Thomas Swan mercator Gilde predicte indigena
    j saccus j quarterium v clavi lane
Thomas Camby mercator Gilde predicte indigena per Willelmum Byrde executorem suum
    j saccus dimidius vij clavi lane
Willelmus Bird mercatore Gilde predicte indigena
    vj clavis lane

Georgius Car mercatore Gilde predicte executor testimonii Thome Herryson
j saccus dimidius vij clavis lane
Rogerus Raw mercator Gilde predicte indigena
j saccus j quarterium iij clavi lane
Georgius Bird mercator Gilde predicte indigena
ixClx pelles lanute
CC pelles shorlinges et morlinges valor xxx s.
Mv^{xx}pelles agnellorum valor cviij s. iiij d.
Georgius Selby mercator Gilde predicte indigena
j saccus j quarterium iij clavi lane
Georgius Conyngham mercator Gilde predicte indigena
j saccus iij quarteria j clavus lane
Robertus Harden mercator Gilde predicte indigena
ij saccos v clavi lane
Willelmus Harden mercator Gilde predicte
j saccus dimidius x clavi lane
Willelmus Alen nuper mercator Gilde predicte indigena per Johannem Alen executorem suum
x sacci v clavi lane
Clx pelles shorlinge et morlinges xx s.
Johannes Alen mercator Gilde predicte indigena
iiij sacci j quarterium lane
Robertus Brigham mercator Gilde predicte indigena
iii quarteria unius sacci lane
Georgius Stalper mercator Gilde predicte indigena
iiij sacci iij quarteria lane
Jacobus Buke mercator Gilde predicte per Willelmum Swan attornatum suum
iij sacci viij clavi lane
Willelmus Swan mercator Gilde predicte indigena
j quarterium unius sacci et ij clavi lane

Examinatur

Summa
Lane lxij sacci j quarterium xj clavi
Pellium lanutarum MCxl
facientium iiij saccos iij quarteria
Pellium vocatarum shorlyng et morlyng DCCCClx pelles
C^{m} per vj^{xx} facientium iiij saccos iij quarteria
valor vij li.
Pellium agnellorum MCCxx pelles
C per vj^{xx} facientium vj saccos dimidium xx pelles valor vj li. xj s. viij d.
Pellium tannatarum siccarum Clxx pellium
facientium xvij dacras valor viij li. x s.

[*Membrane 14 face*]

Diversis et singulis ad quos presentes littere nostre pervenerint salutem. Nos, Aldermannus et seniores iurati communitatis mercatorie Hanze Alamanie Londonii in inclito Anglie regno residentes, notum facimus per presentes certificando quod Johannes Smit nauta, Henricus van der Mole, Johan Resse et Georgius Lindenbergh, mercatores sunt et existunt de Hanza predicta; in cuius rei testimonium signetum nostri communitatis presens in margine inferiore impressum sub anno domini millesimo quingentesimo die vero mensis Junii x^{mo}.

[*Membrane 15 face*]

Diversis et singulis ad quos presentes littere nostre pervenerint salutem. Nos, Aldermannus et seniores iurati mercatorum Hanze Alamanie Londonii in regno Anglie residentes, notum facimus certificando quod Thomas Oldehoff nauta est de Hanze predicta; in cuius rei testimonium signetum nostra communitatis presens est impressum sub anno domini millesimo quingentesimo die vero mensis Maii septimi.

13. Particulars of account of William Baxter, controller, from Michaelmas 1499 to Michaelmas 1500

E 122/108/5

The ten membranes are each 230 mm. wide, and measure in length 595, 685, 690, 640, 650, 695, 665, 680, 640 and 630 mm. Their condition is good.

The account follows that of the collectors, no. 12 above, closely. Baxter omitted the departure of the *Anne de Gowe* on 2 September, but this was entered by another hand at the foot of the last membrane. There is no record there of the roll's delivery to the Exchequer. The heading to the account is given below.

[*Heading to William Baxter's account, E 122/108/5 m. 1*]

Rotulus Willelmi Baxter, contrarotulator domini Regis in portu ville Novi Castri super Tinam et in singulis portubus et locis eidem portui adiacentibus, de custuma et subsidio dicti domini Regis lanarum, coriorum et pellium lanutarum ac parve custume necnon subsidii tonagii et pondagii, a festo Sancti Michaelis Archangeli anno regis predicti usque idem festum tunc proximo sequens, scilicet per unum annum integrum.

Index of Places and Persons

Persons are identified as controllers, collectors, shipmasters (sm), alien merchants (al), or Hansard merchants (han); persons not so identifed occur in the records as English merchants. With some shipments the shipmaster is recorded separately acting as a merchant.

Where a place or person appears more than once on a page this is shewn by *, except within a run of pages.

Subject Index and Glossary

In each entry references are grouped as exports (exp:) or imports (imp:). Where an item appears more than once on a page this is shewn by *, except within a run of pages.

ANALYSIS. Under the heads: Clothes and personal ornaments. Equipment etc., agricultural; commercial or industrial; domestic; military; religious; for ships. Foodstuffs, drink and medicine. Produce and raw materials, apart from foodstuffs. Products and manufactures not in metal or wood, apart from clothes. Products in metal. Products in wood. Receptacles.

Clothes and personal ornaments, see beads, belts, bonnets, brooch, caps, clogs, comb, cramery, eyelets, girdles, glasses, gloves, hats, laces, lacing points, mantles, pin(s), purses, ribbon, rings, shoes, thread, wyvern.

Equipment etc., agricultural, apart from receptacles q.v. below, see bill-shafts, brushes, crooks, horseshoes, knives, millstones, packthread, saddles, saws, tar, windles, winnow.

Equipment etc., commercial or industrial, apart from receptacles q.v. below, see alum, anvil, ash, balances, brushes, compasses, counters, crooks, elsin *al.* awl blades, graters, grindstones, knives, millstones, nails, needles, packthread, paper, preems, reeds, saws, shuttles, slays, soap, tailors' shears, teasels, whetstones, wire, wool-cards.

Equipment etc., domestic, apart from receptacles q.v. below, see balances, battery, bells, beds, brushes, bullions, candles, candlestick, candlewick, chafers, chest, comb, counters, coverlets, crooks, cup, cupboard, cushions, frying pans, glass, graters, grindstones, hangings, harp strings, jesses for hawks, kettles, knives, lute strings, mats, mirror, needles, packthread, pan, pins, playing cards, pot, querns, razors, soap, stools, tables, thread, ticks, trays, trenchers, troughs, whetstones, whistles.

Equipment etc., military, see bowstaves, bucklers, sallet, staves, swords, tasses.

Equipment etc., religious, see beads, candles, table image.

Equipment etc., for ships, see bumpkins, canvas, compasses, crooks, eyelets, masts, oars, pitch, ropes, spars, tar.

Foodstuffs, drink and medicine, see alegar, almonds, apples, barley, barleymeal, beer, brimstone, butter, cheese, comfits, corn, cumin, eels, figs, filberts, fish, flour, fruit, garlic, ginger, grilse, herring, honey, hops, licorice, malt, maslin, meal, mudfish, oatmeal, oil, onions, onionseed, oranges, oyster, pepper, raisins, rice, rye, saffron, salmon, salt, seal blubber, spice, stockfish, sugar, verjuice, wine.

Produce and raw materials, apart from foodstuffs q.v. above, see alum, ash, bast, brimstone, coal, copperas, cork, dross, feathers, flax, galls, hemp, iron, lead, litmus, madder, oak, oil, oxhorn, pitch, reeds, resin, seal blubber, silk, slays, steel, stone, tallow, tar, teasels, wax, weld, woad, wool.

Products and manufactures not in metal or wood q.v. below, apart from clothes q.v. above, see beads, beds, bricks, candlewick, candles, canvas, cloth, coverlets, cramery, eyelets, glass, grindstones, hangings, harp strings, hides, jesses, lute strings, mercery, merchandise, millstones, mortlings, packthread, paper, playing cards, querns, ropes, saddles, skins, soap, stickleather, sticklings, stone, thread, thrums, ticks, tiles, whetstones.

Products in metal, see anvil, balances, battery, bells, brooch, bucklers, bullions, chafers, dross, elsin *al.* awl blades, frying pans, hoops, horseshoes, kettles, knives, nails, needles, pan, pin, plate, pot, razors, rings, saddler's nails, saws, skins (gold), swords, tailors' shears, whistles, tasses, wire, wool-cards.

Products in wood, see barrels, barrelheads, beads, beds, bill-shafts, boards, bowstaves, bullions, bumpkins, cans, chest, clapholt, coffer, counters, deals, masts, oars, pot, rafters, rods, shuttles, slays, spars, staves, stools, tables, trays, trenchers, troughs, wainscot, windles, winnow.

Receptacles, see bags, barrels, baskets, cans, chest, coffer, kits, purses, shitvat, windles.

Expressions of Quantity

aughkindell, aughtyndele, an eighth part, used of eels.
ame, alme, measure of Rhenish wine, sometimes 50 gallons.

bale, canvas container, contents varying with commodity, often used of flax, madder and woad.
ballet, small bale.
barrel, about 31 gallons liquid, also used for dry goods.
bolts, rolls, used of cloth.
bond (bundys), similar to bundle, used of flax.
boxes.
buc', unidentified, used of silk.
bunches (bonches, bounches), varying with commodity.
bundle (*bundellus*).
butt, cask.

C, for *centum*, literally a hundred, but with certain commodities signifying a "long hundred", e.g. five score (100) woolfells, but six score (120) shorlings, morlings or lamb fells; with iron, 112 pounds.
carte, synonymous with fother q.v.
chalder (*celdra, cheldra*), measure of capacity varying with commodity; with coal, about 1 ton in the late fifteenth century.
clout (clute), a cloth containing a recognised number of pins or needles.
clove (*clavus*), see nail.
cradle (credylle), used for glass, perhaps a measure of weight.

D, five 'hundreds", see C.
dicker (dacre, dakyr, deker), ten when used of hides or knives, but varying according to commodity.
dimidius, half, used to qualify other expressions; see also *semi*.
dolium, see tun.
dozen (*dossena, duodena, dussena*), a quantity of twelve; or a piece of narrow wool cloth, 12 yards long, the equivalent of a quarter of a cloth of assize for customs purposes.

ell (*ulna*), a measure varying with country of origin, in England 45 inches.
ends (*finis*), separate pieces of iron.

fardel (*fardellus*), package.
fasse, unidentified, used of basts, and so perhaps a 'bundle'.
fat, see vat.
firkin (ferkyn), small cask, with a capacity one quarter of a
barrel.
finis, see ends.
fother (foder, fothyr), *al.* carte, measure of weight, varying over time in respect of lead, but about 19½ hundredweights in the fifteenth century.
full, a set of three, used of kettles.

garba, see sheaf.
girth, see great.
graunt, see great.
great (grett), sometimes indicating quality, as for salt, i.e. coarse; but generally, like graunt and gyrthe, indicating size, as for e.g. combs, pins.
gross (gros, groce, grosse), twelve dozens.

half, see *dimidius, semi*.
hogshead, cask containing one quarter of a tun, or 63 gallons; also used for dry goods.
hernes barell, i.e. iron barrel.

keg (kagge), used for honey.
kentall, see quintal.

last (*lastum*), varying in quantity according to commodity, e.g. 20 dickers of hides, 200 wainscots, 12 barrels of osmunds, 600 bundles of flax.

libra, a pound.
loaves (loves), used of sugar.

M, ten 'hundreds', see C.
mat (matte), a container, used of kettles.
maund, bag
measure (*mensura, mesura*), used here of corn, perhaps signifying one bushel.

nail or clove (*clavus*), a quantity of wool, weighing 7 pounds.
nest, a set, used of counters.

pack (pak), used of linen
pannus, see above in Subject Index and Glossary.
panier (panyer), used of glass.
paperes, parcels, used of points and bonnets, presumably containing a recognised quantity.
pare (*par*), a pair or a set, as of rosary beads; used also of playing tables, and woolcards.
parvus, petty, small, applied to a wide range of commodities or their containers.
pecia, a piece (pece).
pipe (pyp, pype, *pipa, pippa*), cask, one half of a tun, or 126 gallons; also used for dry goods.
plaustrum, plaistrum, plaustratum, a cart load, or weight of two M, or 2240 pounds.
pocket (poket, pukette), a small poke.
poke (pok), canvas container, used for feathers, hops, madder and wool.
puncheon (ponshon), cask, one third of a tun or 84 gallons.

quarter (*quarterium*), as a measure of capacity, could be 8 bushels; as a weight, 28 pounds, but of wool, as a fraction of a sack, 91 pounds.
quintal, one hundredweight approximately but varying with commodity; used of wax

ream, used of paper
rolls (rollys, rowles), used of canvas.
rood (rode), a measure of Rhenish wine.
roundlet (rondlett), a small cask, also used for dry goods.

sack (*saccus, seccus*), in customs acounts for wool a weight of 364 pounds.
sarpler (*sarplera*), a canvas container in which wool was packed for shipment, of no fixed weight.
semi-barellus, half a barrel.
semi-pecia, half a piece.
sheaf (schyf, shive, *garba*), used of teasels.
shock (skoke, scok), 60 pieces, used e.g. for trenchers.
sort (sorte), a measure of fruit, perhaps weighing 224 pounds.
stone (ston), 14 pounds.
sum (some), a measure of various commodities, used of bullions.

tops (toppes), baskets, used of fruit.
tun (*dolium*), used of wine it contained 252 gallons; used of iron it indicated a weight of twenty C, or 2240 pounds.

ulna, see ell

vat (fatte), a cask or tub with a capacity of 8 bushels.
virga, a yard, i.e. 36 inches.

warp (warpe), a quantity of earthenware, perhaps a weight of potters' clay.
way (wey), varying in weight according to commodity; with salt it was 140 pounds.
wisp, a measure of steel, presumably amounting to a handful, the general meaning of the word.

xx, a score, i.e. 20.

PORTS

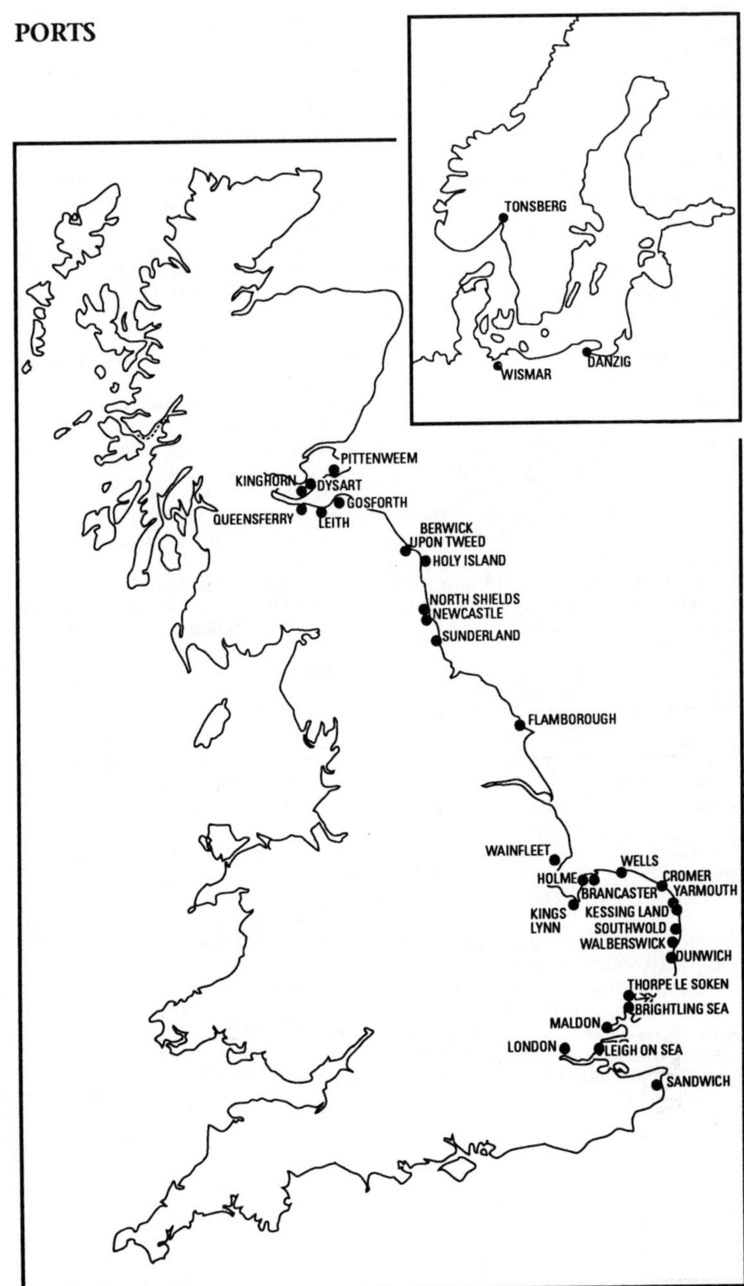

TONSBERG
WISMAR
DANZIG
PITTENWEEM
KINGHORN
DYSART
GOSFORTH
QUEENSFERRY
LEITH
BERWICK UPON TWEED
HOLY ISLAND
NORTH SHIELDS
NEWCASTLE
SUNDERLAND
FLAMBOROUGH
WAINFLEET
WELLS
HOLME
CROMER
BRANCASTER
YARMOUTH
KINGS LYNN
KESSING LAND
SOUTHWOLD
WALBERSWICK
DUNWICH
THORPE LE SOKEN
BRIGHTLING SEA
MALDON
LONDON
LEIGH ON SEA
SANDWICH

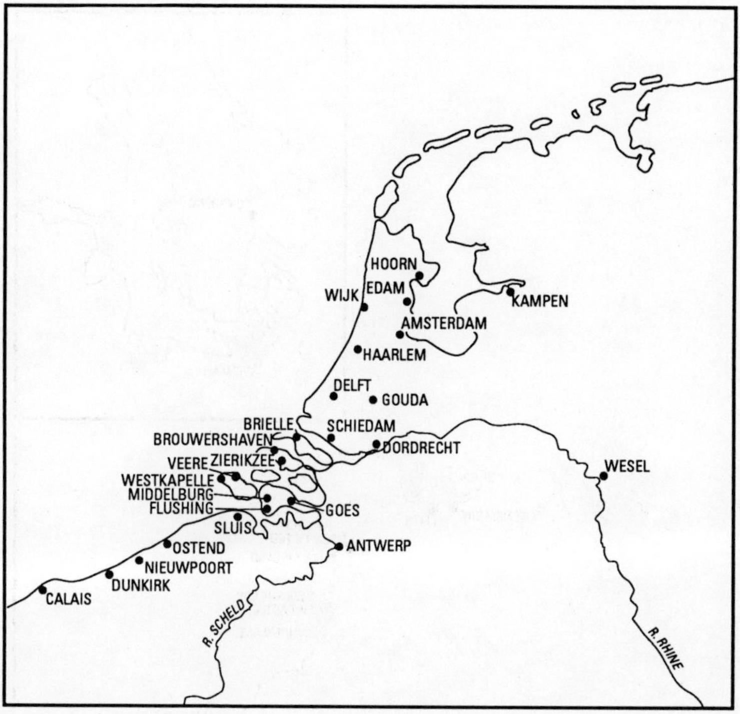

HOORN
EDAM
WIJK
KAMPEN
AMSTERDAM
HAARLEM
DELFT
GOUDA
BRIELLE
SCHIEDAM
BROUWERSHAVEN
DORDRECHT
VEERE
ZIERIKZEE
WESTKAPELLE
WESEL
MIDDELBURG
FLUSHING
GOES
SLUIS
OSTEND
ANTWERP
NIEUWPOORT
DUNKIRK
CALAIS
R. SCHELD
R. RHINE

BOULOGNE
ETAPLES
ABBERVILLE
LE TREPORT
AMIENS
DIEPPE
R. SOMME
HARFLEUR
ROUEN
HONFLEUR
CAEN
R. ORNE
R. SEINE
LE CONQUET
GROIX
GUERANDE
SOULLANS

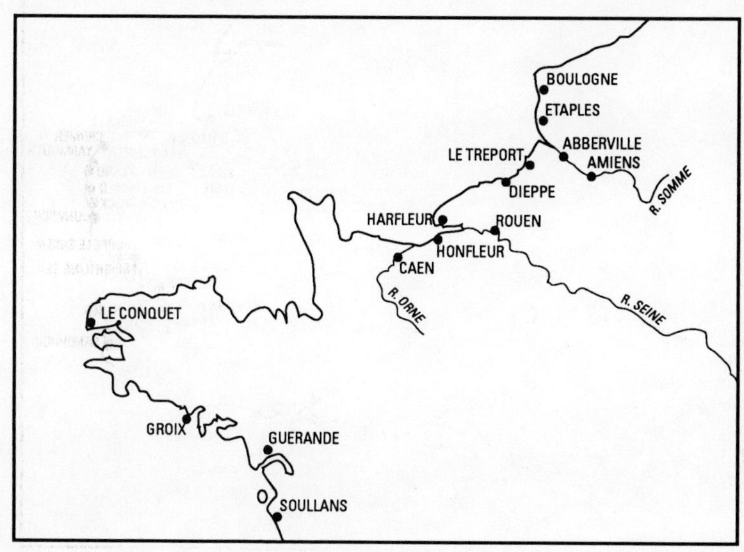